Grounds for Play

A

Book

The Philip E. Lilienthal imprint
honors special books
in commemoration of a man whose work
at the University of California Press from 1954 to 1979
was marked by dedication to young authors
and to high standards in the field of Asian Studies.
Friends, family, authors, and foundations have together
endowed the Lilienthal Fund, which enables the Press
to publish under this imprint selected books
in a way that reflects the taste and judgment
of a great and beloved editor.

Grounds for Play

The Nauṭaṅkī Theatre of North India

Kathryn Hansen

UNIVERSITY OF CALIFORNIA PRESS
Berkeley · Los Angeles · Oxford

University of California Press
Berkeley and Los Angeles, California

University of California Press, Ltd.
Oxford, England

Library of Congress Cataloging-in-Publication Data

Hansen, Kathryn.
Grounds for play : the Nauṭaṅkī theatre of North India / Kathryn Hansen.
p. cm.
"A Philip E. Lilienthal book"—P.
Includes bibliographical references and index.
ISBN 0-520-07273-1 (cloth)
1. Nautanki. 2. Folk-drama, Hindi—History and criticism.
3. Theater—India. I. Title.
PN2884.5.N38H36 1992
792′.0954′1—dc20 91-15291
CIP

Printed in the United States of America
9 8 7 6 5 4 3 2 1
The paper used in this publication meets the minimum requirements of American National Standard for Information Sciences—Permanence of Paper for Printed Library Materials, ANSI Z39.48-1984. ♾

To Carla and my parents

بازیچۂ اطفال ہے دنیا مرے آگے

ہوتا ہے شب و روز تماشا مرے آگے

This world is but a child's play
    before my eyes.
Night and day the spectacle unfolds
    before me.

—*Mirza Ghalib*

Contents

Illustrations

Acknowledgments

The research undertaken for this book received generous financial support from several sources. A fellowship from the Shastri Indo-Canadian Institute enabled me to carry out the first round of fieldwork in India in 1982. A two-year grant from the Social Sciences and Humanities Research Council of Canada funded subsequent trips to India in 1984 and 1985 and provided for research assistance and expenses. The Social Science Research Council (New York) through its postdoctoral fellowship program offered me a maintenance stipend during 1984–85. Additional help came from the University of British Columbia in the form of faculty research grants (1981–84). I wish to express my gratitude to these agencies for their timely assistance.

Institutional support played an important role throughout the development of this project. My first debt is to my home institution, the University of British Columbia, for accommodating my requests to be released from teaching responsibilities in academic years 1983–85 and the second term of 1987–88. During 1983–85 I was associated with the Center for South and Southeast Asian Studies at the University of California, Berkeley. Bruce Pray kindly made available to me the administrative facilities of the Institute for International Studies and the Sponsored Projects Office; I am grateful to Bruce along with Karen Beros and Jeri Foushee for their patience and cooperation. In 1988 the Southern Asian Institute of Columbia University was my gracious host; Ainslie Embree and his staff offered me physical space, most precious of commodities in Manhattan, and in that stimulating environment I completed the first half of the manuscript.

Here I must also thank Maureen Patterson and the personnel of the South Asia library at the University of Chicago for their assistance during research visits in 1982. Other libraries that contributed substantially to this project were the India Office Library and the British Library (formerly the British Museum) in London. I am indebted to them not only for access to their unrivaled collections but for their permission to reproduce many of the illustrations that appear in this book.

In India my activities were coordinated through the Shastri Indo-Canadian Institute in Delhi. I especially appreciate the efforts of P. N. Malik, who expedited everything from government clearances to travel arrangements and accommodation. Thanks to the India International Centre, I enjoyed a high standard of comfort and security, even during the Delhi riots of 1984. The officers of the national Sangeet Natak Akademi, in particular Jiwan Pani, suggested avenues for research and assisted in the acquisition of tape recordings and photographs. I am grateful to R. S. Malhotra for opening the academy's archives to me. I further extend thanks to the Uttar Pradesh Sangeet Natak Akademi in Lucknow and the Archives and Research Centre for Ethnomusicology of the American Institute of Indian Studies in Delhi for their help in my research.

My deepest sense of obligation is reserved for the many individuals who accepted the legitimacy of my inquiry and attempted to quell my curiosity, giving of their time, hospitality, experience, and knowledge. Why they should have done this so unquestioningly still puzzles me, but there is little doubt that without their willingness I would never have written this book. Ron Hess inspired me at the outset with his vivid documentation of Nauṭaṅkī in Banaras, while Alan Entwistle's gift of Nauṭaṅkī recordings from All-India Radio was an unexpected windfall. Similarly, a world was revealed when Shrivatsa Goswami invited me to Vrindavan for the Rās Līlā season. Nemichandra Jain, Amritlal Nagar, Mudrarakshas, Habib Tanvir, Ashok Chakradhar, Urmil Thapaliyal, Raj Bisariya, Jugal Kishor, and others shared their expertise. From the community of Nauṭaṅkī artists, I am indebted to Giriraj Prasad, Ram Dayal Sharma, Pandit Kakkuji, Phakkar, and Malika Begam, who responded to my probing with trust and candor.

During the painstaking process of transcription and computer editing, I received able assistance from Ann Cherian and Arpita Mishra. Dave Fern played many roles from ace receptionist to stalwart Macintosh operator. Tara Sinha enlivened the collating of texts with her charming synopses and sympathetic manner. In the musical analysis, I benefited by repeated consultation with Kay Norton, who was diligent beyond the call of duty.

It would be difficult to mention the numerous colleagues and friends who commented and advised as this book evolved. More than they may be aware, their affection and concern sustained me and proved invaluable to my forward progress. On the long home stretch, Carla Petievich, Yvonne Hansen, and Linda Robbins in their own ways gave me the necessary strength of heart to finish. I also owe many thanks to my editor, Lynne Withey, for her gentle persistence and clarity. The last credit goes to Bitiya and Mehndi, who simply witnessed and believed.

Note on Transliteration

This book contains words from Hindi, Urdu, Sanskrit, and other Indic languages. In general, foreign terms are transliterated following the scholarly conventions in practice for those languages. The differences between the Hindi and Sanskrit romanization systems are few. In most Hindi words, the final "a" is dropped, e.g., *sūtradhāra* (Skt.), *sūtradhār* (Hin.). To facilitate pronunciation, I have rendered the five sounds च, छ, श, ष, and ऋ as ch, chh, sh, ṣh, and ri for Hindi, while preserving the standard c, ch, ś, ṣ, and ṛ for Sanskrit. In the case of dramaturgical terms common to Hindi and Sanskrit, context determines the chosen spelling. The invocation of a Sanskrit drama is *maṅgalācaraṇa,* of a Hindi drama *maṅgalācharaṇ.* Urdu words are romanized following their most frequent spellings in Devanagari script. The *izāfat* construction is represented by *-e-*, e.g., *badr-e-munīr, bahr-e-tavīl.*

Variant spellings are often found in the Hindi texts of this period. I have reproduced the inconsistencies of my sources, transliterating titles as printed. However, when referring to a class of stories, I have adopted the most common spelling, e.g., Ramlal's *Puranmal,* but in most versions spelled *Pūranmal.* Anglicized spellings indicate words that have become common in English, e.g., Koran, guru, Shudras, Awadh. Personal names appear without diacritics, with the exception of authors' names transliterated in the appendixes. The popular surname *siṁh* is spelled as Singh except in textual references, e.g., Amar Singh Rathor (hero's name), *Amar siṁh rāṭhor* (title of drama). Following Hindi usage, I have chosen to speak of Ram instead of Rama but have used *Rāmāyaṇa* and *Mahābhārata* even when referring to Hindi versions of the epics.

Introduction

The Indian subcontinent possesses a rich theatrical history spanning many centuries. As in other parts of Asia, theatre here brings together storytelling, mime, poetry, song, and dance in a multifaceted spectacle. Many of the premodern forms of Indian theatre have religious roots, and earlier scholarship has focused on these genres, stressing the function of theatre as sacred ritual or doctrinal instruction. Less known are the secular stages such as Nauṭaṅkī, although their folkloric interest and musical complexity arguably surpass those of sectarian theatre. Previous oversight of these forms may owe something to the prejudice against profane amusements held in certain sectors of precolonial Hindu and Muslim society, as well as among British officials and Indian elites schooled in Victorian taste. Political authorities, orthodox believers, and aspirants to respectability have tried to suppress popular cultural practices in many places and times. Nonetheless, secular theatre has enjoyed great renown in India, particularly during the last two hundred years, and forms like Nauṭaṅkī have played a significant role in the cultural and social processes of the period.

Although clowning, melodrama, and ribaldry are certainly not absent from the staging of devotional dramas in India, Nauṭaṅkī and other secular theatres are unabashedly concerned with entertainment. Performances of Nauṭaṅkī provide pretexts for fun, grounds for play in the workaday lives of ordinary people. Play, or "ludic behavior" in the eyes of anthropologists, is a deeply creative activity. Just as it gives the growing child an opportunity to experiment and learn new ways of being, play at the societal level allows the exploration of new models and symbols. Cultural forms of play possess the potential to regenerate and change society. As Victor Turner has proposed, they may reveal structures, "social dramas," that are universal to human experience.[1] But even if the cross-cultural study of play had not established its "human seriousness," we would still wish to know more about the traditional modes of recreation among Indians, if only to counterbalance the still-prevalent image of the subcontinent as pious and otherworldly.

Even as they entertain, the traditional Indian theatres such as Nauṭaṅkī supply "pictures of the world," "selections of things worth attending to," just as newspapers, cinema, and television do.[2] Theatrical shows, together with epic recitations, ballads, songs, folktales, and so on, comprise the principal media of communication in societies characterized by limited literacy and technology. In premodern India, these traditional media were at the core of communication.[3] In the broadest sense then, this book is an inquiry into communication, specifically into a medium of communication that has today been displaced by the more powerful mass media. How did beliefs, values, and knowledge of events flow from one group to another before radio, films, and TV? The study of Nauṭaṅkī cannot fully answer this question, but it can point to interesting information from an overlooked source. Through the frame of the Nauṭaṅkī theatre, we gain access to a particular set of scenes that people in North India regularly encountered. We find enmeshed in their vivid details certain shared understandings of the world—and certain recurring puzzlements. We learn how some important ideas circulated and how they fared in new circumstances.

In addition to transmitting ideas and pictures of the world, communication—whether traditional or modern—serves a vital function in the construction of an ordered, meaningful cultural world. An anthropologically based definition of communication understands it as "a symbolic process whereby reality is produced, maintained, repaired, and transformed."[4] This implies that the media of communication not only reflect social reality; they also bring it into existence. To study communication is therefore to "examine the actual social process wherein significant symbolic forms are created, apprehended, and used."[5] It follows that Nauṭaṅkī has contributed to the formation of North Indian culture. Together with other cultural practices, it has generated a set of meanings that render the experience of its society comprehensible to its own members. Communication cannot be separated from its interactive relationship with community. The shared perceptions that make communities possible, the experience of a common life, are unimaginable without communication. Communities create their distinctive forms of communication, and they are produced and reproduced by them. Through media such as theatre, people work their common experience into understanding and then disseminate and celebrate it with others.[6]

Since these processes occur in historical time, the task of understanding communication entails attention to historical conditions and the experience of particular peoples. This book attempts to weave Nauṭaṅkī into a well-defined historical fabric, using both documents and oral accounts from a variety of sources. My discussions of texts, themes, schools, music, and meter are organized into chronological narratives, not because I insist on a linear model of evolution but because it is a convenient way to relate these materials to the context of social and political change. Few South Asian folklore and performance studies have explored the historical resources that allow us to gain interpretive nuance. This study moves beyond speculation to comment on specific connections between cultural representations and social structures as they shift over time.

The historical experience of a particular community contributes to its self-representation in cultural performance. However, different groups within a society do not possess the same experience. They struggle over their definitions of reality, and their struggles inform the content of the traditional media. Contests between groups also partially determine the reception of the communications media and hence affect their meaning. This contentious aspect of communication directs attention to heterogeneity as a trait of cultural practices and interpretations. "Culture must first be seen as a set of practices";[7] alternatively, it is composed as a range of meanings within a single practice. In specific terms, Nauṭaṅkī is only one among many cultural forms competing among a multiplicity of social groups. Each possesses different interests and has its own ways of appropriating the information communicated in performance.[8]

The conflictual nature of social process in India (as elsewhere), together with the multiple strands of literature, philosophy, and social thought contained in the plays themselves, suggest that any unified reading of the Nauṭaṅkī cultural text may miss the mark. Instead, this study approaches its subject from several different positions. By animating diverse voices, I make audible the chorus of meanings occurring within and among texts. This chorus is a characteristically Indian one: polyphonic, improvisatory, with overlapping textures, not harmonic and architectural. The focus on intertextual connection and contention may highlight the ways in which diverse groups receive the messages of the theatre and incorporate, modify, or subvert them. Rarely does communication simply serve the hegemonic interests of the state as described by the Frankfurt school. Nor do the traditional media of third-world countries ordinarily contain univocal expressions of popular resistance. The media of communication instead are "definite forms of life: organisms, so to say, that reproduce in miniature the contradictions in our thought, action, and social relations."[9]

I begin with two chapters on identifications. Chapter 1 introduces Nauṭaṅkī through a decentered approach, juxtaposing several narratives, and chapter 2 positions Nauṭaṅkī in relation to conventional anthropological guideposts. The next two chapters trace the social history of the form, chapter 3 recalling the community of theatre and recitational practices from which Nauṭaṅkī emerged and chapter 4 attending to its subsequent segmentation into lineages, authors, and texts. In chapters 5, 6, and 7, I explore the play of meanings within Nauṭaṅkī narratives, searching out the contradictions in social relations lying beneath the turns of dramatic structure. Here I probe conflicted areas such as political authority, community identity, and gender difference, listening closely for resonances with historical conditions. Chapter 8 attempts to make palpable the pulse of musical life within the form. In the concluding chapter 9, I recapitulate the themes of the preceding chapters, extending the implications of this study to wider contexts.

The research project that gave rise to this book took on its own life in the eight years I worked on it. I came to the subject of Nauṭaṅkī through my studies of modern Hindi literature. Trained to view a text as a composite of strategies, I had learned to gauge the artistry of Indian fiction by Western critical yardsticks. Yet the author I chose for my dissertation, the novelist Phanishwarnath Renu, was a master of regionalism. I could not understand his work without immersing myself in the folk culture and dialectal speech of rural Bihar. As I analyzed and translated Renu, I took an excursion into anthropology and folklore, where the seeds of this project germinated. Anthropology alerted me to the importance of cultural performances; folklore studies acquainted me with the large corpus of oral and written narrative in North India; Renu's fiction informed me of the existence of the Nauṭaṅkī theatre.

Quite soon I realized another happy convergence. I had formed an avid interest in Indian music since my first days in India. Because traditional pedagogy depends on a close student-teacher relationship, music gave me the opportunity to participate in the culture as a partial insider, deepening my insights in many areas. Yet my musical training had little connection with my academic research or university teaching. Nauṭaṅkī as a musical theatre gave me a means of bridging the gap. The sung repertoire of Nauṭaṅkī, I soon learned, was rich in melodic types related to the ragas of classical Hindustani music; to describe these required formal analysis of poetic meters, a skill I had acquired from literary studies. The project thus allowed me to combine my knowledge of Indian music with my expertise in Indian literature and folklore.

In this way my training structured my orientation to the project. I approached Nauṭaṅkī as a performance tradition of primarily verbal and musical dimensions, focusing on the complementarity of literary text and sung performance. Fortunately I encountered ample research materials on both counts. The collections of Darius Swann and Frances Pritchett directed me to the large repertoire of Sāṅgīt texts (Nauṭaṅkī librettos) circulating in India.[10] The first texts to come into my possession were photocopies from the filmmaker Ron Hess. Following this auspicious start, I visited Chicago in 1982 to catalogue Pritchett's collection and augment my own. During trips to India in the summer of 1982 and the winter of 1984, I purchased more Sāṅgīts in Delhi, Lucknow, Mathura, and Jaipur.

Meanwhile I learned of the old Sāṅgīts housed in the Oriental Manuscripts and Printed Books division of the British Museum and in the India Office Library in London.[11] I first visited the London libraries for three weeks in May 1983, returning for two weeks in October 1984. Working in the austere conditions of these remarkable institutions, I accumulated two copybooks of notes and entered catalogue details on hundreds of index cards. Eventually I obtained photocopies of certain texts and a number of rare photographs of illustrated Sāṅgīt covers, including those reproduced in this book.

Acquiring information about Nauṭaṅkī musical performance proceeded along several lines. During three trips to India in the summer of 1982, the winter of 1984, and December 1985, I sought out live performances as well as firsthand reports of all kinds. Beginning in the capital and moving out to the hinterland, I interviewed government officials, intellectuals, theatre directors, and performers, gradually working down the hierarchical rungs from those who control cultural policy and funding to those who carry on the surviving traditions. While making my own field recordings, I also gained access to valuable tapes in the archives of the Sangeet Natak Akademi and All-India Radio. Additionally I discovered that commercial records and cassettes of Nauṭaṅkī were on sale in shops; videotapes of recent Hindi films such as *Tīsrī Kasam* provided further examples of musical style.

The musical dimensions of Nauṭaṅkī were quite adequately represented in the radio, commercial, and archival recordings I acquired. Opportunities to view and record Nauṭaṅkī performances in natural situations were, by contrast, not plentiful. I repeatedly expressed my desire to witness full-length Nauṭaṅkī shows, but very few came to my notice. It is perhaps significant that Nauṭaṅkī singers I met all identified themselves as "former" artists who had now retired from the profession; that fairs, festivals, and municipalities have banned Nauṭaṅkī performances in recent years because of communal violence and other incidents of "criminal activity"; and that troupes reportedly constitute themselves only on receiving a concrete invitation to perform. Beyond these impressions, I must disavow possessing the ethnographic evidence or authority for definitive comment on the extent of Nauṭaṅkī as a living practice during the years of my research.

Instead of arranging for a commissioned performance, I used my time to view styles of theatre across a broad spectrum, ranging from modern Hindi plays to urban productions of Nauṭaṅkī and other folk performances as well as to Rās Līlā dramas in the pilgrimage setting. All these performances taught me a good deal not only about the specificity of particular practices but about the broad character of recitational music theatre, its communicative appeal, and its impact on audiences. From these performances I gained insights applicable to Nauṭaṅkī, even analogies for a Nauṭaṅkī no longer widely accessible. I count them as important sources of learning about the performative dimensions of North Indian folk theatre.

There is no need to detail the chain of evolving thoughts that intervened between the collection of data from the field and the completion of the writing of this book. Every project of similar size perhaps begins in one stage of a scholar's development and ends in another. The questions keep changing as new stances emerge from the flux of academic discourse. Recent influences on my work require little elaboration here, with one exception. During the last decade, feminist studies have compelled many of us to reconsider the boundaries between academic disciplines as well as our own categories of analysis. Feminism has reached far into the academy, in that feminist studies "have proposed new ways of thinking about culture, language, morality, or knowledge itself."[12] Though my project's original structure did not emerge from the presently available feminist perspectives, it bears the impress of feminist thinking and tries to open up areas of future inquiry.

Feminist theory postulates that gender differences are not inherent but are constructed by culture. The "differences" might be expanded from gender roles to include notions of sexuality, love, marriage, family, kinship, and community. Given the importance of the traditional media in the creation and maintenance of culture in societies like India, these media can be assumed to play an important role in the production of gender differences. In my view, Nauṭaṅkī theatre as well as myth, epic, and popular cinema do not reflect actual social relations, gender differences, and power alignments but rather produce and perpetuate them. They frame paradigms of gendered conduct that assist both women and men in defining their identities, inculcating values to the young, and judging the actions of others. The representation of women in Nauṭaṅkī is thus of interest less as a portrait of what women are than as a projection of what they should be.

In Nauṭaṅkī, representations of the female body, womanly conduct, and other aspects of gender difference occur at several levels of the performance. In the dramatic texts of the genre, gender roles and relations are contained within narrative structures. The heroines of Nauṭaṅkī stories are analogous to the role models from the Hindu epics, the Sitas and Savitris, in their capacity to shape behavior and serve as cultural ideals. What kinds of women do we find within the fictional realm of Nauṭaṅkī? Do Nauṭaṅkī heroines reiterate the Sita paradigm, or do we find alternative models? Is there any expression of resistance to patriarchal definitions of womanhood? Given the diversity of Nauṭaṅkī texts, we might anticipate that the corpus of tales would encompass a range of behaviors and, further, that models of womanly conduct would vary in accordance with historical conditions.

Women are present at another level in Nauṭaṅkī, conceived as the entire system of the performance, or the theatrical text. Before the main drama begins, the female performer sings and dances in a seductive manner, a role that often clashes with her later appearance as upright queen, wife, or daughter-in-law. The transactions between the actress or female impersonator (the gendered performer) and the male spectator play with the possibilities of exhibitionism and voyeurism. Here too gender roles are being reproduced, but in an arena labeled forbidden and dangerous. What meanings are attached to the performance of the eroticized actress? How does she fit into the system of gender difference operating in society?

These questions utilize the category of gender to understand issues of textual signification. Beyond them lies a larger inquiry into gender and performance in Indian society. What is the social status of female performers? What has been their contribution to the performing traditions in music, dance, storytelling, and other media? How does women's participation affect the prestige of a cultural performance? Are cultural forms themselves gendered, that is, identified as masculine or feminine? As we learn more about the involvement of women in the production of cultural media, we restore them to their rightful position as bearers of tradition. But we also acquire an empirical base to examine a more far-reaching hypothesis: that culture itself is structured by gender difference, and that any explanation of cultural practice must include the category of gender.

CHAPTER ONE

The Name of the Nauṭaṅkī

First Meeting

Once in a land far, far away, there lived a princess of peerless beauty. She dwelt cloistered in an impenetrable palace, surrounded by dense groves and watched over night and day. Distant and inaccessible though she was, her name had reached all corners of the country. Here was a damsel whose delicacy put even the fairies to shame. The radiant glow of her body made the moon's luster pale. Her eyes were like a doe's; she had the voice of a cuckoo. When she laughed, jasmine blossoms fell. In the prime of her youth, she maddened men with her lotus-like breasts and the three folds at her waist. Whenever she set foot outside, she was as if borne aloft on the gusts of wind, like a houri of paradise. Such was her supreme ethereality that her weight could be measured only against a portion of flowers.[1]

This princess was known in many different regions of India. She appeared under a series of names, each incorporating the word *phūl,* meaning "flower." In Rajasthani folklore, she was called Phulan De Rani, and she was pursued by a prince who was the youngest of seven sons.[2] In the pan-Indian tale of two brothers named either Sit and Basant or Rup and Basant, princess Phulvanti weighed only one flower.[3] In Sind and Gujarat, she was known as Phulpancha (five flowers) because the fifth flower caused the balance beam to tip. Here too she was associated with a two-brother team, Phul Singh and Rup Singh, the younger of whom was her suitor.[4] In the Goanese account, her name was Panchphula Rani, as it was in one North Indian version.[5] The Punjabi tale styled her Badshahzadi Phuli or Phulazadi, "Princess Blossom" as translated by colonial collectors.[6]

In the latter half of the nineteenth century, when most of these tales were recorded, a drama called *Princess Nauṭaṅkī* (*Nauṭaṅkī shāhzādī*) was also being performed. It employed a music-laden style popular in rural Punjab and Uttar Pradesh.[7] Nauṭaṅkī was Panchphula literally weighed in a different coin. *Nau* means "nine" and *ṭaṅk,* a measure of silver currency equivalent to approximately four grams. Thus Nauṭaṅkī: a woman whose weight was only 36 grams. Nauṭaṅkī was the princess of Multan, flower-light, fairylike, whose fame had traveled far and wide. She was the beloved of the Punjabi lad Phul Singh, younger brother of Bhup Singh. Her story is still being told.

> What is it like, this roving theatre? What is its name, do you know? This is Nauṭaṅkī. That's right, Nauṭaṅkī! The chief attraction of village fairs in Uttar Pradesh. Several days before the fair starts, the tents and trappings arrive on a truck and are set up at a fixed spot. A large tent is stretched out to form a hall. At its head, a good-sized stage is erected and adorned with curtains. All the arrangements are made for the lighting. In front of the stage, places are fixed for the audience to sit. A big gate is put up outside, and a signboard attached to it with the name of the Nauṭaṅkī. As soon as the bustle of the fair gets underway, the main performers arrive on the scene. Then at a fixed time an announcement is made and the Nauṭaṅkī commences. The same individuals you watched putting up the tents and curtains now appear before you on stage, acting out roles and singing and dancing.[8]

NAVBHĀRAT TIMES INTERVIEWER: Your name has become almost a synonym for Nauṭaṅkī nowadays. When and how did you become associated with it?

GULAB BAI, FAMOUS NAUṬAṄKĪ ACTRESS OF KANPUR: This is the result of my fifty-five years of self-sacrifice. My father was a poor farmer. He was the one who had me join Trimohan Lal's company in 1929. I was only eleven years old at the time. With Trimohanji's guidance, I worked in the company for roughly twenty years. In the beginning, I got about 50 rupees a month, which later rose to 2,000 rupees.

NAVBHĀRAT TIMES: After working in Trimohan's company for so many years, why did you decide to leave and form your own separate company? And how did you become successful at operating it?

GULAB BAI: That decision grew out of an unfortunate incident. My sister fell off a balcony and was seriously injured. I asked Trimohanji for money for her medical treatment. He put me off with "Come back tomorrow." I told him any number of times that her condition was deteriorating, but he wouldn't listen to me. So that was when I left the company. Later I got together with my sisters Pan Kunwari, Nilam, Suraiyya, and Chanchala Kumari, and we formed a separate company. We organized the costumes and props and so on and started playing for wedding parties. The audiences praised us. In that way, we started up, with our own dedication and others' blessings.

NAVBHĀRAT TIMES: Up until now how many performances have you given?

GULAB BAI: It's difficult to tell exactly how many performances there have been. But by 1942 I had performed approximately twenty thousand times.[9]

MALIKA BEGAM, NAUṬAṄKĪ ACTRESS OF LUCKNOW: Previously, big officers used to call for us every day. They'd summon the Nauṭaṅkī company managers and tell them to make the necessary arrangements. Then all the big officials, their wives, all the best gentry, all kinds of people would come. . . . The public was extremely fond of Nauṭaṅkī. Whenever a program was over and we were leaving by bus or train, all the students, leaders, and so on brought bouquets and bade us farewell. Such respect, how can I tell you? . . . When we were on stage, there could be a dead body lying at home, but when we went on stage, we thought that if we were playing Laila, we were Laila; if we were playing Shirin, we were Shirin. We forgot our everyday reality, whatever we were.

KATHRYN HANSEN: How many people were in your company?

MALIKA BEGAM: At that time, including labor, there were eighty. It depended on the scale of the company. If it was small, then fifteen, twenty, twenty-five men; if large, then eighty or a hundred, including labor. There were four managers in each of the big companies.

KATHRYN HANSEN: How much did you make back then?

MALIKA BEGAM: Sometimes 2,500 rupees a month, sometimes 2,000.[10]

The Hindi author Phanishwarnath Renu describes the encounter of a cartman and a Nauṭaṅkī actress in his short story "The Third Vow."

> Everybody had heard of Hirabai, the actress who played Laila in the Mathura Mohan Nauṭaṅkī Company. But Hiraman was quite extraordinary. He was a cartman who'd been carrying loads to fairs for years, yet he'd never seen a theatre show or motion picture. Nor had he heard the name of Laila or Hirabai, let alone seen her.
>
> So he was a little apprehensive when he met his first "company woman" at midnight, all dressed in black. Her manager haggled with him over her fare, then helped her into Hiraman's cart, motioning for him to start, and vanished into the dark.
>
> Hiraman was dumbfounded. How could anyone drive a cart like this? For one thing, he had a tickle down his spine, and for another, a jasmine was blooming in his cart. Only God knew what was written in his fate this time!
>
> As he turned his cart to the east, a ray of moonlight pierced the canopied enclosure. A firefly sparkled on his passenger's nose. What if she were a witch or a demon?
>
> Hiraman's passenger shifted her position. The moonlight fell full on her face, and Hiraman stifled a cry, "My God! She's a fairy!"
>
> The fairy opened her eyes.[11]

Alternative Etymologies

To educated Indian ears, the word *nauṭaṅkī* sounds a bit uncouth, with its hard consonants and nasal twang. Hindi dictionaries do not include the term before 1951. It occurs in neither Thompson's *Dictionary in Hindee and English* (1862) nor Platts's *Dictionary of Urdu, Classical Hindi, and English* (1884). Of the Hindi-English dictionaries currently in wide use, Chaturvedi and Tiwari's *Practical Hindi-English Dictionary* contains no entry, and the *Mīnākṣhī hindī-aṅgrezī kosh* says simply "folk-dance, village-drama." Nor does the unabridged *Hindī shabd sāgar* (1968) mention Nauṭaṅkī in its ten volumes. Ramchandra Varma's *Prāmāṇik hindī kosh* (second edition, 1951) appears to contain the first dictionary definition: "a type of renowned drama occurring in the Braj region in which they act and sing *chaubolā*s (quatrains) to the accompaniment of the *nagāṛā* (kettledrum)." The most detailed entry is in the fifth edition of the *Mānak hindī kosh* (1964): "A type of folk-drama performed among the common people, whose plot is generally romantic or martial, and whose dialogues are usually in question-answer form in verse. It contains a predominance of music and *chaubolā*s are sung in a particular manner accompanied by the *dukkaṛ* (paired drums) or *nagāṛā*."

What explains the late occurrence of these definitions? And why does the lexical silence persist? Sampling the dictionaries would lead us to believe that this folk art is obscure and insignificant. But dictionaries are slanted mirrors of language and society, reflecting the linguistic tapestries constructed by social, political, and economic forces at different moments of history. We might wonder if a censorious intent is at work, an effort to expunge Nauṭaṅkī from the authorized indexes of the language. We begin to suspect from its omission that Nauṭaṅkī may not rank with the prestigious, officially approved performance genres of modern India. Why then this attempt to exclude Nauṭaṅkī from the canons of acceptable speech?

Part of the reason may be the uncertainty of its etymology. Most of the generic labels for folk theatre in North India are derived from words meaning "stage, play, show, processional theatre," for example, the Māñch of Madhya Pradesh (from Sanskrit *mañcakam,* "stage"), the Rām and Rās Līlās of Uttar Pradesh (Sanskrit *līlā,* "sport, play"), Maharashtra's Tamāshā (Arabic *tamāshā,* "entertainment, spectacle"), Bengal's Jātrā (Sanskrit *yātrā,* "procession, pilgrimage"). In the parallel etymology conjured by Hindi scholars, *nauṭaṅkī* has been traced to *nāṭaka,* the Sanskrit high drama, via a hypothetical term *nāṭakī.* The argument is inconclusive in the absence of references to *nāṭakī* in the dramatic literature. Taking another approach, Hindi novelist Amritlal Nagar explains the term as the theoretical admission price, *nau ṭaṅkā,* nine silver coins, or as the fee paid by a patron for sponsoring a performance, *nau ṭākā,* nine rupees. Others believe the word refers to a distinctive music and drumming style, *nav ṭaṅkār,* "new sound." [12]

Beyond these speculations, folklore preserves the story of Nauṭaṅkī, the beautiful princess of Multan. The dramatized romance of Phul Singh and Nauṭaṅkī (although it may be older) first appears in published form as Khushi Ram's *Sāṅgīt rānī nauṭaṅkī kā* (The musical drama of Queen Nauṭaṅkī) in 1882 (fig. 1). R. C. Temple lists "Rani Nautanki and the Panjabi Lad" in his index of legends collected from the Punjab in the 1880s. In the early 1900s, folk-drama poets from the Hathras area, Govind Chaman, Muralidhar, and the famed Chiranjilal and Natharam team, composed their much published versions of the story; they had many imitators (fig. 2). The popularity of the tale grew with repeated performances, as the folk theatre moved out from the Punjab region and Haryana into Uttar Pradesh and Bihar in the twentieth century.[13]

The traditions of the Nauṭaṅkī theatre, moreover, include a metastory. The name of the princess Nauṭaṅkī became so famous that it came to signify the theatre genre itself.[14] Such semantic extension is not

Fig. 1. Title page of *Sāṅgīt rānī nauṭaṅkī kā* by Khushi Ram (Banaras, 1882). By permission of the British Library.

श्रीगणेशायनमः ।

॥ उस्ताद इन्द्रमन ॥

सां० नौटंकी ।

जो सज्जन असली चहैं,
इन्द्रमन कृत ख्याल ।

देख लेउ तसवीर में,
खास चिरंजीलाल ॥

फोटो-स्वर्गीय उस्ताद चिरंजीलालजी ।

जिसको नथाराम के उस्तादं चिरंजीलाल
हाथरस निवासी ने बनाया और
चिरंजीलाल के पोते बांकेलाल ने
रामनारायण प्रेस मथुरा में बाबू राधारमण भार्गव के प्रबंध से छपवाया ।

उर्दू हिन्दी सांगीतों का सर्वाधिकार बांकेलाल को है ।

बिना मुहर की पुस्तक चोरी की समझी जायगी ।

Fig. 2. Title page of *Sāṅgīt nauṭaṅkī* featuring portrait of the author, Chiranjilal (Mathura, 1922). By permission of the British Library.

unknown to classificatory practices in North India. The name of a protagonist may designate a story, as well as the poetic meter used to tell that story, the musical motif associated with the meter, and finally the performance genre as a whole. For example, Alha is the name of a twelfth-century Rajput hero whose exploits were set down in the *Ālhā khaṇḍ* of Jagnaik. *Ālhā* refers to the martial saga, which engendered a specific performance style called Ālhā, sung in the *ālhā* meter, to a tune recognized by listeners as *ālhā,* practiced by *ālhā gānevāle* (Ālhā-singers)—which now includes other topics along with the original story of Alha.[15] Another example is Dhola, hero of the medieval Rajasthani epic *Ḍholā mārū. Ḍholā* is also the classifier of a North Indian ballad form.[16] So too "Nauṭaṅkī" names the beautiful princess, her well-known tale, and the unique theatrical style in which her story is performed. In popular usage, *nauṭaṅkī* also refers to an item in the performance repertoire, as in the question, "Which *nauṭaṅkī* did you see?"[17]

Having clarified the issue of etymology, let us return to the question of Nauṭaṅkī's absence from the lexicons. A clue may be discovered in the unusual association of a folklore genre with a female character. Whereas the *Ālhā* and *Ḍholā* epics are named for male warriors, this art draws its title from a princess. The fetching Nauṭaṅkī of legend may be intent on conquest, but her territory is the heart, not the battlefield. Does this make her theatre less noble than the epics of the heroes? What is implied when a theatrical tradition is identified with a woman, a supremely desirable woman? The nomenclature linking this folk theatre with the female gender may be the most singular indicator of its nature. It suggests the sociolinguistic and cultural veils that have cloaked Nauṭaṅkī in mystery thus far.

The Journey

Many men had tried to attain the enchanting princess Nauṭaṅkī but none had succeeded. One day the Punjabi youth Phul Singh returned home from a hunt. He impatiently ordered his elder brother's wife to fetch him cold water, get his food ready, prepare smoking materials, and make up his bed. She rebuked him sharply, telling him to go win the hand of Nauṭaṅkī if he wanted a woman to serve his every need. Affronted, Phul Singh vowed not to return home again unless Nauṭaṅkī came with him. Alarmed at his rash words, his sister-in-law retracted her dare. His father begged him not to leave home, and his mother offered to marry him to some other bride. But Phul Singh was adamant.

His heart now inflamed by the passion of pure love, he said farewell to family, friends, wealth, and country, and set off on his quest. He journeyed for many days on horseback, until at last he reached the fort of Multan. He entered the city and soon came to the garden of the princess Nauṭaṅkī.

As Phul Singh entered Nauṭaṅkī's private garden, he was accosted by a *mālin,* an old woman gardener, who warned him away. He begged to stay overnight, winning her consent finally with a gift of money. Phul Singh helped the *mālin* weave a special garland to present to Nauṭaṅkī, affixing a gem of his own. When the princess saw it, her left eye throbbed, her breast quivered, and she sensed her future husband was near. But she said nothing and demanded that the *mālin* produce the maker of the unusual wreath. Phul Singh directed the *mālin* to disguise him as her newlywed daughter-in-law and lead him into court. Decorated in full feminine array, Phul Singh at last beheld his beloved, but he could not speak his heart for fear of revealing himself. Nauṭaṅkī was enchanted by the lovely young girl she saw before her. Overcome with desire, she decorated her bed with flowers and invited the bride to come lie with her.

DHARMYUG INTERVIEWER: Sometimes you're here, sometimes you're there—how do you like all this traveling about?

MASTER SURKHI, A NAUṬAṄKĪ ACTOR AND TROUPE MANAGER: Don't ask, mister, it's a gypsy's life. You can imagine what it's like: loading all the tents onto the truck, traveling, digging a well at a new place, drinking the water. Deciding on the site, then putting up the tents. But what can I do? I have no choice. The whole burden falls on my shoulders now. When I worked as a laborer in Babu Khan's company, I never worried about anything. In those days, I put on airs and made demands. Now I have to put up with all the airs of my own performers. Always I'm the one responsible for their welfare. It's a huge botheration, sir, running this company. On top of that, I have to deal with the intimidation, the extortion from the police, the bosses, and the thugs in the cities. Get them free passes to the shows. And the heaviest tax falls on Nauṭaṅkī companies. It's more than they charge the circus or drama companies. Sometimes we get caught in a storm and the whole kit and caboodle gets wrecked. One night at the Rampur Exhibition there was a terrific rainstorm—don't even ask! All the tents were ripped up, everything a shambles. The hall totally flooded with water. There are a thousand hassles, but how can we go on crying about them?

The tented hall overflowed with people. Tube lights and naked bulbs lit up the sea of faces. Huge painted curtains covered the stage, while below a musician stood at an old-fashioned foot-pumped harmonium. To one side of the stage sat the aged *nagāṛā* player, sticks poised to beat on his kettledrums. Beside him another drummer braced his *ḍholak*. With a flourish, the percussionists began the overture, regaling the audience with a volley of drum rolls. Then the joker entered, an odd toothy character in greasepaint and motley costume. Screwing up his face, he announced the arrival of his "wife."

The first dancer came onto the stage, a fleshy young lady with a huge bun of hair, arching painted eyebrows, and excessively red cheeks. Her sari was slung below the navel. She fluttered her eyelids at the audience and, pouting, saluted the musicians and gestured for them to start. As the song began she danced, revealing every limb and contour of her body. The audience hooted and shouted, and dug deep into their pockets for rupee notes that were passed to a boy on stage. With the note came the name of the donor. The dance stopped, and the boy announced the donor's name over the microphone. The dancer smiled and set her body in a suggestive pose. "I wish to thank that kind gentleman, Mr. ______, and my darling public," and she thrust her hips lewdly and continued with her dancing.

MALIKA BEGAM: Now those big people don't like to come. Why? Because the wrong type of women have come into this, women who are not artistes. They learn a few songs—I mean, the prostitutes. Their profession has been banned so they've entered this one. Imagine, when these women come amidst the public, sit there, grab their clothes, do this and that and somehow earn a tip, then theatre is a thing quite distant. If they give a push, thrust their bodies, and beg for a tip, it's no matter of shame for them. But for me it is the same as dying. At the most, I can say thank you like this [gestures with *namaste*], no more. If it's a special occasion, some big leader, someone to pay respects to, that's all I can do. I can't do all that just to get a tip. These people have fouled the atmosphere.

Forbesganj was Hiraman's second home. Who knows how many times he'd come to Forbesganj carrying loads to the fair. But carrying a woman? Yes, one time he had—when his sister-in-law came to live with her husband. They put a canvas enclosure around the cart, just as Hiraman was doing now.

The fair was to open tomorrow. Already a huge crowd, and the camps were jammed with tents. First thing in the morning Hirabai would go join the Rauta Nauṭaṅkī Company. But tonight she stayed in Hiraman's cart, in Hiraman's home.

Next day, Hiraman and his two companions entered the eight-anna section. This was their first look inside a theatre tent. The section with the benches and chairs was up front. On the stage hung a curtain with a picture of Lord Ram going to the forest. Palatdas recognized it and joined his hands to salute the painted figures of Ram, princess Sita, and brother Lakshman. "Hail! Hail!" he uttered as his eyes filled with tears.

Dhan-dhan-dhan-dharam! rolled the drums. The curtain rose. Hirabai immediately entered the stage. The tent was packed. Hiraman's jaw dropped. Lalmohar laughed at every line of Hirabai's song, for no good reason.

"Her dancing is incredible!"

"What a voice!"

"You know, this man says Hirabai never touches tobacco or betel."

"He's right. She's a well-bred whore."

Renu's Actress

The word Nauṭaṅkī first entered my vocabulary when I read Renu's Hindi short story, "The Third Vow." Set in his home district of Purnea in Bihar, the story follows a rustic cart driver as he hauls an unusual load—a Nauṭaṅkī actress—to a rural fair. During their journey, a tender and sheltered friendship develops between the illiterate laborer Hiraman and the urbane, glamorous Hirabai. The friendship somehow survives the disorienting experience of the fair, where Hiraman attempts to protect himself and Hirabai from the common view that the Nauṭaṅkī theatre is disreputable and its actresses dissolute.

Renu writes into his text the sensory dimensions of experience, the sounds and smells, the feel of the countryside. The lurch of the cart into the ditch, the fragrance of night jasmine, the crescendo of kettledrums, the tingle of fear and pleasure down the spine: these details carry the reader into a palpable realm where emotion and sensation intermingle. Meanwhile, the story creates a rich contextualization of Nauṭaṅkī, evoking the theatrical experience in rural India, and telling us much about the mythic meanings of folk theatre for its audience.

Renu places Nauṭaṅkī in the premodern landscape of India's northern plains. In this world of villages, cartmen, loads, and country fairs, transport by rail or truck is yet to come. Goods—be they legal or contraband, tied down or unwieldy, inanimate or dangerously alive (as narrated in the tales of Hiraman's cloth smuggling, bamboo hauling, and tiger transporting, all activities he has now foresworn)—move on creaky-axled cart beds drawn by recalcitrant bullocks. The carts wind down dusty tracks, or stray off to less-worn paths, crossing dry riverbeds and pausing beneath the occasional shade tree for respite from the sun. The sites of fairs and markets are the nodes in this network of tracks, bringing together drivers and their customers, and offering opportunities for camaraderie, entertainment, and relaxation.

This is a psychic world of limited compass for its inhabitants. Its boundaries are marked in tens of miles rather than hundreds. Hiraman's map includes his village, his "second home" of Forbesganj, and of course, the road. Names like Kanpur and Nagpur, large cities to the west and south, are well known to Hirabai, worldly woman that she is, but to Hiraman, with his childlike literalism, they signify only "Ear City" (*kān pur*) and "Nose City" (*nāk pur*).

Theatre by its nature is concerned with illusion, disguise, and even duplicity; in many societies it evokes distrust and hostility.[18] But in rural India, the suspicious enterprise of theatre is made stranger still by differences in power, culture, and status that separate city and village. The arrival of any citydweller in the village arouses a fear of exploitation and degradation; suddenly the villager's knowledge and authority appear deficient by comparison. Nonetheless, contact with certain categories of outsiders—traveling preachers, itinerant entertainers, or in the new age, campaigning politicos—offers a periodic means for the village to obtain both amusement and information. Such visitations are temporary and may not impose a challenge on the existing pattern of life, yet the outsider retains an aura of fascination and fear. The safest attitude seems one of deference.

It is natural then that the cart driver Hiraman should react with apprehension, even terror, when he first encounters an actress, Hirabai, late one night. He fears she might be a demoness or a witch: dangerous residues of repressed female rage, who return after a woman's death to torment her former oppressors. Instead, in the moonlight Hirabai's face reveals her to be a fairy (*parī*), an equally unearthly but beneficent supernatural. *Parī*s are the residents of heaven in Indo-Islamic mythology, counterparts to the *apsarā*s of Hindu legend, and they appear in many late medieval narratives as well as in the drama. Ethereal, unweighable, borne on the breeze, the fairy is a paragon of beauty, the ideal form of the beloved.

As the story advances, Hiraman domesticates this otherworldly being—paradoxically, by deifying her. He interprets her kindness in conversing with him as a boon of the goddess, an act of grace. To Hiraman, it is as though one of the celestials is riding in his cart, a reference to the practice of publicly parading the temple idol in a cart during annual temple festivals. The dedication and service that Hiraman offers to Hirabai—his protection of her inside the canopy, his ritualized offering of food and drink, and his constant attentions—are the appropriate gestures of a devotee toward the divine. All these behaviors are justified and symbolized through the appellation he gives her, "Hiradevi," Hira the goddess.

The status attached to god or goddess implies a hierarchy, the worshiper figuratively and literally placed beneath the deity. Yet in India, the relationship a worshiper enjoys with the divine is intense and volatile in affect. A widespread cultural metaphor likens the deity and the devotee to lovers in the most intimate emotional bond. Within this mode, opportunities exist for the worshiper to invert the hierarchy and "dominate" the chosen deity with demands, pleadings, and offerings. Hiraman's deification of Hirabai keeps her at a safe distance, but it also provides a known avenue of approach. His response illustrates the comfortable adulation heaped upon theatre artists and other celebrities by the rural audience. "Gods from another realm" is one way in which they can be appropriated and rendered manageable.

Against this cluster of admiring attitudes stands the complex of prohibitions and taboos associated with all secular entertainments, but especially dance, theatre, and film in India. Hiraman, an innocent, has never seen a theatre show or motion picture, largely because he fears his sister-in-law's disapproval. When he meets his fellow cartmen in Forbesganj, they make a pact that none will mention their Nauṭaṅkī experience back in the village. The basis for their circumspection is guilt by association, for "company women" are reputed to be prostitutes. This widely held perception challenges Hiraman and torments him throughout his stay in Forbesganj, but he continues his protective behavior toward Hirabai, brawling with audience members who "insult" her and later suggesting she abandon acting and join the more respectable circus.

No specific information is presented in Renu's story about Hirabai's sexual life, and to the end the reader remains in the dark (as does Hiraman), unable to determine if Hirabai ought to be ranked as a goddess or a whore. This authorial withholding is one of the sources of bittersweet ambiguity in the story. Beyond the text, however, the selling of sexual favors is not essential to the definition of a stage actress as a prostitute, either in North India or in other societies. Gender roles in this agriculturally based patriarchal society are defined in spatial terms, with women occupying private inside spaces and men public outer ones.

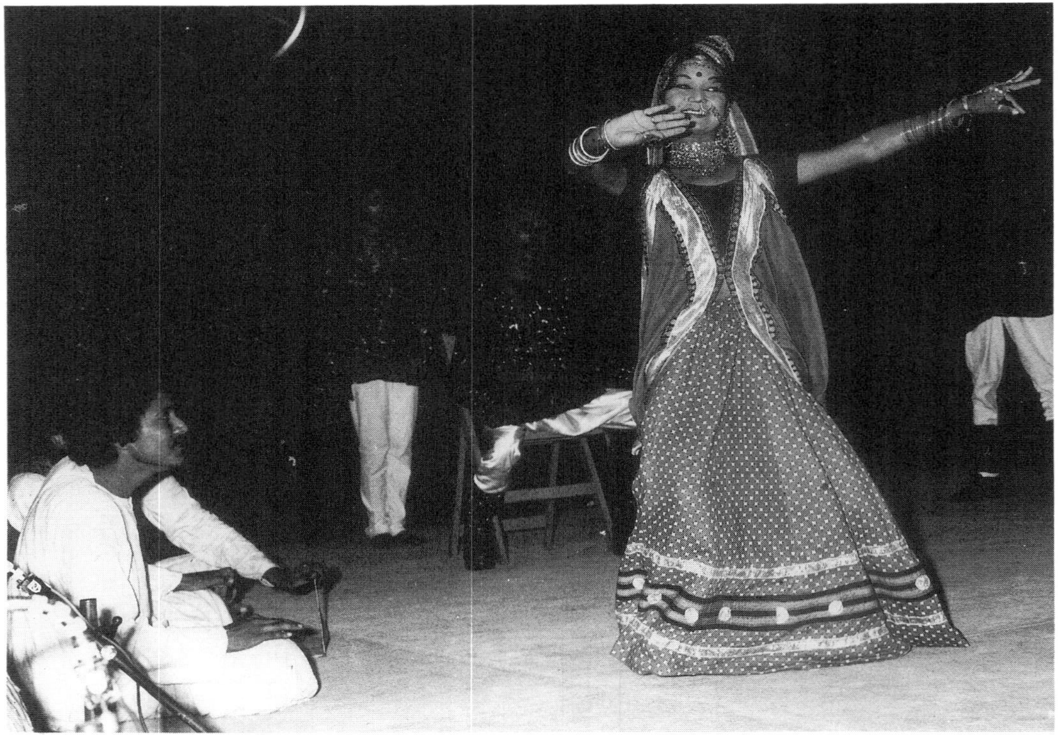

Fig. 3. Dancing girl performing in *Sultānā ḍākū*. By permission of the Sangeet Natak Akademi.

Women are valued for their domestic labor and for their reproductivity, which must be controlled for the perpetuation of pure family and caste lines. Enclosure, whether effected by *pardā* (the curtain or screen of a segregated household), by the canopy of a bullock cart, or by a veil or sari-end drawn over a woman's face, is conceived as necessary to preserve a woman's chastity and, by extension, her menfolk's honor. Since the social construction of gender places "good women" in seclusion, women who appear in public spaces (such as on stage) are defined as "bad," that is, prostitutes. Subjected to the gaze of many men, they belong not to one, like the loyal wife, but to all (fig. 3).

Clash and Conquest

> Phul Singh, who was so close to the object of his desire, trembled with fear of discovery. He asked Nauṭaṅkī why such a lovely princess as herself was as yet unmarried. She replied:
>
> Listen, most excellent gardener girl,
> I am weighed in flowers until now.
> No man has proven worthy of me,
> So I've remained single, in spite of my budding youth.
> Seeing you, my friend, a wave surges in my heart.
> Oh sweet, if only one of us could be changed into a man,
> We could spend the whole night making merry in bed,
> Happily embracing, giving and taking,
> Drinking the cup of union.
>
> Phul Singh recommended she pray for a boon and, as Nauṭaṅkī closed her eyes and prayed to her *pīr* (saint), removed his disguise. All obstacles now eliminated, the two spent the night together.
>
> In the morning, Nauṭaṅkī was weighed in flowers as usual, but this time the scale tipped; she was heavier from her contact with a man. When the king, her father, discovered the insult to his honor, there was an uproar in the palace. He ordered Phul Singh to be arrested and brought before the *kotvāl* (chief of police). Nauṭaṅkī tried to buy her lover's release by offering the *kotvāl* her necklace. But Phul Singh was sentenced to hang. The grieving lovers were parted, as Nauṭaṅkī promised to meet Phul Singh once more.

GULAB BAI: There's one incident I'll never forget. It was when I was with Trimohan's company, during the period of the British Raj. Some antisocial elements had entered the hall and were sitting in the audience. The police were having a hard time controlling them. So the British *kotvāl*, one Mr. Handoo, declared that *we* were a threat to law and order, and he had us banished from the city.

"Where's the man who said that? How dare he call a company woman a whore?" Hiraman's voice rose above the crowd.

"What's it to you? Are you her pimp?"

"Beat him up, the scoundrel!"

Through the hullabaloo in the tent, Hiraman boomed out, "I'll throttle each and every one of you!" Lalmohar was assaulting people with his bullock whip. Palatdas sat on a man's chest pummeling him.

The Nauṭaṅkī manager rushed over with his Nepali watchman. The *kotvāl* rained blows on all and sundry. Meanwhile the manager had figured out the cause of the fracas. He explained to the *kotvāl,* "Now I understand, sir. All this trouble is the work of the Mathura Mohan Company. They're trying to disgrace our company by starting a brawl during the show. Please release these men, sir. They're Hirabai's bodyguards. The poor woman's life is in danger!"

The *kotvāl* let Hiraman and his friends go, but their carter's whips were confiscated. The manager seated all three on chairs in the one-rupee section and told the watchman to go and bring them betel leaf by way of hospitality.

At the gallows two executioners, one wicked and one merciful, debate over Phul Singh's fate. Suddenly Nauṭaṅkī storms the execution ground, dressed as a man and armed with sword and dagger. Phul Singh is content with this last glimpse of her, and he says goodbye to the world as the noose is placed about his neck. But Nauṭaṅkī pulls out a cup of poison and prepares to commit suicide, vowing to die as Shirin died for Farhad and Laila for Majnun. As the executioners advance to pull the cord, she rushes with her dagger and drives them off. She then turns her sword on her father, demanding he pardon her lover at once. The king consents to the marriage and the two are wed on the spot. Phul Singh, his mission accomplished, returns forthwith to the Punjab with his new bride. The story ends with a blessing for the audience: "Thus may all lovers gain the fulfillment of their desires."

Hiraman turned his head when he heard Lalmohar's voice. "Hirabai's looking for you at the railway station. She's leaving," Lalmohar related breathlessly. Hiraman ran to the station.

Hirabai was standing at the door to the women's waiting room, covered in a veil. Her hand contained the coin purse Hiraman had given her for safekeeping. "Thank God, we've met," she held out the purse. "I had given up hope. I won't be able to see you from now on. I'm leaving!"

Hiraman took the purse and stood there, speechless. Hirabai became restless. "Hiraman, come here inside," she beckoned. "I'm going back to the Mathura Mohan Company. They're from my own region. You'll come to the fair at Banaili, won't you?"

Hirabai climbed into the compartment. The train whistled and started to move. The pounding of Hiraman's heart subsided. Hirabai wiped her face with a magenta handkerchief and, waving it, indicated "Go now."

The last car passed by. The platform was empty. All was empty. Hollow. Freight cars. The world had become empty. Hiraman returned to his cart.

He couldn't bear to turn around and look under the empty canopy. Today too his back was tingling. Today too a jasmine bloomed in his cart. The beat of the *nagāṛā* accompanied the fragment of a song.

He looked in back—no gunnysacks, no bamboo, no passenger. Fairy . . . goddess . . . friend . . . Hiradevi—none of these. Mute voices of vanished moments tried to speak. Hiraman's lips moved. Perhaps he was taking a third vow—no more company women.

Gender and Genre in *Nauṭaṅkī shāhzādī*

Two journeys concluded: Phul Singh returns home with princess Nauṭaṅkī, Hiraman leaves Hirabai behind. Beginnings sparked by impatience, greed, curiosity, desire. Breaks from family, ejection from home, travels on the open road. Middles strewn with obstacles, clashes, danger, and fear. Disguise and counterdisguise, wooing and counterwooing. Different endings. Phul Singh completes the quest, makes his conquest, lives to bestow his good fortune on the hearers of his tale as reward for their listening. Hiraman, reputation and purse intact, loses his heart and his innocence. His third vow—not a blessing but a warning, compressed confession of comic defeat.

Renu's account is a modern fairy tale, departing from traditional narratives in the ambiguity of its ending. The short story provides an excellent account of the connection between theatre and its rural audience. The mixture of fascination and fear focused on the exotic, prohibited category of womanhood represented in the Nauṭaṅkī actress could not be more eloquently described. *Nauṭaṅkī shāhzādī* (Princess Nauṭaṅkī) parallels Renu's tale, reproducing a structure of avoidance and attraction between the sexes analogous to the troubled relations between theatre and society. If *nauṭaṅkī* became a byword for the theatre, as the metastory asserts, then the *Nauṭaṅkī shāhzādī* drama must have paradigmatic value for the genre as a whole. Its preoccupations, particularly its problematic construction of gender roles and sexuality, require attention if the meaning of this story to the theatre it names is to be understood.

At first glance, the romance of Phul Singh and princess Nauṭaṅkī simply retells the age-old tale of a proud young man pursuing a distant and difficult love object. The tale's narrative syntax is familiar to both the folklore of South Asia and the larger Indo-European tradition. It begins with a rupture in family life (the quarrel between Phul Singh and his sister-in-law), the imposition of a task (winning Nauṭaṅkī as bride), the hero's vow to fulfill the task, and his departure from home. The next stage consists of various obstacles (the journey, the garden, the palace) and strategies for overcoming them (magic objects, helpers, disguise), resulting in the hero's successful wooing of Nauṭaṅkī. Then a second stage of difficulties ensues, when the hero is apprehended and punished for his amorous actions. After this section, the heroine emerges as the rescuer, creating a mirrorlike pattern of counterdisguise and counterwooing. The conclusion proceeds from her victory, the couple is reunited, and they return home to a restored order.[19]

This story, as narrated in the *chaubolās* of Chiranjilal and Natharam, Govind Chaman, and Muralidhar, early poets of the Hathras branch of Nauṭaṅkī, acquires the Indo-Islamic coloration typical of the genre. Internal allusions link it to the body of tales and motifs common across the region, causing it to blend with other familiar stories in the hearer's mind. Characteristically, when Phul Singh declares his resolve to leave home and seek Nauṭaṅkī as his wife, he calls his period of separation from family "forest dwelling" (*banvās, ban khaṇḍ*), terms used ordinarily to describe Ram's years of exile in the forest in the *Rāmāyaṇa*. Phul Singh's departure is also repeatedly compared to the act of renunciation of a yogi or fakir (*yogī* and *faqīr,* Hindu and Muslim ascetics respectively), especially as parents and friends try to dissuade him from venturing forth. In just the same way, Gopichand (and other kings) are warned against renouncing the world in the cycle of Gopichand-Bharathari. Phul Singh's well-wishers urge him to forsake the tragic path of love, citing the failure of famous couples to achieve union.[20] Laila and Majnun, Shirin and Farhad, Hir and Ranjha, all of whom are the subjects of other Nauṭaṅkī plays, are held out as precautionary examples, while Phul Singh vows to strive unto death for his beloved, citing the evidence of love's power from the same set of stories. These allusions not only legitimize Phul Singh's venture and enhance his heroic status, they bring about an overlapping of tales and motifs traceable to Sanskritic and Islamic sources, illustrating the eclectic borrowings of popular culture.

An experienced reader of Indian literature will notice in *Nauṭaṅkī shāhzādī* other elements common to classica' and medieval tales. The formulaic scene of leavetaking, with effusive demonstrations of pathos and attachment offered by family and friends, suggests the departure of Ram in the *Rāmāyaṇa*, although the Tamil genre of farewell lament known as *ulā* may predate that epic.[21] The two-brothers theme, more prominent in folktale than dramatic versions of the Nauṭaṅkī story, similarly has pan-Indian roots.[22] Stock characters like the *mālin* recall the procuress (*kuṭanī*) of Sanskrit drama as well as regional folklore. And the motif of changing sex to gain access to a woman is an old one found in medieval Sanskrit fiction.[23]

But there is more than continuity and commonality here. *Nauṭaṅkī shāhzādī* is a romance, a tale concerned primarily with love and conquests that occur in the region of the heart. Its themes contrast with issues of honor, territory, and war in North Indian martial narratives like the *Ālhā khaṇḍ*. Yet if love is *Nauṭaṅkī*'s principal focus, it is love with a novel twist. Consider a few anomalous scenes. First, the drama opens with a vituperative refusal by the hero's sister-in-law to supply him with domestic assistance. Her outburst leads to the hero's being launched into exile against the will of his family. Later, at the climax of the first stage of wooing, the princess makes explicit sexual overtures to an attractive young woman (actually Phul Singh in disguise), and at her insistence he eventually joins her in bed. Near the end, the princess charges into her father's court and holds a sword to his neck, threatening his death if her lover is not released. At these junctures, the actions of bold aggressive women dominate the stage, robbing attention from the hero. The very title of the drama suggests that the princess is more important than the male protagonist. Most romances in North India are identified by the names of a pair of lovers, for example, *Lailā majnūn, Benazīr badr-e-munīr*, and *Shīrīn farhād;* but the present story is not remembered as *Nauṭaṅkī phūl siṁh*. What does the stress placed on female characters and actions signify?

A close reading of the drama reveals that it is charged with a double-edged eroticism. Incidents, images, and characters repeatedly focus awareness on the pleasures and pitfalls of sexuality. Much as Hirabai, the actress on the Nauṭaṅkī stage, focuses the spectator's alternating attraction and avoidance, the princess in *Nauṭaṅkī shāhzādī* functions as a textual concentrate of desire and fear. A difficult, even dangerous, dimension to sexuality first arises in the chastity test, a folklore motif common to Panchphula, Phulpancha, Nauṭaṅkī, and others. Although these princesses are defined as lightweight, pure, and fairylike in their virginal state, sexual contact with a man taints them. Loss of chastity literally weighs them down. No longer capable of floating in air, they become heavy and drop down to earth. This dichotomous representation of the weight of the female body proceeds from a cultural proclivity to exalt the chaste presexual woman, raising her to the pedestal of insubstantiality, immortality, and fairyhood, and conversely to regard with dread the gross material nature of the sexual woman. The "heaviness" resulting from sexual contact may allude to the possibility of pregnancy and the ensuing threat to family honor should the woman (like the princess Nauṭaṅkī) be unmarried. Because of the patriarchal imperative to restrict female fertility, the consequences of inappropriate sexual activity come to be viewed as heavy burdens not only by women but by those males (especially fathers and brothers) who are enjoined with controlling unmarried women's conduct in society.

The fact that the princess is weighed in flowers has further significance within the Indian vocabulary of eroticism. Flowers and other vegetative forms are symbols of fertility in Indian literature, and the mention of flowers in a poem often initiates a romantic mood. Flowers, like body weight, encode a socially and culturally defined ideal of femininity. The notion of a princess light as a flower conjures up the delicate refined beauty prized in the aristocratic female. A cultural practice relevant to the motif of flower weighing is the public weighing of kings and princes on festival occasions (especially birthdays), ordinarily against quantities of gems or coins, as a royal demonstration of wealth and largesse; the coins were afterwards distributed. The flower weighing of the female thus constitutes a declaration of her worth as well as her freshness and excellence; a high price must be paid for her acquisition by a suitable male. The flower imagery does not stop with the chastity test. Phul Singh's name means "flower" (albeit coupled with the martial surname, "lion"), and his meeting with Nauṭaṅkī takes place soon after his tour around the royal garden. Significantly, he is led by the gardener woman, who guides him on the path to sexual initiation. Where there are flowers, deflowering is not far off.

In the drama's first scene, the potency of Phul Singh's repressed manhood is intimated through the motif of returning from the hunt. (The association of blood lust with sexual lust goes back at least to the Sanskrit drama *Śakuntalā,* where King Dusyanta entered the stage pursuing a deer in a similarly impassioned state.) Immediately upon the play's opening Phul Singh rushes in to his sister-in-law, wife of his elder brother. The relationship between a younger brother (*devar*) and his elder brother's wife (*bhābhī*) has been classified by anthropologists as a "joking relationship" in North India. The two affinal relatives, more or less equal in age and status, may enjoy a high degree of intimacy. Within this affect-charged bond, the sister-in-law sometimes plays an initiatory role, teasing the unmarried man.[24]

The potentially volatile nature of the *devar-bhābhī* relationship underlies the start of *Nauṭaṅkī shāhzādī*. In several versions of the play, the sister-in-law throws her arms about Phul Singh's neck, and in the earliest Khushi Ram edition, she beckons him to come to her and "fulfill her heart's desire." Phul Singh is impatient after his outing and storms in, expecting his sister-in-law to fetch him cold drinking water, prepare his food, provide his smoking materials, and make up his bed so he can relax. He is outraged when she insolently refuses and makes her own suggestive demands. Whereas he has approached her in her nurturing role as maternal surrogate, she counters as a potential sexual partner. The discomfiture of the hero could hardly be clearer.

Subsequently, Phul Singh's sister-in-law recommends he acquire his own wife to serve him. Here she is daring him to prove his maturity and his manhood, which she suggests is not to be achieved by bragging and commanding but rather to be won through a demonstration of valiant effort. Does he succeed in matching her expectation, pursuing the object of his quest and winning Nauṭaṅkī in a manly way? At first it seems he does. Phul Singh's resolution holds firm as he leaves his home, rides off to Multan, and penetrates the garden of the princess. He gets little chance to show his mettle en route; whatever difficulties he may have surmounted in other versions consist in the extant texts of not knowing the way. Although he manifests more wit than physical strength in making an ally of the *mālin*, he nevertheless succeeds in gaining access to Nauṭaṅkī's apartment.

As he approaches the object of his desire, however, he moves further from the unalloyed masculinity that would seem essential for the completion of his task. Perfecting the disguise necessary to gain entry, he decorates himself as a bride capable of outdoing even the charms of his beloved. The *mālin* assists him in washing his hair, parting it and applying vermilion, making up his eyes, putting jewelry on his limbs, dressing him in blouse, underskirt, and sari, reddening his mouth with betel leaf, and seating him in a palanquin.

This preparation sets the stage for his entry into the palace and the tremendous peril of his encounter with the princess Nauṭaṅkī. The play mounts to a high point of comic tension as her uninhibited declarations of love confront Phul Singh's simultaneous panic and attraction. After all the trials Phul Singh has endured to reach Nauṭaṅkī, her very forwardness now poses the greatest danger of all. In her state of excessive desire, Nauṭaṅkī breaches convention and unabashedly approaches a same-sex partner. The crypto-lesbian seduction scene functions in the text to suggest the enormity of the female sexual appetite and simultaneously to titillate the audience with the projection of a male fantasy. Faced with such an aroused, voracious female, Phul Singh is unable to make a sexual conquest. He is reduced to passivity and, calling on his wits again, stages a sham miracle to regain his control and assert his manhood.

Phul Singh eventually accomplishes the deflowering. But as a result of his personal victory he incurs the wrath of the social order, embodied in Nauṭaṅkī's father, the king. The princess's daily weighing-in betrays the nocturnal rendezvous. Parental authority and societal norms are offended; Phul Singh must be punished. As Phul Singh pledges his willingness to die for love, he seems incapable of mounting any campaign of resistance. Rather than rise up against society's harsh judgment, he waits for Nauṭaṅkī's return. Finally she enters brandishing a sword. When she threatens to slice off her father's head, the king capitulates and offers the lovers the protection of marriage, the mode of male-female sexual relationship permitted by society.

In these final moments, the heroine Nauṭaṅkī assumes the stance of the *vīrāṅganā*, the warrior woman who protects her people by marching into battle and defeating the enemy. Her authority to rule symbolized in her sword, she is not unlike the powerful goddess Durga, who saved the world by vanquishing the buffalo demon while riding on a lion. The *vīrāṅganā* reveals a model of female heroism based not on self-sacrifice and subservience to the male but on direct assumption of power combined with righteousness and adherence to truth (*sat*). While North Indian history records the rule of half a dozen queens of this type, folklore and popular culture supply additional instances of a heroine transforming herself into a *vīrāṅganā* at a critical juncture.[25]

When princess Nauṭaṅkī's violent energy bursts out near the end of the play, she is anything but the ethereal fairy whom Phul Singh earlier sought. In opposition to the dainty and virginal image of woman as fairy, her warring and decapitating aspect seems an extension of the sexually aggressive countenance she presented in the courting scene. Nonetheless, it is this overpowering female alone who is effective in saving the condemned Phul Singh. The intervention of the princess as *vīrāṅganā* allows several interpretations. Perhaps this scene replays a male fantasy of bondage and domination by a female. Possibly it is a disguised lament, a metaphorical expression of the individual's powerlessness in major life decisions such as marriage. Or it may be a remnant of goddess worship linked to possession cults. All are plausible in part, but here we note simply the reversal of gendered modes of conduct that has occurred in the course of the drama. Phul Singh, once strong and active vis-à-vis a slight, powerless female, has become feminine in order to accomplish sexual union with her. Now at the marriage he appears weak, passive, ineffectual, while his woman, dressed as a male, is transformed into a "heavy," dominant, victorious warrior.

As in most romantic comedies, the attainment of the love object ends the story. Marriage concludes the play; it symbolizes both the restoration of society's law and the taming of unruly womanhood. In addition it resolves the hero's crisis of maturation that erupted in the initial scene. The two requirements for Phul Singh to develop to maturity were to prove his manhood through sexual conquest and then to learn the proper social place for sexuality, namely subsumed in marriage. These stages correspond to the two steps of courtship in the plot: the initial seduction of Nauṭaṅkī by Phul Singh and Nauṭaṅkī's counterseduction of Phul Singh via the rescue. Through this narrative pattern the hero, at first an inexperienced adolescent dependent on an elder brother's wife, is transformed by the end into a proper adult, complete with his own wife.

However satisfying the conclusion of marriage to the narrative's symmetrical design, one suspects that it will not resolve the hero's inner division with regard to women. Will his beloved return to her former docile self, or will he have to make do with a warrior for a wife? The cycle of being attracted to the distant female and avoiding the woman at closer quarters seems destined to replay itself over and over. Summarizing the gender relations contained in *Nauṭaṅkī shāhzādī,* one might say that Phul Singh's saga has consisted of a series of challenges comprised of encountering woman and taming her. It is a series that knows no end, however, for the elusive woman keeps escaping his grasp, threatening to tame him instead.

Implicit in this reading of the text is the premise that woman is consistently represented as object, as the other. The female of the text *is seen* by the male who occupies the subject position rather than *seeing* from an independent position as subject. Given the problematics of male sexuality, her image is therefore the eroticized double born of both desire and fear. She oscillates between fairy and warrior, light and heavy, attractive and dangerous—a being essentially alien, outside, and unknown. The male gaze attempts to possess and contain her.

It is this obsession with the otherness of woman, this almost fevered exploration of conflicted male positions in regard to her, that the evidence of the *Nauṭaṅkī shāhzādī* text suggests is intrinsic to the Nauṭaṅkī theatre. Beyond the verbal script considered so far, nonverbal dimensions of the Nauṭaṅkī stage emphatically fix the female body as the locus of this preoccupation (see fig. 3). The erotic dancing, the facial gestures and articulation during singing, the reputation of actresses as prostitutes, and other performative features of Nauṭaṅkī, guide the spectator's interest unerringly to the women on public display. Not only the Nauṭaṅkī story, the entire Nauṭaṅkī theatre revolves around this seductive image of woman. Beguiling, beckoning creature, caricature of men's own craving, she commands the attention of her admirers and dares them to approach.

CHAPTER TWO

Situating an Intermediary Theatre

Bharata's Origin Myth

An old myth attributed to Bharata, the great sage of India's performing arts, relates the origin of the theatre. Bharata takes as his starting point the Vedas, the almost obligatory entry into any discussion of Indian cultural phenomena, but he immediately departs from protocol by suggesting the limits of their scope. For—as Bharata tells it—whereas the Vedas were accessible to the highest classes in society, they were not even to be overheard by Shudras (the lowest of the four orders or *varṇas*), women, or non-Aryans (outsiders, *mlecchas*).[1] For this reason the gods, under the leadership of their king, Indra, approached the creator god, Brahma, and asked him to produce something that all manner of people could enjoy, something that would be a source of diversion and entertainment, a plaything (*krīḍanīyaka*).[2] Accepting the validity of this appeal, Brahma assembled a new art by taking the best from each of the four Vedas. From the Ṛg Veda he took the recitation of words (*pāṭhya*), from the Sāma Veda music and song (*gīta*), from the Yajur Veda gestures and acting techniques (*abhinaya*), and from the Atharva Veda sentiments or emotions (*rasa*). Thus was created the Fifth Veda, the Nāṭya Veda, or Theatre.

This myth comes at the beginning of a great treatise describing the practice and theory of the performing arts, the *Nāṭyaśāstra,* probably composed between the second century B.C. and the second century A.D.[3]

It serves as a defense of the theatre, insofar as it is addressed to the educated classes who associated theatre with actors of low social standing. To this end, the story employs several time-honored strategies for legitimizing its subject. First, it ascribes a divine origin to the theatre, tracing the rationale for its existence to a request of the gods and naming its inventor as the creator god himself. Second, it constitutes the theatre out of older esteemed entities, the four sacred Vedas, from which its various elements are borrowed. Third, it names the theatre in relation to them, adding it as a sequel to their number: the fifth Veda.

At the same time that it proposes theatre as a new Veda, the myth sets out its very different purpose, nature, and social context. The functions of theatre are defined in this passage as pleasure, amusement, recreation—not ritual efficacy, religious instruction, or mystical realization.[4] From the beginning, theatre is designed as a composite art, a multimedia spectacle employing language, movement, musical sound, and feeling, in contrast to the predominantly verbal character of the Veda with its emphasis on the supremely potent Word (*vāk*). Further, in its relation to society, theatre is to belong to the people, cutting across hierarchies and including all ranks and classes within its embrace.

Buried within this story are enduring oppositions between the sacred and the profane, the pure and the impure, the high and the low, which are often viewed as essential to the structure of Indian society. One reading of the myth suggests that theatre belongs to the lower extreme in these hierarchies, especially in the implied contrast to the first four Vedas. Theatre is profane in relation to the scriptures' sacred authority, it is a mixture of forms aimed not at purifying but at entertaining, and it is associated with debased social groups. Indeed the maligning of theatre—and its adherents—has a lengthy history in India, predating Bharata in its origin and continuing to the most recent period. The *Nāṭyaśāstra* myth may be an early recorded apology for an art form that had long been considered lowly, corrupting, and impure.

The myth at the same time seems to say that theatre abrogates categories. Theatre is the great leveler. It holds all spectators in its compass by its universal appeal. The all-embracing character of theatre as described in the *Nāṭyaśāstra* is not intended simply as praise. Though it may be hyperbole to declare the Nāṭya Veda the summation of the Vedas, no doubt the theatre that Bharata knew did include almost all the arts of his time. As the *Nāṭyaśāstra* says, "There is no wise maxim, no learning, no art or craft, no device, no action that is not found in the theatre."[5] The detail of Bharata's text amply illustrates the statement. With its six thousand verses, it is the most elaborate treatise on theatre and its production ever written.[6] Moreover, the theatre, as mediating agency in a complex society, brings together an assortment of castes in the performance spaces created in temples, exhibition halls, and other public venues. In both senses then, theatre moves beyond classes and categories. It fuses, socially and artistically; it merges and transcends.

Bharata's origin myth not only outlines the ancient concept of theatre and social attitudes toward it, it demonstrates the persistent tension between the utility of categories and the limits of compartmentalization. A rhetorically astute scholar, Bharata introduces his topic in terms familiar to his audience. He begins by situating theatre in relation to the schemes of knowledge developed in the past. He identifies theatre as the fifth Veda, an apt procedure given the meaning of *veda* (from the Sanskrit root *vid*), "that which is known." And yet theatre is so obviously not a Veda; it is distinct from the four Vedas in ways that are suggested by the mere mention of them, and this too Bharata knew and intended his audience to know. The Vedas provide the reference point for establishing theatre as a respectable entity, and they also mark the point at which theatre diverges and takes its own trajectory.

The same dilemma confronts us in trying to situate the Nauṭaṅkī theatre within the systems of knowledge available to contemporary scholarship. Multiple approaches suggest themselves, each with its own conceptual framework. This chapter will explore some of the categories that have been utilized in the past, within two systems of reference. First, it describes Nauṭaṅkī in relation to the immensely varied field of theatre in South Asia and compares the genre to a number of other theatrical genres past and present. Second, it explores Nauṭaṅkī's connections within the rich realm of South Asian folklore, including its relations to nontheatrical genres such as folktale, folk song, legend, and epic. Insofar as the primary referent is the cultural environment of the Indian subcontinent, the discussion is grounded in the excellent body of research published by South Asianists in recent years. From the outset, however, it may be noted that some conceptual distinctions current in this scholarship are inappropriate to a complex cultural phenomenon such as Nauṭaṅkī. As this chapter explores how Nauṭaṅkī may best be described, it attempts to clarify the social and cultural situation of the theatre and to outline its broad dimensions in a manner of interest to both the specialist and the general reader.

Boundaries of Language, Region, and Religion

The theatrical arts of twentieth-century India comprise a panoply of forms, few of which are known or ever witnessed outside the country's borders. Those forms characterized by spectacular costumes and brilliant choreography seem to be the ones most frequently transported to Western soil, perhaps because of the commodity value of an image of India as "exotic." For audiences in South Asia, however, there are theatrical traditions in every region and at every level of society, and in all probability theatre has been present during every historical period. Theatre, having many species, has served many purposes. It has provided an arena for the savoring of aesthetic delight by the cognoscenti as expounded in the *rasa* theory of Sanskrit drama, and it has served as staging ground for symbolic inversions during rites of reversal such as the Holi festival. It has disseminated moral and religious messages to audiences accessible only by oral pathways of communication, and it has spoken eloquently through the languages of mime, costume, and music.

Within this variety of forms, Nauṭaṅkī belongs to the set of theatres whose historical evolution has been quite recent. These theatres rely on spoken vernacular languages that themselves developed only several hundred years ago. Nauṭaṅkī employs the languages based on the Khari Boli dialect, a form of speech that probably took linguistic shape during the eighteenth century in the Delhi and Meerut districts. Its written form emerged in the nineteenth century, and it now possesses two literary variants, Hindi and Urdu, the official languages of India and Pakistan respectively (together with English). In India alone, speakers of Hindi or Urdu composed 43.2 percent of the population in the 1971 census, forming the largest single group.[7] The area in which these languages are spoken extends at present from the western Punjab in Pakistan to Bihar in eastern India, a distance of about one thousand miles, and from the Himachal area in the north to the Deccan plateau in the south, again about one thousand miles. This linguistic region is loosely indicated by the term "North India," despite the unsuitability of the phrase after 1947. Beyond these bounds, speakers over a large territory including much of urban South Asia understand Hindi and Urdu in its lingua franca form, Hindustani.

The Nauṭaṅkī theatre of North India is linguistically identified by its use of Hindi and Urdu and its prevalence in the region where these languages are spoken. As a regional form, it is comparable to theatres found in other linguistic territories (largely coinciding in independent

India with state borders). These include the Jātrā of Bengal (which employs Bengali), the Tamāshā of Maharashtra (in Marathi), the Bhavāī of Gujarat (in Gujarati), and others. This is not to say that localized forms of speech never appear in Nauṭaṅkī performances. Depending on the background of the performers and the audience, dialects may be used. Specific song genres draw on literary dialects such as Braj, Awadhi, and Bhojpuri, and older texts tend to use grammatical endings characteristic of the Braj dialect. However, the predominant medium of Nauṭaṅkī theatre is Khari Boli Hindi or Urdu.

Nauṭaṅkī, Jātrā, Tamāshā, and other regional theatres have been shaped by late medieval historical circumstances in each geographical area, and they show marked regional traits beyond language, such as distinctive styles of dress, headgear, ornaments, and makeup, as well as song types, musical instrumentation, dance forms, and gesture language typical of each region. Among themselves, these regional theatres share a number of features: they make extensive use of music and dance, though in somewhat differing ways; their verbal textures are primarily poetic, but they also employ prose, often improvised; their vocabularies of acting, gesture, and costume are stylized; their stage techniques are informal and their productions have sparse props and scenery.

Several authors have referred to this class of vernacular drama forms together with their regional stages as the "traditional theatres" of India. According to Darius Swann, the term denotes "those forms which are distinguished from folk theater by clearly defined and recognized forms and a literature of some merit. Moreover, these genres, which have been passed on for generations by composers and performers, have depended upon the common people for patronage in contrast to the Sanskrit theater which, in its full flowering, catered to a restricted upper-class clientele."[8] Kapila Vatsyayan similarly describes "a certain commonality of approach which distinguishes these forms from purely tribal or village participative activity on the one hand and on the other, from the highly stylized individual expression of dance-forms commonly called 'classical' and normally associated with the urban."[9] That is, the traditional theatres occupy an intermediate position between the simplest folk forms of drama and the highly elaborate Sanskrit theatre. Both reference points, the folk drama and the Sanskrit theatre, will be analyzed in greater detail shortly.

The traditional theatres may be subdivided into those whose dominant ethos is sacred or religious (*dhārmik*) and those whose ethos is secular or worldly (*laukik*), a distinction made by practitioners and scholars alike. The secular character of Nauṭaṅkī is readily observable, for unlike the two religious theatres of the Hindi region, the Rām Līlā and the Rās Līlā, Nauṭaṅkī is not oriented toward the praise of particular deities (such as Ram or Krishna), nor are its performances connected to annual religious festivals (e.g., Dashahara or Krishna Janmashtami, common occasions for Rām Līlā or Rās Līlā performances, respectively). Nauṭaṅkī is first and foremost an entertainment medium, and its lively dancing, pulsating drumbeats, and full-throated singing generate an atmosphere considered by many to be opposed to religion and morality. Nor does the theatre draw its characteristic subjects from the pan-Indian religious epics, the *Rāmāyaṇa* and the *Mahābhārata,* even in their local forms, as do most traditional theatres including nonsectarian ones such as the Terukkūttu of Tamilnadu. The social organization of troupes has no connection with religious institutions or priestly groups, and performances are not viewed as in any way auspicious or ritually efficacious.

In the political sense, Nauṭaṅkī's secularism is displayed by its almost equal attention to topics identified with Hindu and Muslim cultural traditions. Islamic romances such as *Lailā majnūn* and *Shīrīn farhād* are favorite stories in Nauṭaṅkī, and one finds many other tales that may have accompanied advancing armies from the Middle East, entered the narrative lore of North Indian Muslims, and then found their way into the theatre. The blend of Urdu and Hindi diction in the texts, together with the inclusion of metrical types from both Hindi and Urdu prosody, also point to a mixed nonsectarian heritage. Muslims and Hindus participate together in the formation of troupes, and Nauṭaṅkī audiences may be drawn from either or both communities.

Nauṭaṅkī does address certain semireligious topics drawn from the popular strands of devotion and morality common to Hindus and Muslims. Exemplary stories such as that of King Harishchandra (originally found in the *Mārkaṇḍeya purāṇa,* a Sanskrit compendium of mythology), legends of saints promoting asceticism (*Gopīchand, Bharatharī, Pūranmal,* and others), tales of self-sacrificing devotees (*Prahlād, Dhurūjī*), and accounts of miracles and magical feats are examples. Their popularity may have been greater in the nineteenth century, when the theatre was evolving from the performance practices of heterodox religious sects. In other instances, Nauṭaṅkī plays communicate folk concepts of good and evil, the proper conduct of men and women, the nature of spiritual liberation, and similar topics. The element of instruction is often counterbalanced by the ribaldry and debunking of authority expressed in the theatre's nonverbal codes. But just as sexual innuendo, comic relief, and satire may disrupt the piety of a Rās Līlā or Rām Līlā performance, the profane Nauṭaṅkī does not overlook the religious leanings of its audience.

As far as is known, Nauṭaṅkī performances are not and have never been occasions for spirit possession, either on the part of performers or observers. Specific tales included in the Nauṭaṅkī corpus such as that of Guga, also called Zahar Pir, a saint-deity worshiped by the Chamārs (untouchables) in Punjab, are sometimes performed during rituals of possession.[10] In these rites, the narration or enactment of the *Gūgā* story is controlled by specialist participants associated with the cult. Worshipers take part in a procession or other group movement, and the ritual context encourages a lessening of distance between performer and believer. The procedure in a Nauṭaṅkī show is quite different. Performers are professionals from outside the community, organized as a company discrete from community members. Their advertising techniques (placards, drumbeating, public crying) signal a separate space designated for entertainment, and the demarcation of a stage area together with the erection of tents, seating arrangements, and so on keep their activities at a distance from the members of the audience. The absence of ritual possession in this theatre may indicate a general cleavage between North and South Indian oral performance, insofar as the other traditional theatres in the north seem to lack the element of possession, as do most epic recitations.[11]

Urban-Rural Cultural Flows

Among the secular theatres of Hindi and Urdu, Nauṭaṅkī as a traditional theatre may be further distinguished from the modern urban stages found in cities such as Delhi, Lucknow, Jaipur, and Bhopal. The urban stage received its impetus for growth in the nineteenth century when Western theatrical practices were introduced into India through amateur dramatics organized by the British for their own amusement. Colonial educators also influenced the development of Indian theatre by teaching their pupils the classics of Western drama. The modern (post-1850) theatre modeled on these precedents took a number of forms, from the popular commercial stage organized by the Parsi community, to school- and university-based drama clubs, to the urban elite theatre movement. While the Parsi theatre drew on the old repertoire of Indian classics in addition to new social dramas and Western imports (especially popularized versions of Shakespeare), the urban elite theatre in Hindi produced new scripts by Hindi authors as well as translations from important Indian and foreign playwrights.[12] In stagecraft, acting techniques, and thematic material it emulated the Western theatre, although recently there has been a significant attempt to "Indianize" the urban stage and work out a synthesis with folk traditions, including Nauṭaṅkī.[13]

The urban stage is a largely middle-class phenomenon found in the major cities throughout India; in Bengal and Maharashtra it has enjoyed a broad base of support and flourished for more than a century. For various reasons, the Hindi-speaking area has not proven as fertile a ground for urban elite drama. Only in recent years have several permanent companies grown up in Delhi and the provincial capitals, usually assisted by subsidies from the federal and state governments. One of the factors limiting growth appears to be the relatively slow erosion of agrarian ways of life in this region. The middle-class audience is still somewhat parochial in its tastes, and the artistic gains of the few successful directors are quickly offset by the prevailing preference for cinema and television.

In contrast to the urban stage, the Nauṭaṅkī theatre relies not on the patronage of a Westernized middle class or on its imported substratum of ideas and texts. Rather it is rooted in the peasant society of premodern India. This does not mean that its province is strictly rural or that it is even a village form in the usual sense. Several anthropologists in their studies of North Indian oral culture have not listed Nauṭaṅkī among the genres mentioned by the village people.[14] Nor is Nauṭaṅkī related to the seasonal, life-cycle, or devotional rounds of activity that generate many forms of folk poetry. Its actors and musicians are not likely to be represented in a randomly chosen village. Nauṭaṅkī players are specialists who are recruited primarily from the cities and towns of a given area, from where they move out to tour the countryside.

The rural order with its social, economic, and cultural structures infuses Nauṭaṅkī; yet its audiences are not limited to the farmers, agricultural laborers, and artisans in the villages. Within towns and cities, communities of working-class migrants are ready listeners for performing troupes. Factory employees, transportation workers, domestic servants, and lower-ranking clerks and salaried personnel, whose manners and allegiances may be relatively untouched by urban life, create the demand—in the city itself—for more traditional forms of entertainment. In addition, Nauṭaṅkī, like other public performances in the nineteenth and twentieth centuries, has enjoyed the patronage of the predominantly Hindu mercantile class that emerged in the urban centers as successor to the Mughal and post-Mughal aristocracies, filling their place as cultural guardian.

Although many Nauṭaṅkī actors are from low castes, the theatre includes a broad range within its personnel. The participation of the artisan castes appears to have been particularly significant. The legendary poets and singers of Hathras, Ustad Indarman, Chiranjilal, Ganeshilal, and Govind Ram, were all Chhīpīs, a *jāti* (caste) of cloth printers and dyers. Natharam Gaur, the most famous poet of their school, was, however, a Brahmin. Shrikrishna Khatri Pahalvan, founder of the Kanpur branch, can be identified from the back covers of his early plays as a tailor (*darzī*). Nauṭaṅkī troupe members in the Banaras region in the late 1970s were drawn from Muslim entertainer castes such as Ḍafālīs (who play the *ḍaf*, a large drum), Bhāṭs (musician-genealogists), and Chamārs.[15] In 1982, Pandit Kakkuji of Lucknow was wearing a *janeū* or sacred thread, a sign of high-caste status, and he described himself as a Brahmin. He had lived and worked among Muslim actors like Ashiq Hussain and Malika Begam for years, and since retiring from performing he made his living by stitching costumes. Female performers are said to be from the low castes of *beṛin* or *naṭin,* traditionally associated with singing and prostitution.[16]

Nauṭaṅkī is now identified in India as a form of folk theatre (*lok-nāṭya*).[17] Nonetheless, it does not fit neatly into the category of "folk drama" as used by Western folklorists, especially where "folk" designates village-level social organization. According to Roger Abrahams, "Folk drama exists on a village or small-group level. The performers are members of the community and therefore known to most of the audience. The dramas are given on special occasions only, most commonly a seasonal festival."[18] Nauṭaṅkī employs professional actors usually residing outside the village, and it has no regular connection to seasonal celebrations. In comparison with the Sāṅg of rural Haryana, for example, which does involve "village resident musicians," Nauṭaṅkī appears almost urban.[19] On Abrahams's scale, Nauṭaṅkī would belong to the category "popular theatre," which he defines as "often [arising] from folk theater but the players are professional and the audience comes from places other than the community in which the players live."[20] Abrahams's third category of "sophisticated drama" would describe the elite Hindi stage described above.

The designation "popular theatre," however, introduces a new set of ambiguities. Its possible meanings include "well liked" and "of the people," as opposed to an established power or government. In the second sense, " 'popular theatre' is applied to cultural/educational activities in which the popular classes present and critique their own understanding of the world in relation to a broader aim of structural transformation."[21] People's theatre or popular theatre in this sense is usually aligned with progressive political parties or third-world development programs. In the former usage, "popular" may refer to any commercially successful endeavor, often in an urban industrialized context, and has a more pejorative connotation.[22] In addition, popular theatre may be construed as a practice within "popular culture," meaning the culture of everyday life unbounded by class or social group.[23]

As a further qualification to Nauṭaṅkī's traditional or folk character, we must consider the ongoing processes of change, particularly as village and city interpenetrate. In the twentieth century, the lives of both village and urban dwellers have altered under the influence of educational opportunities, new technologies, and consumer goods. Nauṭaṅkī has consistently appropriated the modern values and tastes of its consumers and has brought the clash of old and new onto its stage. Contemporary stories have joined the older repertoire, as witnessed in *Dhūl kā phūl,* a tale of two college students whose bicycles collide, causing them to fall in love. Under the impact of the celluloid medium, tunes and dance items from cinema are now incorporated into most performances, and Bombay films provide the plots for the latest Nauṭaṅkī dramas.

Within this rapidly growing market-based economy, Nauṭaṅkī may even be viewed as a phenomenon of mass culture. Nauṭaṅkī now reaches audiences more through the electronic media—records, cassettes, films, and television—than through the older mode of face-to-face contact. Print reproduction of Nauṭaṅkī play scripts may have contributed to the standardization of the genre and facilitated its reception as a commodity. However, because the printing of drama pamphlets has been a constant of the Nauṭaṅkī tradition for almost a hundred years, the print medium itself cannot be considered responsible for "removing" the stories "from the transmission process of folk traditions," as has been the case with some other South Asian folk genres.[24]

Thus, rather than define Nauṭaṅkī as either a city or village form we might more appropriately view it as one conduit in the cultural flow that connects the urban centers and the hinterland in the ongoing process of exchange between them. For over a century, this theatre and its personnel have carried the stories, poetic forms, music, beliefs, and attitudes of different groups of people back and forth, linking the villager and the urban dweller, the educated and the illiterate, the Hindu and the Muslim. The traveling theatrical troupe brings rural ideology and reference to the migrant worker in the city; it takes back to the village the latest in urban social history. The same exchange occurs between different parts of the geographical territory linked by Nauṭaṅkī, as regionally specific elements (song genres like the Rajasthani *māṇḍ* or Banarasi *kajarī*, for example) are transported to other parts of the country. The audience too is mobile, including within it groups who move between village, town, and city: migrant industrial workers in the factories of Lucknow and Kanpur, artisans in craft centers like Banaras, agriculturalists visiting market towns like Hathras, and seasonal laborers such as the rickshaw pullers found in every Uttar Pradesh city.

Nauṭaṅkī's portability allows it to bridge urban and rural folkways and create an interstitial cultural space between categories. Because of its flexible contextual boundaries it is best characterized as an *intermediary theatre,* in two senses. The first refers to the intermediate level of complexity, as described by Swann and Vatsyayan, between simpler village-based forms and either an elaborate classical or an urban theatre. The second follows from the present discussion, namely that the intermediary theatre functions as a mediating agency between different populations, regions, classes, and ways of life.[25]

Parameters of the Folk and the Classical

A recent collection of essays on Indian folklore examines the connections between the categories of "folk" and "classical," noting overlapping themes, rhetorical strategies, and psychological dynamics.[26] This analysis discusses the categories without specifying the criteria for the "classical" in the context of South Asian performance. In this and other studies, a performance genre is assumed to be "classical" if its verbal texts are in the Sanskrit language (or classical Tamil in some instances) and predate the modern period. In the case of the Indian theatre, the classical tradition would comprise the twenty or so dramatic texts written by Sanskrit playwrights between the first and ninth centuries A.D. together with the performance practices associated with them. "Folk" is the remainder, what is left. The non-Sanskrit traditions are thereby termed the "folk" theatres, a category including forms as divergent as the Kūṭiyāṭṭam of Kerala (which incorporates the texts of Sanskrit dramas and in the view of some scholars uses old, "classical" performance conventions)[27] and the Jātrā of Bengal (which is primarily urban, commercial, and modern in its topical political themes).

Not only are the "folk" theatres ill served by this residual classification; the presence of folk elements in the Sanskrit theatre is glossed over. Sanskrit drama as known from extant texts was more accurately Prakrit drama, the Prakrits or spoken dialects being used to represent the caste, class, and gender of most of the characters except the male protagonist. Songs were composed in Prakrit by the musicians of the theatrical troupe, possibly following folk models.[28] Comic interludes were often interpolated drawing on folk humor and dialectal usage. These elements facilitated the reception of the drama by spectators of diverse backgrounds.

Other uses of "classical" are indicated by contemporary cultural forms as disparate as Hindustani and Karnatak classical music, classical Indian dance, and classical Urdu poetry. These "classical" performance arts to varying degrees thrive today, unrestricted by period or language. Such expressive arts demand an alternative definition of the classical. I suggest that instead of looking internally to textual strategies, themes, or codes as determinative, we give consideration to the sources of a tradition's authority, its modes of reproduction, and its relation to dominant social groups. I propose a three-part definition that may help identify the *classical* in Indian performance. First, a textual authority must be present that legitimizes and governs the art form. (The Hindi word for "classical" is *shāstrīya,* "based on a learned text.") This authority need not be a single text, nor need it be in written form; there may be a set of authenticating commentaries, oral traditions, or guidebooks. Second, this textual tradition must be studied and passed on by trained specialists (gurus, teachers, scholars, or performers) who control reproduction of the art form. Third, the producers, performers, and their institutions must be supported by a dominant social group. In premodern times, courts and temples most frequently acted as patrons; nowadays sponsorship comes from government agencies, corporations, and cultural institutions constituted from elite groups.

This definition serves to clarify the classical status of several traditions. Classical Indian drama had its *Nāṭyaśāstra* and was supported by the Gupta dynasty and later kings. Classical music and dance in modern India have developed under state and bourgeois patronage, being raised to the national level from quite narrow regional origins, following the study of earlier texts, including in the case of dance the evidence from temple and rock sculptures. In the case of classical Urdu poetry, the prior "text" is a parent tradition such as Persian poetry; its rules circulated among the literati while Urdu poetry developed in its shadow. The Mughal and post-Mughal courts had a stake in maintaining the prior Persian cultural identification and therefore patronized Persian-influenced Urdu poetry.[29]

A corollary of this definition would be that an art form or tradition becomes classical as it achieves recognition over time. Classical forms may often be those that have emerged as the most successful in the struggle for remuneration by powerful donors. The competition for support and prestige characterizes the representation of most traditions, regardless of their textual origins. In the India of today, the folk arts must compete for official patronage in an urban environment. Forces within and outside the Nauṭaṅkī tradition exert persistent pressure to "classicize" the form in the expectation of garnering funds for impoverished artists and setting up training institutes. Nauṭaṅkī artists intent on enhancing their status cite as textual authority the recent Hindi monograph written on their tradition, substituting its anecdotes for their personal experiences in interviews. When performing for government agencies, they discard their traditional instruments (harmonium, *shahnāī, nagāṛā*) for those associated with classical music (*tāmbūrā, tablā*) and give their tunes the prestigious designation of "ragas." Similar trends are under way in other regional performance traditions as they jockey for position in a postcolonial cultural milieu pervaded by conflict for limited resources.

So far, these efforts on behalf of Nauṭaṅkī have fallen short of the artists' objectives. Nauṭaṅkī has neither achieved significant government sponsorship nor spruced up its image sufficiently to make believable its claims to classicism. Nonetheless, the fact that Nauṭaṅkī as an intermediary theatre aspires to this sort of legitimacy is telling and brings the folk-classical contrast into the context of power, government regulation, and competition for social, political, and economic rewards. Scholars may find it possible, as Blackburn and Ramanujan do, to conceptualize folk-classical as a continuum rather than a hierarchy.[30] They maintain that both folk and classical traditions are "coexistent and available (in varying degrees) to everyone, as codes switched by rules of context."[31] To the ordinary practitioner of a marginalized and dying art, however, the possibility of coexistence barely occurs. He or she is much more concerned with the reality of survival and the necessity of catering to the authorities who may bestow financial favor. Context is thus not a neutral variable; it may be a matter of life or death. The naming of art forms as folk or classical is a privilege that continues to reside with those who have power and status in the society. The performers themselves rarely achieve this stature.

Terms like folk and classical are therefore inadequate when used in an essentialist way to indicate inherent differences located within the cultural forms. The hegemony of the classical continues to control and contaminate the folk forms, even as they are appropriated by the middle class as "ethnic," "indigenous," and "fashionable." The present study cannot hope to locate itself outside this dialectic. We cannot be immune to these cultural negotiations, but we can make reference to them and consider their influence on our perceptions and our interpretations.

It remains to discuss the relation of the traditional or folk theatres of India, with Nauṭaṅkī as our case in point, to the classical Sanskrit drama. They share a number of stage conventions. They divide performance time into several segments, beginning with the symbolic construction of the performance space, its ritual sanctification, and the worship of deities, followed by musical overtures played on various instruments (to attract and settle the audience), introductory dance items (to entertain and warm them up), and finally the entrance of the stage manager-director (*sūtradhāra*) who formally invites the audience to view the play. All these activities constitute the *pūrvaraṅga* (literally, pre-theatre); they are present in abbreviated or expanded form in the traditional theatres and in Sanskrit drama performance. Then there are the rhetorical features of the verbal text: its formulaic invocation (*maṅgalācaraṇa*) and epilogue (*bharatavākya*), the alternation between prose and poetry, use of different speech levels or dialects, and conventional modes of address, soliloquy, and offstage dialogue. Character roles also show similarities: the usual array of hero, heroine, villain, and servants is supplemented by the *sūtradhāra* (also called *raṅgā* or *kavi*), who often appears at intervals after the introduction to comment on the play in the manner of the early Greek chorus, and also the ubiquitous clown or jester, the *vidūṣaka,* who may act as a foil for the *sūtradhāra*. The dramatic entertainment is in both cases multitextured, mixing speech and recitation with song, instrumental music, dancing, and mime.

Baumer and Brandon account for the similarities between the folk and Sanskrit theatres by several theories. First, Sanskrit theatre may have developed from prior forms of popular or folk theatre. Second, contemporary regional forms may be "degraded remnants" of ancient Sanskrit theatre. Third, classical and regional theatre may have developed simultaneously but independently with little interchange between them.[32] Recently in India, scholars have claimed that theatres like Nauṭaṅkī are the surviving fragments of a continuous tradition traceable to the Sanskrit drama. The argument for this position is as follows. The *Nāṭyaśāstra* lists ten major types of drama (*rūpaka*), but other Sanskrit dramatic treatises mention various "minor" or near-dramatic forms termed *uparūpaka* in which music and dance played a larger part. According to V. Raghavan, these *uparūpaka*s evolved from folk dances and folk plays that were "taken, refined, refashioned, and fitted into the classical technique and framework."[33] The *uparūpaka*s or dance-dramas came into prominence when Sanskrit drama declined, and they are considered the link to the present-day forms. Another intermediate stage of development may be the *saṅgītaka,* or "musical drama," a term used in Sanskrit texts of the fifth through the eleventh centuries but absent from Bharata.[34] This word is etymologically related to *saṅgīta* and *sāṅgīt,* words used to identify the musical librettos of theatres such as Nauṭaṅkī. Thus Nauṭaṅkī is viewed as the most recent descendant of the largely vanished medieval theatrical tradition represented by the *uparūpaka* and *saṅgītaka,* which grew from the Sanskrit drama and replaced it some time after A.D. 1000.

In the face of the difficulties surrounding the reconstruction of performance styles from textual sources, the hypothetical linkages (Sanskrit *rūpaka* to vernacular *uparūpaka* to contemporary forms) are beyond proof, especially given the paucity of evidence for the connecting medieval period. Contemporary observation of the existing regional theatres leads one to marvel more at their differences, suggesting a relatively recent historical evolution rather than lineal descent from a single progenitor. The theory relating traditional theatre to Sanskrit drama may then be speculative and untestable. But to dismiss it would be a mistake, because it is useful for understanding the place of traditional theatre—not necessarily with respect to ancient drama—but in India today.

In the last twenty years, a serious reappraisal of indigenous theatrical forms has occurred in intellectual and artistic circles across India. The regional theatrical arts, formerly considered degraded, corrupt, and moribund, have been reassessed as vital to the cultural diversity of independent India. Their status has been enhanced through urban revivals, direct government support, and scholarly research.[35] The suggested historical link to Sanskrit drama has validated the claims of these theatres to recognition and appreciation. Here again the "classicizing" tendency is at work, dulling the distaste evoked by unrefined "folk" forms of culture. The supposition of classical roots for the folk theatres has therefore become close to official policy. What is visible is a linkage constructed in the service of the ideology of national integration, summed up by the motto "Unity in diversity." Given the political dimensions of culture in independent India, the story of Nauṭaṅkī will inevitably begin in ancient glory.

Folk Theatre as a Genre of Folklore

If we accept Roger Abrahams's definition of folklore as "a collective term for those traditional items of knowledge that arise in recurring performances," we perceive that Nauṭaṅkī theatre is part of the folklore of India.[36] Nevertheless, as Abrahams points out elsewhere, folk drama has been little discussed in the folklore literature, and its recognition as a discrete genre has been somewhat belated.[37] Western scholarship on folklore traditions of India has first focused on the narrative genres, especially the oral or folk "epic" and the folktale, and secondarily on the smaller forms such as the folk song, riddle, and proverb. Folk theatre may have escaped notice because of its dual citizenship, being perceived as "theatre" more often than "folk." Whatever the reasons, the neglect must be remedied. Folk theatre shares so much with other genres of folklore in South Asia that the problem is not whether to consider it as folklore but how to delineate clearly its connections with other folklore genres.

The issue of generic classification is far from solved for the other folklore forms, however. Theoretical discussions of generic interrelations have only recently appeared in the South Asian folklore literature.[38] Many valuable detailed studies of specific traditions suffer from a lack of precision in the use of genre labels, in part resulting from the confusion between Western-based analytical modes of classification and indigenous taxonomies.[39] The difficulty is compounded by the multitextuality of the better-known Indian stories. Gene Roghair notes that the Telugu *Epic of Palnāḍu* exists in a wide range of media:

> It can be found in the form of modern verse; unedited palm-leaf manuscripts in both classical and folk metres; edited scholarly publications . . . ; motion pictures; elementary school reading texts; novels; stage plays; radio plays; . . . rice-transplanting songs; *burra katha* . . . ; articles in weekly magazines; paintings; sculpture; . . . and extended oral narratives.[40]

This multiplicity is not unusual and could be documented for many folk narratives in India today.

Similarly, the stories found in the Nauṭaṅkī theatre are for the most part not unique to this performance genre. The Princess Nauṭaṅkī story itself is present in prose tales in several regional languages as well as in metrical ballads, folk plays, and modern dramas. The stories of the saintly followers of Guru Gorakhnath such as Gopichand, Bharathari, Puranmal, Guga, and others circulate as myths, legends, ritual narratives, oral epics, and poems all over North India. Magical tales of adventure such as the Rup-Basant cycle have multiple versions, including dramatic and folktale forms.[41] The martial themes of the Ālhā recitational tradition are also favorite stories in Nauṭaṅkī theatre, and the Amar Singh Rathor theme is common to Nauṭaṅkī and the puppet theatre of Rajasthan. Contemporary topics such as the bandit queen Phulan Devi, based on journalistic accounts and hearsay, occur not only in Nauṭaṅkī but in the Hindi lyric genre *bārahmāsī,* in the Bhojpuri genre *birahā,* and in the Ālhā style.

Nonetheless, the hypothesis I propose is that Nauṭaṅkī as a theatrical genre possesses conventional modes of communication between audience and performers that set up expectations of a certain type and establish the genre's identity with relatively low levels of ambiguity. The purpose of defining the genre's boundaries is not to erect rigid classificatory walls but to understand the dimensions of performer-audience interaction signaled by a Nauṭaṅkī drama as distinct from other related folklore genres. As Abrahams asserts, "Genre analysis provides a common frame of reference by which such conventions of form and use may be compared and thus permits one genre or group of genres to cast light on others, either within one group or cross-culturally."[42] The identification of Nauṭaṅkī's unique generic traits would help us contrast it to the genres that border it. We may then extend this system of relations to other parts of South Asia and even beyond, where folk drama, folk narrative, folk song, and folk dance reside in close proximity.

Narrative content alone is an insufficient determinant of Nauṭaṅkī since other genres of North Indian folklore share the stories. Content is just one element in a triad of criteria that Western folklorists use to name traditional genres. In Abrahams's terms, content, form, and context are the significant variables that separate generic categories. Dan Ben-Amos uses slightly different language with the same basic meaning when he distinguishes prosodic, thematic, and behavioral levels of folklore.[43] Content or theme refers to the story, the sequence of events of a narrative genre. Form designates the prosodic structure of the genre and its possible use of music, dance, and painting and extends to literary analysis of dramatic structure, rhetorical strategies, and other textual features. The last criterion, context or the behavioral aspect, names the customary usage of the genre, its connection to social structures, its appropriateness to certain settings, and the characteristic interaction between audience and performers. Taken together, these levels of analysis provide a descriptive framework for a folklore genre that identify it as a member of a class of objects and simultaneously distinguish it from other members within that class.

In terms of content, Nauṭaṅkī belongs to a large group of narratives that includes the various legends and tales known to the North Indian region. The reservoir of potential Nauṭaṅkī narratives is fed by oral and written accounts from Arabic and Persian romances, Sanskrit epics and Puranas, folk epics of Rajasthan, Punjab, and Uttar Pradesh, legends of saints, kings, and local heroes, popular novels, historical events, newspaper accounts, and popular films. Within this class, Nauṭaṅkī exerts certain preferences in its choice of subject matter. We have noted the genre's lack of dependence on pan-Indian epic materials and the low level of religious content manifest in the stories. Nauṭaṅkī themes tend toward the martial and romantic, with social dramas based on contemporary life entering in the modern period.

At the formal level, these stories are structured according to a musical and prosodic plan distinctive to the genre. The overall texture is antiphonal, alternating sung recitation of verses with musical passages using the same melodic and rhythmic motifs performed by an ensemble of percussion (typically the *nagāṛā* or kettledrum), wind instruments (*shahnāī,* clarinet, or flute), and harmonium. The tunes are largely dictated by the meters of the verses, and over twenty different meters may be used. However, the bulk of narrative discourse is composed in the ten-line stanzaic form *dohā-chaubolā-dauṛ,* and dialogue frequently occurs in the meter *bahr-e-tavīl,* consisting of two long lines. Prose also appears in improvised passages often of a humorous or topical nature, and it is more prevalent in certain styles of Nauṭaṅkī (such as the later Kanpur style influenced by the Parsi stage).

The sophisticated formal apparatus of Nauṭaṅkī employs the verse patterns and conventions of Hindi poetry (seen in the *dohā* and *chaubolā*) as well as regional folk genres such as the lyric forms *dādrā, ṭhumrī, sāvan, holī, māṇḍ, lāvanī,* and so on. It also draws on the traditions of

Urdu classical prosody, borrowing verse types such as *ghazal, sher, qavvālī,* and others. Similarly, the musical materials show some features of classical Hindustani music, including a rudimentary raga structure, the use of metered cycles (*tāla*), and rhythmic cadences of three repetitions (*tihāī*). In these formal features of music and meter, the *intermediary* character of the genre is again visible, the mediations occurring here between Hindi and Urdu poetics on the one hand, and folk and classical music on the other.

The relative complexity of the performance form is consistent with the professional status of the actors and singers, their lengthy apprenticeship (often beginning in childhood), and the specialization of roles within the troupe. However, not all performers are equally accomplished. Formal complexity accordingly varies with the performer's expertise. This introduces the question of the relationship between the degree of formal elaboration and gender. In a comparison of women's folk songs with those of men, Ved Vatuk observes that men's songs in Hindi and Punjabi tend to use regular end rhymes and meters related to the "high" poetic tradition, whereas women's songs use repetition patterns (refrains) instead of rhyme and a looser prosodic structure.[44] Vatuk's work suggests a continuum of metrical complexity associated with gender that would identify male performers with traditions like Nauṭaṅkī that are metrically and musically quite intricate. Folk genres such as the prose tale, the lyric song, and others performed by women tend to be shorter and lack the complexity of the epic and drama.

Another attempt at constructing a gender-based dimension for genre is that of A. K. Ramanujan, who reworks the classical Tamil division of *akam/puṟam* to suggest a continuum stretching from domestic "interior" tales told primarily by women to public "exterior" performances by males. As Vatuk does, Ramanujan identifies the women's domain with less formulaic, less complex uses of language, and men's with the elaborate techniques of the professional bard.[45] Though on the face of it this argument may appear to state a correlation found in a number of folklore genres, such an equation of form with gender is of limited application. It assumes a traditional, unchanging ideal (to some) of unschooled secluded women. Rather than remain indoors, many Indian women work in the fields, in animal husbandry, in quarrying, road building, and construction; they haul water and firewood daily; they travel on pilgrimages or to weddings and festivals, and they visit relatives; in short, their lives take them into the exterior world on a regular basis, and folklore activity undoubtedly occurs on these occasions. Regarding women's knowledge of sophisticated forms, it is well known that as professional singers and dancers they carried on the traditions of the performing arts for long periods when men's expertise in these areas had almost died out through lack of court patronage. Women have excelled in literature, music, dance, and theatre for centuries in India, and they still play a very important role in the performing arts, including the folk arts.

Before the introduction of female actors, men impersonated women in Nauṭaṅkī as they did in other traditional theatres. Around the 1920s women joined Nauṭaṅkī troupes and began to sing and dance the female roles; a similar process had occurred in the theatres of Bengal and Maharashtra earlier. Considering the importance today of women as actors, singers, dancers, and even as troupe managers in the Nauṭaṅkī theatre, we could not characterize it as a male or male-dominated institution. Nor could we explain its formal sophistication as a result of the determining presence of males. Women use the same meters and musical materials as men do; their art is in no way stylistically inferior because of their gender.

Although we know very little about the performance art of women in India, we must not assume that their performance is less formally sophisticated than that of men, or that it is exclusively tied to the hearth and limited to private interior contexts. Only recently with the expanding body of knowledge generated by feminist studies have we recognized that much of women's history has been lost or suppressed in societies around the world. Definitive study of women's participation in the cultural processes in India remains a project for the future. Nonetheless, we can assume from the partial evidence available that women have taken a significant part and that their activities have been extremely varied. Until the subject is thoroughly researched in its own right, to summarize the complex relations that may exist between folklore genres and female performers, audiences, and performance contexts would be premature.

Ramanujan's use of the *akam/puṟam* dichotomy in reference to folklore genres leads into the third element of generic classification, the interaction between audience and performer. The identification of interior and exterior contexts sets up one way of looking at this variable. Ramanujan's continuum places the folktale at the extreme of interiority, where an intimate, often familial, connection exists between performer and audience. At the other extreme, the theatrical performance represents maximum exteriority and professionalization, with a public (and therefore depersonalized) relation between audience and performer. According to this model, both the formal nature of the genre and its subject change to some extent when the performance moves from an interior domestic space into an outer public one. Although Ramanujan does not explain it in this way, the greater distance between the exterior nonfamilial audience and the public performer may necessitate a more redundant, verbally ornamented, repetitive (formulaic) style to bridge the relatively greater gap in experience and affect between speaker and hearer. The domestic context, in contrast, assumes an affinity of feeling and a shared substratum of interaction. The communication is therefore sparser, less redundant, more economical in its means.

The concept of interpersonal distance between audience and performer is central also to Abrahams's way of perceiving the contextual dimension of folklore genres. Abrahams outlines a continuum of relations between performer and audience extending from total interpersonal involvement to total removal. At the extreme of involvement, he lists the conversational genres, such as jargon, slang, traditional similes and metaphors, and the discourse of address, appeal, and assault: proverbs, spells, curses, prayers, charms. At a slightly greater degree of distance are the play genres, such as riddles, jokes, verbal contests, debates, spectator sports, and finally rituals, folk plays, games, and dance-dramas. In folk drama, "contact between performers and audience is almost completely severed—this is what is meant by the term 'psychic distance.' "[46] However, the degree of audience involvement in folk drama is still greater than that present in the "fictive genres," in which dramatic movement must be envisioned by the mind's eye rather than being present in visual form on stage. This group includes the "great" narrative forms of folklore, the epic, ballad, lyric, and legends, as well as work songs, traditional sermons, and so on. Finally Abrahams's spectrum includes static genres such as painting, sculpture, and design, which present the extreme of removal between audience and performer, relying not at all on performance or verbal communication.

Whereas Ramanujan's model emphasizes the spatial component of context, Abrahams focuses on the quality of communication embodied in the genre's conventions, ranging from the completely dialogic and participatory to the univocal, professional, and ultimately even nonverbal. Nevertheless, a considerable degree of compatibility exists between the two models. Both stress the conventional separation of audience and performer in a publicly enacted theatrical event, a separation that may be ensured by verbal as well as visual and spatial means. This separation distinguishes theatre from debate and verbal contest on the one hand, in which respondents have an equal role, and from religious ritual on the other, in which audience members often participate both as officiants and as recipients. Abrahams, however, makes a unique contribution by specifying the crucial distinction between folk drama and narrative forms, namely the *acting out* of the story, so that makeup, costumes, and movement visually represent the narrative events to the audience. Abrahams is undoubtedly correct in asserting that the techniques of theatrical representation bring the audience closer to the performance, closer to the action and the emotions of the characters, than a recitational mode that employs no dramatic role-playing. A performance genre that mimes human action through the artifice of stage acting—showing the audience the actions of the story, not simply talking about them—is fundamentally different from one that simply narrates.

Following this reasoning, a Nauṭaṅkī enactment of a story from the *Ālhā* epic (to take one possible example) belongs to one genre, and the *Ālhā*'s epic recitation belongs to another. We would perceive this distinction if we listened closely to the formal structure of the performance, especially the meters and tunes used, but grounds for confusion exist even here because Nauṭaṅkī has incorporated the characteristic meter of the *Ālhā* epic, the *chhand* (also known as *ālhā chhand* or *bīr chhand*) into its prosodic texture. We could also look for the ubiquitous *nagāṛā* and other musical instruments typical of Nauṭaṅkī. We could more easily discern the difference between the folk theatre Ālhā and the epic recitation *Ālhā* by a simple visual survey of the costuming, makeup, physical movement, as well as the possible presence of a raised stage, painted curtain, or otherwise demarcated performance space signifying the dramatic mode of representation and the generically unique relationship of audience as spectators to performers as actors.

Despite the similarity of story material then, the folk theatre possesses its own performance praxis, and it secures its own objectives through a generically defined grammar. This is not to argue that dramatic and narrative genres are always easy to separate in Indian folklore. Within the dramatic texture of Nauṭaṅkī, for example, some narrative passages occur in which a character describes her or his own movements and actions in the third person, usually to relate an abbreviated series of events. The folk theatrical traditions, including Nauṭaṅkī, also bring on stage a narrator (the *kavi, raṅgā,* or *sūtradhār*) who makes connections between segments of action by means of narrative speech. On the other side, epic performers from narrative traditions such as the Panduvani of Chhattisgarh embellish their singing with many physical gestures, including facial expressions, brandishing of weapons, and energetic body movements.[47] The presence of a "second," the singer-respondent present on the stage who prompts the main performer with "And then what happened?" and other verbal cues, also brings an element of dramatization to the performance style of many South Asian epics. Still, epic performances as a class will tend to have conventions in common, as will folk drama performances, and though both classes incorporate elements from other genres, the approach of each is sufficiently distinct to ensure its own identity.

To summarize the discussion, we may best define Nauṭaṅkī according to two referential schemes. As an *intermediary theatre,* it is representative of the class of theatres in India that have flourished in the more industrialized, semiurbanized environment emerging from agrarian society. It belongs to the public life of the community, employs professional personnel, and depends on a sophisticated level of social organization for its commercial survival. As a *folklore genre,* it is a relatively long and complex form, related to oral epic and other narrative genres in content, but distinct from recitational forms in its dramatic mode of performance and in its own sophisticated formal grammar.

Nauṭaṅkī as conceptualized here is certainly folklore, but it is not folklore as "timeless" or "immortal." The historical moment figures significantly in Nauṭaṅkī's rise and development, and the theatre has already gone through tremendous change. We must further qualify these categories and continua in a historical perspective, by erecting another axis for comparison. That perspective provides the focus in the next two chapters. For now, suffice it to say that folklore is the product of its age. Folk theatre in India—especially in its recent manifestation as intermediary theatre—has a spongelike quality that allows it to soak up whatever is current, controversial, or salable—whether it be new songs, dances, plots, topical references, jokes, or puns. One trait of a large form like Nauṭaṅkī, moreover, is that it can maintain a framework (much as the traditional epic did) so that generic integrity persists even with the continual implantation of new materials. This integrity is somehow greater than the sum of the parts named by content, form, and context. It is carried forward by a tradition that includes texts as well as performance events, lineages of poets as well as rival performing troupes. No one locus is sufficient to define the elusive unity of this mediating art.

CHAPTER THREE

The Landscape of Premodern Performance

The community life of late medieval North India was enlivened by a number of performance traditions of a mainly local and oral character. Many of these arts, including those of a theatrical nature, went into eclipse during the period of cultural redefinition and reform that occurred in the late nineteenth and early twentieth centuries.[1] More recently, shifts in historical method together with cultural and political processes at work in India have stimulated a reassessment of the premodern cultural landscape and sparked an effort to restore it to Indian social history. This chapter contributes to that process by examining significant traditions of theatre and performance predating the emergence of Nauṭaṅkī in the late nineteenth century. My endeavor is to describe a "community of forms," to adopt Raymond Williams's phrase, a historically specific set of practices located in an evolving social environment.[2] In the process I hope to refurbish some dim corners of North Indian culture and challenge some earlier preconceptions.

Before the twentieth century, the theatre now identified as Nauṭaṅkī was known as Svāṅg. This term is still used to refer to the art of mimicry and impersonation in general as well as to specific skits. The word *svāṅg* and its variant *sāṅg* are related to *sāṅgīt,* a term employed from the midnineteenth century onward as a generic marker for the libretto or musically rendered dramatic script. "Nauṭaṅkī," originally the name of a heroine and the musical stage play based on her story, came into wide parlance replacing the term Svāṅg around 1920. "Svāṅg" is even now the label applied to the Nauṭaṅkī form by its practitioners in the Hathras-Braj region, and it is a widely understood synonym for Nauṭaṅkī among scholars of Indian theatre.

A recognizable Svāṅg folk theatre appears in the midnineteenth-century Sāṅgīt texts, lodged in the India Office and British Library collections. Early dramas like *Prahlād sāṅgīt* (fig. 4) and *Gopīchand rājā kā sāṅg* (fig. 5) contain the thematic and metrical seeds that later flowered into the full bloom of the Hathras and Kanpur styles of Nauṭaṅkī. Scholars in India have shown some reluctance to push the theatre's historical narrative further back. The predominant opinion is that drama was sadly missing for the many centuries between the decline of Sanskrit drama around A.D. 1000 and the appearance of nineteenth-century urban drama. Shrikrishna Lal, for example, declares that there was an "absence of Hindi dramas" before those of Bharatendu Harishchandra, the "father" of modern Hindi drama.[3] Following Somnath Gupta and influential earlier critics Shyam Sundar Das and Ramchandra Shukla, he posits reasons for this assumed absence, ranging from Muslim rulers' theological disapproval of dramatic representation to the overwhelming popularity of bhakti poetry. To the extent that Lal and other authors acknowledge folk theatre, they identify it with the Līlā spectacles of religious pageantry. Accordingly, when Svāṅg emerges as a secular folk theatre, they attribute to it the same religious roots as the Līlās, namely medieval devotionalism.

Collating information from a variety of colonial, literary, and ethnographic sources, I propose to demonstrate that the Svāṅg stage constituted an incremental development in a preexisting arena of public entertainments, influenced both by evolving folk traditions and by court-based and urban performance styles. In the first part of this chapter, I look specifically at the twin theses of indebtedness to the Līlā traditions and the "absence" of performed dramas before 1850. I then consider several folk streams that enriched the early Svāṅg, including the Khyāl folk stage of Rajasthan, an agonistic verbal art called Turrā-Kalagī, and the narrative corpus of minstrel mendicants of the Nath sect. In the second section, I examine the contributions of Indo-Islamic court culture, which entered the popular milieu through the intermediary of Urdu drama. Finally I turn to the urban Parsi theatre, a pan-Indian commercial network, to trace its role in the evolution of the performance practice called Nauṭaṅkī.

Fig. 4. Title page of *Prahlād sāṅgīt* by Lakshman Singh (Delhi, 1866). By permission of the British Library.

Fig. 5. Title page of *Gopīchand rājā kā sāng* by Lakshman Singh (Delhi, 1877). By permission of the British Library.

Devotional Drama in Hindi

Two folk traditions of religious drama, the Rām Līlā and Rās Līlā, developed in North India some time before the secular Svāṅg. Dedicated to the sectarian deities Ram and Krishna, the Līlā theatres likely originated with impersonations of the gods at annual festivals. Their current forms date from the bhakti period of Hindi literature, when vernacular devotional poetry found a home in the hearts of the Hindu population. The Līlā dramas wed episodic enactment of the lives of Ram and Krishna with the singing, dancing, and recitation of poems from this newly flowered literature.

The Rām Līlā is based upon Tulsidas's narrative of Ram's adventures, the *Rāmcharitmānas,* a long poem composed in the Awadhi dialect.[4] Chanted passages from Tulsidas's text intersperse with song, drama, and pageantry to explicate the story. This form of the Rām Līlā began soon after Tulsidas's death in 1624 and, according to legend, was first enacted by his disciple Megha Bhagat. In the nineteenth century the royal house of Banaras undertook sponsorship of the Rām Līlā at Ramnagar on a massive scale, employing large numbers of actors and specific locations in the city to represent the story's geographical settings. This grand Līlā is performed over a period of days, culminating in the festival of Dashahara, when Ram finally defeats the forces of evil. It is attended by hundreds of thousands of spectators who follow the procession as an itinerant audience of worshipers.

Whereas the most famous Rām Līlā is linked with the geography and people of Banaras, the Rās Līlā's homeland is Vrindavan and the Braj area, where pilgrims come to worship Krishna, born among its simple village people.[5] Temple courtyards and pavilions form stages for dozens of Rās Līlā shows held every year at Krishna's birthday. The performances are bipartite, comprising circle dances (*rās*) by boys playing female devotees (*gopīs*) and dramatic episodes (*līlās*) from Krishna's life. As foci of religious emotion and musical embellishment, the verses of poets like Surdas and Nanddas, written in the Braj dialect, punctuate these incidents. The Rās Līlā may have achieved this form as early as the sixteenth century.

Alongside these celebrated Līlās, scores of less elaborate representations of the Ram and Krishna stories are performed by wandering drama companies and residents of city neighborhoods. The artists who play in these rustic shows are not dogmatic about the difference between devotion and entertainment, and the deity's story is intermixed with much singing, dancing, and comic improvisation.[6] These folk Līlās provide an important avenue of access to devotional Hinduism for people all over northern India.

The Līlā theatres, particularly in their village and neighborhood forms, established a practice of popular drama that in a general sense created a foundation for the later Svāṅg and Nauṭaṅkī. Common conventions such as open-air performance, use of music and dance, and mythological story material link these theatres, but a more explicit genetic relationship at the regional level is difficult to verify.[7] Indeed, a set of contrasts distinguishes the theatre of devotion from its secular counterpart. On the one hand, the Līlā plays are meant to inspire reverence and love for God, and they often produce audience emotion approaching rapture; the actors, prepubescent Brahmin boys, are worshiped as divine incarnations (*svarūp*). On the other hand, Svāṅg and Nauṭaṅkī shows evoke merriment, lust, wonder, even fear; their performers are considered outcastes and prostitutes. The Līlās function within a religious matrix presided over by priests, patrons, and high-status interpreters. Nauṭaṅkī relies on its commercial appeal, offering diversion in exchange for a price. The language of the Līlās is elevated and literary, whereas Nauṭaṅkī is composed in the spoken tongue, accessible to all.[8]

The Līlā traditions may therefore be considered precursors of Svāṅg to the extent that they created a receptive climate for dramatic performance, accustoming viewers to theatrical representation. Since theatre was well established in India in ancient times but appeared to lapse when the use of Sanskrit for literary composition declined, we may more aptly state that the Līlā theatres perpetuated the folk stage in an era of transition. Under the guise of devotional religion, the Līlās kept the traditions of folk theatre performance alive, until altered circumstances in the eighteenth and nineteenth centuries gave rise to a new secular drama.

Early References to Svāṅg

Popular entertainments of a nondevotional sort were not absent in the fifteenth through the eighteenth centuries. References to a variety of public diversions abound in the literature of the period. The sayings attributed to Kabir, who probably lived in the second half of the fifteenth century, contain many allusions (mostly derogatory) to dramatic entertainments termed *tamāshā* (show), *svāṅg* (skit, mime), and *khel* (play, game).[9] In the *Āʿīn-e-akbarī* Abul Fazl describes a group of performers termed *bhagatiyā* who dress in disguise, sing, and "exhibit extraordinary mimicry."[10] In Maulana Ganimat's masnavī *Naurang-e-ishq* (1685), an extended description occurs of a group of *bhagatbāz* artists who play instruments and perform impersonations.[11] Other sources suggest that mimics, actors, and acrobats (*bhāṇḍs*, *naqāls*, *naṭs*, and others) informally circulated throughout the region.[12]

Controversial evidence also exists in the form of about three dozen texts composed between the early seventeenth and midnineteenth centuries in Braj Bhasha. Several of these are original compositions on epic and religious themes, but most are translations from Sanskrit.[13] Most texts style themselves *nāṭaka,* the Sanskrit dramaturgical term for "serious drama." Nonetheless, much disagreement exists over whether the texts should be viewed as poems or as dramas. Bharatendu Harishchandra, Ramchandra Shukla, Shyam Sundar Das, and Somnath Gupta consider them poetic compositions, citing the lack of divisions into acts and scenes, conventions for stage entrances and exits, and prose dialogues. Gopinath Tivari, breaking with received wisdom, holds that the texts were modeled on folk drama styles and were actually performed.[14] He cites internal evidence from the texts, such as mention of the curtain and backstage area, references to the stage director (*sūtradhār* or *kavi*), instructions regarding dance and physical movement, mention of vocal projection, and details regarding historical occasions of performance. Tivari's argument seems quite convincing, but it would be impossible to verify without study of his manuscript sources.

According to Tivari, the word *svāṅg* first appears in Hindi dramatic literature in these plays.[15] Possibly the first text to term itself *svāṅg* is the Braj Bhasha *Hāsyārṇava* written between 1686 and 1689 by Rasarup.[16] An eighteenth-century example is the *Mādhava vinoda* by Somnath Chaturvedi (1752).[17] The word *svāṅg* occurs in two lines in the play.[18] Other references to *svāṅg* occur in the many versions of *Prabodha chandrodaya.*[19] The Braj Bhasha dramas differ from nineteenth-century folk Svāṅgs in several ways: their language is literary Braj, the meters are *dohā, chaupāī,* and *savaiyā,* and the performances most likely occurred in court, not on a public stage. The word *svāṅg* thus apparently refers to dramatic art in general; later it came to signify a specific genre of folk theatre. Nonetheless, these early plays point to the presence of secular dramatic poetry that *naṭs* and other professionals probably performed well before the nineteenth century.

Khyāl Theatre of Rajasthan

The same group of Braj Bhasha dramas also contain the word *khyāl* referring to drama. The word *khyāl* is polysemous within the context of the performance arts of North India. At least three discrete fields are now designated by the term: the classical Hindustani vocal genre, in vogue since the seventeenth century;[20] the folk theatre of Rajasthan and its texts, written in Marwari and other dialects; and the Hindustani folk poetry composed extempore and sung in the genre *lāvanī*. At an earlier time, these fields perhaps overlapped: the *khyāl* poetic style possibly became associated with a type of singing that in turn influenced the classical musical form (or vice versa); the folk theatres may have adopted *khyāl* poetry, or the poetry may have come to be dramatically performed. The issue is complicated by the several etymologies available for the word. Derived from Arabic *Khayāl,* it means "imagination, thought, memory," connotations appropriate to the musical senses of the term (and possibly to poetry), whereas *khyāl* from Hindi *khel* means "amusement, play," an etymology more apt for folk theatre.[21]

Leaving aside the Khyāl form of classical music, let us look further at the Khyāl theatre and *khyāl* folk poetry. Somnath Chaturvedi in *Mādhava vinoda* was perhaps the first to use the term *khyāl* in reference to his play.[22] Another early use of the term is in Dhonkal Mishra's *Prabodha chandrodaya,* dated 1799.[23] The term *khyāl* thus appears to have been in circulation in the eighteenth century among poet-playwrights writing in Braj Bhasha. This usage connects these plays to a larger group of dramatic texts called *khyāl,* performed by folk troupes in Rajasthan and elsewhere in the late eighteenth and nineteenth centuries.

The earliest description of this Khyāl folk theatre was published by John Robson in 1866.

> In the principal cities and towns of that country, during the weeks following the Holi crowds assemble night after night around elevated spots of ground or *chabūtras*, which supply a ready-made stage, and on which rude attempts at scenery are erected, and the players continue acting and singing accompanied by an orchestra of tom toms, on till late at night, or early in the morning, and for weeks and months afterwards, the favourite refrains and passages may be heard sung in the streets and markets.[24]

Robson reproduces five short plays in the Devanagari script with information on their history and performance.[25] He collected the manuscripts from actors' handwritten scripts, supplemented by transcriptions from commissioned recitation. Citing the local view that the *khyāls* are "not . . . literature at all," he asserts, "Yet there can be no doubt that, for good or for evil, they do constitute a literature, the most popular in Rajputana at the present day." Further, "[these *khyāls*] show us an indigenous drama, in the course of formation, rude and imperfect, but original and containing all the elements of growth."[26]

Perceptively linking this drama with the martial and romantic ballads of Rajputana, Robson refers to an anecdote regarding its origin.

> The brave and accomplished, but unfortunate, Ram Singh, King of Jodhpur for a short time in the middle of the last century, had a great fancy for hearing the recitals of the bards and other poets at his court. Among them was a Pokurn Brahman, called Jasu Lal, who was especially distinguished for the spirit of his compositions. One day, when reciting one of his pieces, he dressed in the character which he described and accompanied his declamation with appropriate action. This pleased the prince greatly, and he desired that it should be repeated. On the next occasion Jasu appeared in one character and a companion of his in another; and between them they recited and acted a dialogue. To listen to this became a favorite amusement with Ram Singh, though not with his nobles, who often found themselves the butt of Jasu's pleasantry and of the King's laughter; and, if we may believe tradition, this had not a little to do in estranging them and causing them to transfer their allegiance to Bhakta.[27]

This passage implies that the Khyāl began in Rajasthan around 1750, and another reference to "hundreds" of *khyāls* that had been previously composed suggests a tradition with substantial development behind it by the middle of the nineteenth century.[28] According to Robson, the "ballad parentage" remains visible in the style of dialogue and singing. Most of the singing was done by one individual or by a pair who alternated stanzas.[29] This structure is congruent with the question-answer format of the Turrā-Kalagī tradition prevalent at the same time.

Robson's collection contains the first record of a folk theatre based in rural Rajasthan dating to the mideighteenth century. Other authors confirm these suppositions about the age of Khyāl.[30] Soon after Robson's handpenned manuscript was published in 1866, Khyāl librettos started being printed by local Indian presses. Numerous Khyāls in Devanagari type dating from the 1870s are contained in the British Library and India Office Library.[31] These documents illustrate the further development of the Khyāl theatre. Published from Bombay, Poona, Delhi, Banaras, and especially Calcutta, the Khyāl texts appear to have followed movements of theatrical personnel across western and northern India.[32] The titles, however, indicate Rajasthani origins for most of the plays, being primarily based on local romances (*Ḍholā mārū, Pannā bīramde,* and *Sadābrachh sālaṅgyā*) as well as martial (i.e., Rajput) stories (*Rāṇā ratan siṁh, Ḍūṅgar siṁh*). Some titles are synonymous with nineteenth-century Svāṅg themes: *Gopīchand bharatarī, Benazīr badr-e-munīr, Pūranmal,* and *Harishchandra.*

The Khyāl tradition of folk theatre continues to the present. Now a regional form distinguished by the use of Marwari and other Rajasthani dialects, particular meters, distinctive costuming, and specific story material, it possesses several subvarieties. Nanulal Rana of Chidava (1858–1900), the most prolific playwright in the British library collections, originated the Shekhawati style. His contemporaries in the same school in eastern Rajasthan included Prahlad Ray Purohit, Ujiram Teli, Jhaliram Nirmal, and Bhan Kavi. Lachhiram of Kuchaman (1867–1937) established the Kuchaman style based near Jodhpur.[33] One of the most knowledgeable researchers of Khyāl reports that two hundred printed dramas have come to light, and the oldest is purported to go back three hundred or four hundred years.[34] *Khyāl*s performed in the area neighboring the Braj region share certain characteristics of Svāṅg and Nauṭaṅkī: playing of the *nagāṛā* drum and meters such as *chaubolā, bahr-e-tavīl,* and *lāvanī.*[35]

Some scholars suggest that the Agra-Bharatpur region, on the border between Uttar Pradesh and Rajasthan, was the original home of Khyāl theatre, and that Khyāl spread throughout the north in the late eighteenth and nineteenth centuries, undergoing linguistic changes in the respective regions it entered.[36] According to this diffusionist hypothesis, as the commercial structure of the folk theatres developed and the cultural and linguistic identity of each region solidified, the separate character of the theatres evolved to the point where the Khyāl of Rajasthan, the Nauṭaṅkī of Uttar Pradesh, the Sāṅg of Haryana, and the Māch of Madhya Pradesh are now considered discrete genres. This argument requires modification, however, when we incorporate the evidence of the poetic tradition, also called *khyāl,* which came to inhabit the same territory in roughly the same period. Although the Khyāl theatre based in Rajasthan set the stage for the emergence of Svāṅg to the east, traditions from the south had been at work too, strengthening the foundations of folk expression.

Lāvanī Poetry and the Turrā-Kalagī *Akhāṛās*

While the Khyāl theatre grew out of bardic recitations, the poetic tradition of *khyāl* developed from philosophical exchanges between heterodox religious sects. The ancient practices of public debate of scripture (*shāstrārth*), extemporaneous poetic composition (*samasyāpūrti*), and musical dialogue (*savāl-javāb*) are all visible in the unique Turrā-Kalagī tradition. In it, two opposing groups direct questions and answers to each other, using the song type *lāvanī* or *khyāl*, accompanied by the drums *ḍholak* and *chaṅg*. The Turrā is commonly described as advocating the Shaivite position and the Kalagī as arguing for the supremacy of Shakti. Each group is organized as an *akhāṛā*, wears a distinctive color, and exhibits its ensign on its drum in the form of a crest (*kalagī* and *turrā* both refer to the crest or plume affixed to a turban). The competition or contest between the parties is known as *daṅgal*.[37]

Turrā-Kalagī apparently originated in Maharashtra and became a prominent form of popular poetry in the eighteenth and nineteenth centuries. Various theories have been espoused concerning its origins;[38] accounts indicate that a range of religious topics may have informed the poetry of this genre. The dispute turned on dualities not limited to Shiva versus Shakti; it would typically oppose *puruṣh* and *prākriti*, *brahm* and *māyā*, or *nirguṇ* and *saguṇ*.[39] Debates that began as metaphysical exchange would often end in verbal abuse and even physical violence. The dialogue form of religious discourse occurred even earlier in a type of Marathi folk poetry known as *goṇdhaḷ*. This too is a recitational tradition using two opposing sides, performed originally to propitiate the goddess Amba and to enact Puranic incidents and heroic ballads.[40] Both the *goṇdhaḷ* and the Turrā-Kalagī traditions fed into the Tamāshā folk theatre of Maharashtra, which reached its height in the late eighteenth and early nineteenth centuries. In Tamāshā performances, a serious philosophical discussion between Shiva and Parvati generally occurs using question-answer *lāvanī* singing, following the erotic female dance known as *gaulaṇ*. Showing the clear influence of Turrā-Kalagī, this section is known as *jhagṛā* (fight) or *savāl-javāb* (question-answer).[41] Performers of Tamāshā identify themselves by their allegiance to the Turrā or Kalagī parties.

In Bengal a similar performance practice known as Kabi or Kavi flourished. "The Kavi is sung between two parties, and there are wit-combats between the two parties relating to Sakti, Siva, Krishna and other mythical topics. One party sings after the conclusion of the other."[42] Here too the Kabiwalas had connections with the theatrical traditions of Jātrā, and by the midnineteenth century they had established a substantial following among the affluent in urban Calcutta as well as in the hinterland. The *Calcutta Review* of 1851 noted the tendency toward obscenity: "The animus of the Kavis is rivalry. Two bands under different leaders are with each other in winning the applause of the audience. . . . They indulge in the songs of the most wanton licentiousness and to crown the whole [*sic*] with calling each other bad names."[43]

It is assumed that the Turrā-Kalagī troupes and their *lāvanī*s traveled northward from Maharashtra, possibly when entertainers followed the camps of the Maratha army in the eighteenth century. Turrā-Kalagī was taken up in Madhya Pradesh, where it is still practiced as a folk song form.[44] The institution eventually reached northern India. In Saharanpur in Uttar Pradesh, Turrā-Kalagī troupes and their competitions were described by Chaube in 1910.[45] At some time between 1750 and 1850, Turrā-Kalagī further developed its dramatic potential and moved its performances to a raised stage, with costumes, incidental singing and dancing, and new story material. In Madhya Pradesh this folk stage was known as Māch or Māñch (from Hindi *mañch*, "stage").[46]

In Rajasthan Turrā-Kalagī became associated with the Khyāl folk theatre, where it led to a separate style called Turrā-Kalagī Khyāl centered in Chitor and Ghosunda. Its performances focused on story material found in the oral traditions of the region, and the organization of performers into rival *akhāṛā*s under the Turrā and Kalagī symbols and the *daṅgal* competition continued. When one group presented its latest play, its opponent attempted to obstruct the performance and then started up its own drama on the same theme as soon as the first group had finished.[47]

As the Svāṅg folk theatre evolved, it absorbed the social organization and competitive character of Turrā-Kalagī.[48] In Sāṅgīt texts, the poet's affiliation with a Turrā or Kalagī *akhāṛā* is referred to in invocatory or colophon verses. Thus, "We bear the guise of the Turrā faction"; "Nattha the Brahmin and Madan enter the arena with the crest on their drum (*chaṅg*)"; "Maharaj says, Raghuna leads the party in the *daṅgal.* / Flaunting the crest on the drum, he deals blows to the pride of the enemy."[49] The boasting typical of the Turrā-Kalagī style is also evident here: "No one has achieved victory over those who wear the *turrā*"; "The enemy's claims turn to water, / The drums are played forcefully, / Chhitarmal's clamor reigns supreme—in the *daṅgal.*"[50] The poets often sought supernatural protection to survive the poetic combat. The famous Hathras poet Indarman invokes the goddess Bhavani thus: "Come sit in my throat, goddess, and sing 3,600 ragas . . . / Protect the honor of your servant. / Drink the blood of the wicked. / Be gracious to me now, / Uphold my respect today in the assembly."[51]

The term *khyāl* was used by Hathras poet-playwrights of the late nineteenth century as a synonym for *sāṅgīt, svāṅg,* and *sāṅg.*[52] The signature *dohā* that came to adorn the covers of Chiranjilal's and Natharam's Sāṅgīts reads, "Gentlemen seeking the authentic *khyāls* of Indarman should buy and read those with the name of Chiranjilal."[53] Similarly, another *akhāṛā's* poet says at the end of his play: "This *khyāl* was sung by Vaidya Chiranjilal. In seven days he composed this *svāṅg.*"[54] These uses of *khyāl* indicate the assimilation of the Turrā-Kalagī conventions to the Svāṅg theatre, and they show how *khyāl* poetry had by now merged with a relatively undifferentiated theatre known by the same name, Khyāl.

Another legacy of the Turrā-Kalagī tradition was the mode of dramatic discourse found in all the related forms—Svāṅg, Sāṅg, Bhagat, Khyāl, and Māch. Typically only two actors appear on the stage at once, and they engage in sung dialogue in question-and-answer form.[55] The influence of Turrā-Kalagī is also apparent in the growing popularity of *lāvanī* poetry. As a result of the dispersal of Marathi folk artists throughout the subcontinent, poets of Gujarati, Rajasthani, Hindi, and even Tamil came under their influence and adopted the *lāvanī* form. Though in Marathi the *lāvanī's* character was predominantly erotic and lyrical, it was adapted in these languages to new uses. The use of the *lāvanī* for nondramatic Hindi poetry had become well established by the second half of the nineteenth century.[56] The cover illustration of one of the popular *lāvanī* chapbooks is shown in figure 6. Such collections contained verses by Hindu and Muslim poets on devotional Krishnaite themes and on Indo-Islamic topics, for example, the love between *āshiq* and *māshuq* (lover and beloved).[57] The activities of *khyāl* and *lāvanī* poets in nineteenth-century Lucknow are also described by Sharar.[58] Bharatendu Harishchandra, the father of modern Hindi drama, was very fond of this form and would sit on the pavement with *lāvanī* singers to learn their compositions; his own *lāvanīs* were published as well.[59] This folk style of poetic composition is still extant.[60]

It is clear then that during the nineteenth century the popular stream of *lāvanī* poetry was incorporated into several North Indian theatres: Khyāl in Rajasthan, Māch in Madhya Pradesh, and Svāṅg in Uttar Pradesh. Many varieties of *lāvanī* meters appear in Sāṅgīt texts beginning in the 1890s. The rich *lāvanī* tradition fertilized the developing Svāṅg, particularly as it established itself around Hathras in the late nineteenth century. *Lāvanī* continues to be an important category of verse composition in twentieth-century Nauṭaṅkīs.

The discussion so far shows that a secular folk theatre existed across

Fig. 6. Title page of *Lāvanī navīn bilās* by Nanhu Lal (Banaras, ca. 1873). The group leader plays a large tambourine (*ḍaf*) and holds the *akhāṛā*'s banner. He is accompanied by musicians playing the sitar and cymbals while an enthusiast smokes a pipe (*chilam*). By permission of the British Library.

a broad sweep of territory in North India from at least the mideighteenth century on. Known under various names (Khyāl, Māch, Svāṅg, Sāṅg), this folk stage was related (and perhaps directly indebted) to a tradition of spontaneous poetic composition, initially disseminated by followers of non-Brahmanical religious cults. While the poetry of the Turrā and Kalagī parties became more overtly dramatic, the emerging stage preserved the aesthetics of competition, improvisation, and partisanship typical of secular performance art, in contrast to the devotional drama that canonized the words of medieval saint-poets and inculcated surrender to religious emotion. We turn now to other sources of the early Svāṅg, which confirm the notion that the religious roots of Svāṅg and Nauṭaṅkī, such as they were, lay not in devotionalism but in the iconoclastic teachings of Yoga, Tantra, and Shaktism.

Nath Yogis and Narrative Folklore

Along with the bards of Rajasthan and the Shaiva and Shakta *lāvanī* singers, another unusual population contributed to the early Svāṅg theatre. The ascetics known as *sādhūs*, especially the followers of Guru Gorakhnath in the Punjab, originated several frequently told Svāṅg tales, principally *Gopīchand* (see fig. 5) and *Puranmal* (fig. 7). In contrast to the Līlās focusing on divine heroes incarnate in flesh and blood, the Nath yogis stressed faith in ascetic renunciation, magical beliefs, and Tantric mysticism. The Nath yogis (*nāths*, *yogīs*, or *jogīs*) are followers of saint Gorakhnath. Because of the initiatory rite of inserting a heavy earring (*mudrā*) into the pierced cartilage of each ear, they are known as *kānphaṭā* (having split ears). Tales such as Gopichand's embody their beliefs: emphasis on conquering death and achieving immortality of the physical body, and rejection of sensual pleasure, especially congress with women.[61] They worship Gorakhnath as one of the nine Naths (lords, masters) and reckon Gopichand as one of the eighty-four Siddhas (adepts).[62]

The Naths were largely responsible for spreading Tantric beliefs and terminology among the masses of northern and central India, through their popular sayings or *Gorakh bānī.* Yogis of the Nath sect established a formidable reputation among the villagers as curers, magicians, and masters of the occult. Most important for our purposes, they also functioned as singers, musicians, and popular entertainers. Through songs and stories such as that of Gopichand, they elaborated a redoubtable body of folklore to spread their sectarian message. Nath oral traditions

Fig. 7. Title page of *Sāṅgīt puranmal kā* by Ramlal (Meerut, 1879). By permission of the British Library.

are one of the main sources of the early Svāṅg stories, and the yogis themselves may have been a primary conduit to the popular stage.

The Nath community had a substantial geographic reach. Its chief pilgrimage sites and monastic centers ranged from Hing Laj in Baluchistan, to Dhinodhar in Gujarat, Tilla in Punjab, and sites in Nepal, Bengal, and Bombay.[63] Nath yogis lived in settled caste units as well as in monasteries, and they also traveled in bands. Toward the end of the eighteenth century, these bands gained an unusual degree of political and economic clout in the absence of a strong central authority. Ascetic orders were heavily involved as mercenaries and traded, lent money, and owned property.[64] The proportion of religious mendicants in the population has been estimated by Bayly to be 5 percent around 1880 and significantly larger a century earlier. Briggs, reviewing census figures for the late nineteenth and early twentieth centuries, concludes, "simply, Kanphatas are very widely scattered and are exceedingly numerous."[65]

Not all Naths were bards, but the evidence from various caste groups suggests the sizable domain of their storytelling art. Briggs notes the involvement of many *jogī* groups in playing musical instruments, singing ballads, and preserving religious songs.[66] Raghunathji describes a Bombay beggar caste known as *gopīchandā*s engaged in the same activities.[67] In Banaras in the nineteenth century, Sherring mentions the *bhartharī*s, "a sect of devotees who . . . carry a musical instrument in their hands, on which they play, while they sing the exploits of Raja Bhart."[68] Recently, *jogī*s in Meerut district, Uttar Pradesh, have been noted as singers of the oral epic of *Gūgā,* while in Rajasthan members of a Nath householder caste preserve the epic of Raja Gopichand.[69] Other authors document the important role played by *jogī*s in the singing of ballads and transmission of folklore in North India.[70]

Although *jogī*s have been professional raconteurs perhaps for centuries, there is no explicit evidence of their organization into dramatic troupes in the nineteenth century or earlier. The number of Svāṅg stories of the period featuring the character of Guru Gorakhnath do indicate a substantial assimilation of Nath yogi lore, either through their direct involvement or through an intermediate agency. The measure of the Nath yogi contribution can be glimpsed in the first ethnographic account of the Svāṅg stage, Richard Carnac Temple's *Legends of the Panjab,* which includes four complete Svāṅg texts, three of them on Nath themes. Temple, a captain in the Bengal Staff Corps, collected an impressive body of folklore from the Punjab in the late 1870s and early

1880s. His three-volume work, published in 1884, contains the Svāṅgs *Rājā Gopī Chand, Guru Guggā, Sīlā Daī,* and *Rājā Nal,* all composed by one Bansi Lal. He also includes metered texts of *The Song of Pūran Bhagat* and *The Marriage of Hīr and Rānjhā* and a prose version of *The Adventures of Rājā Rasālū*—all stories based on Nath lore.

Other nineteenth-century collectors like Abbott, Crooke, Steel, and Swynnerton attest to the popularity of Nath folklore and its particular association with the Punjab in their versions of *Gūgā, Rasālū, Hīr Rāñjhā,* and *Pūran.*[71] Further documentation of the staging of *Gopīchand* and other Nath themes is provided by Pandit Hiranand Sastri, who describes performances in the Punjab on the "modern and mundane" heroes Gopichand and Puran.[72] The Gopichand story is called "the greatest favourite," and the manner of singing calls to mind the Turrā-Kalagī tradition, with "two parties, each sitting on the tops of two different houses and there singing songs in turn by way of dialogue about midnight."[73] These colonial accounts go a long way toward filling the historical gap in our knowledge of Svāṅg and Nauṭaṅkī. They identify the recitational and performative practices that converged to enrich the early Svāṅg stage and document the prevalence of a secular theatrical art in place in various locales by the midnineteenth century.

To recapitulate, this theatre did not spring suddenly from northern Indian soil: there was no dearth of indigenous theatrical entertainments—no critical "absence of dramas"—before the introduction of Western theatre under the British Raj. Nor was the Svāṅg theatre an outgrowth of medieval devotionalism. On the contrary, secular antecedents of Svāṅg carry its history well back into the eighteenth century and suggest an independent line of evolution. Chief among these was the flourishing folk stage of western Uttar Pradesh and Rajasthan termed Khyāl, whose librettos predate the earliest known Sāṅgīt texts. The emerging Svāṅg stage was also heir to the spontaneous poetry tradition of Turrā-Kalagī and *lāvanī,* as well as to the narrative lore of the Naths, a prominent yogic order in northern India. These little-known performance arts all contributed to the formative stage of Svāṅg.

Court Theatre and the *Indarsabhā*

The folk antecedents for Svāṅg were augmented by midnineteenth-century theatrical developments in the princely establishments of the ruling elite, as well as in the urban centers where British-bred bourgeois culture was forming. The court and city as cultural loci were not isolated from the rural-based traditions already surveyed, but each lent to theatrical performance a unique set of conditions and conventions. It is only in examining each tradition separately that the panorama of premodern theatre comes to life, and the emergent and combinatory nature of Svāṅg and Nauṭaṅkī takes on comprehensible shape.

Theatre was a principal pursuit of a number of kings across northern India in the period from 1600 to 1850, and they patronized theatrical performances held in their palaces as well as in public to amuse and edify the populace. Passing reference has been made to Braj dramas such as *Hāsyārṇava* and *Mādhava vinoda* commissioned by or performed in the presence of royalty; the legendary connection between the Rajput courts and the early Khyāl theatre has also been noted. The exact relation of court performances to the local drama traditions and available vernacular texts is a topic requiring research beyond the scope of this book. It would be particularly useful to know more about performance styles and their affinities to the secular folk traditions. For the present, we scan the range of court-related theatre, culminating in the appearance of Urdu drama in association with the midnineteenth-century court of Lucknow.

A flourishing court theatre based upon the Vaishnava movement was patronized by the ruling dynasties of Mithila, Nepal, Bundelkhand, and Assam from the fifteenth to the nineteenth centuries.[74] About a hundred plays were written by thirty-five dramatists during these four centuries, inspired in the main by the devotional songs of Vidyapati and Chandidas and traceable ultimately to Jayadeva's *Gīta govinda,* written at the end of the twelfth century. Suniti Kumar Chatterji describes these dramas as "elementary dialogues of two or more actors accompanied by songs," and they appeared first in Bengal and northern Bihar (Mithila), spreading thence to Assam, Orissa, and Nepal.[75] The themes came from the Sanskrit epics and Puranas but also included the folk epics of eastern India, such as *Rājā gopīchandra.*[76]

The Malla kings of Nepal were great patrons of drama from whose courts in Patan, Bhatgaon, and Kathmandu come many of the surviving play texts. Although the Mallas' native language was Newari, a Tibeto-Burman tongue, various Indo-Aryan languages spoken in the vicinity were widely understood. The plays contain a mixture of dialects: stage directions in Newari; prose conversations in Bengali, Maithili, Kosali, or Awadhi; and songs in Maithili and other dialects.[77] One of these plays, *Harishchandra nrityam,* was written in 1651 by Ramabhadra Sarman for performance in the Indrayatra, a large festival held in the streets and squares of Kathmandu. Cassiano Beligatti, a padre en route to Tibet, wrote an extensive account of Indrayatra performances he witnessed between 1725 and 1750. Although he mentioned no specific titles, his description corresponds to the features inferred from the *Harishchandra nrityam* and other manuscript sources.[78]

Another Kathmandu manuscript, *Kriṣhṇacharitopākhyān nāṭakam*, dated 1835, was enacted during the Indrayatra for nine days, by a troupe of 238 Newari performers. It was put on at the British residency before a mixed audience of Nepali court officials, Indians, and Britishers. The familiar *Kriṣhṇa līlā* from the tenth book of the *Bhāgavat purāṇa* formed the story. This play is written in Khari Boli Hindi, and Shardadevi Vedalankar claims it to be the earliest extant manuscript of a performed drama written in the modern vernacular.[79]

In the Bundelkhand region of Madhya Pradesh, theatre prospered at the court of Gangadhar Rao (reigned 1835–1853), husband of Lakshmibai, Rani of Jhansi. A man of sophisticated taste, Gangadhar Rao was a patron of theatre and made stage appearances himself on occasion.[80] *Shakuntalā* and *Harishchandra* were two of the dramas exhibited in his court; the names of female dancers and scene painters have been preserved from the period. The plays were full of instrumental music, singing, and dancing, with conversations spoken in prose. This theatre survived until the end of the nineteenth century, when the noted Hindi novelist Vrindavan Lal Varma viewed some of its plays.[81] We do not know whether any texts were preserved from the Jhansi court theatre.

The last of the Nawabs of Lucknow, Wajid Ali Shah (reigned 1847–1856), ranks among the preeminent royal patrons of the arts in nineteenth-century India. Seated on the throne at the time of the British takeover of Awadh, Wajid Ali has been alternately praised for his magnificent court with its aesthetic refinement and condemned for his moral decadence and inattention to administration.[82] Several important performance genres such as the Kathak style of dance and the light classical song form *ṭhumrī* received his early support, and a host of minor forms thrived too.[83] In the theatrical realm, the Nawab encouraged the Radha-Krishna themes found in other North Indian courts. Attracted to song and dance from childhood, he established a *rahasḵẖānā* (drama hall) where the amorous exploits of Krishna and his female devotees were enacted, and he maintained a *parīḵẖānā* (harem) for the ample provision of female artists.[84] Hearsay has it that Wajid Ali himself participated in these private sports in the role of Krishna. He also penned a skit, *Rādhā kanhaiyā kā qissā,* first played in Huzur Bagh in 1843.[85] Upon ascending the throne, he adapted several Persian-style romances for the stage and sponsored performances of them in Qaisar Bagh.[86]

During the reign of Wajid Ali, a drama by Aga Hasan Amanat entitled *Indarsabhā* was staged in Lucknow. This play has long been considered the first written in the Urdu language. Opinions differ regarding the circumstances of its debut. Ram Babu Saksena, Somnath Gupta, and Annemarie Schimmel assert that Amanat was a courtier of Wajid Ali, and that he was commissioned to write *Indarsabhā* for a court performance. Saksena and Gupta also cite the oral tradition that the Nawab played the title role of Indra for the opening.[87] Masud Hasan Rizvi ("Adib"), however, attempts to disprove Amanat's association with Wajid Ali Shah, maintaining that Amanat was never present at court owing to paralysis of his vocal chords. He recounts Amanat's own story, namely that the play was written at the suggestion of friends as an exercise in poetic virtuosity. Adib postulates that the *Indarsabhā* was intended for a popular stage and was premiered before the common citizens of Lucknow, although Amanat may have imitated the king's *rahas* performances.[88]

Another controversy concerns European influence on the *Indarsabhā.* Given the absence of antecedents for theatre in the Indo-Islamic tradition, several Urdu literary historians have opined that the *Indarsabhā* was based on Western opera, introduced into Lucknow's court by visiting European musicians.[89] John Pemble notes that European music was in general not popular at court, and he concludes that operatic influence "does seem far-fetched."[90] From another perspective, Hindi literary historians have linked the *Indarsabhā* to the Indian folk traditions, claiming Amanat's play as a vital bridge between ancient Sanskrit dramatic works and more recent regional theatre.[91]

Regardless of whether it was ever produced in court, the *Indarsabhā* set a new standard for popular drama in North India. The work fuses Hindu and Muslim elements of plot, meter, and language in a form more indicative of its Indian and Awadhi origins than anything European. The events take place in the court of the mythic Indra, king of the gods, who sits in state encircled by fairies. Sabz Pari (emerald fairy) has been smitten by love for Gulfam, an earthly prince. Through the intervention of Kala Dev (black genie), she smuggles Gulfam into Indra's heaven. Displeased at this infraction, Indra casts Gulfam into a well and clips the wings of Sabz Pari. The *parī,* however, is undaunted and, singing irresistible songs in the disguise of a *jogin* (female mendicant), eventually earns her lover's release. Indra grants his blessings to the couple, and the lovers are reunited.

Replete with pageantry, fantasy, and romance, the *Indarsabhā* was a multimedia piece incorporating narrative, poetry, dance, and music within the visually opulent setting of Indra's heaven. King Indra, originally a Vedic deity, had by late medieval times become an emblem of the lordly human monarch, particularly in his hedonistic aspect. He was often depicted surrounded by a harem of beautiful dancing girls.[92] This Hindu icon, with its popular symbolic relevance to India's Muslim kings, is wedded in the *Indarsabhā* to a story of Islamic origin. The *parīs* and *devs* belong to the *dāstān* storytelling tradition imported from Persia.[93] Specific motifs seem to be imitated from several Urdu romances, including Mir Hasan's *Sihr-ul-bayān* and the *Gulzār-e-nasīm.*[94]

Whereas *Gopīchand* was the favorite nineteenth-century drama of folk derivation, the *Indarsabhā* achieved pride of place in the newly spawned Indo-Muslim theatre. It earned immediate fame and soon appeared on stages all over India. The manuscript became a runaway bestseller. The first edition was published in Kanpur in 1853 (fig. 8).[95] The publishing peak occurred in the 1870s; during that decade, thirty-three editions were published from major cities in Uttar Pradesh and Bihar, as well as Lahore, Bombay, Calcutta, and Madras. The title *Indarsabhā* was stolen by several imitators, the most successful being Madarilal.[96] Many Urdu dramas on the theme of a fairy succumbing to love for a mortal were written, using the word *sabhā* or *majlis* (referring to the "aerial assembly") in the title.[97] Bharatendu Harishchandra even wrote a one-act parody entitled *Bandar sabhā* (The monkey assembly).[98] The reputation of the work spread to Europe; it was translated into German by Friedrich Rosen in 1892.[99]

The *Indarsabhā* phenomenon dominated the theatrical world until the era of the talking cinema. Henceforth, aristocratic Islamic prototypes of costume, scenery, language, music, and story matter were widely emulated. The fact that Muslim rule in India virtually ended three years after the play appeared added to rather than detracted from its prestige, for the image of Indra with his delight-inducing assembly came to represent the precolonial past in all its splendor and carefreeness. The emerging Indian elite may have scorned this nostalgic attitude as reactionary, defeatist, and decadent, but for the less sophisticated audience of popular theatre, the Indo-Muslim monarchy signified power and

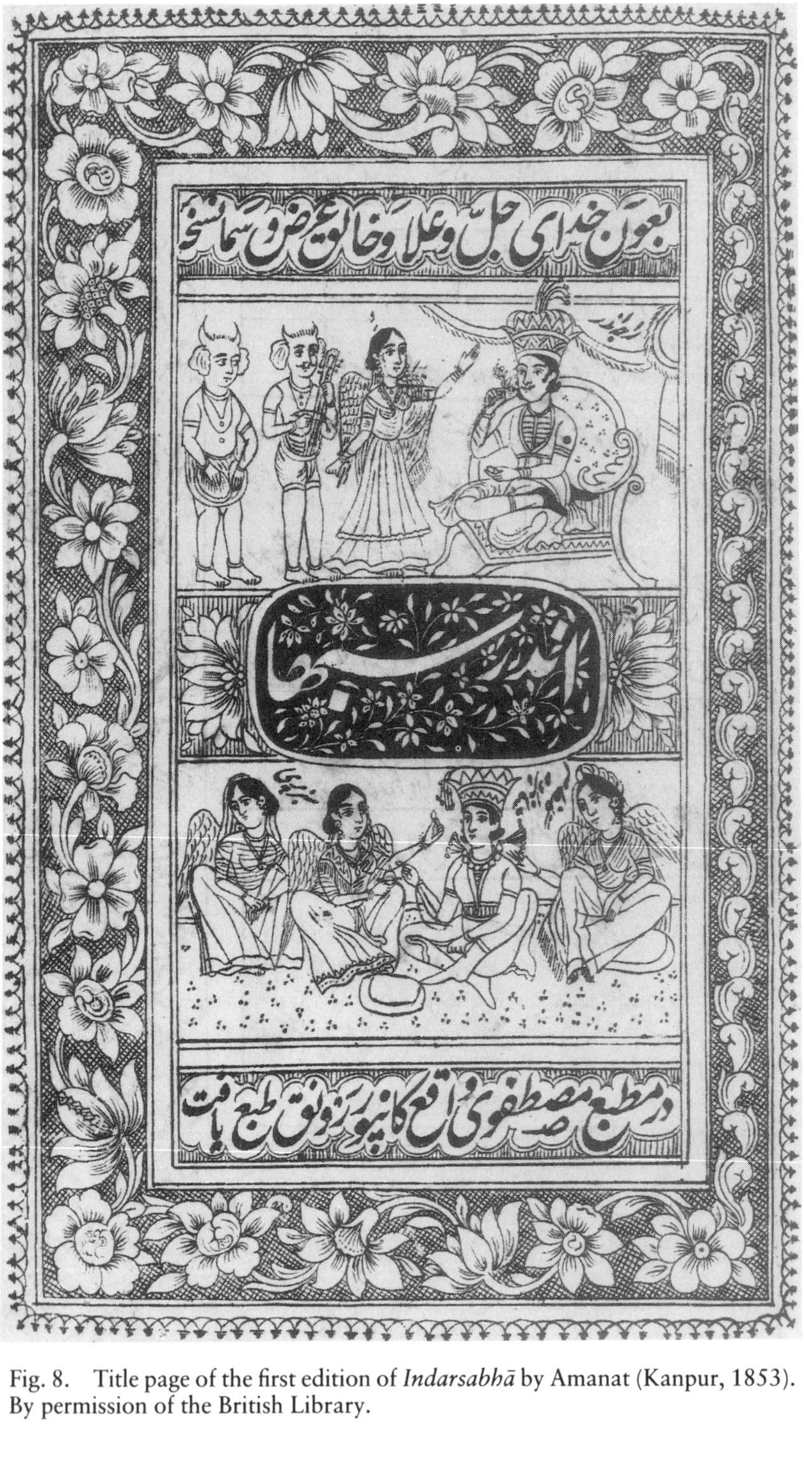

Fig. 8. Title page of the first edition of *Indarsabhā* by Amanat (Kanpur, 1853). By permission of the British Library.

privilege. Feudal attachments remained strong, and they continued to dominate the popular culture of North India even as the first signs of a postfeudal reformist ethic in playwriting emerged.

After the *Indarsabhā*, the Svāṅg theatre became heavily imbued with Islamic flavor. Backdrop curtains painted with palace arches and pillars conjured up the courtly ambience, as did Nawabi styles of dress, headwear, and ornaments. The aristocratic tone of the *Indarsabhā* was imitated by adopting Urdu diction and modes of address. The folk vocatives *beṭājī* or *pyārejī* (son, dear) used in early Sāṅgīt texts gave way to flourishes like *lak͟ht-e-jigar* (piece of my liver, i.e., son or daughter) or *jān-e-man* (beloved of my heart). Stories based on Islamic materials, *Syāhposh, Benazīr badr-e-munīr, Lailā majnūn,* and others, became more frequent Svāṅg topics. These influences are clearly visible in the Hathras Sāṅgīt texts from the turn of the century.

The *Indarsabhā* in this manner accelerated a process that transplanted court-based styles of music, dance, and poetry to a popular milieu. The perennial movements of exchange between refined and folk forms accelerated in the rapid breakdown of the patronage structure after the annexation of Awadh. Performers in search of employment must have turned to the rapidly growing theatrical sphere for survival. In consequence, styles such as Kathak, *ṭhumrī,* and *ghazal* were transplanted to the popular performance sphere, where they met less discriminating but not unenthusiastic patrons and audiences. By the same token, poetic meters and song forms moved from the court to the public milieu. The *Indarsabhā* text contains the earliest instances of the *chaubolā* meter, the six-line *chhand* that became the standard *dohā* plus *chaubolā* of Svāṅg, as well as a variety of *ghazal* verses and many types of folk songs (*basant, holī, dādrā, sāvan,* and *bihāg*). This metrical and musical diversity went hand in hand with the new style in stagecraft, and it stimulated the Svāṅg poets in Hathras to incorporate a greater variety of verse types into their plays—a trend quite marked by 1900.

Urban Theatre and the Parsi Stage

With the proliferation of Urdu dramatic activity following the success of the *Indarsabhā,* Indo-Muslim manners and messages—vestiges of feudal privilege—became embedded in the North Indian theatrical vocabulary. Yet the court as a social institution had collapsed, and the means of sustaining dramatic activity became concentrated instead in the economic networks for entertainment developing in the cities. Foremost among these was the so-called Parsi stage, a broadbased commercial theatre whose appeal and influence extended far beyond the ethnic group from which it took its name.[100] It developed around 1850 from Parsi-organized amateur groups in Bombay like the Elphinstone Club, which were active in presenting English and Indian drama classics.[101] Soon full-fledged professional companies were being floated by Parsi businessmen who were themselves theatre buffs. Many of the leading actors, also Parsis, held shares in these companies; several of them went on to form their own companies. Khurshedji Balliwala, the famous comic, founded the Victoria Theatrical Company in Delhi in 1877, while in the same year Khawasji Khatau, the "Irving of India," established the rival Alfred Theatrical Company.[102] Dozens of companies sprang up across the subcontinent, attaching the phrase "of Bombay" to their names to associate themselves with the prestigious urban theatre.[103] Muslims, Anglo-Indians, and a certain number of Hindus joined the companies, but the organizational reins remained largely in Parsi hands.

In a short time the demand for Parsi theatrical fare spread to all parts of India. The major companies routinely toured between Bombay, Lahore, Karachi, Peshawar, Delhi and the Gangetic plain, Calcutta, and Madras. Balliwala and his troupe ventured as far as Rangoon, Singapore, and London.[104] Parsi shows were the primary form of dramatic entertainment consistently available to urban audiences in greater India for almost a century. In consequence, the influence wrought by this stage on the development of modern drama and theatrical practice, and on the folk styles of performance, has been substantial. The Parsi stage exerted a major impact on the emerging Marathi and Gujarati theatres, as well as on new drama in Hindi, Bengali, Tamil, and other regional languages.[105]

Much of the initial inspiration for the Parsi stage came from British-sponsored dramatic efforts in their colony. English-style playhouses were erected in Bombay and Calcutta in the late eighteenth century, and the native elite was invited to attend English-produced performances from time to time and even to act in selected roles. Later the Parsi companies played in the same halls and took over the material culture of European theatre: the proscenium arch with its backdrop and curtains, Western furniture and other props, costumes, and a variety of mechanical devices for staging special effects. Artists from Europe were commissioned to paint the scenery, and the latest in "elaborate appliances" were regularly ordered from England, so as to achieve "the wonderful stage effects of storms, seas or rivers in commotion, castles, sieges, steamers, aerial movements and the like."[106] The British example also influenced advertising and scheduling. Playbills boasting the latest Saturday evening performance were distributed throughout the city, and in the auditorium, spectators perused the "opera book" or program containing the lyrics of the latest songs.[107] This eager embrace of things European was characteristic of the Parsi process of assimilation to Western culture in the nineteenth century—a process in which the Parsis, aided by economic prosperity, a nonhierarchical social structure, and lack of religious taboos, were considerably ahead of their Hindu and Muslim compatriots.[108]

The early playwrights of the Parsi stage, K. N. Kavraji, E. J. Khori, and N. R. Ranina, were themselves Parsis. Gujarati being their mother tongue, it became the first language of the Parsi theatre.[109] By the 1870s the large companies had adopted the practice of hiring Muslim *munshīs* (scribes) as part of their permanent staff, and Urdu became the principal language of the stage. Zarif and Raunaq were prolific authors who worked for the Original Theatrical Company of Bombay in the 1870s and 1880s.[110] The renowned companies of Delhi, the Victoria and the Alfred, engaged two Hindu authors, Vinayak Prasad ("Talib") and Narayan Prasad ("Betab") respectively, who continued the practice of writing in Urdu but also put into Hindi a certain number of plays (*Harishchandra, Gopīchand, Rāmāyaṇa, Mahābhārata*).[111] The most prominent author associated with the New Alfred Company was Aga Hashra Kashmiri, an Urdu playwright best known for his reworking of Shakespeare's tragedies; he later turned to composition in Hindi.[112] Radheyshyam Kathavachak was an important Hindi writer also employed by the New Alfred. He composed epic-based works such as *Vīr abhimanyu* and *Prahlād.*[113] The Parsi stage was never a bastion of linguistic purity. Urdu and Hindi, the two literary forms of the North Indian lingua franca, were most accessible to the largest number in the audience and were therefore the most widely employed. However, productions in non-Hindi-speaking areas freely drew on other regional languages—Gujarati, Marathi, and Bengali—for comic skits, improvised interludes, and songs.

In important respects aside from language, the Parsi theatre revealed its distinctive Indian character: it employed Indian subject matter and included a great deal of music and dance. These characteristics were a natural legacy of the Indian dramatic tradition; the existing folk drama much influenced the Parsi theatre while it exerted a countereffect on indigenous theatre. The first Indian-produced dramatic performance in Bombay is said to have been a Hindustani version of *Rājā gopīchandra,* written and directed by Vishnudas Bhave in 1853. Composed in Hindustani mixed with Gujarati and Marathi, this production provided the impetus to Parsi groups to adopt songs, dances, and mythological subject matter in the style of the folk theatre.[114]

Hindu epic heroes and heroines—Harishchandra, Prahlad, Nala and Damayanti, Savitri, and Shakuntala—were extremely common on the Parsi stage. It is likely that the dramatists, rather than looking to Sanskrit literature for their inspiration, knew the versions of these stories current in popular culture and based their plays on them. At the same time, Urdu playwrights brought the stock Islamic romances to the fore: *Shīrīn farhād, Lailā majnūn, Benazīr badr-e-munīr,* and *Gul bakāvalī* were common titles here. Fairy-mortal romances, modeled on the *Indarsabhā,* were also extremely popular. The Parsi theatre's sizable repertoire of mythological and legendary plays thus drew on the same stratum of North Indian popular culture as the nineteenth-century folk theatre and with equal alacrity embraced non-Indian subject matter side by side. Shakespeare provided a rich store of plots, and the prestige of the bard's name went unsurpassed on the Parsi stage. The Shakespearean stories were heavily Indianized, characters being reassigned names, castes, and communities, geographical settings transferred to Asia, and motivations and story lines adjusted to fit the Indo-Muslim environment.[115]

The music and dance of Parsi theatre, although difficult to document, appear to have been liberal in measure and hybrid in manner. The "orchestra" often consisted of harmonium and *tablā,* played by accompanists who, seated in the wings or pit, "also in many cases do duty as prompters."[116] The use of a chorus for the opening invocation is described by Yajnik in a colorful passage:

> In the midst of the noise and bustle of the Urdu theatre, opened an hour before the performance, one hears three bells at short intervals and with the third bell a thundering gun shot is heard as the drop-curtain, gorgeously painted with mythological legends, goes up. The chorus girls sing a prayer or a "welcome" to the accompaniment of the harmonium and rhythmic drum beats. This song ends with an offering of flowers to the distinguished patrons and with garlanding the portraits of the pioneers of the respective company or of deities. Then the action commences.[117]

This ceremonial opening parallels the preliminary rituals of Sanskrit drama and traditional folk theatres. The Kanpur style of Nauṭaṅkī inherited the practice of employing a chorus for the *maṅgalācharaṇ,* as seen in Shrikrishna Khatri Pahalvan's plays.

The musical style has been variously described: "tuned to the traditional modes (Ragas)" and "in the chaste classical style," or as consisting of "slipshod Parsi and semi-European tunes."[118] Partial manuscripts of two plays, *Jahāngīr shāh aur gauhar* of unknown authorship and Raunaq's *Benazīr badr-e-munīr,* contain the names of classical and semiclassical ragas such as Bhairavī, Soraṭh, Desh, Pīlū, Kālingaṛā, and Kalyāṇ at the headings of the *ṭhumrīs*, *ghazals*, and other songs. An initial phrase occurs in quotes, the opening line from an already well-known song, as an indication of the tune to follow.[119] Actual practice may have considerably undermined this classical basis in favor of novelty and catchiness. Theatre tunes were easy to memorize and circulated freely in the bazaars in the period before sound films, filling the place now occupied by Hindi film songs.[120]

When women were admitted to the Parsi stage around 1880, an innovation commonly credited to Balliwala, they were recruited primarily from the ranks of professional singers and dancers. Their crowd-pleasing tactics were a big draw, and solo dancers "were rewarded by the audience with currency notes and coins amidst shouts of 'Encore.' "[121] The better-known actresses, Khurshed, Mehtab, and Mary Fenton, achieved their fame as least partly on the basis of genuine talent. Boy actors gifted with sweet voices, good looks, and physical graces were also employed by many professional companies to play the heroines' roles and perform dance items, and "boy companies" became a popular item in certain regions.[122]

Available scripts show that a typical scene in a Parsi stage play consisted of a variety of songs and verses (in forms such as *ṭhumrī, ghazal, lāvanī, sher, musaddas, mukhammas, savaiyā,* or simply *gānā*) connected by prose dialogues. In early plays, dialogues were composed in rhymed metrical lines; actors spoke them with great emphasis to project the lines to the back of the hall. Later prose became predominant, although rhyme at the end of sentences remained. In such stylistic matters much mutual influence is visible between the North Indian folk theatre forms such as Svāṅg and the Parsi theatre in this period.

Although the Indian elite saw in the Parsi theatre vulgarity, sensationalism, and lack of aesthetic standards, the humbler sections of society thrilled to the mystique of English company names like the Corinthian, the Victoria, and the New Alfred. The sumptuous fittings of the Parsi stage, replete with elaborate painted scenery, fine costumes, exotic Anglo-Indian actresses, and tricks of stagecraft augmented the allure. Such shows may have been commonplace in the numerous theatrical houses of the big cities, but in the provincial towns the spectacles no doubt overawed the populace. No wonder then that the Bombay companies were eagerly sought as the purveyors of all that was current and stylish in theatre. They were widely emulated wherever they performed, particularly in the cities of Uttar Pradesh such as Banaras, Lucknow, and Kanpur, where they enjoyed an enthusiastic following.

The exchange between the urban Parsi theatre and the simpler, more rustic Svāṅg and Nauṭaṅkī operated in both directions. Stories, songs, and stage techniques moved back and forth at different times. Early on, the Parsi theatre drew from the themes and conventions of the folk theatre. A common core of stories is found in both theatres in the period from 1850 to 1900.[123] Once the Parsi theatre's popularity was established, this process reversed itself. An old story like *Harishchandra,* known first in folk legend, was adapted for the Parsi stage and gained a tremendous following in the nineteenth century. Its new prestige fed back into the folk theatre, where in the Nauṭaṅkī of the early twentieth century a dozen versions of the story suddenly appeared.[124] Similarly, the *Rāmāyaṇa* story and selected episodes from the *Mahābhārata,* like *Vīr abhimanyu* and *Shravaṇ kumār,* were not originally part of the repertoire but became common Nauṭaṅkī themes after Betab's and Radheyshyam's plays succeeded in the Parsi companies.

The Kanpur Nauṭaṅkī of Shrikrishna Khatri exhibited this influence from the Parsi theatre. Many of Shrikrishna's plays contained a comic subplot and focused on contemporary social themes. Formal features such as the use of the chorus and the large proportion of prose showed movement away from the all-verse, individualistic Hathras style, as did its imitation of the Parsi vogue in curtains, painted scenery, costuming, music, and dance. In this way the Parsi theatre acted as a barometer of cultural change, showing the folk theatres new directions of proven popular appeal. After 1920 the Bombay cinema not only inherited the personnel, sensibility, and repertoire of the Parsi stage but took over the modeling role as well, supplying innovation to the Nauṭaṅkī stage.

In reviewing the material presented here we see clearly that the world of North Indian theatre in the nineteenth century was crisscrossed by a number of intersecting performing practices. These practices, developed in the context of specific socioeconomic conditions and the cultural systems associated with them, may be distinguished as folk, courtly, and urban. Yet the mutual exchange and imitation that occurred among them obliterated clear lines of difference. From this swirl of transformed tradition, the Svāṅg theatre distilled its own singular identity. The Khyāl folk stage and the competitive arenas of improvised folk poetry framed its formal parameters and agonistic ethos. Nath yogi lore as well as Rajput chivalric and romantic legends and popular Indo-Islamic tales supplied its narrative substratum. In its performance praxis, it incorporated the visual symbolism, stagecraft, and linguistic resonance of both the Urdu drama and Parsi stage. These multiple streams collided and competed and, as they did, Svāṅg and Nauṭaṅkī continued to absorb and blend them. In the next chapter we pursue the historical narrative through the subsequent phases of development, using as source material the large Sāṅgīt literature of the last hundred years.

CHAPTER FOUR

Authors, *Akhāṛās*, and Texts

Although the textual evidence is scanty for much of the dramatic literature predating Nauṭaṅkī, plays of the Svāṅg and Nauṭaṅkī traditions have been published in chapbook editions since the arrival of the printing press in northern India. Beginning in the 1860s, dozens of popular publishers have engaged in disseminating Nauṭaṅkī booklets; the repertoire of stories now numbers over four hundred. These folk plays have been fortuitously preserved against the hazards of time, despite their fragile form and lowly status. By an act of Parliament in 1867, printed playscripts dating to 1866 were collected and sent to the India Office Library and the British Museum in London. Cheaply produced contemporary versions can still be purchased on the street in certain markets in India. The dramatic literature of Svāṅg and Nauṭaṅkī is a unique resource in its large size, chronological span, and link with a surviving performance practice. Its texts afford an exceptional opportunity to study a single folk genre in rich detail.

Insofar as this literature has never been fully documented, this chapter first specifies the location of contemporary and historical textual resources and then chronicles the sequence of poets, plays, and themes and their changes over time. By noting titles that recur from decade to decade and among authors and publishers, we plot the continuities that bind the genre into a distinct identity. Simultaneously we illuminate aspects of the social process of cultural production characteristic of North India in this period. Thus we focus on the means of production (the evolution of the printed text and its various formats), the producers of the text (the publishers), and the internal organization of authors (poetic lineages or *akhāṛās*). The chapter may consequently be read as a specific exercise in the sociology of culture as well as an extended addendum to canonical literary history.

The Sources of Sāṅgīt Texts: Old and New

The scripts of Svāṅg and Nauṭaṅkī, or more accurately librettos, are termed *sāṅgīts*; this label or its abbreviation (*sāṅ.*) is almost invariably part of the title. Platts's *Dictionary of Urdu* defines *sāṅgīt* as "a public entertainment consisting of songs, music and dancing." However, as a printed rubric it denotes simply "musical drama." The origin of the word is disputed: it may be an adjectival form of the Sanskrit *saṅgīta* (music) or a compound of *sāṅg* (mime, drama) plus *gīt* (song).[1] In any case, the term distinguishes this class of texts as intended for musical performance, in contrast to poems or tales meant for silent reading or unaccompanied recitation.

Sāṅgīt manuscripts and booklets are probably as old as the theatre itself. Before the printing press came to India, handwritten scripts circulated among communities of actors and helped them memorize parts; they were sometimes collected by patrons.[2] Lithography made possible their duplication and publication, and it is in this form that they are preserved in the nineteenth-century collections of the libraries in London. With the introduction of inexpensive Devanagari printing in the 1880s, the Sāṅgīt entered the era of mass communication and became widely printed and reprinted, bought and sold.

Nowadays Sāṅgīt chapbooks can be purchased from pavement sellers specializing in popular literature.[3] These mobile retailers are usually found in a city's old sectors near a temple or market, their wares spread on the ground by day and packed up in a strongbox on a bicycle rack every night. The vendor who deals in Nauṭaṅkī Sāṅgīts is likely to stock a variety of other items: collections of *bhajans* (hymns), *vratkathās* (women's religious narratives for fasting days), astrological almanacs, folk poems on martial legends like the *Ālhā*, traditional joke books (like *Ghāgh-bhaḍḍarī*), *lokgīt* anthologies (women's songs, marriage songs), sex manuals, how-to guides, cheap editions of Hindu devotional texts (*Rāmcharitmānas, Bhagavad-gītā, Hanumān-chālīsā*), discourses by spiritual masters, film magazines, romances and paperback novels, and detective stories; all are in Hindi. This fare contrasts with the stock at more prestigious sites—railway bookstalls, bookstores, hotel lobbies—where most material is in English, prices are higher, and packaging is more durable.

Among the popular publishing houses that supply the street vendors through a far-reaching distribution network, the most prolific publisher of Sāṅgīts is Shyam Press in Hathras. Other popular publishers include Dehati Pustak Bhandar (Delhi), Shrikrishna Pustakalay (Kanpur), Babu Baijnath Prasad (Banaras), and Bombay Pustakalay (Allahabad). These publishers advertise their current lists in conveniently subdivided catalogues, and on making a personal visit one can order specific Sāṅgīt titles uncut from the warehouse. In the late 1970s Frances W. Pritchett collected approximately one hundred contemporary Sāṅgīt texts from such publishers and donated them to the Regenstein Library of the University of Chicago, where they are accessible to researchers.

Older Sāṅgīts from the nineteenth and early twentieth centuries are held in the Oriental Manuscripts and Printed Books division of the British Museum (BM) and in the India Office Library (IOL), both now part of the British Library system in London. In 1867 the British Government of India passed the Press and Registration of Books Act (Act XXV of 1867), requiring that one copy of every printed or lithographed book issued in India be forwarded to the Secretary of State for India in London. The law was originally introduced to enable the Raj to tighten its control over Indian publications and apply stricter censorship.[4] However, it had the salubrious secondary effect of creating an unparalleled collection of books from India. The India Office Library (and in certain instances the British Museum) became the repository for these books and developed into a virtual copyright library for Indian publications.[5] In this way the British authorities, who probably had less use for chapbooks of folk plays than for most types of indigenous literature, unwittingly ensured the preservation of a comprehensive body of folklore.

The British Museum holdings of Hindi, Panjabi, Sindhi, and Pushtu books are catalogued in a three-part publication beginning in 1893, with a supplement for Hindi books in 1913, and a second supplement in 1957. The Hindi acquisitions of the India Office Library are listed in two published catalogues of 1900 and 1902; the 1903–1944 catalogue of Hindi books is unpublished and must be consulted in the library itself.[6] Within these catalogues Sāṅgīt texts are not easy to locate, although they are listed by author and crosslisted by title or by "subject" (often literary genre). The difficulty stems from a British-designed taxonomy that overlooked or did not perceive the connection between the Sāṅgīt and the indigenous folk stage. In very few cases are the Sāṅgīt works listed under the drama sections of the subject indexes. In the earlier catalogues, Sāṅgīt texts are primarily classified as "Literature: Tales and Fables—Verse." The 1913 catalogue distinguishes between "Poetry—Narrative" and "Poetry—Historical," placing ordinary Sāṅgīt titles under the first and Sāṅgīts on the *Ālhā* epic theme in the second category. In the 1957 supplement, however, these are collapsed into the category "Literature: Poetry—Narrative and Historical Poems." Occasionally Sāṅgīts on saintly figures appear under the heading "Poetry—Mythological." These subject indexes point to the bibliographers' confusion regarding the genre and suggest a lack of awareness of its performance context. Similarly, individual bibliographic entries characterize the Sāṅgīt first as a "legend in verse" or "metrical legend," and later mostly as a "ballad." Only occasionally is the performative character mentioned, as in the description of *Sāṅgīt pūran mal kā* (1878), "a popular romance, in a dramatised form," or Khushi Ram's *Sāṅgīt rānī nauṭaṅkī kā* (1882), "a love-tale, in verse, adapted for the stage." Looking in the title index under Sāṅgīt rather than in the subject index is therefore the quickest method of locating these plays, except in the earliest catalogues that lack the title index.

Of the two London collections, the British Museum has the better resources for study of nineteenth-century Sāṅgīts, and the India Office Library is superior for those of the twentieth century. The British Museum contains a total of 56 Sāṅgīt texts published between 1866 and 1912, plus another 109 published between 1913 and 1957. In the India Office Library, some 28 titles (including 10 duplicates of British Museum items) were published before 1902, and approximately 280 Sāṅgīts appeared between 1903 and 1944.[7] By any calculation these are remarkable resources, all the more so considering the lack of attention they have received until now.

With samples of texts from every decade of the last one hundred twenty years, the history of Nauṭaṅkī as a folk literature lies open for study. Recurring stories, characters, and motifs can be easily identified, formal structures of language and meter can be historically analyzed, and the styles of different authors, schools, and regions can be contrasted. Furthermore, the printed Sāṅgīt yields valuable self-contextualizing information. Advertisements on back covers help to reveal the consumer audience for popular texts. Prefaces by editors may explain how a play came to be published, under what constraints, or with what purposes in mind. Sometimes a poet's colophon includes descriptions of dramatic troupes, the roles and function of their personnel, and the musical instruments used. Invocations directed at patrons provide information on the circumstances of performance. As a result, although the libretto was originally devised as an actor's guide, in its published form it is a self-referencing document that supplies important clues to the evolution of the theatre.

Lithographed Sāṅgīts: 1866–1896

From the inception of British collection of vernacular works in 1867, two types of North Indian folk drama occur in large numbers: the Rajasthani *khyāl* (or *khel*) and the Hindustani *sāṅgīt* or *sāṅg*. We have considered the development of *khyāl* and its relation to Svāṅg and in the previous chapter have determined that the Khyāl folk theatre probably preceded the printed Sāṅgīts by about a hundred years. The earliest preserved Sāṅgīts in the British Library are *Prahlād sāṅgīt* (1866) and *Gopīchand bharatarī* (1867), both written by one Lakshman Singh (also known as Lakshman Das) and published from Delhi. Each of these was reprinted many times, indicating their great popularity; sixteen editions of *Prahlād* and twenty-seven of *Gopīchand* were published between 1866 and 1883 (see figs. 4 and 5). Two editions of *Prahlād* and three of *Gopīchand* were written "in Persian characters," that is to say, in Urdu. The fact that multiple copies exist almost from the start of British collecting suggests an already established tradition of Hindi and Urdu folk drama. As with the *khyāls* of Rajasthan, we conjecture that Sāṅgīt texts were copied and circulated before printing was known in the region. It therefore seems probable that these two texts were composed sometime before 1866; how much earlier we cannot say.

The widespread availability of the Sāṅgīt of *Gopīchand* was noted by G. A. Grierson, who published a fragment of the text in the *Journal of the Asiatic Society of Bengal* in 1885. "There is no legend more popular throughout the whole of Northern India, than those [*sic*] of Bharthari and his nephew Gopi Chand. . . . A Hindi version of the legend can be bought for a few pice in any up-country bazar."[8] The story concerns the conversion of a king to the ascetic way of life that Guru Gorakhnath embodied. The Sāṅgīt has remained a popular classic for over a century. I recently discovered contemporary reprints of the original edition in markets in Hathras and Jaipur (fig. 9).

Thematically related is the story of Harishchandra, a generous king

Fig. 9. Title page of recent reprint of *Gopīchand bharthari* by Lakshman Das (Delhi, n.d.), collected from Jaipur bazaar in 1984.

who comes to earthly ruin by speaking and living the truth but who in the end receives salvation. A version by Jiya Lal was published in both Hindi and Urdu scripts in the 1880s. The Gopichand and Harishchandra plays, with their example of abdication of kingly duties for a renunciant's life, are medieval morality tales, inculcating otherworldliness and pursuit of spiritual perfection. Other popular Sāṅgīts too exhorted the faithful to renounce power and follow the example of the saints; the titles *Puranmal* (or *Pūranmal, Pūran bhagat*) (see fig. 7) and *Dhurūjī* both refer to spiritual exemplars admired in the late nineteenth century. The theme of kingly asceticism, popular for millennia in the subcontinent, may have gained prevalence in the disturbed political conditions of eighteenth- and nineteenth-century North India. Loss of power and title was part of everyday reality for the nobility, while the people experienced a dwindling of confidence in the moral authority traditionally expected of kings. The age demanded a model of virtue for future rulers and consolation for privilege usurped.

In counterpoint to these dour dramas of dispossession, the fantasy world of princes and princesses and of fairies and demons played on the nostalgia for bygone days that also preoccupied the late nineteenth century. The *Indarsabhā* of Amanat was the prototype, a play that dominated the Urdu theatre for over seventy years. Its theme of love between a fairy and a prince was a legacy of the Persian *dāstān* and had parallels in Indian folklore, as evidenced by the story of the fairylike Princess Nauṭaṅkī who weighed only thirty-six grams. The formula of combining ribald love scenes (preferably between celestial women and mortal men), titillating cross-dressing, and bold melodrama featured in a number of popular romances of this period: *Rūp basant, Saudāgar vo syāhposh,* and *Benazīr badr-e-munīr.*

Between 1866 and 1896, thirty-two titles appear as lithographed Sāṅgīts in the London collections. Half of them treat religious themes (seven legends of saints, nine stories from Ram and Krishna *līlās*); more than a third are romances (nine Hindu or regional, three Islamic), and only a handful are heroic and contemporary stories (two martial chronicles, two modern stories). The most popular as measured by reprintings were the legends of saints (*Gopīchand, Pūranmal, Rājā harishchandra, Dhurūjī, Prahlād*) followed by the romances *Rūp basant* and *Saudāgar vo syāhposh*. The plays were most frequently published from Delhi by Mishra Bhagvan Das of Brahman Press and by Munshi Naval Kishor; from Meerut by Pandit Hardev Sahay of Jnan Sagar Press and

Lala Natthumal Seth of Jvala Prakash Press; and from Banaras by Munshi Ambe Prasad.

It is difficult to ascertain much about the authors at this time. Rarely does the author's name appear on the title page. Instead the poet usually mentions himself in an invocatory verse, where he speaks as a suppliant requesting blessings from the deity:

> Lachhman is your servant, Lord, protect my honor.
> (*Gopīchand,* 1870)
>
> Baldev is your servant, give my heart knowledge.
> (*Krishṇalīlā,* 1868)
>
> I am your servant: my name is Dalchand the wise.
> (*Soraṭh,* 1878)
>
> Ramlal joins his palms and bows his head at your feet.
> (*Puranmal,* 1878)

Infrequently a bit of biographical information appears at the end of the work. Jiya Lal, author of *Harichandra* (1877), describes himself:

> I am head of the guards, a Jain scribe by caste.
> In the world my name, Jiya Lal, is famous.
> My name Jiya Lal is famous, my hometown is Faraknagar.
> In Chhaproli I received this story already composed.[9]

The fragmentary information that is available seems to suggest high-caste backgrounds for many authors and publishers in this period, for example, that of Brahmin, Kayasth, Jain, Rajput, and other literate castes.

The manuscripts are handcopied by scribes with highly ornamented covers featuring illustrations of central scenes and characters. Often the pages of text are also illustrated in a manner similar to folk styles of painting of the time. The widespread use of visual images together with printed text suggests a midway point on the continuum between simple images and learned books, comparable to the chapbooks of sixteenth- and seventeenth-century France. Such materials, in the view of Roger Chartier, suggest the multiple uses to which a text could be put.[10] For the literate classes the text constituted reading matter, while for those unable to read the pictures outlined the narrative, served as a basis for oral (including memorized) recitation, and rendered the written word a familiar part of everyday life.

The appearance of these texts is remarkably similar from one publisher to another, the handwriting of the scribe being the most individualizing feature. The plays are most frequently thirty-two pages in length, and the page size is 6″ by 9½″. Urdu versions of some are published separately or back to back with the Devanagari. The title is boldly displayed in Devanagari and often Urdu as well, with the publisher's details appearing at the bottom of the page. In the early manuscripts, the poetic lines are penned running on continuously with no indentation. Only stanza numbers and full stops are inserted to show where lines end. In later texts, lines and stanzas are separated and centered on the page, and the characters' speeches are prefaced by indications such as "reply of the queen to the king." The names of the meters are specified in full or abbreviated form in all the manuscripts of the period.

In the early period no differentiation into rival arenas or *akhāṛās* occurred, as far as we can tell. Competition among publishers and fear of plagiarism were, however, of some concern. The cover of *Sāṅgīt budre munīr kā* (1876) carries a fifty-word plot summary instead of the usual illustration, and the back cover issues this admonition:

> All publishers take note that this Sāṅgīt Budre [*sic*] Munīr, or Fairy Princess, was very carefully corrected and published by Pt. Hardev Sahay, after taking permission from Lala Dhannulal's son Munshi Basant Ray and Munshi Umrao Singh. No one may publish it without permission.

Such warnings frequently accompanied the publication of new material, together with notices proclaiming the play's authenticity.

How widely distributed such lithographed plays were we cannot determine, for the title pages bear no mention of the number of copies printed, as later ones did. These plays contain no references to troupe organization or details of performance. However, there is little doubt that the impetus for the creation of these dramas was the presence and continuing expansion of a Hindi and Urdu folk stage in the region around Delhi, Meerut, and Banaras.

Natharam and the Indarman *Akhāṛā* of Hathras: 1892–1920

At the close of the nineteenth century, major changes in the organization, style, and subject matter of Svāṅg took place. The popular theatrical activity that had been diffused over a fairly expansive area converged on the town of Hathras, where the most visible changes occurred. Hathras is in the district of Aligarh in western Uttar Pradesh. Located in proximity to both the Vaishnava pilgrimage sites in Mathura district and the former Mughal capital at Agra, Hathras became an important independent Jat kingdom under the chieftain Daya Ram in the early nineteenth century. The area around Hathras was renowned for its unusually rich commercial agriculture, with cash crops of indigo and cotton providing the base for a prosperous economy.[11] It continued to flourish even after the British seizure of Daya Ram's kingdom in 1817 and the revolt of 1857.[12] The town had a large population of moneylenders (*sāhūkārs*); together with the wealthy agriculturists they formed a sizable patron class to the service groups, including artisans and performers. Affluent individuals like Hanna Singh Dalal are said to have squandered fortunes on the maintenance of Svāṅg members, construction of their houses and stage facilities, and expenses of special events.[13] As a railway junction later in the century Hathras continued to thrive, a commercial center in a predominantly agricultural region. The constant flow of travelers to festivals and fairs ensured a ready audience for the folk theatre.

The organizational basis of Svāṅg acquired greater structure and visibility with the development of the *akhāṛā* system in Hathras. The *akhāṛā* (wrestling-ground or arena) was already associated with teams and lineages of folk poets of *lāvanī* and *khyāl*. The first and foremost of the Hathras Svāṅg *akhāṛās* was founded by a poet named Indarman, who immigrated from Jahangirabad in Bulandshahr district sometime in the 1880s.[14] A Chhīpī (from the artisan caste that prints cloth), he was prevailed upon by his fellows in Hathras to visit and initiate them into the art of poetic improvisation for which he was well known. As a devotee of the goddess, Indarman enjoyed the reputation of a seer and, although he himself was illiterate, exerted a spiritual leadership among his followers. The most prominent of these were Govind Ram and Chiranjilal, both Chhīpīs and prolific poets in their own right. Under their leadership, the Indarman *akhāṛā* began exhibiting Svāṅgs in Hathras, probably in the 1880s.

Although it is said that Indarman only dictated verses to his disciples and authored no Svāṅg himself, a text has come to light in the London collections that is almost certainly a composition of Indarman—but whether he was the Indarman of Jahangirabad and Hathras we cannot be sure. The work, *Khyāl pūran mal kā* (1892), is not a Rajasthani *khyāl* but a Khari Boli Sāṅgīt in the style that soon became the standard for the Sāṅgīts of Hathras. One of the first to be printed using machine-made type, it was published in Calcutta by Ganesh Prasad Sharma. Indarman's name does not appear on the title page, but it is scattered in signature verses in at least ten places throughout the play, in various forms such as Indarman, Indraman, Indar, or Inda.[15] New poetic structures characterize the text, and it bears a distinctive cover design, lending credence to the idea that it was an innovative work. The meter *dauṛ* is introduced for the first time here.[16] The title page is enclosed by a simple border, with the name of the play printed at the top, then the publisher's name, mention of registration under Act XXV of 1867, a small picture of the elephant god Ganesh, and lower on the page the address and name of the printer, the Christian era date, number of copies printed, and price. This bare but elegant format became the basis for Hathras Sāṅgīt covers in the following years.

Whereas we know little about Indarman, we are on firmer ground with his most illustrious disciple, Natharam, called Nathuram or Nathumal in his early plays and later renowned as Natharam Sharma Gaur. Born in 1874 in the village of Dariyapur to a Brahmin family, Natharam came to Hathras as a child guiding his blind father, Bhagirathmal, and singing for alms. With his sweet voice and charm, he attracted the attention of Indarman's disciple Chiranjilal and was soon adopted into his *akhāṛā*, where he learned the arts of singing and dancing as well as reading and writing. He quickly became a star, playing the female parts with irresistible flair; he later revealed great skills as a poet, organizer, and publisher.

The Indarman *akhāṛā* had its headquarters at Kila Darvaza in Hathras. Nearby was a temple, Dauji ka Mandir, where an annual festival was held. Natharam rehearsed and presented a new play every year for the large crowds who frequented the festival (*baldev chaṭ kā melā*); after building up a reputation in this way, he was invited to tour outside the city. Around 1890 Natharam and his teacher Chiranjilal organized a professional troupe that earned a tremendous reputation as it traveled throughout northern India. The eager reception that greeted them is attested in the earliest Sāṅgīt attributed to Chiranjilal and Natharam, *Chandrāvalī kā jhūlā* (1897):

ANNOUNCEMENT

Let it be known to all good men that the entertainment of the troupe from Hathras has been shown in various places in Kanpur, and many gentlemen have gathered for it and all their minds have been pleased. Seeing the desire of these good men, we have published the same entertainment, *Chandravali's Swing* or *The Battle of Alha and Udal*, for the amusement of their minds, so that whenever they read it, they will obtain happiness and remember us. Take heed, this opportunity will not come again. Make your purchase quickly, or the chance will slip away and you will be left wringing your hands. All of Indarman's books are available from us.[17]

This statement suggests that the publication of a Sāṅgīt followed its performance in a given locale, in response to popular demand for the text.[18] Note that by 1897 Indarman's name was famous enough to warrant the claim that "all of Indarman's books are available from us."

This play is another early example of the new typeset format. The cover drawing has disappeared; instead, an image of Ganesh adorns the top of the page. Prominently placed in the middle is a list of all the meters and melodies included in the text. Whereas the older Sāṅgīts contained only a few meters, such as *dohā, chaubolā, kaṛā,* and *rāganī,* the Hathras poets employed a plethora of verse types, giving greater variety and virtuosity to their singing style.

Subject matter in the period from 1890 to 1910 was also changing. While the old stories still held their own, episodes from the martial epic of Alha and Udal enjoyed particular esteem. By 1902, the Chiranjilal and Natharam team had published ten episodes from the *Ālhā* cycle, and the number kept increasing through the next two decades.[19] The famous *Amar siṁh rāṭhor,* another tale of Rajput valor, was first published in 1912. Unlike the earlier saintly legends and make-believe romances, these tales are based on historical events in the not-so-distant past. This celebration of India's warring heroes in folk theatre parallels the resurgence of political activism in the early twentieth century, suggesting that a model of confrontation may have begun to replace the older attitude of religious quietism.

Several turn-of-the-century Sāṅgīts yield interesting details about the personnel of the troupe of Chiranjilal and Natharam. The following description closes *Ūdal kā byāh* (1902):

> The Indar *akhāṛā* in Hathras is like the court of Lord Indra:
> The teachers (*ustāds*) are Ganesh and Chiranji and the director (*k͟halīfā*) is Gobind.
> Jivaram Das and Parshadi are servants of Vishnu's lotus feet,
> Madan, Janaki, Hira, and Lachchha are known throughout northwestern India.
> Natharam the Brahmin seeks the shelter of Bhairav and Kali,
> Dulari and Udayraj dance circles around the king.[20]

The first line compares the entire troupe to the assembly of lord Indra, the glamorous image of the *indarsabhā* frequently invoked in popular culture. The second line refers to Natharam's trio of gurus, Govind, Ganesh, and Chiranjilal. The "servants" may be musicians or other supporting staff (cook, barber, or laborer) but were clearly Vaishnavas, as opposed to Natharam's Shaiva or Shakta proclivities. Madan, Janaki, Hira, and Lachchha appear to be renowned actor-singers; Dulari and Udayraj specialized in dance. The feminine names "Janaki" and "Dulari" probably indicate female impersonators.

In the standard closural apology the poet alludes to the young Natharam's high caste, physical grace, and poetic talent and begs forgiveness for errors or offense committed.

> The Sāṅgīt is concluded, the heart pleased and free of sorrow.
> The lord's servant, Chiranjilal, lives in the city of Hathras.
> Thanks to him, the coquettish Brahmin boy Nathamal lives
> happily,
> A jewel of the Gaur lineage, creator of spontaneous poetry.
> May all good men read this and deem his effort a success:
> Excuse his errors and wrongs, knowing him to be a child.[21]

Up to 1910 Chiranjilal and Natharam's plays were all published in Kanpur. Perhaps the initial demand for printed Sāṅgīts was greater in Kanpur, or possibly Devanagari printing facilities did not reach Hathras, a smaller town, until later. It is conceivable that the *akhāṛā*'s poets only amassed sufficient capital to finance a local press after 1910. Shyam Press of Hathras, which was originally owned and operated by Natharam Sharma Gaur and is now in the hands of his son, Radhavallabh, began its publishing activities about 1925.

The true authorship of the Sāṅgīts printed under Natharam's name is difficult to determine. Although approximately fifteen plays list Chiranjilal and Natharam as joint authors, how the poets divided the labor between themselves is unknown. By 1908 either Chiranjilal had died or his influence had diminished, for a verse speaks of him as the *ustād* in the past tense.[22] Natharam then began taking sole credit for some of his earlier collaborations with Chiranjilal.[23] Several plays first published between 1910 and 1920, such as *Sāṅgīt harishchandra,* have clear references to Natharam in their colophons and may be his own compositions. After 1920, most plays published under the Indarman *akhāṛā* name were credited to Natharam, but probably few were wholly his work. By then the *akhāṛā* had attracted a number of ghostwriters who were turning out Svāṅgs in Natharam's style on new themes.

During the period from 1920 to the present, Sāṅgīts of the Indarman *akhāṛā* were issued and reissued in very large numbers under the name of Natharam. Many of these were actually written by Ruparam of Salempur, who started employment with Natharam around 1920.[24] He composed a number of stories that present new types of heroes and heroines, contemporary or recent historical characters who are in pursuit of justice. These may be outlaws in the service of the poor, such as

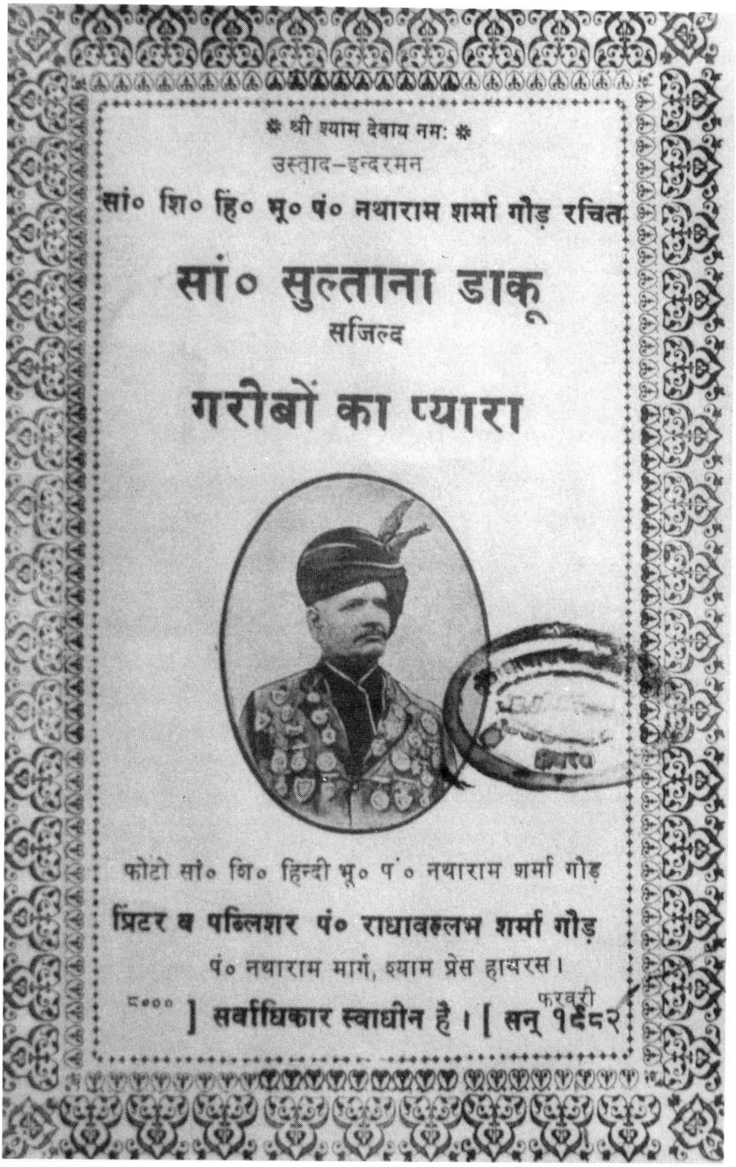
श्री श्याम देवाय नमः

उस्ताद–इन्दरमन

सां० शि० हिं० भू० पं० नथाराम शर्मा गौड़ रचित

सां० सुल्ताना डाकू

सजिल्द

गरीबों का प्यारा

फोटो सां० शि० हिन्दी भू० पं० नथाराम शर्मा गौड़

प्रिंटर व पब्लिशर पं० राधावल्लभ शर्मा गौड़

पं० नथाराम मार्ग, श्याम प्रेस हाथरस।

८०००] सर्वाधिकार स्वाधीन है। [सन् फरवरी १९८२

Fig. 10. Title page of *Sultānā ḍākū* by Natharam Sharma Gaur (Hathras, 1982). The actual author is Ruparam and the likely date of composition in the 1920s. The portrait of Natharam and cover details are typical of this most popular *akhāṛā*.

Sultānā ḍākū (fig. 10), women warriors avenging their husbands in battle like *Vīrāṅganā vīrmatī*, or ill-treated daughters and daughters-in-law, *Shrīmatī mañjarī*, *Andhī dulhin*, and *Beqasūr beṭī*. Ruparam also prepared texts for such classics as *Lailā majnūn*, *Hīr rāñjhā*, *Bhakt pūranmal* and *Rūp basant*, and he continued writing under Natharam's imprint even after the latter's death in 1943. Rupa's distinctive signature line appears at the end of the plays:

> Enough! Rupa's pen stops here. (*Vīrāṅganā vīrmatī*, pt. 1)
> Natharam says, "Rupa, stop your pen now." (*Sultānā ḍākū*)
> Natharam the Brahmin says, "Rupa, stop your pen." (*Andhī dulhin*)[25]

Using an assortment of clues, I have attempted to assign approximate dates of first publication to many of "Natharam's" Sāṅgīts. It appears that a minimum of twenty-six were first published between 1897 and 1920. From 1921 to 1940, new publications totaled fifty, and in the categories after 1940 and undated, thirty-seven appeared.[26] The Indarman *akhāṛā* was thus the most successful and long-lived of the Hathras *akhāṛās* in producing and publishing Sāṅgīts. Its texts, considered the authoritative versions of Nauṭaṅkī in its present stage of revival, are still reprinted and sold.

The poet Govind, one of Natharam's acknowledged teachers, was another major figure in the Indarman troupe between 1900 and 1910. Using the name Govind Ram or Govind Chaman, he published a number of plays, some under the Indarman imprint, some in conjunction with or under the tutelage of an *ustād* named Tota Ram.[27] These were mostly published by Babu Gokulchand Publishers in Aligarh and Umadatt Vajpeyi of Brahman Press in Kanpur.

Govind's pen name *chaman*, meaning "garden," appears in an opening *dohā* that occurs in several of his plays, praising the author and his poetic virtuosity.

> *dohā* This history is in the form of a garden (*chaman*), whose root is prosody (*piṅgal*):
> It contains various meters (*chhand*) and melodies (*rāginī*), the many classes of flowers.
> *chaubolā* The many classes of flowers bloom on every garden bough,
> Green foliage appears on each branch, each poetic category.
> On every trunk sprout strange and unusual forms of verse (*raṅgat*),
> Each tree of literature the gardener-poet waters as he composes.[28]

Govind Ram's plays also include details of the Indarman troupe, the names of its members, and their respective roles and functions.

In the city of Hathras, the Indra *akhāṛā* wears the crest of victory
as its mark.
Its poets, Radherai, Baldev, Kalan, and Murshad are full of the best qualities.
Ustad Tota Ram is a mine of wisdom and knowledge.
Ganpati and Miyan Muhammad are not vain of their learning and skill.
The director Govind Ram always narrates the Svāṅg.
Chiranjilal ever performs the latest turns of phrase.
Parshadilal instructs the group so humorously.
Natharam the Brahmin, Madan, Janaki, and Hiralal too are singers,
They uphold their teachers' respect and from this achieve victory.
Ramlal Chaubeji sings the praises of the Lord.[29]

The continuity in personnel between this and earlier descriptions confirms that Govind was associated with the same *akhāṛā* as Chiranjilal and Natharam.

Other Hathras *Akhāṛās*

The three decades before the arrival of motion pictures (1890–1920) witnessed a proliferation of playwriting and theatrical activity in Hathras. These were heady days for Svāṅg; in addition to Chiranjilal, Natharam, and Govind Ram of the Indarman *akhāṛā,* poets such as Muralidhar and Batuknath Kalyan were producing plays by the dozens. The *akhāṛā* system fostered competition among troupes, and performances often took place in a contest situation or *daṅgal.* In this atmosphere of rivalry, poets naturally suspected that others might plagiarize their compositions. The practices of providing a signature couplet (*dohā*) on the cover of the play, identifying the *ustād* of the *akhāṛā,* and later picturing the author himself, perhaps originated as devices to prevent literary theft.

Around 1900, the page size of printed Sāṅgīts was reduced to its present 5″ by 8½″. Two vertical lines of a signature *dohā* flanked an image of Ganesh at the top of the page. For the Chiranjilal and Natharam team, the *dohā* read,

> Gentlemen seeking the authentic Indarman *khyāl*
> Should buy and read those with the name of Chiranjilal.[30]

After Chiranjilal's death, when Natharam began publishing plays under his own name, he changed it:

> Those gentlemen who especially seek the priceless plays (*khyāl*)
> of Indarman,
> Read "Natharam" in the imprint and gladly purchase them.[31]

Note that the term *khyāl* was still being used to refer to the Hathras Svāṅg.

After the Indarman *akhāṛā*, the second in importance was the *akhāṛā* best known by its poet, Muralidhar Ray (or Muralidhar Kavi). Muralidhar was the disciple of one Pandit Basudev, or Basam, whose name is invoked in his plays.[32] This *akhāṛā* is further connected with the names of Sedhu and Salig.[33] In *Sāṅgīt samar malkhān* (1907), Muralidhar pays homage to Salag, Sedhu, Basam, and Ballabh.[34] The London collections contain several published plays confirming the authorship of Salig (or Shaligram) and Sedhu, although whether they constituted two persons or one remains unclear.[35] The publication dates do not help much to construct the lineage of this *akhāṛā*, but the fact that Nihalchand published most of Muralidhar's plays as well as those of Shaligram and Sedhu Lal (and may have been related to Shaligram) links these individuals into some sort of unit.

Nine Sāṅgīts by Muralidhar are available in London; these are primarily incidents from the *Ālhā* epic cycle or romances (*Nauṭaṅkī shāhzādī, Siyeposh*). A prolific writer, Muralidhar seems to have been in close competition with the Indarman *akhāṛā*. The subjects chosen, manner of telling the story, style of printing, and cover design are so similar that one suspects a good deal of borrowing and mutual influence. Muralidhar's publisher, Nihalchand Bookseller of Aligarh, claimed to have an exclusive contract with the popular poet, for the inside covers feature a notice declaring, "All of Muralidhar's plays are published by Nihalchand by right." Nihalchand also seems to have been preoccupied with respectability: "We publish no obscene, vulgar, or impure plays . . . and we are having such plays written as will benefit the country."[36]

The third Hathras *akhāṛā* that developed in this period was known as the Nishkalank (blameless) *akhāṛā*. Its founders were Sahdev, Mukund Ray, and Shivlal. The chief poets, Muralidhar Pahalvan (the wrestler) and Natharam Jyotishi (the astrologer), bore names that are identical in part with members of the first two Hathras *akhāṛās*, namely Muralidhar, disciple of Basam, and Natharam of the Indarman *akhāṛā*. This confusion may have been intentional—a ploy to lure unsuspecting customers to buy their plays. Natharam Jyotishi's son, Chhitarmal Jyotishi, and one Jiman Khan also composed poetry for this group.

The IOL and BM catalogues do not always distinguish Muralidhar Kavi, disciple of Basam, from Muralidhar, disciple of Mukund Ray; as plays by "Muralidhar" are the second most numerous after those of

Natharam, their correct identification is often problematic. To make a distinction we must examine the title page. The signature *dohā* surrounding the Ganesh of Muralidhar's *Pūranmal jatī* (1915), for example, reads:

> The founder of Nishkalank was Shri Ustad Mukand,
> Its pure poetry is composed by Shivlal, Muralidhar, and
> Harnand.[37]

This identifies the poet as Muralidhar of the Nishkalank *akhāṛā*. Nishkalank's publishers were Lala Hotilal Motilal and Buddhsen Bhagvan Das, both of Hathras; these publishers' lists on the back covers indicate that about thirty or forty Sāṅgīts, with *Ālhā* episodes again dominating, had been published by 1915. Ram Narayan Agraval says that this *akhāṛā* was supported by Hanna Singh, a wealthy merchant through whose largesse a permanent stage for the troupe was constructed. Their gathering place in Hathras was at Sadabad Darvaza. A number of Nishkalank's Svāṅgs, such as *Māh-e-rukh̲* and *Māh-e-chaman*, are still remembered as occasions of great pomp and display. Hanna Singh was famous for riding through the streets and distributing rupee coins and guineas to the crowd.[38]

The fourth Hathras *akhāṛā* was that of Batuknath Kalyan, whose main poet was Vaidya Chiranjilal (notice again the similarity in name to another poet). This *akhāṛā* was possibly the first to publish its plays in the Braj region, for three of its *Ālhā* episodes, *Brahmā kā byāh*, *Malkhān kā byāh*, and *Ūdal kā byāh*, were published in Mathura in 1902 by Lala Hotilal Motilal. The cover *dohā* does not mention the founders of the *akhāṛā*; rather it emphasizes the authenticity of the text:

> When you find a jewel, don't settle for glass.
> Read from start to finish, and pick the true from the false.[39]

The word "jewel" (*chintāmaṇī*) may be a pun on the name of one of the troupe's actors; the final *lāvanī* mentions a Brahmin, Chunni Chintaman, who sings verses, as well as a possible guru, Siriya, who has died and gone to heaven. Reference is also made to Raghuna (or Raghunath), the troupe's patron. Agraval indicates that this troupe was famous for its extravagant procession employing many decorated elephants on the occasion of the performance of *Bahoran kā byāh*.[40]

Apart from these important and well-remembered *akhāṛās*, a number of lesser poets were also writing Sāṅgīts in the Braj area at this time. The London catalogues list a dozen or more such writers before 1920, who composed on romantic, martial, and social subjects. We can also measure the scope of publication by examining the lists printed on the backs of Sāṅgīt covers. Nihalchand Bookseller, for example, claimed to have published eighty Sāṅgīts by Hathras poets by 1913. Significantly, many of these dramas were published in Urdu script also. Nihalchand notes that thirty-five of the eighty had already appeared in Urdu and the rest were in the process of publication in Urdu.[41] From this it is clear that Hindi and Urdu readers alike sought Svāṅg texts, indicating the mixed following that the dramatic literature enjoyed.

The custom of featuring the poet's or *ustād*'s picture on the title page became established by 1920. A 1915 version of *Gorakh machhandar nāth* by Chainaram and Khumaniram Mistri sheds light on the reasons for the practice: "The purpose of giving photographs in this book is to show that these are good men who are completely worthy, and as their troupe is in need of every item and they require assistance, their pictures have been given here." Other reasons may have been to publicize actors or directors whose faces were well known and to help semiliterate purchasers make the correct choice. At first full-page portraits were included as frontispieces to the plays (see fig. 11 of Trimohan Lal from *Ālhā manauā* and fig. 13 of Shrikrishna Pahalvan from *Malkhān samar*). Eventually the photographs were integrated into the cover design, occupying the center of the page where detailed lists of the contents and meters had previously been placed. The image of Ganesh now vanished, and the Sanskrit blessing, "hail to Ganesh" (*śrīgaṇeśāyanamaḥ*), was poised at the top of the page.

Extension of Nauṭaṅkī to Kanpur: 1910–1930

As the Hathras Svāṅg spread to other regions in the second decade of the twentieth century, the term *nauṭaṅkī* became attached to this performance style. Virtually every poet in his own way retold the popular tale of the princess Nauṭaṅkī. Evidence of early use of the word to indicate the genre occurs in Shiv Narayan Lal's *Sāṅgīt sundarkāṇḍ rāh nauṭaṅkī*, "The musical play 'Sundarkāṇḍ' in the Nauṭaṅkī manner." *Rāh* means "road, way; manner, method; custom, fashion," and here designates the performance genre. At the back the author states:

Submission

These days Nauṭaṅkī is becoming extremely popular. But there is fear of the character being corrupted by books on bad subjects. Therefore I have adapted

> the Sundarkāṇḍ of the revered *Rāmāyaṇa* in the style of Nauṭaṅkī (*nauṭaṅkī ke rāste nikālā hai*). If my readers appreciate this, then gradually I will bring out all the *kāṇḍ*s [of the *Rāmāyaṇa*].[42]

The declaration by Shiv Narayan Lal points to public objections to the corrupting influence of Nauṭaṅkī performances, matched by greater self-consciousness among poets regarding the reception of their work. Moralistic condemnation of the theatre emanated from several quarters. The Dramatic Performances Act of 1876 established a legal basis for the colonial government to prohibit performances deemed defamatory and threatening to the government as well as those likely to deprave and corrupt persons present.[43] Social reform movements such as the Brahmo Samaj and Arya Samaj also sternly criticized popular theatre, and by this time their messages had extended to the smaller urban centers. Authors and publishers had been subject to strict censorship ever since the registration act of 1867. It is thus not surprising to find the competitive publisher Nihalchand Bookseller admonishing his prospective authors:

> *Notice* [English word]: We require intelligent and educated poets to write superior Sāṅgīts. Let those who are accomplished in the business of writing *dohā, chaubolā, kaṛā, lāvanī, dādrā, qavvālī, bhajan, bahr-e-tavīl*, and so forth compose true Svāṅgs on subjects pleasing to us and they shall collect their reward. Let them not damage the country by writing lewd and impure *jhūlnā*s and so on, boasting of being poets.[44]

Shaligram, the schoolmaster-cum-*ustād* of the Basam-Muralidhar *akhāṛā*, likewise imparts a lesson to the poets of his day:

> *Lesson*
>
> Among those who write Svāṅgs are particularly foolish and ill-educated men who compose vulgar, impure, plotless, and completely useless (*mahā raddī*) Svāṅgs and do a great disservice to the country. Such people should not trouble themselves in vain with this kind of writing . . . because they do not enhance their personal esteem; on the contrary they increase their ill repute.[45]

Shaligram goes on to advise the singers of *jhūlnā*s not to indulge in verbal abuse of one another's female kin but rather to fill their songs "with sentiments of devotion and valour."

These statements imply that vulgar language and erotic topics were part and parcel of Svāṅg and Nauṭaṅkī in the early twentieth century. At the same time, the countervailing effects of colonial censorship, curiously reinforced by the reformist social agenda of the nationalist movement, were beginning to be felt. Just as the mass appeal of the Svāṅg stage became recognized, some quarters attempted to convert Svāṅg and Nauṭaṅkī to a more edifying form, one beneficial to the building of moral character. The impact of the new political ideology seemed to intensify just as Nauṭaṅkī took root in Kanpur. It left a clear mark on the early career of Shrikrishna Khatri Pahalvan, the founder and chief proponent of the Kanpur style.

From the end of the nineteenth century, Hathras troupes had performed regularly in Kanpur, and the Sāṅgīts of the Hathras *akhāṛās* were published there in large numbers. Kanpur's history was intertwined with the military and economic purposes of the British Raj. It was one of India's largest grain markets in 1810. The stationing of ten thousand British troops in its cantonment caused the population to rise dramatically in the early nineteenth century. As with the area of Hathras, the lands around Kanpur were very fertile; in response to the army's demand for fruits, vegetables, and tobacco, "an island of relative agricultural prosperity was created in the midst of the depressed middle Doab."[46] After the opening of railway lines connecting the city to Calcutta and Lucknow in the 1860s, the industrialization of spinning and tanning turned Kanpur into a manufacturing center surpassed only by Bombay, Calcutta, and Madras. In 1901 the semiindustrial male labor force was estimated at twenty-seven thousand.[47] Rapid social mobility characterized the society, especially among the lower castes, yet westernization in the sense of interest in British education, culture, nationalist politics, or even religious life scarcely existed. These conditions helped create both the audience and commercial structures that sustained popular entertainments like Nauṭaṅkī, while minimizing the reformist opposition that might have put a damper on such activities.

Kanpur began to develop its own brand of Nauṭaṅkī sometime around 1910. One of the first local *akhāṛās* was that of *ustād* Chandi Lal and poet Bhairon Lal, whose *Jagdev kaṅkālī* was published in 1914 by Umadatt Vajpeyi of Brahman Press, Kanpur. Chandi Lal was introduced as a "resident of Kanpur" on the title page, and thirty-one titles appear on the back cover in a publication list, indicating an already well developed playwriting tradition based in the city.[48]

The poet Tṛimohan Lal was an important link between the Hathras Svāṅg and the new Kanpur Nauṭaṅkī (fig. 11). A native of Kannauj, about fifty miles northwest of Kanpur on the Ganges River, he went to Hathras to become a disciple of Indarman but later established his own troupe in Kanpur and published all his plays there and in Kannauj.[49]

त्रिमोहनलाल, कन्नौज सिटी

Fig. 11. Portrait of Trimohan Lal of Kannauj, frontispiece to *Ālhā manauā* (Kannauj, 1920). By permission of the British Library.

Trimohan was a good *nagāṛā* (kettledrum) player as well as organizer, and Agraval credits Trimohan with instituting scene changes following Parsi theatrical practice. He is also said to have introduced female singers to the Nauṭaṅkī stage.[50] Curiously, his compositions are described on their covers as *phūlmatī krit* (made by Phulmati), a usage usually indicating the poetic mentor or guru rather than the actual author. Phulmati is a female name, and this strange heading suggests that Trimohan Lal composed his plays in conjunction with or for a certain Phulmati. It is possible that Phulmati was an actress or perhaps a transvestite.

Trimohan Lal's plays carry his picture on the title page plus the following *dohā:*

> Beware the false book, pay attention please.
> This is the real sign: identify the photo and buy this.[51]

Most of his Sāṅgīts from the early 1920s are catalogued under the name of the twosome, Manni Lal Trimohan Lal, but nothing is known of Manni Lal.[52] A recently reprinted copy of Trimohan Lal's *Khudādost sultān* (1977) contains the name Yasin in the colophon, evidently a ghostwriter; many of his plays may have been composed by Yasin.[53]

Explicit political comment and concern with contemporary events are noticeable in several Kanpur plays that retell the tragic massacre at Jallianwala Bagh in Amritsar. One of these, *Rāṣhṭrīya sāṅgīt julmī ḍāyar,* written by Manohar Lal Shukla in 1922, bears an unusual cover image in allegorical style (fig. 12). A whip-flailing policeman named Martial Law holds the mantle of a woman named Afflicted Punjab, threatening to disrobe her while she prays to Lord Vishnu (an allusion to Draupadi in the *Mahābhārata*). The law books, labeled Vyavastha, lie unattended on the ground, while in the corner a male figure resembling Mahatma Gandhi, named Satyagraha, sits sadly in contemplation. After recounting the historical incident from a child's point of view, the play ends with an element of wish fulfillment, when the collective ghost of the murdered citizens comes to the evil General Dyer seeking revenge, beats him up, and forces him to release the prisoners he arrested.

Shrikrishna Khatri Pahalvan

Just as the Indarman *akhāṛā* and its leader, Natharam, dominate the Hathras Svāṅg, so Shrikrishna Khatri Pahalvan's name is synonymous with the Nauṭaṅkī of Kanpur. As troupe organizer, actor, author, and

Fig. 12. Title page of *Rāṣhṭrīya sāngīt julmī ḍāyar* by Manohar Lal Shukla (Kanpur, 1922), on the incident at Jallianwala Bagh. By permission of the British Library.

publisher, his influence extended to all aspects of the Kanpur stage in the 1920s and continued for forty years or more.[54] It seems that Shrikrishna made his living as a tailor before he became firmly established in the Nauṭaṅkī business. The reverse covers of several plays feature advertisements for his shop: "Every type of tailored clothing is sold wholesale, such as coats, shirts, kurtas, women's jackets, waistcoats, three-piece suits, two-piece suits, and so on." Obviously he was also a wrestler (*pahalvān*). His Sāṅgīts carry a full-length portrait of the poet, standing in a proud posture clad only in a loincloth (fig. 13).

Shrikrishna's early plays dealt with historical figures such as Haqiqat Ray, Maharani Padmini, Shivaji, and Virmati, who defended Hindu faith and territory against Muslim armies and were in most cases martyred. At this time, Shrikrishna was under the influence of the Arya Samaj, a Hindu reform movement espousing the superiority of ancient Vedic civilization. Several of these plays were published expressly for the Āryā Sāṅgīt Samiti of Kanpur, and the Samiti's name is listed on the covers. There are also internal references to the Samiti and the founder of the Arya Samaj, Dayanand Sarasvati. The *maṅgalācharaṇ* of *Mahārānī padminī* (1919) concludes with: "May everyone spread the objectives of the Sāṅgīt Samiti." This play also closes with a moral lesson based on the promulgations of the Arya Samaj:

> Friends, fellow Indians, awake from your stupor!
> India produced goddesses like this one, who burned themselves
> on the pyre and saved their honor.
> If you wish the country to progress, take steps to preserve the Hindu faith.
> Rani Padma was burnt to ashes. Hail Dayanand! The story is finished.[55]

Similarly, in *Haqīqat rāy*, reported to be Shrikrishna's first play:

> Look, friends, at Haqiqat's sense of duty.
> He got beheaded to uphold the Vedic faith.
> This only is my request: don't abandon your religion.
> Hail Dayanand! The story is finished.

The cover page of *Mahārānī padminī* includes the following note: "Warning! It is strictly forbidden to perform this Svāṅg with dancing." This unusual prohibition was probably intended to protect the reputation of the Āryā Sāṅgīt Samiti, since it could not afford to be seen countenancing *nāch*. (Dancing of course remained an important element in Kanpur Nauṭaṅkī.) These texts indicate the strong influence of the Arya Samaj on the young Shrikrishna, when he accompanied his treatment of patriotic historical subjects, a feature of his output until around 1930, with a Hindu revivalist tone bordering on communalism.

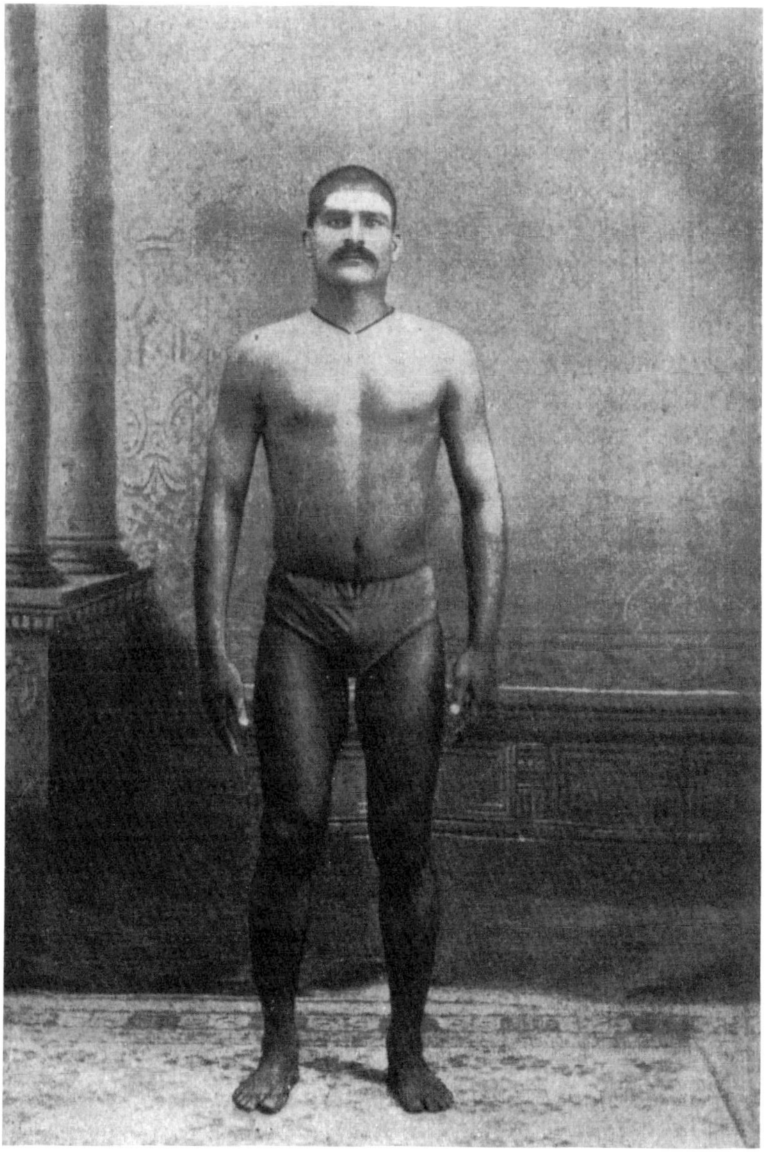

श्रीकृष्ण पहलवान कानपुर.

Fig. 13. Portrait of Shrikrishna Khatri Pahalvan of Kanpur, frontispiece to *Malkhān samar* (Kanpur, 1920). By permission of the British Library.

Later he turned to the middle-class social milieu that characterized the comedies of the Parsi theatre, choosing characters from the nouveau-riche Seth class and their servants, as well as government employees, students, and other contemporary figures. Examples of these subjects in the London collections are "The Eye's Magic" (*Āṅkh kā jādū*), "Devotion to the Husband" (*Pati bhakti*), "The Loyal Accountant" (*Vafādār munīm*), "The Valiant Manjari" (*Shrīmatī mañjarī*), "The Punjab Mailtrain" (*Pañjāb mel*), "Flute Girl" (*Bāṅsurī vālī*). Some of these stories were based on current Parsi plays or film hits.

The title page of *Vīrmatī* (1921) contains the characteristic *dohā* of Shrikrishna's early plays:

> The imprint gives information on the name and the mark;
> Inside is the photo of Shrikrishna Pahalvan.

The same play mentions two important co-writers in the colophon:

> Panna the poet's pen has stopped and Lakshmi Narayan says it is morning.

A number of early plays are listed under the dual authorship of Pannalal Shrikrishna; possibly Pannalal's contribution was comparable to that of Ruparam who worked for Natharam of Hathras. Lakshmi Narayan's name stands alone in the colophons of several Sāṅgīts. As with the other famous poets, it is impossible to determine which plays published under Shrikrishna's picture are truly his own compositions.

In the early days, Shrikrishna's plays were published by Umadatt Vajpeyi, the leading popular press in Kanpur, but eventually he opened his own publishing concern, Shrikrishna Pustakalay in the Chauk. According to his son, Pooranchandra Mehrotra, who now operates the press, seventy-five million copies of Shrikrishna's books were published and sold up to 1971. A 1987 publication, *Sāṅgīt vīr vikramāditya,* lists over one hundred Sāṅgīts of the Great Shrikrishna Sāṅgīt Company. Shrikrishna received the annual award of the Sangeet Natak Akademi, Delhi, in 1967.

Another popular poet of Kanpur, judging from the London collections, was Chhedilal, who often composed with Devidas. Seven of his Sāṅgīts, mostly on older themes like *Lailā majnūn, Sultānā ḍākū, Amar siṁh rāṭhor,* and *Vīrmatī,* were published between 1928 and 1932. Other Kanpur poets like Madhoram Gulhare appear to have been competing with Shrikrishna as the popularity of Nauṭaṅkī spread in this region.

Recent Developments

Beyond Kanpur, publishers in all the major towns of Uttar Pradesh sought out popular plays and encouraged the local troupes by publishing their scripts. The IOL has a particularly large collection of Sāṅgīts for the period from 1920 to 1942. Although most were composed by minor poets, a list of the cities in which they were published gives an idea of the geographical extent of Nauṭaṅkī's popularity: Ambala and Amritsar in the Punjab; Bhiwani, Hisar, and Sirsa in western Haryana; Beawar in Rajasthan; Jhansi and Jabalpur in Madhya Pradesh; south as far as Bombay; Meerut, Moradabad, Bulandshahr, and Aligarh in western Uttar Pradesh; and Lucknow, Kanpur, Etawah, Gonda, Allahabad, and Banaras in eastern Uttar Pradesh.

Toward the end of this period, playscripts in the distinctive style of the Haryana Sāṅg appear in the London collections. Pandit Dipchand of Khanda, one of the founders of this tradition, is represented by two plays, *Rānī mahakde va jānī chor* (1927) and *Nauṭaṅkī shahzādī* (1932), both published in Muzaffarnagar. The IOL contains fourteen Sāṅgīts dated between 1937 and 1939 published by Lakhmi Chand, the most famous exponent of Haryanvi Sāṅg. These are mostly on subjects familiar to Nauṭaṅkī, such as *Lailā majnūn, Prahlād,* and *Hīr rāñjhā*. The metrical treatment is different, however, the verse form *rāganī* replacing the *chaubolā;* the language is the local dialect, Haryanvi. The music in Haryana Sāṅg is simple and resembles folk song, in contrast to the virtuosity of the Hathras Svāṅg.[56]

Since the 1940s, Nauṭaṅkī performance has been in a decline, caused in large measure by the powerful impact of cinema and television on the traditional performing media. Competition from the Bombay commercial films has exerted particular pressure on Nauṭaṅkī. But surprisingly, the printing and reprinting of Sāṅgīt chapbooks proceeds unabated. The small presses all over North India continue to churn out new covers for the old texts, changing the date each year as the publication runs reach into the tens of thousands. The classic stories dominate the field, and the most esteemed texts for purchase remain those of Natharam and Shrikrishna.

New tastes and trends in popular culture, however, are also quickly absorbed. Two of the latest texts to join the repertoire are *Jay santoṣhī mā,* based on the fashionable religious film lauding the goddess Santoshi, and *Phūlan devī,* a product of the cult following enjoyed by the low-caste heroine of the 1980s, the "bandit queen" Phulan. The fascination with goddess figures and valiant women central to these stories is perennial in North India but has acquired new significance in a time of changing gender roles and expectations.

Also visible in recent additions to the Sāṅgīt literature is the impact of the official public culture of postcolonial India, which appropriates Hindu mythology and Sanskritic religious ideology in the service of politics. Dramas based on Sanskrit sources previously unknown to the Nauṭaṅkī repertoire are appearing for the first time, such as the *Sāṅgīt vīr vikramāditya* of the Shrikrishna *akhāṛā* published in 1987. I suspect that the 1988–89 Doordarshan (Indian television) fifty-two-part serialization of the *Rāmāyaṇa,* followed by the *Mahābhārata* and *Rāmāyaṇa* part two in 1989–90, will lead to a spate of new Nauṭaṅkī plays based on the Hindu epics. The cycle of creativity and imitation continues to revolve, throwing up both novelty and reiteration of the old, in response to changes in public demand, whatever their origin.

Perspectives on Change

We can view the historical development of the Sāṅgīt literature over the last one hundred twenty years from several perspectives. We can first trace a geographic movement, beginning with the early texts published in Delhi, Meerut, and Banaras, followed by increased activity in Hathras and the Braj region, a shift eastward to Kanpur, and then a gradual extension outward to areas as distant as Rajasthan, Madhya Pradesh, and eastern Bihar. This movement corresponds to the establishment of printing facilities in the areas where the Nauṭaṅkī theatre attracted large public followings and achieved viable institutional structures. Its two foremost centers—Hathras and Kanpur—remain as active foci of publishing even though their performance traditions have faded away.

Despite their frequent shifts of locale and multiplicity of publishers, the format, content, and manner of distribution of Nauṭaṅkī chapbooks have been consistent over time. This suggests a network of exchange and borrowing that is corroborated by the publishers' repeated attempts to reduce plagiarism. As a folklore genre disseminated through the print medium, the Nauṭaṅkī literature exhibits a relatively standard form, enabling its ready recognition and separation from other popularly published genres. Whether such stabilization of the printed package has affected the performance text is a question of interest, but it lies beyond the scope of this research.

The evolution of *akhāṛā* structures is another dimension of Nauṭaṅkī history illuminated by the examination of printed texts. Except for the first twenty or thirty years of its history, this folk theatre has been organized into lineagelike groups of poets and actors whose names, faces, and disciples are given on Sāṅgīt covers. The *akhāṛā* connection serves here as a sort of advertising device. More significantly, the *akhāṛā* provides cohesion among the performers, sustains the initiation and training of upcoming poets and singers, and supplies a mode of internal organization that is both affiliative and hierarchical. Identification by *akhāṛā* is the chief criterion by which an aspiring poet establishes his legitimacy, much as adherence to a guru or *gharānā* bestows credentials on adepts of other Indian systems of knowledge, as in music, dance, or spiritual practice.

The alliance to an *akhāṛā* reinforces group identity in a situation where caste, religion, and geographical origin place few constraints on the participation of performers. The history of printed texts demonstrates that rivalry among *akhāṛās* parallels rivalry among publishers, as a particular *akhāṛā* tends to be published by a single publisher and publishers vie for steady contracts with leading poets. The elastic economic network generated in this process has no doubt contributed to the growth and expansion of the Nauṭaṅkī tradition, enabling authors and publishers to benefit from commercial sales.

Within the covers of Sāṅgīt plays a wealth of narrative diversity meets the eye. What at first appears an inchoate mass reveals, to closer analysis by periods, the clear impress of historical change. As the nineteenth century slowly turns into the twentieth, the hoary saints and imaginary princes yield to heroes with firmer historical and regional identities. The old stories with their timeless universal themes continue to attract listeners, even as the appeal of contemporaneity consistently grows. By 1920 or so, everyday situations from various sections of modern life routinely appear, along with a sprinkling of English words appropriate to these contexts. The increasing realism present in folk theatre literature parallels the emergence of realistic conventions in the modern urban literatures in roughly the same period. However, in Nauṭaṅkī narratives realism coexists with traditional elements; contemporary characters accumulate alongside the existing stock of fantastic, supernatural, and legendary figures rather than replace them or nullify their popularity.

The emergence of certain hero types within the contexts of colonialism and nationalism as well as changing conceptions of political authority will be our subject later, as will the connection between the folk theatre and social reforms relating to the family, community, and women. At this point, let us summarize certain facts about the political circumstances of the time that bear on the interpretations that this chapter's textual history suggests. First, government censorship of published literature and of public performances was a political reality throughout the period, placing strict limitations on the expression of nationalist or anti-British sentiments. To convey political messages under such conditions, poets had to adopt covert strategies. The fictional, poetic, or dramatic representation of Indian historical figures vanquishing ruthless aliens was a common ploy. The apparent shortage of politically explicit Sāṅgīts, seen thus, likely masks the more widespread circulation of nationalist sentiments clearly visible in texts such as *Sāṅgīt julmī ḍāyar*.

Second, the pressure on publishers and poets to "purify" their language, content, and performance practices was not only an echo of Hindu reform movements like the Arya Samaj but constituted an external form of state suppression, aimed at controlling any public exuberance that might acquire a volatile political character. Third, the geographic areas where Nauṭaṅkī flourished were not early centers of Western-style education, nationalist activism, or religious reform. This fact was fortuitous in several senses, for until recently folk theatre has tended to disappear when "modernizing" forces become ascendant. The poets of Nauṭaṅkī were by all indicators provincial but literate men who were not unaware of changes in the climate of ideas within their home regions. References to social and political reality in their plays may have become manifest somewhat later than they did in the consciousness of urban elites but probably before the new consciousness spread to illiterate laborers and the peasantry.

CHAPTER FIVE

Kings, Warriors, and Bandits

The little-known dramas of the Svāṅg and Nauṭaṅkī theatre offer a fascinating source of lore to those interested in the popular culture of North India. The plays encompass a broad range of themes, drawing on varied sources such as Islamic storytelling, the Hindu Puranas, regional heroic legends, the lives of saints, historical incidents, and even motion pictures. To a greater degree than the religious dramas and elite literature of the region, Nauṭaṅkī embodies the taste and values of the ordinary person. Bawdy, comical, frankly entertaining on one level, the plays are also deeply conservative and at times surprisingly idealistic. They are concerned with central issues in Indian culture—the nature of moral virtue, the proper exercise of political authority, the conflict between romance and family, the heroism of women.

While Nauṭaṅkī texts are fictional and show an imagined realm, their contours match the shape of lived experience. The narratives offer structures, ordered sequences of suspense and release, that compel attention to particular themes and issues. Critical junctures in the story lines direct audience response to areas of anxiety and conflict, inviting the spectators to participate in the playful construction of meaning. In the next section of this book we plunge into the rich world of Nauṭaṅkī's narratives. Through examining the core stories of the genre, we seek access to the problems and preoccupations of the everyday world of folk theatre and its participants.

The most important concerns of the plays invite schematic grouping into several areas, despite the number and variety of Nauṭaṅkī narratives in existence. Whereas indigenous practice categorizes Sāṅgīts by themes such as religious (*dhārmik*) or devotional (*bhakti ras*), martial (*vīr ras*), and social (*sāmājik*), I have chosen a somewhat different approach. Many Nauṭaṅkī dramas confront aspects of social life in which morality is conflicted or problematic. Each major area of conflict forms the topic of one of the next three chapters. The areas are the exercise of power and the proper use of wealth; romantic love and group loyalty; and the strength of women and the dangers of sexuality. Within each area Nauṭaṅkī's narratives articulate an assortment of responses that probe some of the most troublesome dilemmas in the consciousness of North Indians.

Questions regarding the basis of political authority and its relation to moral conduct and spiritual perfection are at the center of a group of well-known dramas going back to the earliest phase of the Sāṅgīt literature. The figure of the renunciant king, displaced from his title and wealth, haunts these accounts. Other dramas incidentally portray kings moving about disguised among the poor or tell of beggars who profess to royal origins. A common motif running throughout the genre is that of the aristocratic daughter or son, abandoned at birth and brought up by kindhearted low-caste folk. In all these tale types, the boundary between kingship and common humanity is crossed over, either by conscious choice or an accident of fate. What is the difference between plebeian and king? these plays seem to ask. What makes one a pauper and another a prince? How are wealth and privilege distributed in society? Who is really entitled to rule?

Whereas scholars often discuss the culturally sanctioned divinity of kings in India, the folk plays of Svāṅg and Nauṭaṅkī, I argue, intimate that the prerogatives of royal office proceed not from a king's godliness but from his simplicity and willingness to pursue virtue—especially by living among the poor. According to the ideal Nauṭaṅkī worldview, the king and the beggar share many qualities. The true king is as uninterested in material gain and privilege as the naked ascetic. This lesson animates the exemplary heroes Gopichand, Harishchandra, Puranmal, Dhuruji and others who abandon their kingdoms to follow the path of spiritual enlightenment.

Somewhat later in the history of Nauṭaṅkī, when the legendary saint-kings are supplemented by historical heroes from the *Ālhā* cycle and other Rajput tales, the kingly qualities of generosity and adherence to truth are joined by traits of loyalty, fearlessness, and defense of honor.

In more recent dramas, the old monarchical order fades and a new system of patronage arises: the bandit king is the proletarian hero who redistributes wealth to the lower classes in dacoit dramas like *Sultānā ḍākū*. A double-stranded thread weaves through these different sets of tales: political authority is legitimized on one side by identification with the lowly and downcast, and on the other by submission to a truth higher than possessions or power.

Kings Who Abandon Their Thrones

The great ruler Harishchandra exemplifies the kingly paragon: learned, judicious, beneficent, and utterly devoted to truth. His most common epithets in the Nauṭaṅkī theatre are *satyavādī,* "he who speaks truth," and *satyasindhu,* "ocean of truth." Truthfulness, or adherence to *satya* or *sat,* signifies more than not telling lies. It connotes an attitude of righteousness extending to all aspects of conduct, guided by a constant searching to determine the nature of truth. In practice, holding to truth means fulfilling promises, following up on bonds of trust established in good faith. Harishchandra is also famed for his generosity; he is a great bestower of gifts, a *dānī.* It is Harishchandra's penchant for keeping his word coupled with his largesse that precipitates his fall when, tricked by the gods, he gives away more than he has.

> Harishchandra, ruler of Ayodhya [or Avadhpuri], is a rich and virtuous king who has performed ninety-nine sacrifices (*yajña*) and must accomplish only one more to gain liberation. Indra, the king of the gods, feels threatened by Harishchandra's escalating fortunes, and he sends the sage Vishvamitra to obstruct the king. Vishvamitra in the form of a boar uproots a garden in the vicinity of the palace, and when Harishchandra comes to slay him, he changes his disguise to that of a Brahmin. Challenging the king's reputation as a truth sayer, he requests two boons, and Harishchandra agrees. He commands that the king bestow his entire kingdom upon him as a religious donation (*dān*), and on top of that he asks for his priestly honorarium (*dakṣhiṇā*). Since Harishchandra has given away all he possesses with the first boon, he is forced to sell his wife and son into slavery in order to pay off the second.
>
> The king, his wife, Taravati, and their son, Rohit [or Rohtas], journey to Banaras. A Brahmin purchases Taravati and Rohit, but an untouchable buys Harishchandra and sets him to work at the cremation ground collecting the tax on dead bodies. He suffers not only the pollution of the death rites but hard labor, starvation, and the indignity of servitude. One day Rohit is bitten by a snake and dies. When Taravati brings his body to the cremation site, Harishchandra is compelled to

> demand the tax that she is too poor to pay. Denying herself the modesty that is her only remaining possession, she shreds her sari and gives Harishchandra a piece of it instead of the tax. After Rohit's body is cast into the Ganges, Vishvamitra retrieves it and brings it to Taravati, raising rumors that she is a witch. Because untouchables serve also as executioners, Harishchandra is appointed to behead her. However, just as he raises his sword, the gods appear. Harishchandra is cleansed, reunited with his son, and given direct passage with his family into heaven.[1]

As recorded earlier in the epics and Puranas—where rulers and priests often competed for power and merit—this myth may once have been intended to warn against the hubris of excessive virtue among the royalty.[2] By its nineteenth-century appearance in theatre, however, the display of Harishchandra's forbearance had become a set piece, comparable to the labors of Sisyphus or the torments of Job.[3] The king's suffering induces pathos because of its lack of provocation; it comes upon him randomly, as every good person's hour of trial seems to come. If even the most mighty and lauded individual in the land can suddenly find himself shorn of all privilege, degraded and outcast, how tenuous the happiness of any human being must be. The story reverberates with familiar slogans on the inscrutability of destiny. It recommends a course of action that rewards acceptance of subjugation and diligent perseverance—if not in this birth then surely in the next.

Within this framework, the folk theatre works its magic in the mode of exaggerated contrasts of feeling. The Nauṭaṅkī text exploits the ironies of lost rulership especially through the tender figures of the wife and child. These pawns in the king's moral battle with the gods become foci of intense pathos and melodrama. Harishchandra is not only unable to protect his kingdom; he cannot help those who are his most intimate dependents. As he witnesses their degradation, he suffers doubly for his incapacity to succor them. The ultimate blow is of course Rohit's death and Taravati's near death, in which he is an unwilling accomplice. Through the reversals written into the story line, the narrative dismantles pat metaphysical explanations, exposing the contradictions at the heart of the moral system. It is not enough that the king pursue truth with utmost vigor. The drama deconstructs the very concept of truth, distilling its ultimate cruelty and blindness to human desire. Let us take the most memorable scene in the drama, when Harishchandra is called upon to execute his own wife. The act of beheading Taravati has the radical potential to undermine the truth of the king. It dramatizes the possibility that his descent to untouchability has destroyed his former capacity for virtue: he is beyond the pale socially *and* morally, not only unable to do good but compelled to do evil. The wife's murder is necessary as the logical extension of the reversal in the king's fortunes, denying the accumulation of goodness as much as wealth. However, the king is prevented from reaching this outer limit of truth—now equated with the murder of a virtuous woman by her husband, a most despicable untruth—by the deus ex machina. Harishchandra's acceptance of the patently immoral act of wife-slaughter as a moral imperative consummates his surrender to the gods; they are satisfied and demand no further sacrifice. For both the king and the audience that identifies with him, the prospect of that horrific deed is sufficient to effect a transformation of awareness. Truth itself is unknowable, difficult to discern, and irrevocably intermixed with untruth.

This final blurring of truth and untruth is anticipated throughout the drama by multiple instances of illusion and disguise, building to paranoia on almost a cosmic scale. As Harishchandra plummets down the social ladder, reality is less and less what it seems. Most of the havoc is created by Vishvamitra, appearing first as a boar in the garden, then as a Brahmin, then as a beggar on the ghat, and even as the snake in the garden. But the treachery that Harishchandra confronts is not just Vishvamitra's trickery; it is the caprice of the gods. The inversion of appearances in this world is the gods' *līlā,* play making for their own amusement. But to human beings, especially humans unguided by discernment, this world in its unknowability is duplicitous and anxiety-inducing in the extreme. This story shows a hero struggling to free himself from the same existential confusion that afflicts each of us at moments, to lesser degrees.

Harishchandra's pursuit of truth takes him along a path followed by other kings in these Sāṅgīts. Deprived of his wealth by his generous offer to a Brahmin, he forsakes his throne, his dignity, even his family, to accept an existence at the utter bottom of the social hierarchy. Tormented by the gods and their henchman Vishvamitra, he sacrifices his comforts and prestige for a life of immense hardship, one very similar to that of the wandering yogi. A parallel case from the Indo-Islamic side of the Nauṭaṅkī tradition is that of Khudadost Sultan, the largehearted king of Yaman. Approached by a fakir (a Muslim ascetic) who comes to test his magnanimity, the king swaps places with the fakir for three days, but then the ascetic refuses to return to his former penury. The king, trusting in God's will, exchanges the fakir's clothes for his own and leaves his kingdom for a life of begging, accompanied by his wife and two sons. Hardships befall them; the wife is kidnapped by a crafty merchant, one son is seized by a wild animal, the other falls into the river. Eventually Khudadost's faith and virtue are rewarded, and he is reinstated as king and reunited with his family.[4] The story conforms to that of Harishchandra in its broad outline, but it also anticipates the narrative of Gopichand, in that Khudadost joins the ranks of mendicant ascetics as the means of fulfilling his commitment to perfect virtue.

The ascetic ideal of kingship is perhaps most unforgettably brought to life in the very popular drama of King Gopichand and his uncle Bharathari (see fig. 5). Unlike many mythological stories about Indian saints, the tale of Gopichand in the Nauṭaṅkī theatre is concerned not with his difficult penances (*tapas*) but rather with the emotional torment involved in renouncing the world. The grief endured by the king's kin, especially the abandoned women, is keenly dramatized, as is the vocal opposition from all sides when Gopichand attempts to depart. Each scene pits an opponent of renunciation against its supporter, who in most cases is Gopichand himself. The debates test Gopichand's resolve; they require not metaphysical argument so much as the fortitude to resist the demands and pleadings of his near and dear ones. In meeting these challenges and proving the firmness of his intentions, Gopichand progresses from a neophyte unaware of the full meaning of his vows to an initiate ready to follow his guru into the forest.

> Gopichand rules in the city of Dhara, unsurpassed in wealth and fame. One day as he is administering justice, he is summoned to his wife's chamber. She has prepared a special feast and decorated their bed. Before joining her, he excuses himself to go pay his respects to his mother, the queen Mainavati. Upon seeing his handsome form, Mainavati begins weeping. She can think only of his mortality and begs him to renounce the world and take on the robes of a yogi. Only by renouncing the world can he attain the glory of an immortal body. Gopichand resists her request. How can he abandon his family? His 1,600 wives will curse him; his 1,250 unmarried daughters will bring shame upon him. Mainavati insists he forsake illusion and attachments, and finally he relents. She urges him to become a disciple of Gorakhnath under the tutelage of her brother Bharathari, an initiate.
>
> Gopichand rubs ash on his body and goes to meet his queens, who receive him weeping and wailing. He then leaves the palace for the forest, where he meets Bharathari and asks to go to Gorakhnath. Bharathari tries to dissuade the young Gopichand. He warns him of the difficulties of the path, and explains that the real meaning of Yoga lies not in leaving behind possessions but in abandoning all ties of love and

fondness for others. Then Bharathari takes Gopichand to Gorakhnath. The guru again tries to break Gopichand's resolve. Finally he takes the obstinate Gopichand and performs the act of initiation, cutting the cartilage of both ears. Gopichand must now prove himself by returning to his wives to ask for alms, addressing each as "mother."

Gopichand reenters the palace. His chief queen complains bitterly of the suffering brought by separation from him. Gopichand calls himself her son and, leaving her heartbroken, proceeds to say farewell to his mother. She is pleased with him but sternly warns him not to go to Bengal. His sister Champa lives there, and should she see him as a yogi she will die of grief. Inevitably Gopichand goes to Bengal. His sister's suffering is so great that she swoons and dies. Gopichand's firm resolve begins to crumble. Overcome with guilt, he calls on his guru for guidance. Gorakhnath arrives and resuscitates Champa by uttering Om in her ear. Champa, rising from the dead, curses her mother. Gopichand finally resorts to a trick that makes her palace appear to be on fire; vanishing, he proceeds to the forest with his guru.[5]

This is a story brimming over with pathos and tears. The departure of Gopichand—beloved king, master, husband, and nephew—is greeted by every character except Mainavati with copious displays of weeping. The phrase *rovat zār bezār* (weeping bitterly) is used to describe the reaction of kin as Gopichand successively encounters his queens, his uncle, the maids, and finally his sister. In its emotional impact, the drama is a downward spiral in three stages. It begins with the pleasures of sensual enjoyment (*bhog*), represented by the opulence of the king's court and the enticements of the women's chambers. This leads to the ascetic denial accomplished by embracing *yog* (union, as with the eternal). And what eventually follows is *viyog:* separation, loss, and bereavement, the consequences of the act of *yog* for ordinary mortals, for those who are left behind.

Gopichand's conscious decision to renounce contrasts with Harishchandra's willing submission to an unchosen imposed fate, although the consequences are equally severe. Gopichand has enjoyed the best of material existence: wealth, power, and a huge harem of women. The hyperbolic number of wives is repeated more than any other attribute of his worldly life, to suggest the limitlessness of sensual indulgence available to him—a fantasy of desire unbounded. Moreover, Gopichand knows fame, the adulation of the populace; his stature is mirrored in the eyes of all who gaze upon him. The relinquishment of this multiform state of desire is a hardship requiring huge reserves of dedication and self-control. His renunciation is not on the face of it an escape from bitter circumstances, and the persuasive force of his example of self-denial is therefore much greater. His renunciation is motivated by the awareness of mortality, by the *prospect* rather than the palpable presence of decay and loss. If for Gopichand even such a distant possibility as death can throw the whole of life into question, how much more compelling for others to forsake lives already lived in adversity. For this exact reason, the contrast between kingly affluence and ascetic poverty has served to dramatize many major Indian narratives of conversion, such as those of the Buddha, Shankara, and others.

Yet Gopichand, like Harishchandra, gets caught in the snares of righteousness despite his best intentions. He is seemingly under siege, buffeted by the contrary demands of duty, voiced mainly by the women in his life. In the opening scene Gopichand allows the temptations of his wife's company to disrupt him in his administration of justice (*nyāy*), the customary dharma of the king. This prelude to the drama's main action casts the king in the archetypal mold of the benevolent and just ruler—and then shows him drop his work to proceed to the women's quarters, preening himself in the glass on the way. Before he surrenders to his chief queen, however, he accedes to the dominant will and superior spiritual insight of his mother, who urges him to forsake his role as narcissistic consumer, as *mahābhogī,* and leave the world. Gopichand at first resists this formulation of his duty, because abandoning the kingdom would entail neglecting his wives and failing in his sacred duty to ensure that his daughters marry. How can he reconcile the requirement to protect the weak with the solitary vow to renounce all ties?

In fact at a deeper level, the drama raises the question of the true ability of the king to rule—not only to rule the populace, but to rule over his womenfolk and ultimately over his own emotions and desires. Seemingly pushed and pulled by the strong female personalities around him in the first part of the drama, Gopichand exchanges his loyalties to them for unswerving devotion to his spiritual guides. He severs his connections with the palace, returning to beg alms from his wives and by this gesture bringing tragedy to their lives. Warned not to confront his sister with his ascetic countenance, he defies the ban and precipitates her death from uncontrollable grief. Gopichand's unfeeling dismissal of family obligation proves him a practiced initiate, an ascetic who not only controls the urges of the body (*tan vash karnā*) but gives up emotional attachment, killing the instincts of the heart (*man mārnā*). While such undaunted asceticism glorifies Gopichand's spiritual estate, the drama implicitly puzzles over the consequences for the body politic.

The net of familial ties symbolizes the king's responsibilities to the community and the kingdom. What is to become of the populace, especially the unprotected and unjustly wronged? The laments of the women seem to echo the silent despair of the people, left defenseless in the wake of the king's retreat.

The dilemma posed in this drama proceeds from the profound recognition that righteousness and the exercise of power are not easy to reconcile. For Gopichand, the problem simply stated is, to rule or not to rule? But simplicity does not resolve the crisis of political authority; neither side of the equation offers a satisfying answer. The Harishchandra and Gopichand narratives struggle to find a modus operandi, a way to reinstate kingship on the basis of truth and justice. As if playing with possibilities, they avoid linear logic and circle back and forth between positions. They demonstrate the limitations of absolute standards of virtue to mortal kings caught in the contradictory circumstances of everyday life. The ideal of ascetic denial and detachment is proffered as a model for kingly conduct, yet the pursuit of that path seems to lead inexorably to the forest and away from political life—away from the problem rather than toward a solution.

From the perspective of the common viewer, these dramas reveal an ambivalent stance toward kingship. That ambivalence goes far back in Indian history, yet events in eighteenth- and nineteenth-century North India may have reinvigorated it within these dramas. Following the breakup of the Mughal kingdom, power was decentralized and eventually reestablished in successor states holding regional dominion, but clashes for local control characterized the period. The seemingly arbitrary transfers of power continued under the British, as land revenue officers sought to "settle" the titles of local rulers and secure allies for their colonizing enterprise. Although the degree of political fragmentation and instability is open to dispute, sectors of the population experienced the weakening of old political entities and were troubled by their perception of it. Kings deposed, tottering and vacant thrones—such was the picture of disarray that left its impress on popular memory, whatever the realities of alliance and consolidation. It is not surprising, then, that some plays should incorporate the perception that entitlement was capricious and the moral foundations of rulership obscure. A secondary notion similarly revealed the cynicism of the age, namely that rulers who clung to sovereignty were likely to be indolent hedonists.

The perception of capricious entitlement is illustrated by the Sāṅgīt of Raghbir Singh, an anomalous tale because of its apparent correspondence to local events and its pictorial reference to the British.[6] Raghbir is a king whom his enemies plot against, poison, and leave for dead. Rescued from a river by a washerman, he assumes the guise of a mendicant and wanders in exile for seven years. Finally he returns to claim his throne, pleading for the restoration of his good name and his hereditary right to rule. But his former subjects cannot judge his tale of exchanged identities, and the story ends without resolution. As if to comment upon the drama's indecisive outcome, the play's cover pictures a British officer, listening to the ascetic's petition with pen in hand, ready to render permanent the inexplicable reverses of fate. A king one moment, a fakir the next—Raghbir embodies the period's pessimism about the viability of kingdoms, voicing the fear of dispossession as well as popular suspicions of spurious claims to royalty.

The second notion inspired another familiar icon: the decadent king, prone to sensual excess and self-indulgence. Even as living examples of the type disappeared, the Sāṅgīt texts inscribed this figure in cultural memory. The plays manifest attitudes of fondness and nostalgia on the one hand, and distrust and condemnation on the other. The wave of enthusiasm generated by the fanciful *Indarsabhā* of Amanat and its multiple imitations illustrates the positive part of the public perception, the fascination with the old style of conspicuous kingly display. The fun-loving Raja Indra, given to poetry and music with his fairylike concubines, was not merely a figment of fantasy; he was a fictional reconstruction of the model actively pursued in the courts of the Nawabs of Awadh and the Nayaks of South India. Similarly, the late medieval romances (mostly of Persian origin) that populate the early Svāṅg seem to perpetuate the fantasy that a good king or prince has no more fitting occupation than to search out the most enchanting women available to him and capture their hearts. The most obvious examples of Sāṅgīts of this type are *Benazīr badr-e-munīr, Gul bakāvalī, Lāl-e-rukh̲ gulfām,* and *Qatl jān ālam.*

This sensual image carries over into plays featuring the renunciant king as well. Gopichand begins the drama as a pleasure seeker who admires himself in the glass en route to an afternoon of pleasure. Yet here the narcissistic self-reflecting stance is hedged with irony, for his limbs will soon be covered in ash, his locks matted on his head, his visage gaunt and dusty. The king as emblem of surfeit is indeed the one destined for and most in need of enlightenment. To the extent that kingship equates with luxury, ease, and excess—as a commoner in nineteenth-century North India might easily have concluded—there is a sense of justice in the king's losing it all. The tremendous influence of the renunciant-king dramas may owe much to the desire among the audience for a reversal of the high status and privilege accorded the frivolous hedonistic king.

While part of the period's response is to look back at faded Mughal splendor and celebrate its lost glory and pomp, the will to reestablish a moral basis for kingship surfaces repeatedly in these dramas of renunciation. The examples of Harishchandra and Gopichand indeed seem to prepare the ground for a future style of leadership, one in which truthfulness, humility, and even poverty constitute the criteria for exercising authority. Of course, Gopichand and Harishchandra are imperfect models of what the audience desires. They do not return from exile to rule, enlightened by their experience as ascetics; Gopichand vanishes and Harishchandra goes to heaven. Elsewhere, however, viable exemplars emerge from within Indian tradition. Ram returns from his sojourn in the forest in the *Rāmāyaṇa,* and saintly followers of Gorakhnath like Puranmal and Risalu combine their kingly duties with moral purity in other Svāṅg stories.[7] As if illustrating the possibilities should the excursion into renunciation be less permanent than Gopichand's, these models suggest ways in which the ascetic and king might merge.

This longing for a renewal of political authority through an ascetic kingly figure was ultimately fulfilled in the historical rise of Mahatma Gandhi to power in the nationalist period. A self-proclaimed admirer of King Harishchandra, Gandhi brought back to public leadership the deep regard for truth heralded in the folk drama.[8] Moving beyond Harishchandra's passive stance of forbearance in adversity, Gandhi realized the dynamic potential of adherence to truth and fashioned it into an activist strategy in the doctrine of satyagraha. He imposed on himself the indigent appearance and inner discipline of an ascetic. Throughout his career he moved in and out of periods of intense seclusion and reflection, like a renunciant repeatedly withdrawing to the forest. Following in the steps of Gopichand, he chose vows of celibacy over the responsibilities of householdership, largely abandoning his wife and children. Gandhi's renunciant style of leadership answered the desires of a population raised on high ideals but accustomed to disillusionment with the political realm. Repudiating the foppish antics of an Indra, he brought political authority back to its roots in moral righteousness. He was exactly what the Svāṅg-viewing public had been waiting for.

Honor, Loyalty, and the Warrior's Code

The Rajput martial Sāṅgīts that proliferated in Nauṭaṅkī between 1895 and 1920 present a somewhat modified picture of political authority, in which the focus shifts from the supreme sovereign, who is often depicted as weak and vacillating, to the champions and nobles of his court. These less exalted players are shown as the true heroes, the men most suited to rule, although they remain subordinate to the monarch until their deaths. The concept of kingship now extends to a circle of valiant men, and it accentuates loyalty, honor, and defense by arms rather than passive endurance and ascetic withdrawal. A bolder, more aggressive style of leadership is celebrated here, but emphasis is still placed on the virtues of liberality, forbearance, and steadfast resolve.

Unlike the ascetic kings Harishchandra and Gopichand, who inhabit a distant age (a *yuga* less debased than the present Kali Yuga) and belong to ahistorical legend, the warriors of these Sāṅgīt texts can be assigned specific dates with some certainty. The Banaphar clan of which Alha and Udal are the chief members took part in the great battle in 1192 when Prithviraj Chauhan of Delhi was defeated and after which North India was lost to the Turks. Amar Singh, the Rathor chief of Mewar, was a vassal of the Mughals Jahangir and Shah Jahan in the early decades of the seventeenth century. In the development of Svāṅg and Nauṭaṅkī, these historical figures demarcate an intermediate stage in the evolution of the hero from mythological giants of the past to citizens of the contemporary world.

Within these stories, regional identification becomes a potent force for the first time as well. Kings like Harishchandra had no particular alliance with a geographical area and were admired universally. Amar Singh Rathor, on the other hand, has specific ties with Rajasthan and is celebrated through its folklore, especially in the puppet theatre (*kaṭhputlī*).[9] Whereas the Banaphars were also Rajputs (although allegedly of mixed blood), the *Ālhā* cycle is associated with the Bundelkhand region of Uttar Pradesh and enjoys its greatest local support in that area. Nonetheless, both stories became well loved in Nauṭaṅkī form in both Hathras and Kanpur and have sustained continued popularity across North India.

The character of Amar Singh shows Rajput chivalry in full flower (fig. 14). A trusted and loyal commander in the emperor's army, Amar Singh can be alienated from his sovereign's affections only by a treacherous plot that develops while he is absent from court attending his

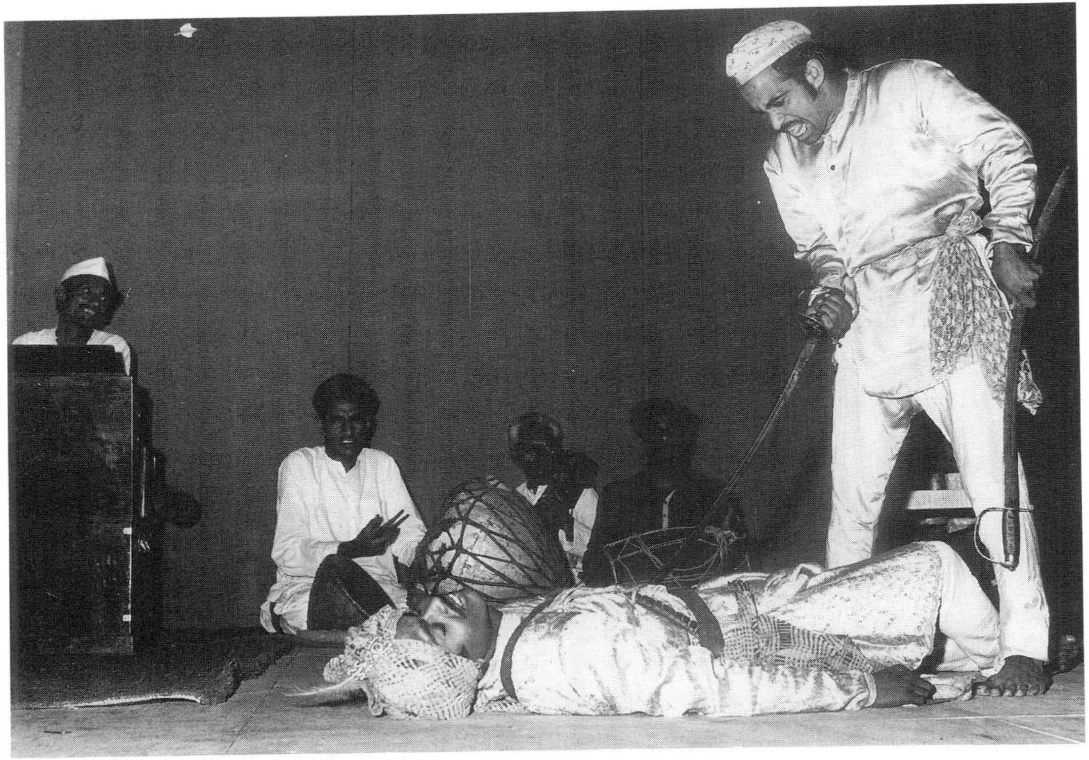

Fig. 14. The death of a Rajput hero, from *Amar siṁh rāṭhor*. By permission of the Sangeet Natak Akademi.

marriage. He is cut down in a deceitful and dishonorable attack by a relative. His death requires a vengeance that almost destroys the king's forces but vindicates the reputation of Amar Singh's nephew, Ram Singh, who is appointed to take his place.

> Amar Singh is the chief officer in Shah Jahan's army, where he lives with his brother's son, Ram Singh. When the time comes for his *gaunā* (consummation of marriage), he requests leave from the emperor and is granted seven days away from court. If he overstays, he will be fined 100,000 rupees for each day he is late. On the way back, Amar Singh meets Narshebaz, a Pathan, and offers the thirsty man water, obtaining a promise of friendship in return.
>
> When Amar Singh does not appear within the seven days, the jealous courtier Salawat Khan instigates Shah Jahan to levy the fine. Summoned to court, the humiliated Amar Singh insults the king and kills Salawat Khan. The emperor is stunned at the outrage and offers a reward for his capture. Arjun Gaur, a relation of Amar Singh's, under the pretense of mediating the quarrel, stabs Amar Singh treacherously as he passes defenseless through a window.
>
> After Amar Singh's death, his widow, Hadi Rani, wants to join her husband on the pyre during the cremation rites. Shah Jahan, however, threatens to bury the corpse, challenging the Rajputs to retrieve it by force. Three attempts are made: first by Narshebaz, and next by Bhallu, Amar Singh's reluctant brother—both warriors are killed in battle. Finally Ram Singh together with Narshebaz's son succeed in getting the body and are promoted to officer rank in Amar Singh's place. With elaborate preparations, Hadi conducts the *satī* ritual and joins the body of Amar Singh; the pyre ignites on its own.[10]

The conflict that breaks out between Amar Singh and his master in this play has nothing to do with territory or the perquisites of power. Rivalry among the nobles provides the ostensible motivation for the quarrel, removing the blame to visibly traitorous agents who *are* greedy for gain. But more fundamentally, the struggle hinges on who is the more honorable man—the king or his commander—and by implication, who is truly worthy of being king. Amar Singh's code of honor has three cornerstones: loyalty, generosity, and courage. As a loyal retainer he does not dispute the king's authority; rather, he shows himself a humble servant when he requests leave, and he obediently returns within the stipulated time. (The same dutiful respect is shown by Narshebaz later in the story when he resigns from the king's service before joining Ram Singh as an ally.) Amar Singh's failure to present himself at court upon his arrival is a lapse attributable to his involvement with his new wife, not an act of disobedience. On the one hand, generosity of heart lies behind this action as well as his befriending of Narshebaz in the desert and his affectionate relations with his nephew, Ram Singh. In a similarly generous spirit of reconciliation he leaves his weapons behind and goes with Arjun Gaur to patch things up with the king, exposing himself to assassination. Amar Singh's angry response to the king's summons, on the other hand, reveals his fierce pride and his ready courage to defend his personal honor. He is insulted by the fine because of the implicit accusation that he is not performing his duty to the king. At this moment, overcome with anger, he kills the villain Salawat Khan and escalates the confrontation between himself and the king.

While the drama underscores Amar Singh's virtues throughout, events prove Shah Jahan to be a vacillating and opportunistic overlord whose weaknesses offer temptation to those around him. Although he resists Salawat Khan's suggestion that Amar Singh is untrustworthy because he is a Hindu, the king is eventually drawn into the web of suspicion created by Salawat's innuendoes and Amar Singh's prolonged absence. After Salawat, the king's brother-in-law, is killed, the king makes a cowardly retreat from the court and turns to his wife for solace. She must taunt him with threats to kill Amar Singh herself before he agrees to avenge her brother's murder. He subsequently offers twelve villages to the man who kills Amar Singh, but when Arjun Gaur comes to claim the trophy and Shah Jahan learns of the treacherous manner of the death, he reneges on his promise—showing a sense of justice, no doubt, but vacillating once more. Perhaps the king's most problematic action is his decision to hold the corpse of the dead warrior until the Rajputs regain it in battle. Shah Jahan's threats to bury the body, following Muslim custom, are offensive to the religion of the Rajputs and run counter to the declarations of Hindu-Muslim unity he made earlier on. His behavior seems baldly opportunistic, the avowed intention being to test Rajput mettle so that he can name a successor to Amar Singh. In consequence, a number of his most talented warriors as well as several Rajputs are killed in a series of battles that inevitably end with the surrender of the body.

Whereas the conflict between Amar Singh and Shah Jahan terminates in the display of the Rajputs' superior force, Amar Singh's inner qualities of fortitude, his strength of heart, and his purity of intention are what truly vanquish the emperor. The drama, so unlike the renunciant-king plays in its martial ethos, in fact reiterates their central premise, the moral basis of political authority. Once more, the superiority of the true leader has to do with selflessness and devotion to virtue rather than exercise of brute strength. In this case, that devotion is manifest in Amar Singh's willingness to lay down his life in defense of a code of honor rooted in loyalty, mutual trust, fearlessness, and benevolence. In certain ways, the independence and defiance represented in the icon of the Rajput warrior correspond to the iconoclasm of the renunciant model of kingship. In both, the true "king," the ideal ruler, is placed at a distance from the actual seat of power.

A similar asymmetry exists in the relationship between the heroes of the Banaphar clan, Alha and Udal of the famous *Ālhā* cycle, and their sovereign, Parmal of Mahoba.[11] As outsiders who are reputedly of lower rank than the Mahoban Chandels, the Banaphars are adopted into Parmal's service when they prove their merit and successfully defend the gate of Mahoba against Kariya of Maro. Parmal is an ineffectual ruler who is a vassal of Jaychand, king of nearby Kannauj. He is overpowered by his much stronger wife, Malhna, and her brother Mahil, the villain of the saga, who is of another clan and has an ancient claim to the Mahoba lands. Alha, Udal, and the other Banaphars perform numerous acts of valor, defending Parmal time and again, but they are banished when they refuse to join the cowardly king in sending tribute to Prithviraj of Delhi. In exile they serve Jaychand of Kannauj, expanding his territory, and later return at Malhna's invitation to defend Mahoba when it is besieged by Prithviraj. Some time after, in the tremendous battle with Delhi, all the champions of Mahoba except Alha and his son are killed while Parmal sits at home; the craven king finally starves himself to death in despondency.

In this complex of legends, the heroes outstrip their sovereign in determination and prove themselves matches for even the mighty Prithviraj. Yet they remain on the fringes of authority, moving back and forth between kings, never coming into their own. Their supposedly low birth inhibits the Banaphars; according to rumor, their mothers were Ahirs (from the cowherd caste) and they are not of full Rajput blood. The tension between birth and merit is highlighted whenever males of the clan seek a marriage alliance. The bride's family always casts aspersions on their origins, refusing to sanction a union. Necessarily preceding each betrothal is a full-scale battle that leads to the defeat of the bride's kin and capture of the not unwilling bride. This coupling of marriage and warfare is visible in the Nauṭaṅkī titles of many *Ālhā* episodes: "The Marriage of Alha, or the Battle of Nainagarh," "The Marriage of Brahma, or the Battle of Delhi."

The *Ālhā* narratives celebrate the same cluster of Rajput virtues as the Amar Singh story and conclude in the same selfless act of fighting to the last breath. But perhaps even more than the account of Amar Singh, the *Ālhā* legends question a hierarchy of clan and caste that divides human beings without respect to their moral qualities. The most worthy characters in the dramas—the Banaphars—are those most subject to insult, rejection, exile, and untimely death. Their trials are not unlike the difficulties of the ordinary person who strives for a sense of belonging in an indifferent world. One's inner worth, one's true nature, is not visible to others, and life entails a series of struggles to assert that truth in the eyes of the world. The Ālhā Nauṭaṅkīs explore a dilemma that haunts the moral reasoning of North Indians, a dilemma that goes beyond the particulars of time and place. How is the virtue manifest in a good person's actions to be reconciled with inferior social and political position? The *Ālhā* tales, although based on a feudal setup, may have helped disseminate a new strand of nationalism, insofar as they proposed armed combat as the appropriate means of righting society's wrongs. Their model of active struggle paralleled the nationalist ideology emerging from leaders such as Bal Gangadhar Tilak and later Subhash Chandra Bose. The Ālhā Nauṭaṅkīs' representation of the forcible redress of injustice thus reinforced the agenda of the activist wing and may in circular fashion have gained in popularity because of the ascendance of such leaders.

Attitudes toward British Rule

This model introduces another dimension to the discussion of indigenous conceptions of political authority. While the British presence met a powerful response in the nationalist movement, how did Nauṭaṅkī texts react? The representation of contemporary events appears rather late in this genre; in 1920 most dramas still eulogize well-known mythological and historical heroes rather than craft more realistic narratives. Nevertheless, two texts stand out that answer political events in this period and offer clues to popular attitudes to the British.

The first is *Dehlī darbār,* a drama describing the festivities following the coronation of George V in 1911. This week-long ceremonial extravaganza was witnessed firsthand by Natharam, the Hathras poet, who describes the events of each day in detail. What most impressed the author were the grandeur and expense of the arrangements, and the promises made by the king: more support to education and the armed forces, debt relief to the "king of Gujarat," the relocation of the capital to Delhi. From the evidence of this text, the new emperor attempted to gain support by acting with traditional largesse, creating an image of himself as a *dānī* (bestower of gifts) and entertaining grandly in the Indian style. His public gestures of generosity imitate the Harishchandra model of kingship, wherein outward acts of kindness are presumed to emanate from a core of righteousness.

The sense of betrayal that overtook the populace when the colonial regime displayed its oppressive side is well documented in the Sāṅgīt *Julmī ḍāyar,* an account of the 1919 massacre at Jallianwala Bagh in Amritsar (see fig. 12).

> The non-cooperation movement against the British government has gripped all Indians, and General Dyer, feeling demeaned by the freedom fighters, decides to put a stop to their activities. A young boy, Madan, looks forward to the meeting in Jallianwala Bagh, thinking proudly of the country's leaders who have tried to restore justice. When he seeks his father's permission to attend, his father warns him that General Dyer is ruthless and he should stay away. Madan prevails against his father, saying that it is no time to sit back, when the country is in the hands of foreign rulers and tyranny is rampant. Meanwhile General Dyer discusses his fears of the enemy's strength with the governor, and they decide that all who attend the meeting should be arrested. Madan senses the impending danger and wants to turn back, but his friend encourages him to be fearless now that Gandhi is their leader.
>
> A crowd gathers at Jallianwala Bagh and the leaders of the meeting denounce the Rowlatt legislation to detain Indians without trial. Just then, troops move in and begin firing at the people. Madan's friends flee, but he is hit by a bullet and falls to the ground. After the soldiers leave, Madan's friends return to find him and carry him home. Madan's parents are distraught, and his father runs out to fetch a doctor. On the streets, General Dyer is still killing and arresting adults and even children. Madan's father too is arrested and put behind bars.
>
> When General Dyer goes to bed that night, an apparition comes to haunt him. The apparition identifies itself as the Ah, the sighs and curses of the people. The Ah attacks the general and threatens to kill him, while the general begs for mercy and promises never to do such misdeeds again. When Dyer wakes up the next morning, he immediately releases all the prisoners, including Madan's father. The father heads straight for home, but it is too late; he finds Madan lying dead.

In the view that emerges from this text, the struggle between the Indian nationalists and the British government is not terribly different from Amar Singh's confrontation with Shah Jahan. It deals less with constitutional freedoms or voting rights or even economic oppression than with honor (*izzat*) and the betrayal of trust in acts of tyranny (*julm*, "cruelty, oppression"). According to the Sāṅgīt text, the causes of the massacre are, first, that through their intransigence in defying certain laws Gandhi and the freedom fighters threaten British *izzat*. General Dyer feels "demeaned" and insulted, much as Shah Jahan did when Amar Singh failed to appear in court on time. Second, Gandhi and other leaders persuade the people that the British have insulted *their* honor, that it is ignoble to be ruled by a foreign power, that acts of "tyranny" (*julm*) are being perpetrated. In addition, ordinary people like Madan believe that higher powers are on their side, that their quest for justice has divine sanction. When the shooting starts, Madan wonders why God has deserted India when He always helps those in trouble; He came to aid Draupadi when she was in distress and destroyed the evil and proud kings, Kamsa and Ravana. Events seem to have cruelly shattered this reliance on a higher truth, yet faith in divine intervention emerges later in the Sāṅgīt when the ghost, a manifestation of the popular wish for revenge, punishes General Dyer and forces him to change his policy.

Not surprisingly then, attitudes to British authority in these texts appear an extension of the principles that governed attitudes toward Indian kingship. Fulfillment of the benefactor-protector-patron role earned adulation for the British, whereas the dependent populace viewed actions in apparent violation of that role as unjust and meriting defiance. Again, the moral foundation of political authority serves as the essential ground. If the British are positioned within a cosmic order of truth beyond their power to determine events, then resistance is not only possible but ultimately efficacious.

Dacoit Heroes: Serving the Poor

Another set of dramas presents resistance to established power in more explicit and fully developed ways. These are the plays about the dacoits (*ḍākū*), bandits of rural society.[12] Dacoit dramas begin to appear in the Sāṅgīt literature around 1920; although they do not completely displace older story types such as the tales of renunciant kings or episodes from the *Ālhā* cycle, their frequency and continued popularity make them noteworthy. They are remarkable in that virtually every bandit hero known to Nauṭaṅkī is based on a living or recently deceased individual, and that events and conflicts described are contemporary (even when not strictly factual). Thus this subgenre shows the process of myth in the making—folklore visibly emanating from people's lives.

The characters of this recent type are ordinary, even lowly individuals, in contrast to the great kings and warriors of older dramas. The type marks an advance in literary realism comparable to developments in modern Hindi fiction, where storytelling rooted in rural reality comes into its own with Premchand around 1920. A greater degree of particularization is present not only in the characters and events but in the geographic locale. Each dacoit is firmly associated with one place, usually mentioned in the opening *dohā;* this town or village provides an anchor point for the band's comings and goings in the countryside. Although geographic origin may provide the basis of identity, ties of affinity and loyalty are now defined primarily by socioeconomic class rather than clan, caste, or cult. The bandit hero marks the emergence of a proletarian "king," an overlord who is of and for the poor. Earlier dramas placed emphasis on the protective function of the king and the virtue of generosity, but here for the first time, the distribution of wealth concerns society at large and is open to question by the needy, to redress from below as well as above.

The similarity of this tale type to the martial dramas needs to be restated, for they also dispute the hierarchical nature of society. The lowborn warrior, fighting for his rightful place as chief, is not far from the unjustly victimized villager who turns to a life of banditry as a means of correcting social and economic wrongs. Both narratives celebrate the underdog, although the dacoit dramas exhibit greater consciousness of both the class basis of economic privilege and the unrelenting arm of the law. It may be significant that the Chambal valley in western Uttar Pradesh is the part of northern India most associated with dacoits in recent times. This territory is adjacent to Bundelkhand on one side (the region in which the *Ālhā* epic still holds sway), and Rajasthan, the land of Rajput chivalric tales, on the other.

An early example of the structural parallels between the martial and bandit tale types is the Sāṅgīt *Dayārām gūjar.*[13]

> The robber Dayaram is incited by his wife to steal the queen's jewels, which she has dreamed she will wear one day. He successfully stages a holdup at the river where the queen has gone to bathe, killing a large number of the king's men plus their leader. When the king hears of the outrage, he offers a reward of twelve villages for the capture of Dayaram, a challenge accepted by Jafar Khan, a friend of the bandit. Jafar

deceives Dayaram by tying him up while celebrating a sham wedding. Dayaram is sent to jail. The dacoit's younger brother, Chand Singh, goes to rescue Dayaram, challenging Jafar Khan to a fight and killing him. The king allows the brothers to meet in jail, and Dayaram is so happy at seeing Chand Singh that he breaks his fetters. To avoid a struggle with the two brothers, the king offers them both posts in the army on the condition they abandon dacoity.

This drama resembles *Amar siṁh rāṭhor* in a number of ways. The motif of elder brother and younger brother structures both, with Ram Singh (actually a nephew) playing second to Amar Singh and retrieving his dead body, and Chand Singh rescuing Dayaram. Strong women motivate both the heroes' actions, Hadi Rani in the one play and in the other Dayaram's wife joined by her mother. The reward for capturing Amar Singh and Dayaram is the same (twelve villages), and it is a traitorous friend or relation (a Muslim in both cases) who undoes the hero. In both plays the king remains on the sidelines, waiting to reward the valorous men with posts under his command, reestablishing his authority in the end.

A dominant theme in later dramas, the rationale for banditry as redistribution of wealth among the poor, does not appear here; instead the action springs from a woman's greed. As a result, Dayaram does not figure as a particularly noble figure, except in comparison with his wife, although he is certainly a powerful and effective outlaw. The only justification presented for Dayaram's actions is Chand Singh's argument to the king that robbery is the *dharm* (duty) of the brothers, which could refer to birth in a particular caste or tribe. This outlaw hero is barely distinguishable from the upstart warrior whose fame and prowess bring him a modicum of respect. The king must eventually come to terms with the outlaw's power, best accomplished by enlisting him in the military.

The moral dilemmas raised by the dacoit are present in only a rudimentary fashion in *Dayārām gūjar*. In the most enduring of the Nauṭaṅkī dacoit dramas, *Sultānā ḍākū,* the confrontation between the admirable underclass hero and the agents of a colonial government is more problematic (fig. 15).

Sultana is a Robin Hood–like figure who robs from the rich to give to the poor. His rival is Mr. Young ("Young Sahib"), a British policeman assigned to arrest him. The early scenes of the play sketch Sultana's ruthless discipline of his band of men, his fearlessness, and his fondness

Fig. 15. Record jacket of *Sultānā ḍākū* on the Odeon label, purchased in Lucknow in 1982.

for the dancing girl who is his mistress. The dacoit hears a prophecy that he will meet his end when he holds a five-year-old boy on his lap and gives him a thousand rupees.

Both Sultana and Young send spies and launch strategies to outmaneuver each other. Young's efforts consistently fail, despite the fact that Sultana always sends a letter to the police announcing the time and place of his next dacoity. Sultana often dons a police uniform as disguise and steals weapons directly from the police station. Sultana and his gang rob a moneylender, a wealthy merchant, and a landlord. Following the raid on the landlord, Sultana sends half the booty to the city to be distributed among the poor, spending the remainder on uniforms for his men.

Finally Sultana takes pity on a captured messenger of Young's who has a large family and low salary. When Sultana promises to meet him in his village to give him a sum of money, the messenger reports the rendezvous to Young. He then meets Sultana with his five-year-old son

> whom Sultana immediately takes into his arms. Young arrests him; he is tried and sentenced to be hanged. On the gallows, Sultana requests Young to bring up Sultana's nephew and prevent the boy from becoming a dacoit. Admonishing the audience to do good, not follow his example, and vote for the Congress party, he places the noose around his own neck and dies.[14]

Just as in the story of Harishchandra, the dacoit's preeminent virtue is his generosity, which his opponent exploits and turns against him. Sultana's commitment to aiding the poor is illustrated throughout the play. The opening *chaubolā* states: "It was his job to loot the treasuries of the rich / And always bring relief to the poor and helpless." Somewhat later Sultana declares his mission to be that of an equalizer sent by God: "For those who have found wealth and given not a penny to charity, God has made me the enemy. / For those who are poor and have no consoler, I have been born to share their sorrows."[15] When Sultana's mistress complains that they always seem penniless, he explains that he gives all the booty to the poor and the men who work for him. It is his penchant for bestowing gifts that traps him finally when Young's messenger turns informer. Sultana demonstrates other kingly virtues, such as impartial justice, when he shoots one of his own men on a charge of indiscipline.

Consistently admired by the common folk and feared by the well-to-do, Sultana earns even Young's respect, and at the end the two are close to friendship. Yet the relationship between the men—and between the morality of Sultana's egalitarian impulses and the hierarchical authority of the state—is complex and not without its incongruities. Throughout most of the play, Sultana appears to establish a parallel kingdom, a territory in which he reigns through patronage of the poor and intimidation of the rich. He is at once king, chief minister, and head of security, playing these roles through various disguises. By sending reports on his activities to the police, Sultana seems to recognize the legal jurisdiction of the British government. Of course, he may simply be taunting the police for their ineptitude, saying, Catch me if you can. Similarly, he may wear the police uniform for its expediency, from emulation of the police, or out of defiance—or all three.

Once caught, Sultana is at pains to appear a loyal follower of the same order he previously defied. At the gallows, Sultana acknowledges the supremacy of the established rule, requesting that his offspring and the entire population follow the straight and narrow and eschew his model of rebellion. Is he reversing his former position, or is he simply bowing in submission to a higher power, as Gopichand and Harishchandra did when they became renunciants, as Amar Singh and the Banaphars did in service to their less competent lords? Willing self-surrender is an important aspect of kingly virtue, deserving of acclaim in itself.

Difficult to interpret as well is Sultana's exhortation to vote for the Congress party. It may have been tacked onto the play at a later date, perhaps during an election campaign when the Sāṅgīt was being reissued. Or perhaps the slogan originated in the pre-Independence period, which would be particularly plausible if Sultana had been adopted as a popular symbol of anticolonial resistance, much as the Rani of Jhansi was. The words of the Sāṅgīt narrator, however, seem to refute this, inasmuch as they acknowledge the audience's fear of dacoits. They link the vote for Congress with promises to eliminate *badmāsh* elements (scoundrels) and punish every murderer, no matter how "good."[16]

Another puzzling component of the dacoit syndrome is the apparent need to justify the bandit's way of life by reference to early misfortune and victimization. We must know *why* Sultana turned to a life of crime. A drama in which a hero consciously adopts an agenda that counters authority may not satisfy the audience—or the colonial censors—unless it proceeds from an initial provocation. The factual history of Sultana recounted by Jim Corbett states that he was "a member of the Bhantu criminal tribe."[17] Two out of three Sāṅgīt versions are silent on the question of his origins. In the third, Sultana explains during the trial scene that he acquired his habit of robbery as a boy, when his mother asked him to steal a chicken to save the family from starvation.[18] Being poor and being forced to steal for survival is the ideal rationale for a bandit's entry into a career of crime—and the one most common in these plays. The meaning of the rationale is not simple, however. Clearly it enhances the audience's sympathy for the hero, playing on its ready response of sympathy for the child victim. Compassion for the needy, however, offers a simplified form of class analysis, with its implications of the necessity to equalize the distribution of wealth in society and take back from the oppressors what was taken from the poor.

Another text of the same type, Sāṅgīt *Ḍākū mān siṁh*, devotes sixteen out of fifty-four pages to accounting for Man Singh's turn to a life of crime.[19] The hero is a Rajput farmer of the Rathor clan, whose original offense is to beat up a Brahmin named Talfiram who steps ahead of him at the village well. This leads to a jail sentence, a vow to take revenge, and the eventual murder of Talfiram. These episodes dwell not on the poverty of Man Singh as such (although he is a village dairy farmer, not a warrior), but on the affront to Rajput pride and the themes of honor and revenge found in the martial Sāṅgīts. Caste tensions rather than class antagonisms seem to motivate these incidents, although the difference is not always explicitly stated. After becoming a dacoit, Man Singh adopts the code of the underclass hero with its egalitarian ethos. He robs only from the rich, gives money and other assistance to the poor, uses the least violent means to achieve his ends, and avoids looking at women; he instructs his entire gang to behave in the same way. He intervenes in the marriage of a young girl to an old merchant, killing the prospective bridegroom, arranging the bride's marriage to a younger man, and presenting her with a huge dowry. With his gang he also raids several Seths (wealthy merchants) and a landlord. Respected in his community, Man Singh is addressed as *dāū* (elder brother) by persons outside his family and is often depicted together with his community and family.

Journalistic accounts corroborate Man Singh's reputation as local benefactor: "He helped people in their distress, mediated in disputes; in short, he became the uncrowned king of Khera-Rathore."[20] Even the police reported:

> The villagers looked up to him as a friend and a guide and had their disputes settled by him. The poor received generous help from him and the legend about his charities and lavish gifts spread far and wide. . . . His admirers often remarked that he represented the high watermark of dacoity nobly practiced.[21]

He was also known to be a deeply religious man who gave daily offerings to the deities. Yet this "colossus among dacoits" and his gang committed over 1,000 dacoities and 185 murders before he was killed.[22]

In the Sāṅgīt, Man Singh's men roam disguised sometimes as policemen and sometimes as sadhus and elude the police for years. But in the end the police detect the gang and open fire. Man Singh is such a great fighter that he cannot be captured alive; in the climactic scene he and Govind Thapa, his police assailant, kill each other (the actual event occurred in 1955). Like Sultana in his final hour, the dying Man Singh seems to wish his life had been different. "Leaving my home, I wasted my whole life in the jungle, alas! / I became a dacoit, and disgraced my own name. / But I take solace in never having harmed the poor."[23] This play also concludes with a call to support the Congress party.

Similar in many respects to *Sultānā ḍākū*, this drama perpetuates the myth of the noble outlaw, a theme replete with variants in South Asian folklore.[24] Putting this figure in sequence with the king and warrior of earlier Nauṭaṅkī plays, we can perhaps give new meaning to this type of hero. The dacoit at large is, in the words of the journalist, an "uncrowned king," much in the same style as the roving knight with his band of loyal supporters. The precepts of his rule are almost identical with those of the ideal monarch—protecting the people, acting with generosity, enforcing justice, upholding honor. But the dacoit hero differs significantly in not being born to such principles or possessing any hereditary right to rule but rather achieving moral leadership after an experience of life-transforming tyranny. Further, the dacoit moves one step beyond the older models of king and warrior, practicing a primitive communism among his gang and attempting to rectify the class-based disparities of economic privilege in society as a whole. The inequities of a hierarchical society and the proper use of wealth thus become dominant themes in this most modern icon of rulership. The legitimacy of the bandit rests on careful selection of his victims and service to the poor. Through redistributing the booty, refusing to retain it for his own use, the dacoit approaches the saintly level of the kingly ascetic and the heroic death-defying stance of the warrior, who both act from self-denial and endure hardship in pursuit of virtue.

The dacoit in captivity, unlike the dacoit at large, reasserts the authority of the state and preaches conformity to the law, in apparent contradiction of his previous posture of rebellion. Despite the heralding of the poor and oppressed in these plays, a conservative impulse controls their design, serving to reinforce the established order of society through a conclusion in which the final *darshan* (sight) of the dacoit is as antisocial villain. Yet even here, a glow of righteousness tinges the icon of the bandit hero, imbuing him with valor in adversity. The dacoit facing death shows fortitude, humility, and submission to truth, qualities that also ennobled the earlier claimants to kingship. Like the renunciant king and warrior, the dacoit distinguishes himself by surrendering the very authority that empowered him to his limited messianic role. His willingness to relinquish power, to denounce even himself and his former way of life, provide a heroic subtext in conflict with the narrator's exhortation to vote for Congress and eliminate *badmāsh* elements. With his kingly predecessors, the rural bandit ultimately steps to one side, vacating the seat of power, and in so doing he reinforces the recurring concept of the moral basis of rulership.

Beginning with the transit from king to yogi, and moving through the trials of the warrior heroes and bandit kings, we have seen that the transformations in the heroes' roles that occur in Nauṭaṅkī dramas illuminate the qualities inherent in the true king, qualities that coexist in uneasy conflict with the exterior manifestations of power. A moral complex—renunciation of wealth, selfless pursuit of truth, and willingness to submit to a higher authority—runs through these narratives. By its universality of application, it extends the meaning of the texts beyond the king to the householder and the ordinary person. The lessons of perseverance, detachment, and charity are equally relevant to all individuals' daily existence, and should they manage to embrace this inner moral code, they too will rule in their own small kingdom.

In the next chapter, we examine the collision between romantic love and loyalty to family, clan, and community. Again the ubiquitous figure of the yogi provides a point of entry. The mendicant shorn of earthly privilege and desire serves as informing emblem not only of the king, the supreme commander of temporal affairs, but also of the lover, the epitome of passion and sensual feeling. The sufferings the lover must endure to be united with the beloved in Nauṭaṅkī romances are analogous to those of Harishchandra searching for truth or of Sultana seeking justice for the poor. The model of renunciation is once more employed, not as a transcendental path to the liberation of the soul from rounds of rebirth, but rather as a moral response to crises that are fundamental to human existence in the everyday world.

CHAPTER SIX

Paradigms of Pure Love

In contemporary Indian culture, obsessive passion seems to run riot: songs, dramas, novels, films, and magazines loudly declare the inexhaustible craving for romance. Western media images may have given a new face to "love"—an English word now heard everywhere in India. Yet the tradition of romance predates European influence and has strong roots in the lore of village society. In North India long before British incursions, performances popularized a number of oral tales, each focusing on a pair of pining lovers. The concept of love in these folk traditions is distinct from the courtly notion of erotic sentiment (*śṛṅgāra rasa*) of Sanskrit verse and the devotional love of religious poetry (*prema-bhakti*). Indigenous and secular, it manifests itself in the dramas of the Nauṭaṅkī theatre beginning in the middle of the nineteenth century and continuing to the present.

The prevalence of romantic tales presents something of a paradox in North India, as it does in other agriculturally dominated societies. Here and in other places, people view marriage as a pragmatic coupling of families, intended to reproduce clan lines, maintain the domestic economy, and safeguard the rearing of children. The separation of the sexes is the norm, secured through the institution of gender-assigned tasks and spatial divisions consonant with them. Marital alliances are settled early in the life cycle and lead quickly to the assumption of adult gender-specific duties. Romantic love stands in opposition to the rules governing appropriate marriage. The union of hearts and bodies by mutual individual choice is rarely approved, and it may be punished by the strictest measures.

Western opinion often concludes that in such societies "love" is an impossibility. In consequence it interprets their love stories as compensatory outlets for repressed emotional and sexual urges, ways of living out imaginatively an experience for which there is scant opportunity. Although plausible to a point, this view assumes dichotomies between thought and action, imagination and behavior, that may jeopardize an understanding of the cultural construction of love in North India. "Real" and "imagined" love are not essential opposed categories in the Indian tradition. As this chapter will soon elaborate, love becomes most real, most true and compelling, when it takes complete hold of the imagination, even subverting the mental faculties and preventing their normal functioning.

Rather than documentation of a sublimated fantasy, what the Nauṭaṅkī dramatic literature may offer is evidence of the complex ways in which society responds to the emotional lives of its members. The tension that arises between a pair of lovers and their families is one that is amply depicted in these plays, indicating a strong push and pull between individual interests and the group loyalties focused on units of caste, clan, and community. The love experience frequently seems to oppose and undermine the hierarchical order, yet in other situations the social body incorporates it into a more harmonious whole. Once more the Nauṭaṅkī play, through its concrete embodiment of character and incident, explores the moral dilemmas around a difficult issue that touches each spectator. In this process, it ultimately affirms the capacity for loving as an indispensable part of being human.

The Paradigm of Pure Love

Romantic love is preeminently a condition of the heart and is widely acknowledged to be an experience that takes the form of visualizing, yearning, and formulating future plans. The North Indian love complex builds on this foundation by accentuating the intensity of love and the emotional upheaval brought about by its occurrence. In the North Indian romances included in the Nauṭaṅkī literature, the best example of the intense love experience is that found in *Lailā majnūn* (fig. 16). *Majnūn* means "crazed person, madman." The narrative tells of the transformation of Qais, under the influence of love for Laila, from a respected

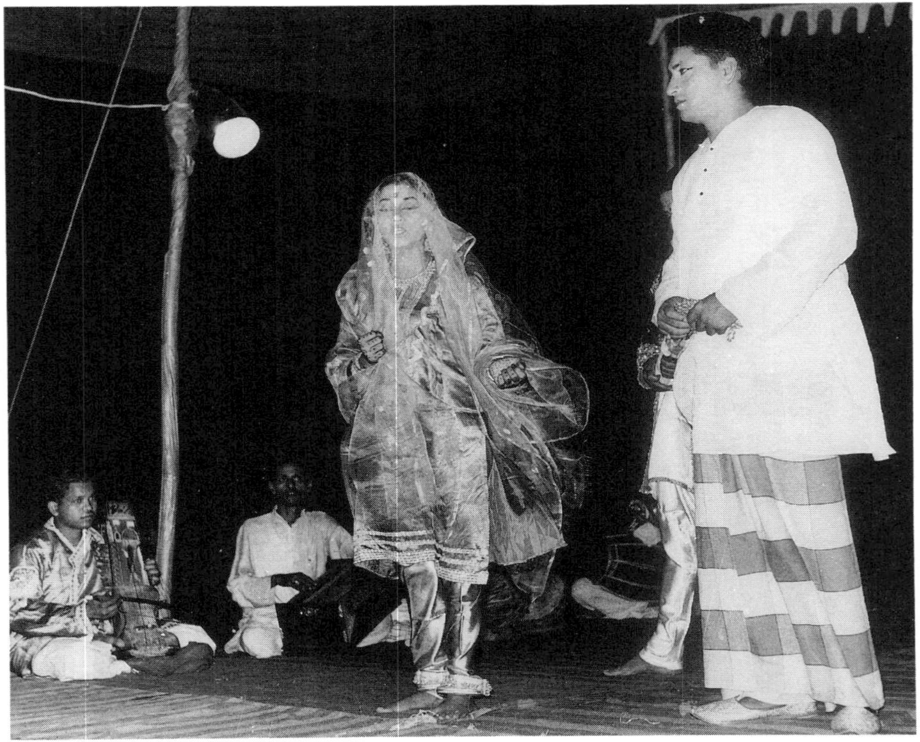

Fig. 16. A meeting of the lovers, from *Lailā majnūn*. By permission of the Sangeet Natak Akademi.

noble to Majnun, a demented beggar who wanders in the forests and wastelands searching endlessly for his beloved. The Nauṭaṅkī version places an almost equal emphasis on the female's experience and allots to Laila an equivalent share of devotion and passion along with an explicit account of the societal obstacles to her pursuit of love.

> Qais is the son of Amir of Damascus, and in Najd rules Sultan Sardar, whose lovely daughter is Laila. Both Laila and Qais attend the same school, and a great love grows between them. Qais loses interest in his studies, spending his hours chanting Laila's name; Laila's family on learning this withdraws her from school.
>
> Distraught at the separation, Qais soon earns the scorn of the townsfolk and is treated as an insane person. Hearing of his son's infatuation, Qais's father takes a proposal of marriage to Laila's father. The families are social equals, but Laila's father is unwilling to marry her to a madman. Qais is invited to the house so that the women may test his mental competence. Qais performs well until he spots Laila's dog, whereupon he loses all semblance of balance and, lavishing hugs and kisses on the animal, releases his crazed passion and scotches his marriage chances.
>
> Qais, now Majnun, takes refuge in the wastes beyond the city walls where he wanders, heartbroken. He encounters Naufil, who offers to help him defeat Laila's father in battle. Unfortunately, they lose the contest. Soon after, Laila is married off to Khushbakht, prince of Delhi. Laila continues to long for Majnun and has nothing to do with her husband. She is ejected from her husband's home and goes to the desert to look for Majnun. In the meantime, Majnun has heard of Laila's marriage and reached Delhi. The two lovers finally meet in the desert.
>
> Their happiness is short-lived. On nearing the city, the pair are spotted and Laila is forcibly taken home by her mother. She is unable to survive the separation this time and pines away to death. When Majnun hears this news, he kills himself in grief. The two lovers are finally united in heaven. The city people bury their bodies next to each other and sing high praises of their immortal love.[1]

This tragic romance with its ending of dual death originated in the Arabian peninsula in the eighth century and has sustained popularity through the centuries in folk and courtly renderings all over the Islamic world.[2] Within the Nauṭaṅkī repertoire, it functions as the prototype of a body of similar romances, its characters being cited frequently within other texts by both aspirants to and opponents of love. Several aspects of the text's treatment of love deserve special note, insofar as they link the tale to others similar to it. First is the spontaneous and unpremeditated nature of Qais and Laila's love. Their feeling for each other arises naturally, when they meet at a young age. The instantaneous origin of true love is often represented in folk romance by such beginnings as an early meeting, the appearance of the loved one in a dream or sight of the painted picture of the beloved, or even the mention of the beloved's beauty and fame. The second characteristic is the complete constancy of the lovers and their devotion unto death. Their love for each other never wavers; they are completely loyal. They spend their entire lives in quest of union, abandoning all other concerns. No obstacle is too great, no misfortune too daunting. Third, the love depicted here is a mutual love. Laila boldly declares her attraction and is as unwilling to be separated from Majnun as he from her. She leaves her forced marriage to go join him in the desert and is the first to die of grief at being parted from him. Fourth and paramount, the tale tells of thwarted and obstructed love. Just as surely as Laila and Majnun's love is perfectly matched and steadfast, it is unattainable. Although the lovers finally spend a brief time together in the desert, society intercedes time and again to separate them. True union comes only after death, their total dedication to each other having removed them, as it were, from this world into another.

All these characteristics lend their love a pure, perfected quality, identified within the tradition by the phrase *pāk ishq* (pure love).[3] An almost unrealizable ideal is supported here: love that is the excessive outer limit of human feeling and attachment. To this romantic ideal the drama counterposes the many obstacles encountered by the lovers as they strive for the fruition of their love. Although some versions mention a preexisting tribal feud between the lovers' families, opposition from Laila's family constitutes the primary impediment in the Nauṭaṅkī account.[4] This opposition is based on the linkage of clan honor to effective control of female sexuality. The family's preoccupation with *izzat* (reputation, honor) necessitates "protecting" Laila, preserving her in a chaste and chastened state until a suitable marriage is contracted. The family's fear of losing *izzat* causes them to withdraw her from school to prevent the lovers from meeting once their love is discovered. Qais is then proposed as a possible marriage suitor and is almost accepted; love may be contained by the institutional forms of society if the lovers are of compatible rank. After Laila's marriage to Khushbakht, however, the chances of the pair's love reaching any socially acceptable outcome are reduced to naught. The natal family's surveillance is replaced by the concern of Laila's affines. They find in her a tarnished unwilling bride and turn her out. When she later meets Majnun, her own family hounds her, wishing to confine her at home, even though her behavior would already have irreparably damaged their reputation. At every turn, her movements are controlled by physical force, but psychological coercion is imposed as well. The play is full of parents' and elders' preachings about female virtue, the importance of family honor, and the social necessity of marriage, all directed to Laila and intended to alter her attachment to Majnun.

The restraints imposed on Laila as a woman in patriarchal society are not present for Majnun as a male. No one attempts to confine him; on the contrary, the text's creators allow him—even force him—to roam far and wide. His unimpeded movement perhaps expresses the unbound freedom of the human spirit in love, although the text also describes him in cliched terms as ensnared, entrapped, and shackled by love's bonds. Nonetheless, as Laila does, Majnun incurs a loss of reputation, although of a different and finally more devastating kind. Whereas Laila is rebuked by her immediate family, Majnun becomes an object ridiculed by society at large. His love and the distraction it brings cause him to slight convention, to behave in inappropriate ways. For this he is taunted and labeled a madman, and he plummets rapidly to the level of an abject beggar. Laila is forced back into the confinement of the family; Majnun is pushed out of society altogether. He is ostracized and exiled to the jungles and wastelands. Through this action, the text asserts that excessive love (which *pāk ishq* is by definition) is also transgressive. It violates the social order, alienating the lover from the ordered balance of human relations. On the one hand, it drives the lover as a social being beyond the pale, making him an outcaste, despised and lonely. On the other, it leads the lover's mind and heart into a territory of untamed feeling, into jungles of overwrought emotion and wastelands of unfulfilled longing.

According to our text then, the experience of love (even, or especially, unfulfilled love) poses a tremendous threat to the social relationships of both parties. In the case of the woman it endangers the standing of her entire family and clan, while for the man it puts at risk reason and human companionship. The only place for romantic love is in an existence contrived beyond society's boundaries—in the barren wilderness, or in heaven. The profundity of society's opposition to the violation compassed by love emerges most forcefully in the tragic endings of many of these narratives. Society exacts its revenge on errant members not only by confining and exiling them, but ultimately by killing them. In most of these stories (and in some versions of *Lailā majnūn*), betrayal figures in this stringent end. The first death occurs when a lover gives up all hope after an antagonistic relative spreads a rumor of the other's death; this leads to a double suicide—each dying for the other, but in falsified circumstances. The treachery motif relieves the lovers of the burden of individual responsibility for suicide and accentuates the malicious and desperate opposition of family and society. In this way, the romantic dramas consistently pit the lovers against family and society in an unequal match, where the superior strength of the many acts against the isolated, separated couple.

From the viewpoint of the larger community, the validity of the family's claims and the apparent necessity of renewing the social order seem to lend moral weight to those who oppose the lovers. Yet the lovers' commitment to each other is not condemned but is commemorated in the Nauṭaṅkī text: the lovers are the heroes, and society is the villain. How does the cause of love gain the moral force necessary to transform Laila and Majnun from antisocial deviants to cultural icons? The predictable answer, in Indo-Islamic scholarship, would be to refer to the mystical allegory of earthly lovers as seekers of the divine. Stories like *Lailā majnūn, Shīrīn farhād,* and *Hīr rāñjhā* come out of the mystical tradition of Sufism, which identifies the lover with the seeker for eternal truth and the beloved with God. In Sufi-inspired literature, the experience of intense love becomes a way of understanding and describing the soul's desire for God. Both love-objects—God the divine beloved and the earthly beloved—are impossible of attainment. Both quests lead the seekers into peril, infamy, even madness and death. The mystical meaning of the romantic text, according to this view, directs the reader to a higher level of truth, which transcends the social ("mundane" or *majāzī*) experience of love to appear as a metaphor for the eternal ("real" or *haqīqī*) love of humans for God.

Such an interpretation no doubt often accompanies the reception of love stories like *Lailā majnūn* in North India today, especially among the educated and orthodox circle of believers. The curious fact, however, is that our Nauṭaṅkī text is noticeably lacking in mystical references. The spiritual allegory is not made manifest; Majnun is never designated as a seeker for God. Majnun simply asks God to help him, that is, to bring him Laila or end his life. During the lovers' separation, there is no mention of the mystical overtones of separation by the characters themselves, the narrator, or a third party. In the absence of an explicit allegory, the tale might still be interpreted mystically by knowing auditors. What seems more obvious, however, is that the earthly romance of the lovers provides sufficient ground for a self-contained narrative at the folk level. An apparatus of translation into Sufistic terms is not necessary to the identity or popularity of the Laila-Majnun tale.

The Lover as Renunciant

Largely shorn of its mystical import in the Nauṭaṅkī theatre, *Lailā majnūn* nevertheless preserves one important motif associated with both the Hindu and Sufi saintly traditions—and that is the characterization of the lover as a yogi or fakir. As in the texts of Gopichand and other renunciant kings, the two terms, signifying the ascetics of the great religious traditions of Hinduism and Islam, are used interchangeably by Nauṭaṅkī poets. By the nineteenth century, the persona of yogi or fakir had become a multivalent referent employed in many narrative contexts. The figure was often conjoined with the icon of the righteous king, as discussed in the previous chapter. The disguise of the renunciant was also used in dramatic situations where deception was the intent, for example, for traveling incognito, infiltrating an enemy's ranks, or entering the women's quarters of a palace. The ascetic ruse played on North Indian society's suspicion of false (and true) ascetics as well as cultural obligations to provide for their maintenance through alms.

Almost universally in late medieval romance, the renunciant role additionally served to convey something of the excessive, selfless nature of romantic love. The lover is invariably compared to a yogi or fakir, and in many instances he takes on the attire of the renunciant either as a temporary expedient or, in a deeper transformation, for life. Even in the popular Indian movies of today, the unshaven gaunt visage of the hero is semiotic shorthand for the yogi or fakir, signifying "rejected or outcaste lover." Interestingly, North Indian romances at one time extended the assignation to love-crazed women as well. The *abhisārikā* of Sanskrit lyric poetry—the woman who ventures abroad seeking union with her lover—was converted into the *jogin*—a female ascetic who makes a journey, enchanting men with her singing and playing musical instruments: an amalgam of Kali-like gruesome physique with the charms of the *apsarā* (heavenly singing girl in classical Hindu mythology). Unlike the *jogī*, the *jogin* appears to have fallen by the wayside with the revision of gender roles in the modern period; other less ambiguous temptresses have usurped her place in cinema and popular culture, if not entirely in folklore.

Returning to the *Lailā majnūn* text, we can see how the representation of the lover as a fakir ennobles his character and highlights the selfless nature of his quest for Laila, building into the text a morality that may have Sufi antecedents yet is not overtly mystical. Like the avowed renunciant, Majnun gives up his attachments to possessions, to his good name, to his kin and community, even to sanity. His search for Laila carries him beyond the gates of civilized society to the edge of the desert, where he lives a hand-to-mouth existence without thought of his own well-being. The religious mendicant is held up as a cultural role model of the egoless search for truth, and Majnun's dedicated resolve and self-abnegation are exemplary traits that qualify him for the life of renunciation. Nonetheless, it would be shortsighted to deny the negative aspects of the fakir figure. Even though the yogi or fakir chooses to renounce the world, an aura of rejection by society envelops him. The beggar, the seeker of love, may be praised for his selfless suffering, but he is also despised, spurned, and taunted for his unconventional appearance and eccentric behavior. The extreme deterioration in Majnun's condition evokes a response of avoidance and disgust, not only in the townsfolk who stone him, but even in the largely sympathetic audience. In this manner the guise of fakir gives palpable shape to the idea of the lover's degradation, a major theme that recurs in many genres of Indo-Islamic literature.

Above all, what renunciation carries here, as in Nauṭaṅkī texts like *Gopīchand,* is a powerful affective component of sadness, despair, pain, and loss. Majnun in the desert is the human spirit in anguish—tormented by failure, by hopelessness, by abandonment. The sufferings of Majnun, like the sufferings of Job or Harishchandra, sustain the narrative on its pathos-driven course. Once more, according to the emotional syntax of folk narrative, degradation leads ultimately to apotheosis. Carried to its dramatic extreme, the pity that Majnun evokes converts to exoneration and veneration. The plot flipflops and suddenly catapults the lovers through the double suicide into the orbit of the immortals.

In short, the slippery ambiguous figure of the yogi or fakir encodes a complex set of messages communicated by the folk theatre (and North Indian society's other cultural forms as well) on the subject of romantic love. Love is uplifting but also demeaning; it is socially unacceptable, yet it purifies the spirit and finally transforms. In his search for the beloved (or more abstractly, for the experience of love itself), the lover is judged and judges himself by the highest moral standards: he must be constant, vigilant, ever willing to suffer. Steeling himself to a stern inner discipline, his goal is nothing less than the perfection of his own being as much as union with another. Yet his diligence brings him into open conflict with society, and he suffers rejection on all sides.

Running through this tremendous idealism and moral fervor surrounding love is a dark commingling of compulsion and tragedy. Although the life of the lover may be the loftiest objective of human effort, the end of the lover's existence can only be death. The lover is compelled to love, driven by a destiny beyond conscious control. Commitment to the path of love allows no alternative, no turning back. Despite the travails of the most dedicated lover, separation remains as the unwavering condition of being in the world. Union with the beloved is a state one never experiences during an earthly life. Love is in no terms an impossibility: rather it is the distinguishing mark of the human condition. It rages through human consciousness, demanding the ultimate in commitment, the best that is within us. Yet as long as we exist as human beings, we are trapped in a state of imperfection, and we fail.

The exacting requirements of love, the lover's difficult passage through sufferings imposed from within and without, and the dim possibility of success—all are implied in the notion of love as renunciation and the lover as renunciant. That these themes are not limited to stories of Islamic origin is confirmed by other romantic tales in the Nauṭaṅkī corpus. The tale of Sorath and Bija, found in *Sāṅg soraṭh,* one of the oldest texts in the Svāṅg collections, has a provenance extending from Rajasthan through Gujarat and Saurashtra. It lacks Islamic characters and references, yet undertones of unhappiness, loss, and tragedy mark the romantic chain of events.

> Sorath, born under an unlucky sign, is abandoned by her father and brought up by a low-caste potter. Because of her beauty she is desired by several men, but she never finds a secure home. In her youth she passes from hand to hand, being sold to a wandering trader (*bañjārā*), kidnapped by one king, and lusted after by another. Finally her true lover, Bija, embarks on a quest to rescue her, assuming the attire of a yogi seeking alms (*bhikṣhā*). The two profess their mutual love and eventually escape from captivity together. On returning to his homeland, Bija is asked to surrender his beloved to his uncle the king and forced into exile. When he returns to the palace as a peacock, the king recognizes and shoots Bija. Seeing the only man whom she loved dead, Sorath immolates herself to become a *satī.*[5]

This story offers a moving account of female misery. The themes of misfortune, abandonment, and abuse all converge on the heroine, Sorath, who seems to represent what happens to a woman when she loses the protection of her male kin. Many men covet and desire her, but no one stands up for her. Nevertheless, through her own inner truth, her *sat,* she survives the circumstances into which she is thrown and cultivates her personal sense of virtue. The trials she endures in the early part of the story prepare her, as it were, purifying her for a genuine experience of love that redeems and literally frees her from her chains.

As in *Lailā majnūn,* society's opposition to the pursuit of romantic love is represented by the obstacle of other males who claim possession of the heroine and confine her. The true lover, Bija, is distinguished from his rivals by his moral superiority: his courage, perseverance, and humility contrast with their rough arrogance. In appearing as a renunciant, Bija outwardly expresses the transfiguration that love may induce; he has taken on the life of self-denial, whereas the other suitors remain traders and kings, masters only of wealth and power. In the end the tyranny of the king does manage to snuff out the pair, yet their joint departure for another realm encodes the immortal nature of love. Tragedy is again a vehicle for lauding the most difficult and worthy of human aims.

A similar structure manifests itself in the great romance of the Punjab, *Hīr rāñjhā,* a widely known folktale also performed as a Nauṭaṅkī play.[6] The earliest extant version was composed by Damodar at the time of Akbar, and in that account as well as the Nauṭaṅkī telling the lovers live together happily at the end although their circumstances differ. According to Damodar, Hir and Ranjha journey as fakirs to Mecca where they attend at the grave of the Prophet, whereas in the Nauṭaṅkī they live peaceably with Ranjha's family.[7] However, in the most literarily respected version, that of Waris Shah, as well as in most variants, the tale concludes tragically.[8] Hir's uncle treacherously poisons her and Ranjha dies of grief, in the classic double-death pattern. Regardless of the variation in endings, all versions recount the depth of hostility between Hir's family and the lovers, which as we might now expect includes an attempt to marry Hir to another man. In all variants, the character of the lover Ranjha acquires vigor and persuasive power through his yogic leanings. We briefly summarize the Nauṭaṅkī plot because it differs from the well known Waris Shah text on a number of points.

> Hir and Ranjha are the offspring of noble families from Jhang Shiyala and Takht Hazara respectively. Appearing one night in each other's dreams, they fall deeply in love. Hir's distraught condition comes to the attention of her family members, who respond with lecturing and

abuse. Her brother, Patmal, threatens to kill her if she shames the family. A folk healer (*bābā*) is sent to cure Hir, but instead she persuades the *bābā* to deliver her message to Ranjha.

Learning of Hir's whereabouts, Ranjha prepares to leave to find her. After many warnings and outpourings from his family and friends, he manages to depart. Dressed as a mendicant *jogī* he crosses various hurdles and eventually reaches Hir's garden, where he encamps until Hir comes to him. The lovers decide that Ranjha should go to work for Hir's brother, Patmal, as a cowherd, so that they may continue meeting regularly. This plan succeeds, and every day when Ranjha takes the cows to the fields to graze, Hir goes to meet him.

One day the lovers are discovered. Patmal tries to kill Ranjha by sending him into a beast-infested jungle. Fearing for Ranjha's life, Hir follows him in the guise of a *jogin.* With the protection of his seventy saints, Ranjha overcomes the vicious animals, and the two lovers meet once again. Patmal now sends Karnu Shah to capture Hir, promising her to him in marriage. Karnu and his men are easily defeated by Ranjha. The lovers, united at last, set off for Ranjha's home, where they find welcome in his family, get married, and live happily ever after.

Except for its conclusion, the Nauṭaṅkī drama works within the same parameters of romantic love as *Lailā majnūn* and other texts, including the Waris Shah poem. If the love of Hir and Ranjha is excessive and overweening, it is also spontaneous and natural: the scenes of the lovers disporting in the fields with the grazing cattle strike pastoral tones that heighten the contrast with the oppressive dictates of clan and kin. The mutuality of feeling from love's inception is another important element, a pattern that appears in Indo-Islamic romances yet is absent from lyric genres such as the *ghazal,* where love is one-sided and the beloved assumes a haughty and cruel posture. Both fall simultaneously in love in a dream, but in the Nauṭaṅkī it is Hir who first manifests the familiar symptoms of love's intensity, risks her position in the family, and makes the initial contact through a messenger. Disguised as a *jogī,* Ranjha journeys to her garden to meet her, and she in turn follows him to the forest in the role of a *jogin* when he is threatened by Patmal. She boldly escapes from home every day to meet her lover in the fields and repeatedly demonstrates her cleverness in plotting various stratagems to meet Ranjha. In the Waris Shah account, the opening events are somewhat different. Ranjha, the unfortunate youngest brother, is cheated out of his patrimony and leaves home to seek his fortune. He meets Hir at the river Chenab, and they fall in love at first sight. Hir demonstrates her boldness by taking Ranjha home and getting him a job as the family cowherd.

The strength of Hir's character is matched by superlative traits present in the hero Ranjha. In the Nauṭaṅkī version, special powers accrue to Ranjha as a result of his protection by seventy saints (*sattar pīr*). Thanks to divine guidance he is capable of performing a series of magical feats in his quest for his beloved.[9] To pass the *bābā*'s identity test he produces milk from a virgin cow. On his way to Hir's garden he crosses over a river seated in the lotus position without a boat. He later kills lions and beasts in the jungle and defeats Karnu Shah's army singlehanded. In all these instances, Ranjha's contact with the supernatural assists him in proving his valor, loyalty, and merit as the true lover of Hir. It also endows his personage with a mysterious attractiveness. Ranjha's powers, whatever their source, are superior to those of ordinary men, and his second identity as *jogī* lends him charismatic appeal, if not precisely moral authority.[10]

The fortitude of asceticism, the magic protection of the saints, the fiery passion of Hir—all are needed in the series of confrontations between the lovers and society. The suspense in the narrative is largely constructed of recurring episodes of family opposition that threaten the couple's relationship. In the Nauṭaṅkī, the chief upholder of family honor and instigator of the trials that besiege the lovers is Hir's brother, Patmal. He insists that his sister's actions bring ill repute (*badnāmī*) to himself and his family, and he assaults her with vile terms of abuse. Predictably he strives to arrange a marriage for Hir, handing over control of her movements to a husband, but the plan fails because Karnu lacks the superiority of arms (and character) to defeat Ranjha. Waris Shah provides a much more complicated series of incidents. The lover's chief opponent is Kaido, Hir's uncle; Hir's marriage, previously arranged with Saida, takes place but does not achieve its purpose of ending the lovers' involvement. Following the marriage, Ranjha visits Hir's town as a yogi, and eventually the lovers elope. The lovers are captured, Ranjha is exiled and Hir returned to her husband's clan. However, Ranjha's curses set the town on fire; fearing supernatural punishment the chief of the clan orders that the marriage of Hir and Saida be annulled. Hir and Ranjha prepare to marry at last. Even as Ranjha approaches Hir's home with his wedding party, Hir's brother and uncle poison her and she dies. Waris Shah's elaboration of plots and counterplots reiterates the structural opposition between the pair and society, highlighting the tenacious endurance of love against the most severe odds. The poet also brings out the dynamism in rural society, in that shifting alliances of elders and friends alternately support and castigate the lovers, and the possibility for rapprochement exists until the end. Nonetheless, the stress imposed on the social fabric is beyond containment. The events tend toward rupture again and again.

Love across Boundaries of Caste and Class

The romances discussed so far feature a pair of lovers who are by birth social equals. In two of the tales, the hero after falling in love declines in rank, becoming unfit as a marriage partner for the heroine: Majnun goes mad and becomes a destitute beggar, Ranjha works as a cowherd and servant to Hir's family. Other Nauṭaṅkīs accentuate the transgressive nature of romantic love and bring out the theme of the lover's self-surrender by situating the lovers in different classes or castes. In these stories, the beloved is ordinarily a princess or daughter of nobility, whereas the lover may be a merchant, an artisan, or other social inferior. It should be mentioned that hypergamy is the normative pattern for marriage in North India, that is, alliance of a groom with a bride whose family is of somewhat lower rank. The transgression inherent in the romantic liaison between the high-born female and lower-born male has two possible outcomes in the Nauṭaṅkī plays. It may provoke an act of treachery leading to the deaths of both lovers—the tragic pattern of earlier narratives—or it may lead to an execution threat and a redemptive counterstrike by the beloved, followed by marriage—a melodrama with a happy ending.

In *Shīrīn farhād,* an example of the former type, the stonecutter Farhad falls in love with queen Shirin while engaged in building a canal for her. Shirin's paramour, the king Khusro, hoping to get rid of his rival, assigns Farhad the task of digging a tunnel through an impenetrable mountain. Farhad recites Shirin's name continuously to invigorate himself, passes the difficult test, and wins her heart. Khusro then plants an old crone who falsely bewails Shirin's demise, causing Farhad to commit suicide; Shirin follows him soon after in death. The lovers Shirin and Farhad, often quoted in the same breath as the example of Laila and Majnun, embody the same brand of intemperate passion that knows no social boundaries. The character of Shirin is particularly impetuous in the Nauṭaṅkī version; she rides forth to find Khusro when they are courting and later takes a bold stand, pursuing Farhad despite the difference in rank between them. She also manifests a certain degree of haughty disdain: at first she rebuffs Farhad and demands that he earn her love. The act of carving through an obdurate mass of stone remains as a striking metaphor for the pursuit of romantic love in North Indian society—the tunneling underground matching the surreptitious designs that lovers must implement to break through society's massive resistance.[11]

Another early addition to the Nauṭaṅkī repertoire, and an example of the melodrama plot, is *Saudāgar vo syāhposh*. This is the tale of a merchant's son, Gabru, who attempts to win the hand of Jamal, the daughter of a minister of state, after being enchanted by hearing her read from the Koran. While visiting Jamal, Gabru is apprehended one night by the king, who is touring the city disguised as a police constable to ensure its safety. Gabru is sentenced to hang; at the scene of the gallows, he waits anxiously for a final vision of his beloved. Jamal at the last moment appears dressed as a man all in black (*syāhposh*), riding a horse, wielding a dagger and sword. She threatens to commit suicide by stabbing herself or drinking a cup of poison. The king is persuaded of the true love of the couple and marries them on the spot.[12]

A similar tale of perilous love between a highly placed valorous woman and a commoner is *Lākhā bañjārā,* which relates the love between a princess and Lakha, the son of a trader.[13] Reminiscent of *Syāhposh* in many details, it culminates in Lakha's being arrested by a policeman while returning from the princess one night, his death sentence by the king, and the appearance of the princess at the gallows to plead with her father for her lover's release. In this story, however, the king does not relent. Lakha is killed, and the lovers are united only after Guru Gorakhnath arrives and resuscitates the dead Lakha. The final events of these two tales are remarkably close to those of *Nauṭaṅkī shāhzādī.* After the discovery of the affair between the princess Nauṭaṅkī and Phul Singh, Phul Singh is sentenced to hang. As he awaits his execution, Nauṭaṅkī suddenly arrives at the gallows, dressed as a man and armed with sword and dagger. She pulls out a cup of poison and prepares to commit suicide, vowing to die as Shirin died for Farhad and Laila for Majnun. As the executioners advance to pull the cord, she rushes with her dagger and drives them off. She then turns her sword on her father, demanding he pardon her lover immediately. The king consents to the marriage and the two are wed at once.

Although details differ, these stories all involve a romantic quest fraught with danger. The danger is expressed not only in the lover's travails in reaching the princess and obtaining her consent to love, but in the life-threatening sentence meted out for the violation of an upper-class woman's honor. The social distance between the lovers increases the risk, particularly for the male. His transgression offends the law of the land and must be punished with execution by the king, while in earlier narratives the opposition was primarily from family and clan and never involved a criminal charge. The high-ranking female, in contrast, ignores family censure and has the liberty to behave in even imperious ways. In each case, the princess becomes her lover's rescuer. She braves public opinion, daring to leave the seclusion of her palace and appear in public; she challenges the chief representative of society's moral order, the king or her father (frequently one and the same), pleading for permission to marry and even threatening violence against him. To carry out her brave resolve, she may adopt the avenging persona of the *vīrāṅganā,* the woman transformed into a warrior figure outfitted with weapons and riding a horse.[14]

On the one hand, we may interpret these tales as lauding the exalted love that dares to overstep lines of caste and community. Romantic love here moves beyond the limits prescribed by the social hierarchies. It reverses the dominance of the upper castes over the lower and of the male over the female, much as tales like *Lailā majnūn* and *Hīr rāñjhā* questioned the authority of elders over the young. The legitimacy of romantic love, as these tales' heroes and heroines continuously recite, resides not in its legal sanction or propriety but in its spontaneity, its irrepressibility, its sheer persistence in the face of opposition. The stories with happy endings seem further to suggest that an affair of the heart having illicit beginnings may transform itself into the approved state of marriage, even of intercaste marriage, once the lovers convince the guardians of the bride of their overwhelming commitment to each other (which they usually demonstrate by their willingness to sacrifice themselves and die). These dramas thus illustrate that within the social domain some space remains for deep feeling. They play on the possibilities within that space, keeping alive the attachment to the ideal of romance while mildly debunking the rigidities of caste and class.

On the other hand, the consistent assignment of the female to the dominating position perhaps proceeds from a feudal concept of hierarchy and a notion of courtly love consonant with patriarchal values. The superior status of the beloved, although bestowing on her undoubted power and privilege vis-à-vis society, gives her the potential to oppress her lover. The Nauṭaṅkī dramas do not particularly stress this configuration; nevertheless, the status differential at least hints at the haughty beloved found in court-based genres of Indo-Persian literature. The high position of the beloved in that tradition provides a means of representing the degradation and social opprobrium that the true lover gladly undergoes. His suffering is testimony to his constancy and moral fitness for the supreme trial of love. We are reminded of the deplorable condition of Majnun, the important difference being that society's ridicule and his own self-abandonment lead to Majnun's becoming an outcaste, whereas in the Urdu *ghazal* for example, it is the beloved herself who is usually responsible for the sufferings of the lover, inflicting pain out of cruelty.

In our Nauṭaṅkīs, the princess Shirin comes the closest to this attitude, although eventually she is won over by Farhad's valor and comes to love him equally. The other princesses respond more favorably to their lovers from the start. Even when they assume the aggressive *vīrāṅganā* guise, their motivation is to protect a suitor's life; they turn their attacks against society and its authorities, not against the lover. Nonetheless, the high status accorded to these heroines erases the obstacles they face as women in patriarchal society, especially in comparison with tales such as *Lailā majnūn* and *Hīr rāñjhā*. The social reality of being female vanishes from the text, yielding to an artificially elevated ideal of womanhood that aggrandizes the male's self-sacrifice and ignores the female's experience. Furthermore, the high-born beloved motif reinforces the association of superior beauty, power, and merit with high caste or class, providing support for the logic of hierarchical organization, even though the narrative ending of intercaste marriage overrides that hierarchy.

The prototypical love affair between a highly placed female and a beseeching subordinate male is generally thought of as an Islamic legacy, just as the prevalence of unrequited love and the tragic ending are traced to Muslim sensibility and considered anathema to the Hindu mind. Within the body of romantic tales found in the Nauṭaṅkī literature, however, the tidiness of these distinctions breaks down. Some classic romances like *Lailā majnūn* or *Shīrīn farhād* that end in both lovers' deaths clearly traveled from the Islamic Middle East to Indo-Pakistan. Others equally tragic (*Hīr rāñjhā, Soraṭh bījā*) have roots in the subcontinent and are thought of as the cultural property of a cross-section of communities. Similarly, the high-status beloved is not limited to one particular religious tradition. It is commonly linked to the Sufi mystical allegory, wherein the earthly beloved (*mahbūb*) is portrayed as lofty and inaccessible because such are the attributes of God, whom the beloved symbolizes. Yet the motif occurs in other contexts where a Sufistic interpretation would be inappropriate.

A good example is found in the *Ālhā* cycle—a story corpus indigenous to the middle Hindu castes of North India. Incidentally, this well-known non-Islamic narrative ends in tragedy, insofar as most of the heroes are killed in a great battle. Within this larger frame a number of smaller battles take place, and almost all revolve around the marriage-capture of a bride whose family is more highly placed than the Banaphar clan of Rajputs who are the suitors. The Banaphar heroes succeed in each of these encounters but only after enduring abuse and insults and resorting to physical combat. In the *Ālhā* legend the high status of the beloved, while calling up the code of chivalry and courtly love, primarily provides a pretext for the Rajput warrior to prove his mettle. Love backed by force triumphs and leads to marriage, reversing the claims of caste distinction.

Intercaste love is a common theme in more recent Nauṭaṅkī stories as well. No particular rule governs the assignment of lower status to the male or female in these stories. Indeed, low status often seems to be associated with rejection by or loss of a parental figure, a plight that affects children of both sexes. In many of these "modern" tales, the hero's or heroine's misfortune leads to a situation of mistaken identity. A low-caste person volunteers to raise the abandoned child, bestowing his or her caste identity upon it. The leading characters, having become adults, subsequently fall in love across caste lines, but the conclusion typically involves a discovery of the original high caste of the abandoned child, and the finale of marriage thus brings together individuals who in fact socially match each other.

The drama *Mālī kā beṭā* (The gardener's son) exemplifies these themes and also incorporates a number of aspects of both the Laila-Majnun story and the melodrama plot.

> The prince Firoz is born to his royal parents after years of childlessness. The dying king wills his kingdom to his son, placing his minister Afzal on the throne to rule until Firoz attains the age of majority. Afzal, fearing loss of his power, has the prince sent to the forest for execution. There he is rescued by a gardener, who takes the boy home and brings him up as his son.
>
> Soon after, Afzal's daughter Shamsha is born. Independent and indifferent to the idea of marriage, she falls in love with Firoz when he delivers her flowers on her sixteenth birthday. The lovers vow to love each other until death and be remembered like Laila and Majnun. They suffer various persecutions from Tagril, Shamsha's suitor, and Afzal.

> When Firoz goes to look for water for the tormented Shamsha, he is stoned by the townspeople. He then proposes to kill himself to give her the blood of his heart (*k͟hūn-e-jigar*) to drink. Finally Shamsha resolves to die rather than marry Tagril, on condition that she be buried next to Firoz. Firoz's last wish is that he meet his father. The gardener appears, reveals the truth about Firoz's birth, and explains Afzal's role in the deceptive execution plot. The nobles turn against Afzal, place Firoz on the throne, and the lovers are married.[15]

The previous pattern of romance between a high-born female and low-born male, ending in a suspenseful execution scene, becomes even more melodramatic here. The narrowly avoided execution is replicated at the beginning of the story, following a sequence in which the boy heir is first abandoned by his dying father and then betrayed by the power-hungry minister. Within this outline, the pathos of the drama is heightened by numerous references to the Laila-Majnun story: the lovers' vows to be remembered like the immortal pair, the pelting of Firoz by the townspeople, his willingness to sacrifice himself for her well-being, and the couple's resolve to die together and be buried next to each other. The theme of passion in defiance of class differences operates as the foundation, the chief departure from earlier tales being that in the end the status of the lovers turns out to be equal. The lovers' compatibility of rank and the revelation of the minister's treachery, rather than the sheer depth of the lovers' feeling, reverse public opinion and pave the way for their union.

The abandoned daughter, counterpart to the hapless boy Firoz, is the focus of sympathy in *Andhī dulhin* (The blind bride).[16] Again a much desired child, Pyari, is finally born to a royal couple, but the queen dies soon after, and the grieving daughter weeps herself into blindness. The king is faced with the impossible task of marrying a disabled daughter and abandons her in the forest. Instead of being raised by a low-caste family, the girl in this story takes to begging. The Nauṭaṅkī proper begins when a certain prince, Jaipal, is forcibly married to Pyari as punishment for disrespecting his father. Through a series of difficult adventures, the couple demonstrate their virtue and constant devotion to each other and are eventually rewarded with the return of Jaipal's father's kingdom and their real identities. Here love prospers despite the unequal stature of the partners and, as in *Mālī kā beṭā,* the apparently disadvantaged Pyari turns out not only to be worthy but to have high rank. A strong ideal of self-sacrifice emanates from this love story, which evokes a sufficient measure of pity through the sad circumstances accompanying the child's "handicap."

The fixation on childhood abandonment in these two dramas (and others like them) points to a questioning of social structures and the stability they are supposed to provide for the young. The stories seem to indicate that the social umbrella made up of family, clan, and caste alliances is not always effective in protecting children. The loss of a parent is a threat not only to the physical and psychological health of the boy or girl, but also to the child's social identity; caste affiliation as well as family connections are easily obliterated by the removal of the guardian figure. Together with this sense of insecurity, the stories show the continuing romantic attraction exercised across caste lines. They repeatedly invoke true love as greater than caste, greater than family. In dramas with the mistaken identity motif, however, love leads to a marriage that conforms to caste rules, fulfilling a conservative desire to reproduce the status quo. These stories confirm, too, the larger rationale that credits moral superiority to high birth: the abandoned children manifest the goodness inherent in their superior birth-status, even when that status is unknown to them. A powerful romantic ideal challenging the social order thus engages with a narrative structure that removes the discomfort of that very challenge and eases it into harmonious marriage within conventional bounds.

Relations between Communities: Hindu and Muslim

We consider last three dramas not directly concerned with romantic love that may shed further light on the issues of birth, loyalty, community identity, and intercommunal relations. In this case, we speak not of differences between castes within the Hindu hierarchy or of classes within Muslim society but of the larger gulf that separates Hindus from Muslims. One of these Nauṭaṅkī plays depicts the enmity between the two great communities as implacable whereas the other two see friendship and trust to be possible, and the two communities aid each other even while respecting the other's separate identity.

The Sāṅgīt of *Dharmvīr haqīqat rāy* (Haqiqat Ray, defender of the [Hindu] faith) reads almost like a document written to foment communal hatred.[17] The story focuses on a young Hindu Punjabi boy who chooses martyrdom over conversion to Islam. After mastering Sanskrit, the child enrolls in an Islamic school with the intention of learning the

Persian language. (In the eighteenth and nineteenth centuries, Persian was the official language of the court and government affairs; knowledge of Persian was a passport to employment.) He quickly becomes the victim of jibes from the Muslim schoolboys. During a religious debate with them, he compares the gods of Hinduism to the god of Islam; for this blasphemy he is brought before a judge and given an ultimatum: convert or die. Ignoring the advice of family, he chooses death and glorifies the fame of the Hindu religion (*dharm*). The drama paints Muslims as intolerant, unjust, and merciless in their demand for the child's death, whereas Haqiqat Ray and his family come across as entirely innocent victims. Perhaps the story originated in a period when Muslims held political control of the Punjab and the difficulties of economic survival for the upper Hindu castes produced religious intolerance and fear.

Against this partial view of communal tensions, two twentieth-century Sāṅgīts deliberately espouse the cause of Hindu-Muslim unity. Both dramas take the viewpoint of the majority Hindu community and describe events that befall their Hindu characters. Muslim characters play significant roles and are exemplars of their communities, as if the dramas intend to dissuade Hindus from prejudice against Muslims. Curiously, both stories commence with circumstances reminiscent of *Mālī kā beṭā* and *Andhī dulhin*. A child is abandoned by its parents and raised in a household belonging to the other community, but in these cases the child's religious affiliation is preserved. In *Shrīmatī mañjarī* (The valiant Manjari), the Muslim boy Jalal and the Hindu girl Manjari grow up as brother and sister, coming to each other's assistance when trouble strikes.

> During an epidemic of the plague a poor Muslim and his wife die, leaving their son, Jalal, an orphan. Seeing the boy starving and ignored by his own community, a Brahmin named Jugal Kishor adopts him. Jugal's wife has also died in the plague, and he has a daughter named Manjari of the same age as Jalal. Jalal is enrolled in an Islamic school and raised as a Muslim.
>
> Some years later Jugal falls ill and is beset by his creditors. Manjari offers to stand as surety for a loan and joins the household of the moneylender Janaki as a maidservant, while Jalal goes out to beg for money to repay the debt. Manjari successfully defends her mistress against a raid by dacoits, earning the title "Shrimati" for her courage. Jalal meets Kamruddin, a merchant, who is impressed by his story of the Brahmin who brought him up, and he gives Jalal the money needed to repay Janaki.
>
> Janaki makes advances to Manjari but is thwarted when Jalal arrives

> to hand over the money. Janaki implicates Jalal in an incident in which Jugal is attacked by Janaki's servant and left for dead. When Jalal is sent to jail, Manjari seeks protection from Jalal's friends, Kamruddin and his wife. At Jalal's trial, Jugal shows up in court alive, and Jalal is proven innocent.
>
> Janaki renews his pursuit of Manjari. This time Jalal arrives just in time to save Manjari's honor, and in his rage he stabs Janaki and kills him. Manjari is suitably married off. Jalal's name becomes immortal after his death (presumably he is executed for the murder of Janaki). The play ends saying, "Not all Muslims are alike. What Hindu would have done what Jalal did?"[18]

The kind-hearted Brahmin functions in this story much as the gardener, the potter, or washerman do in other tales that return an abandoned child from the brink of death. The financial difficulties that beset Jugal Kishor accent the altruism of his action; he is an impoverished individual himself, yet he takes on the rearing of another community's child—and that too without a wife. Jalal repays the debt he owes his foster father for his upbringing by seeking funds to pay off Janaki, by going to jail on a false charge, and by risking his life for the sake of Manjari's honor. In these various ways he proves himself a perfect son and brother, demonstrating that Muslims can be grateful, loyal, and courageous. The relationship between Manjari and Kamruddin reinforces the message of mutual assistance across community lines. When she is threatened by a greedy and lustful Hindu merchant, she seeks shelter with her brother's Muslim friends who take her into their home just as her father took in Jalal. This encounter gives a mirrorlike symmetry to the play's events, the Hindu's rescue of a dying Muslim boy at the beginning of the story answered by the Muslims' harboring of a threatened Hindu girl later on.

This drama is silent on the issue of religious differences between the two communities, never probing into the clash of beliefs that led the youth Haqiqat Ray into his precarious position. Simplistic in its analysis of communal tensions, the drama nevertheless proposes a morality that moves beyond religious creeds and dogmas. This morality may be illuminated through the metaphor of moneylending: an act of good performed for another human being creates a moral debt that the other must repay with interest. Communal relations can be substantially improved—the drama seems to assert—when good acts are viewed as emanating not just from the individual but from the community as a whole and hence deserving of return by the other community as a whole. Thus

Kamruddin "repays" the initial kindness of Jugal to Jalal by offering the money and protecting Manjari, although he "owed" the Hindu community nothing on the basis of his own experience. The story itself ends with a moral surplus on Jalal's side—he has done so much good for Jugal and Manjari that surely the Hindus in the audience will extend themselves to act generously toward Muslims in future transactions.

It is significant that the moral guidance provided by this metaphor preserves the integrity and social boundaries of the two communities. Hindus remain Hindus and Muslims Muslims, even when reared in shared households. There is no hint of romance or sexual commerce across community lines, and indeed Jalal remains celibate—almost a renunciant figure—dying before he assumes any sexual identity. Manjari and Jalal have the relationship of brother and sister instead of the romantic tie between hero and heroine. Their attachment to each other is permeated by a level of devotion, loyalty, and affection comparable to the romantic bond between lovers, but their relationship lacks sexual overtones, holds no potential for marriage, and cannot jeopardize the purity of blood lines in either community.

Another popular play with origins in the Bombay cinema, *Dhūl kā phūl* (Flower in the dust), likewise explores the theme of a child's abandonment and adoption. In this case it is a Hindu boy, the illegitimate offspring of a middle-class couple who meet in college, who is raised by a Muslim foster father and sheltered against the harsh rebuffs of the world until his natural parents accept him back into their hearts.

> Mahesh, the top student in his M.A. class, meets Meena, foremost among the girl students, when their bicycles collide. They fall in love and continue to meet after exams are over. When Mahesh is called home by his father, Meena reveals that she is pregnant. Mahesh promises to speak to his father about their marriage, but once home he is unable to muster his courage and instead agrees to marry another woman, Malti. Meena is forced from her home and gives birth to a son.
>
> Meena goes to Mahesh, who is now a magistrate, asking him to help care for the child. He refuses. Losing hope, she leaves the baby boy in the forest. A Muslim named Abdul discovers the child and tries to find a home for him, but since his religion is unknown, no one is willing to raise him. Abdul himself decides to adopt the child and names him Roshan. He is excommunicated for this act.
>
> At school, Roshan is constantly harassed and taunted for being illegitimate. He begins avoiding school and keeps company with hood-

> lums. One day a thief drops a bag of money in front of him and the police arrest him. Abdul enlists the services of the barrister who is now married to Meena, and she realizes the boy is her son. The case is tried with Mahesh acting as magistrate. In court Meena declares that Mahesh is the child's father and the one guilty for his wicked ways. Mahesh repents and expresses willingness to take Roshan home. He asks that Roshan be returned to Meena and himself. After much discussion about who deserves to keep the boy, Abdul hands Roshan over to his mother and leaves for a pilgrimage to Mecca. The play ends with an exhortation: the two communities should live together harmoniously, as the Muslim did with the Hindu child, for the good of the nation.[19]

This story brings our discussion of romantic love and community loyalty full circle, focusing as it does on the outcome of a love affair between students, a Laila-Majnun tale in modern dress. Times have certainly changed. The powerful attraction between the young people is no longer the *pāk ishq* of olden times; it is mutual and ardent, no doubt, but hardly enduring and certainly not frustrated or unfulfilled. For the first time in the narrative universe examined in this chapter, the corporeality of love intrudes in an unmistakable and rather unwelcome way, leaving behind its debris—the illegitimate child—once the love affair is over. Both Mahesh and Meena attempt to distance themselves from this threat to their social status and, abandoning the boy, go on to successful positions in society. He marries and becomes a magistrate, while she gets a job as secretary to another barrister and later becomes his wife.

The moral focus thus shifts rapidly away from the romantic ideal to the themes of parental responsibility and communal cooperation. Abdul Chacha (uncle), another wholly selfless and guileless Muslim like Jalal, manifests the caring and kindheartedness that alone can save Roshan. His generosity contrasts with the narrow-mindedness of other Muslims, who are unwilling to bring up a child from a different community and who excommunicate Abdul for doing so. Although Abdul gives the child a Muslim name, he does not necessarily raise him as a Muslim; the text repeatedly emphasizes that no one knows the religion into which the child was born. Abdul is intent on providing the boy with a good education and making him a respectable member of society. He is enrolled in the same school as Ramesh, the son of Mahesh and Malti.

In spite of the attention and love he receives from Abdul, Roshan begins to manifest the signs of his troubled background. Shamed for his birth rather than his character, he is driven into the company of rebels and deviants, and his own behavior gradually deteriorates. It is as though the moral lapses of his parents, and his father in particular, are being meted out on him for repayment. His suffering, culminating in the false arrest, seems to proceed not from parental neglect—for Abdul is there—so much as from a kind of curse, a punishment for the irresponsibility of Mahesh and Meena who live comfortably denying their past. Finally the courtroom trial of Roshan forces Mahesh and Meena to examine themselves and begin to atone for the errors of their youth. The sentimental reunion of lost child and guilty parents possesses a moral logic of its own, although Abdul's claim as foster parent seems to wither overnight, and he gets only scant thanks from Meena and Mahesh.

Enclosing both Hindus and Muslims within the impermanent structure of the family of adoption, *Shrīmatī mañjarī* and *Dhūl kā phūl* create a pattern for caring intercommunal relationships. In these plays, the paradigm of romantic love shifts to a paradigm of parental and sibling love, defusing the potential for volatile sexual contact between the two communities. The constellation of moral traits associated with the familial caregiver is in many ways the same as the one that defines the true lover: attachment in the face of society's hostility, defiance of conventional norms, extreme loyalty, self-sacrifice to the point of death. The path to communal harmony offers many of the same hazards as the path to union with the beloved and consequently requires the fortitude and self-sacrifice that characterize the lover as well. Despite these challenges, the dramas point to the clear possibility of cooperation and loving interaction. While not going so far as to extend the concept of romantic love to alliances between Hindus and Muslims, the alternative construct of mutual support at the family level brings the communities into an intimate bond, displacing fears and allowing individuals to explore interaction beyond the rigid perception of essential differences in character.

These dramas, like those on intercaste romantic love, echo the perhaps universal intuition that human beings—whatever their differences—share the capacity for deep feeling. Not all individuals are equally capable of experiencing supreme joy and sorrow, not all are qualified for the test of love. But the ability to feel, to love, and to care is not determined at the outset by affiliation with a particular clan, caste, class, or religion. Loving falls within the range of being human. It is as one human to another that the queen and the stonemason love each other, as one human to another that the Hindu parent fosters the Muslim child. Learning to love is an achievement, a result of striving and endeavor, not a birthright, and therefore it occurs in no greater measure in one caste or creed than another.

The stories analyzed in this chapter definitively prove the case for love, be it the tragic love of the immortal couples, the cross-caste romance of adventuring heroes and high-born heroines, or the familial affection possible between Hindus and Muslims. Love, which most fully stretches and exercises the human heart, is highly valued in the society from which Nauṭaṅkī springs. Those who engage in its often perilous pursuit are praised, glorified, and celebrated in the tales, songs, and dramas that populate North Indian folklore. So great is the appreciation for this most compelling of human emotions that the tales compare the experience of love to the search for God. Given the lofty position love occupies within the culture, it is evident that the lover is not only a fervently moral individual but one who has superior spiritual insight or competence. In this regard the lover is like a mystical seeker, and the act of love is akin to renunciation.

These formulations bespeak an affirmative response to the life of the heart, to the capacity for deep attachment and feeling, and they construct a space within cultural memory for the preservation of love and the lore of past lovers. An analytical reading of love's history, however, reveals within the selfsame texts the hard wall of opposition erected to hold back this mighty emotional flood. Family honor, female chastity, maintenance of clan and caste lineages, social propriety, surveillance of the young, and other societal priorities repeatedly suppress and restrict love. They often threaten the very survival of the lovers and punish their reckless yearning with the ultimate sentence: death. In other instances, the intense attachment of the pair finds fulfillment in the acceptable form of marriage. The obstacles that society places in the path of love serve to magnify the selfless, difficult nature of the quest for union with the beloved, yet it is obvious that more than a rhetorical function feeds the image of familial and social hostility to romantic love. Even in the more recent dramas, where love appears minus some of its medieval grandeur, the plots contrive a harmonious accord between the lovers and their families, confirming the existing social arrangements. The dramas on Hindu-Muslim relations likewise allow helpful interaction between the communities without danger of religious conflict or sexual contact. In this fashion, the established order stands in many of these dramas but only after a contest. The Nauṭaṅkī romances operate as an arena for sorting out the conflicting responses of society to the experience of love, an emotion that poses a profound moral dilemma for North Indian society. Antithetical to many of that society's aims, it emerges over and over to arouse in men and women actions of nobility and self-sacrifice.

CHAPTER SEVEN

Women's Lives and Deaths

The world of Nauṭaṅkī is a strange place, full of disguises, reverses, and contradictions. An almighty emperor struts across the stage and next moment appears as a shirtless beggar. An executioner readies a heedless lover for hanging, only to be accosted by a black-caped, masked apparition—the lady to the rescue. The argument so far suggests that the unusual couplings that riddle Nauṭaṅkī stories—be they of character, incident, or motif—couch meanings that pertain to the moral universe of the audience. Sharp contrasts surprise the spectator into new perceptions, casting light on issues that never fully meet satisfactory resolution.

Perhaps nowhere are startling elements more rife—and more productive of altered awareness—than in the last thematic area of this section, the Nauṭaṅkī's representation of women. Nauṭaṅkī poets delight in describing women as murderers, lustful vamps, warring goddesses, and potent sorceresses. Yet they expound an ideology of female chastity and subservience that belies the powerful posture of so many of the women in their stories. Once again, these plays probe a dilemma with firm roots in Indian society. How may the morality conventionally espoused for women (which is gender-specific, different from that prescribed for men) be reconciled with the ways the Nauṭaṅkī actually presents women: as strongwilled, independent, heroic, dangerous? We may suggest the range of possible answers by comparing a number of narratives in which women play striking roles, roles that accost placid presumptions about the construction of womanhood in North India.

To appreciate the Nauṭaṅkī characters, it may be useful to mention first the mythic female figures most often identified in India: the heroines Sita, Sati, and Savitri who appear in the great epics, the *Mahābhārata* and the *Rāmāyaṇa*. The epic heroine type—the wife who is sacrificing, chaste, and loyal—represents the ideal for female behavior among the high Hindu castes. The ideal may be far from the real experience of many women.[1] Nevertheless, the prescriptive force of the epic heroines remains strong. The story of Savitri, for instance, teaches unswerving devotion to the husband, which if faithfully practiced can endow women with supernatural capacities, even the power to bring back the dead. Passive endurance in adversity is the lesson imparted by Sita, heroine of the *Rāmāyaṇa,* who follows Ram into forest exile. Willingness to suffer self-immolation for the preservation of her husband's honor is enjoined by the examples of Sita's fire ordeal as well as the self-sacrifice of Sati, wife of Shiva. In each case, self-abnegation and subservience to the husband are seen to bestow power upon the wife. She may use this power for various ends but customarily directs it toward the welfare, long life, and good name of her husband and the couple's offspring, particularly the sons. The epic stories do not portray woman as powerless; they define her power as derived from self-effacement in a relationship of subjugation to the male.[2]

Hindu mythology offers another important female paradigm that contrasts with the wifely ideal, namely the mother goddess. The goddess, whether manifest in her benign aspect as Lakshmi or Parvati or in her more menacing form as Kali or Durga, derives her power fundamentally from her status as mother rather than spouse, a role in which she exercises uniquely female control through the ability to generate and nurture life.[3] Outside folk religion, however, her power is often subverted or leashed by subordination to a male deity. Each god in the Hindu pantheon is matched with a consort who is understood as his activating energy or *shakti.* Philosophically the individual goddess consorts may be subsumed under one universal principle or Shakti, of which they are considered manifestations.[4] The Hindu recognition of an underlying female principle has impressed some observers as a more positive formulation of woman's place in the cosmos than that offered by the Judeo-Christian tradition.[5]

Although women in Nauṭaṅkī plays most frequently figure as wives and mothers, they do not necessarily conform to the mythic prototypes of classical literature. In addition to these two roles, women appear in other relationships. A female unrelated to male characters, however, scarcely exists; she is always some man's daughter, sister, or spouse and may act in more than one familial role. The relationships defined by kinship are crucial to understanding Nauṭaṅkī's women, particularly in view of the cleavage that exists in North Indian society between a woman's natal family and her affines (her husband's family). In the patrilineal and patrilocal pattern that prevails over most of this region, the woman departs from her parents' home at (or soon after) marriage and takes up residence with her husband's family, becoming subsumed into it henceforth. When she returns to her parents' for visits, she enjoys the pampered status of daughter (*beṭī*), while in her husband's house she is forever a daughter-in-law (*bahū*), burdened with rules of avoidance of male kin and multiple domestic responsibilities. The transfer of the female from one household to another rarely brings those households together. The wife's loyalties are considered to be forever divided, her heart and child self attached to her birth home, her adult identity, duty (*dharm*), and status lodged with her husband and his relatives.

It goes without saying that men are the heads of household, and that male kin (the father, his sons, their sons) ideally reside together in an extended family. Daughters are shorn away from one family and thrust into the midst of strangers. Because of these practices, women are reckoned an economic, social, and emotional liability, despite the large contribution they make to domestic welfare through the value of their labor and fertility. They are resented in their parents' home because they must be married off (nowadays often at great expense) and distrusted by their husband's family because they come into it from the outside. (The Hindi word for their outsider status is *parāyā*, fem. *parāyī*, the source for English "pariah.")

Beyond this structural inequality, men and women are further divided by separate moral codes. Women's sexuality is strictly controlled by family members, insofar as female fertility provides the "ground" for the male "seed," and chaste women are necessary to reproduce pure lines of caste and clan. Corruption of blood is an evil to be strictly avoided; that the avoidance occurs more through the surveillance of female sexuality than through self-control on the male's part is explained by patriarchal privilege. According to the dominant ideology of gender roles, a woman ought to be exclusive in her sexual and affectional fidelity to her husband; she may not remarry should her husband predecease her. Men, however, may have more than one wife or mistress, either serially or at once. As in other societies, this differential moral code has led to a variety of anomalies and inequities. Colonial

India was notorious for its "problems" of unmarriageable widows (including the occasional incidence of widow immolation or *satī*) and incompatibilities of various kinds such as large age differences between husband and wife. These injunctions and conditions, in brief, form the background against which we must read and understand the Nauṭaṅkī tales about women.

As we did in the preceding two chapters, we approach these narratives on women's lives in loose chronological order. At the center of the first group of dramas dating from the nineteenth century, we find lustful and dangerous women whose actions contravene the code for the ideal wife. These morality tales teach by inverse example; the destructive violence that female desire unleashes turns against the women, and they die untimely and often gruesome deaths—stern warning against following their path. The second cluster of examples paints a less lurid picture, granting its women the strength and nobility commensurate with their high Rajput status. These dramas, by focusing on the pivotal position of the married woman between competing houses or clans, portray women as untrustworthy not primarily because of their sexuality but because of divided familial loyalties. Here and in the dramas of the third group, an affirmative formulation of female agency emerges in the person of the *vīrāṅganā,* the warrior woman who defends righteousness. Moving beyond both paradigms of the chaste wife and the ferocious goddess, the *vīrāṅganā* model combines direct assumption of power with exemplary virtue. Finally, in the protofeminist texts of the midtwentieth-century Nauṭaṅkī, these themes find new contexts. Issues of widow remarriage, working women, and unwed mothers frame perspectives on women's sexuality, family loyalty, and personal freedom that both differ from and restate earlier articulations.

The Dangers of Female Desire

The possibility of polygyny (a man marrying more than one wife) is accepted in the narrative universe of Nauṭaṅkī almost without question. Heroes roam about, acquiring wives and mistresses as part of their quest for adventure and fame, and rarely does this fact spark any particular interest. As might be anticipated, it was not until the social reform movement left its mark on the twentieth-century Nauṭaṅkī that the practice came under scrutiny out of a concern for women's welfare. Two earlier tales, *Pūranmal* and *Rūp basant,* contribute an intriguing commentary on the dynamics of the polygynous family from the prereformist perspective. These dramas generate a debate on the wisdom of a man marrying more than once—not from the standpoint of the possible neglect of the wives (except in a very restricted sexual sense) but from the position of the male offspring. The consequence of remarriage is damage to the unity of the family, inducing the father to murder or exile his son. The responsibility for this painful sundering is placed squarely on the shoulders of the younger second wife, who is conceived as concupiscent, shameless, and vengeful. In this manner, the difficulties created for the family by a practice that privileges men are ingeniously ascribed to women. The lust and guilt of the father are transferred to the young outsider female, and what results is the "lustful stepmother," a folklore motif of wide circulation all over the world.[6]

A prime example is found in the well-known North Indian legend of *Pūranmal* (also known as *Pūran bhagat*) (see fig. 7).

> In the city of Syalkot in Punjab rules the king Shankhpati, who has a wife named Amba and a son called Puran. One day the king receives an invitation to the *svayamvar* (marriage contest) of Phulan, daughter of the king of Kusumnagar. Although Amba tries to advise the king against remarrying because of his advanced age, he replies that as a warrior it would be cowardly of him not to enter the contest, and besides it is the *dharm* of a Rajput to marry several wives.
>
> Shankhpati marries Phulan but is unable to keep her happy. One day Phulan spots Puran and is attracted to him. She coaxes him into entering her apartment with the ruse that she is ill and needs his assistance. Once inside, Phulan reveals her feelings and tries to seduce Puran. Puran is appalled at this advance by one who is related as a mother to him. Further, he is committed to celibacy because of a vow. When he resists, Phulan makes threats and seizes Puran's waistband and sword as he leaves.
>
> In front of the king, Phulan accuses Puran of violating her honor. Showing the waistband and sword as proof, she convinces the king of Puran's guilt. He becomes enraged and sentences his son to death. Puran is killed, his eyes are taken out and given to Phulan to appease her, and his body is thrown into a well. Guru Gorakhnath passes by, revives Puran, and makes him his disciple.
>
> In subsequent episodes, Puran joins Gorakhnath's roving band of yogis. He continues to be pursued by lustful women. When he goes to China, the queen Sundra insists that he marry her, vowing to kill all the yogis who enter her land if he refuses. Later he encounters the princess Rupvati of Sinhaldvip who possesses great magical powers. She traps Puran and turns him into a parrot, but he eventually escapes with his guru's aid.
>
> Puran returns to Syalkot and sees that the garden of the palace has

> completely withered in his absence. As he enters, it turns green again. Hiding his true identity, he elicits Phulan's confession in the presence of the king. Phulan says she simply wanted a son that her husband was unable to give her, and she asks the yogi for forgiveness. Puran blesses her and says she will soon bear a son. He then restores the eyesight of his mother, Amba, who has gone blind with weeping at Puran's loss. Puran reveals his identity and vanishes.
>
> Phulan bears a son named Risalu. Seeing the sadness of his mother, Risalu sets out to find his brother Puran. Before he leaves Amba falls ill, and Puran, who has dreamt that his mother is about to die, comes back to Syalkot again. Amba dies, and Puran conducts her last rites. Puran is persuaded by Guru Gorakhnath to remain in Syalkot. Shankhpati and Phulan retire from the kingdom and take up *sannyās* (the stage of renunciation). After ruling the kingdom for twelve years, Puran hands it over to Risalu. He at last joins Guru Gorakhnath in his forest abode.[7]

The contrast between the two wives of the king, Amba (*ambā,* "mother") and Phulan (*phūlan,* "flower"), is consistently maintained throughout this story, illustrating the split constructed between the ideal female and the bad woman. Amba, the good mother, is nurturing, nonthreatening, and asexual. Like Sita, Savitri, and Sati, she uses against herself the power gained through her position as wife, taking on suffering for the anticipated benefit of her husband and son. She squelches her intuition, acceding to her husband's desire for a second marriage, even though she knows it will bring ruin on the family. Bereft at the loss of Puran, her pride and joy, she sacrifices her eyesight by weeping herself into blindness. For all her virtue accumulated through self-abnegation, she is unable to exert much influence on the course of events. She manages to attract Puran back only when she lies dying. The satisfaction of Puran's conducting her cremation rites seems to be her final (and possibly only) reward.

The chief characteristics of Phulan are her youth, beauty, and flowerlike freshness (she even hails from Kusumnagar, "city of flowers"). These traits imply fertility and sexual readiness and in themselves carry no negative charge. Phulan becomes dangerous insofar as she challenges Puran's lifelong vow of celibacy. Puran is called a *jatī* (or *yatī,* from the same root as and cognate with *yogī*), a man dedicated to control over his senses. Any female presence is a potential source of anxiety to him; it is no accident that all the women in the drama except Amba are portrayed as having sexual designs on him. In Phulan, moreover, attractiveness is coupled with a kinship bond (mother) that makes any hint of sexual contact taboo.

The situation is thus set for an explosive confrontation between Phulan and Puran. Phulan's chief vice, according to the morality prescribed for women, is that she does not suppress her own desires. She takes the initiative, drawing in the young Puran who is close to her in age and a fitter partner than the decrepit king. Her playful attraction is soon converted under his resistance into humiliation and anger. As she fights back at his affront to her pride, she employs the strategy of Potiphar's wife—accusing him of seducing her when she made the advances. Phulan's intentions, given the information available in the story, may not really be so terrible, but she comes across as a wicked mother, crazed by lust, vicious, out of control. Despite this negative characterization, it is important to note that her sexuality becomes dangerous within the context of the polygynous family, her proximity in age to Puran, and her distance from and unhappiness with the king.

Only at the end of the drama does the poet bestow some sympathetic touches on Phulan, tellingly when she confesses to her desire for a son. By bearing Risalu and accepting the mantle of real motherhood (as opposed to her legal motherhood or stepmotherhood in relation to Puran), she becomes a safer, gentler female. She publicly seeks absolution of her sins, an act that mirrors her earlier accusations against Puran, leading to his trial and public sentence. Because of the changes Phulan is willing to make, she and Puran are finally reconciled. For his part, Puran's position of self-righteous celibacy never alters. He resists all female attentions and remains unmarried to the last. His self-control is so perfect that he is even capable of resuming rulership without abandoning yoga. Unlike Gopichand and Bharathari, he is a yogi for all seasons, equally impervious to the temptations of women, wealth, family, and friends.

A similar series of events begins and ends the long saga of *Rūp basant,* an adventure story about the differing fates of a pair of non-yogic brothers.

> King Chandrasen and his queen Rupvati have two sons, Rup and Basant. One day they see a bird whose first mate had died bringing a new mate to the nest. The stepmother bird kills all the babies born of the first mate. Rupvati tells Chandrasen that if she dies, he should not marry, for a stepmother would in similar fashion destroy her sons. The king assures her he will never do such a thing. Soon after Rupvati dies, and the king, remembering his promise to his wife, refuses many mar-

riage proposals. Finally, however, he is persuaded to marry the princess Chitravati.

Chitravati sees Basant and falls in love with him. On one occasion, Rup and Basant are playing ball and the ball lands in her palace. Basant, going to retrieve it, is accosted by the queen, who demands sexual favors. When he refuses to oblige her, she threatens to have him killed. With the maid backing her up, she reports to the king that Basant assaulted her modesty. The king sentences Basant to hang but is convinced by his minister to convert the sentence to exile. Rup vows to accompany his younger brother, and the two leave the kingdom.

When they arrive in Egypt, Basant is bitten by a snake and swoons. Rup, taking him for dead, goes into the city to buy a shroud. The king of Egypt has just died without an heir, and it is proclaimed that the first man to cross the city gates next morning will be crowned king. Rup happens to be the first and becomes king.

Meanwhile Basant is cured by a yogi. He kills a man-eating tiger but then is attacked by guards and left in a ditch. He is rescued by a potter and then is sent to jail. He escapes, joins a merchant ship, and sails the world. He marries a princess, Chandraprabha, is attacked by sailors, jumps overboard, and is washed ashore to be sheltered by a gardener. And so on.

After many adventures, Basant returns to his father's kingdom disguised as a yogi. As he enters the garden, all that had shriveled turns green. The yogi is asked to stay and minister to the problems of the people, and when the king reveals his great sorrow at his childlessness, the yogi indicates that he should learn the real story now from his queen. Chitravati comes out with the truth.

The father goes to Egypt to ask for Rup's forgiveness. Rup relents and the father and sons, finally united, return home. As they touch their stepmother's feet in greeting, she dies. Rup goes back to rule in Egypt, Basant takes over the kingdom from Chandrasen, and the old king retires to a life of meditation.[8]

Once more the willful desire of the stepmother leads to a family rift resulting in the sons' banishment and the father's grief. This triangular structure (father-stepmother-son) is common to several South Asian narratives in which polygyny is the indispensable but often unacknowledged precondition. Best known among them is the *Rāmāyaṇa* of Valmiki. The aged king Dasharatha's young wife, Kaikeyi, demands that Ram, the son of senior wife Kausalya, be sent into exile and her own son, Bharata, be placed on the throne. Dasharatha, under the influence of passion and bound by a previous debt, is forced to grant her wish, even though the sorrow brought on by separation from Ram is so immense that it kills him. The motive that drives Kaikeyi, namely the wish that her son inherit and that the title be stripped from her co-wife's son, is absent from the narratives of *Pūranmal* and *Rūp basant*. However, it lies at the core of the societal suspicion of stepmothers, insofar as a woman's position in an extended family is derived through a male relation, and a woman's own son is her primary economic and psychological asset. It is in the co-wife's interest to put forward her male offspring and diminish the influence of her stepsons. Despite the initial absence of sons born to stepmothers in *Pūranmal* and *Rūp basant,* the family structure resembles the *Rāmāyaṇa* configuration in important ways. In both cases, the narrative follows a sequence of rupture, exile, purification, and return, propelled in the first instance by an aroused and angry woman.

The agency of the female appears prominently in this narrative structure, yet by its articulation it conjures fear and loathing rather than empathy or emulation. Because the Nauṭaṅkī stepmothers assume an overtly sexual stance vis-à-vis the stepsons (an element lacking in the *Rāmāyaṇa*), their desire assumes almost monstrous proportions. The magnitude of horror may owe more to the potential reversal of the hierarchical relationship between father and son than to transgression of an incest taboo. The stepmother and stepson are not in fact related by blood; sexual contact between them would not in itself be abhorrent. What is hazardous is the competition between father and son for sexual possession of the same woman. The implication that the king is impotent to protect his rights over the queen's body undermines his authority as ruler as well as his sense of masculinity. It introduces an element of anarchy into the family structure—and by extension the public family, the kingdom—that seemingly leads only to breakdown.

While these stories impart a horror of the dangerous sexuality of women, especially young attractive women, they also reinforce the stereotype of the stepmother as homewrecker. The stepmother is not content simply to seduce a stepson; she usurps the very role of mother. Insofar as her actions precipitate the crisis that leads to the sons' exile, she orphans her stepsons, depriving them of both their mother's love and father's protection. Even more devastating is the blow to her husband, whom she renders heirless, an immense tragedy for a king. The king's loss of his sons and the sterility of relations between the king and his second wife are represented by the withering of the gardens. The absence of fertility in the kingdom is directly related to the absence of righteousness, specifically the injustice committed by the king in sentencing an innocent son. The symbolism of grief goes even further. The great sadness of the queen Amba manifests in her excessive weeping followed by blindness—the "star of her eyes" (*āṅkhoṁ kā tārā*) having departed and made her vision useless. Similarly, the return of the exiled son in yogi's weeds—a potent visual sign of grief and renunciation—conveys the child's feeling of loss attendant on separation from his parents.

Only the downfall or recantation of the stepmother can balance the moral deficit. Phulan seeks atonement through giving birth to Risalu and making up with Puran. Chitravati, on the other hand, expires as soon as Rup and Basant touch her feet. Their gesture, a display of respect, submission, and forgiveness, so overpowers the unworthy woman that it kills her. Yet lurking just beyond the narratorial castigation of these women lies the inescapable countertruth: the kings opted to marry again. A moral confusion disrupts the stasis of each drama's conclusion. The onus lies on the woman, but is the male free of guilt? The old kings do not die; they go off to meditate, perhaps to ponder the errors of their ways. These dramas in short intertwine a muted but audible objection to polygny. Perturbed in their very structure, they formulate a conflict between the gender ideology that teaches women chastity and submission and a more universal morality that holds both men and women responsible for the control of their sexual activity.

The perception of women as unruly, threatening, and shameless was in India encapsulated in a catchphrase, *strī charitra* or *triyā charitra.* Literally this expression translates as the "moral nature" or "character" (*charitra*) of women (*strī, triyā*). By extension *charitra* means "narrative" or "biography," and so the phrase could also be translated as "the woman's story" or even "herstory." In popular Indian parlance, however, the phrase has a decidedly misogynistic ring, more equivalent to "female trouble" or "women's wiles." *Triyā charitra* became a prevalent folklore theme in North India, one illustrated by a number of stories. The Nauṭaṅkī play of this title, like *Pūranmal* and *Rūp basant,* is preoccupied with the potential infidelity of the young wife. Continuing in their mold, it pictures a woman who is deceptive, sexually voracious, murderous, and beyond redemption.

> The Nauṭaṅkī opens with a reference to the unhappy state of affairs in India where parents for the sake of money marry their young daughters to aged men or to boys who are still children. The latter was the case when Madan Seth of Andher Nagari (the city of darkness) married Champa, his sixteen-year-old daughter, to Panna, ten-year-old son of the millionaire Bhondu.

> Champa, her desires unfulfilled, attempts to seduce a yogi who comes to her house begging for alms. Threatening to accuse him of assaulting her, she cajoles him into entering into an affair. Every night she goes to meet the yogi in the forest. Finally it is time for her *gaunā* (final rite of marriage). Panna and his friend Khushdil arrive to take her to Panna's house. Champa explains her plight to the yogi, and in a fit of jealousy he asks her for her husband's head as proof of her loyalty.
>
> Champa goes to the sleeping Panna, cuts off his head, and carries it back to the yogi. The yogi, shocked at her misdeed, calls her a murderess and sends her away. When she pleads with him, he bites off her nose. Khushdil, who has been watching all the while, leaps out and kills the yogi. In public, Champa tries to cover up by accusing Khushdil of seducing her, cutting off her nose, and killing her husband.
>
> The commotion is overheard by a policeman who brings both Khushdil and Champa before the king. Their stories conflict, and the truth is only ascertained when Khushdil shows the king the piece of nose still caught in the yogi's mouth. Sentenced by the king, Champa goes to her death urging other women not to stray from the path of *dharm*. The lord Shiva revives Panna's dead body, and Panna and Khushdil proceed on their way.[9]

This morbid didactic tale shows the wife, Champa, in a most unflattering light. Here too the young woman's name refers to a kind of flower, suggesting attractiveness and sexual appeal, but her character is short on lovability. Contradictions—or rather juxtapositions signaling clashes in viewpoint—abound in the narrative. Champa flagrantly conducts an affair after marriage, committing the (for women) unpardonable sin of adultery. The text tells us, however, as if in her defense, that she is not yet in the custody of her in-laws, her husband is not old enough to consummate the marriage, and consequently she may not meet the minimal definition of wife. She murders her own husband, but the idea is put into her head by her paramour, the yogi—who turns against her and disclaims all responsibility. Champa is coldhearted and cruel toward her boymate, Panna. But what about the behavior of the ascetic? Aside from fornicating with a married woman every night, he has a peculiar penchant for severed body parts: first the head of Panna and then Champa's nose. The immoral actions of Champa, if not softened by the counterindications in the text, are at least positioned in a moral arena where no one is perfect.

The framing editorial blames society and greedy parents in particular for the unhappiness of young women married to incompatible mates. Like Phulan and Chitravati, Champa is the victim of an inequitable social practice, but with a difference. Whereas they were married to men twice their age or more, she is wedded to a partner who is younger, who is not yet a man. The perspective of social justice, however, is not consistently maintained, and in the punishment meted out to the errant women the flawed marital arrangements are overlooked. Champa is put to death for not following the *dharm* of a virtuous wife, just as Phulan is made to recant and Chitravati is killed by her stepsons' touch. The stress on female duplicity and blackmail (the Potiphar's-wife motif) reinforces the aversion to women inscribed in all three dramas. Champa seduces the yogi by threatening to reveal his alleged designs on her, and she later makes false claims that Khushdil, her husband's companion, tried to seduce her and cut off her nose.

In *Bhain bhaiyā* (Sister and brother) the sexual dimension of male-female interaction is obscured, and murderous greed alone defines the woman's character. The key relationship here shifts from stepmother-stepson or wife-husband to sister-brother.

> While traveling to earn money to maintain his wife and mother, the merchant Uttamchand visits his sister. As he retires for the night, he entrusts her with his bag of jewels for safekeeping. The sister tries to enlist her husband's support in killing her brother for his money. He refuses, and she murders her brother in cold blood.
>
> When the sister returns to her husband, he is horrified and begins beating her. Hearing the uproar, a policeman stops to inquire. Uttamchand's sister accuses her husband of killing her brother, while he maintains that she did it. Finally the king determines the truth by subjecting both parties to an ordeal: a poisonous snake is to be put around the neck of the accused, and whoever succumbs to snakebite will be proved guilty.
>
> The sister refuses to go near the snake, but the husband readily dons the snake, and it does not bite him. The king sentences the sister to a gruesome death. Uttamchand lies dead, and his wife comes to commit *satī* with him. Lord Shiva responds to the prayers of the brother-in-law and resuscitates Uttamchand. Uttamchand, his wife, and his mother return home together.[10]

It is difficult to extract anything but unalloyed gynophobia from this sparse tale. No visible ambiguity clouds the moral positions established: the brother is good, the sister is evil. What makes the story thought-provoking in the Indian context is that ordinarily a high degree of affection accompanies the sister-brother relationship. A woman's brother is considered her protector, her ally, even her companion on an equal footing, and tales about brothers and sisters usually speak of mutual support and devotion. Ritual occasions such as the festival of *rakṣhābandhan* (the tie of protection) symbolically bind brother and sister together, the brother pledging to defend his sister and she to love and worship him. This drama points to an undercurrent of male suspicion and paranoia that the ritual may seek to allay. Are there any limits on the sister's desire for protection? Will she not suck her brother dry, asking more and more in the way of support? Does she care about him at all? Is she not just after his money? *Bhain bhaiyā* details the dark side of brother-sister feeling, adding to the list of dangerous females even the offspring of one's own parents, one's flesh and blood. Not even distinguished by a proper name, the sister meets her end much as her counterpart in *Triyā charitra* does. After the snake ordeal she goes to an ignoble death, whereas the innocent Uttamchand is restored to life—final proof of the law of just deserts (*karmaphal*).

To sum up, this set of narratives revolves around raging female desire, desire that is explicitly sexual in three cases and perhaps obliquely so in the fourth (lust for the brother's jewels). The female characters are all young wives, women who are supposed to conform to the code of personal modesty, obedience, and fidelity exemplified by Sita, Savitri, and Sati. Yet their behavior more resembles that of the decapitating goddess Durga—except that her victim was the demon Mahisha, and these wives' victims are innocent stepsons, husbands, and brothers. In each story the women not only transgress the norms of wifely servility but proceed to commit moral outrages, instigating or perpetrating acts of murder. The women's misdeeds are punished with public shaming, either through the extraction of a confession and pardon or through royal sentencing and execution. Finally, in each story the wronged dismembered males are revived and made whole through the mediation of a renunciant figure, either a yogi, the guru Gorakhnath, or the deity Shiva. They return to their former estate or acquire an enhanced entitlement, while the wicked angry women completely and finally disappear.

The didacticism of these tales with regard to women's roles is transparent. It is unlikely that any spectator would mistake these characters for heroines or models of ideal conduct. Nonetheless, the untamed spunky young brides excite flutters of pleasure and temptation as they flirt with the protagonists—and the audience—on stage. For the moment they draw in the viewer, the voyeur, only to turn suddenly and assume a frightful posture. In converting the male response of attraction into avoidance and fear, the dramas reproduce the ideology of female chastity by means of inverse illustration. They represent the unchaste wife as loathsome, all-devouring, and grossly immoral, teaching a hatred of her that only her ultimate annihilation seems to satiate.

The surface texture of exaggerated values—the wholly good men, the utterly evil women—operates to maintain the gendered sexual conduct that ideologically supports the patriarchal family, polygynous or otherwise. Doubtless the misogyny instilled by these dramas affects the daily lives of women outside the theatre. Much more difficult to discern is that for all of the Nauṭaṅkī's simplification of issues, its reduction of characters to flattened stereotypes, its tired manipulation of melodrama, the theatre creates space for moral examination. It gives voice to a clash of viewpoints, making visible the cracks in the moral edifice. If this set of dramas enjoins self-control upon women, it also asks us—albeit more timidly—to consider the problem of male sexuality. The aging kings indulge in youthful fantasies and remarry, the yogic lover of Champa misbehaves and betrays his vows, and parents still marry off their daughters for monetary gain. The protagonists do not simply have flaws; the foundations of their motivation are open to question. These questions—of intention, accountability, and the universality of moral standards—are not resolved in the course of the Nauṭaṅkī dramas. Viewpoints shift and collide, puzzling doubts remain beyond the apparent smoothness of the concluding deaths and rebirths. Significantly, however, the playing out of conflict on the theatrical stage has reactivated those doubts. The slack, the play, existing within the Nauṭaṅkī narrative allows the probing of right and wrong, the disturbance in the complacency of moral presumption.

Family, Chastity, and the Limits of Loyalty

In the second group of stories, the brother-sister relationship that plunged to such abysmal depths in *Bhain bhaiyā* acquires a more complicated background of family and clan politics. The dynamics of the brother-sister bond are central to the Rajput Nauṭaṅkīs, especially the *Ālhā* plays and *Amar siṁh rāṭhor*. Here we encounter a number of strong women in more positive circumstances than in the preceding stories. In one very popular Ālhā Nauṭaṅkī, *Indal haraṇ* (The kidnapping of Indal), the women are bold, outspoken, and insightful.[11] The story opens with the capture of Alha's son Indal by his bride-to-be, the sorceress Chittarrekha. It ends with the defeat of her clan by Alha's army followed by the couple's marriage. Of special interest is the supernatural power ascribed to Chittarrekha; she turns Indal into a parrot and imprisons him for her pleasure. Other women such as Indal's mother, Machhla, and an older relative similarly exercise magical abilities.

Further, the young women in the drama show their independence by choosing their own husbands, while the older ones inspire their menfolk to action by shaming them and questioning their valor. Machhla precipitates the kidnapping of Indal by insisting that they join Alha's brother, Udal, at the Baithur festival despite Alha's displeasure and forebodings of ill. On several occasions she rouses both Udal and Alha when their will is weak. Similarly, when Alha tries to kill his brother, it is their mother who inspires Udal to resist. Udal's mother-in-law has a vision that enables her to guide Udal in his quest for his nephew, Indal. Women thus seem to possess the inner energy or *shakti* that rises to activate the sluggish male principle.

In the chivalric code of honor and shame, however, this energy is circumscribed by an ideology of purity, powerlessness, and dependence on men. The virtue of a Rajput woman, her *sat* (truth, goodness), lies in preserving her virginity if she is unmarried or staying loyal to her husband once married. A woman may exhibit some independent agency in this regard, the final act of virtue being the supposedly voluntary commission of ritual suicide in the practice of *satī* or *jauhar* (suicide to avoid the dishonor of capture by enemy forces). But for the most part the surveillance of female purity is carried out by men. The duty devolves upon fathers and brothers prior to a woman's marriage, and it shifts to the husband and his clan at marriage.

During an interim period the claims of the two families conflict, as between the marriage ceremony and the *gaunā* (when the woman is physically removed to her husband's residence). Romantic attachments may also circumvent parental authority. Familial consent to a woman's marriage is almost universally withheld in the *Ālhā* epic, because the Banaphar heroes are deemed to be of inferior rank to other Rajput clans. For these reasons, the "protection" of women leads to innumerable clashes. During courtship or even after marriage, women are commonly being "defended," that is, fought over, by their fathers and brothers against their lovers and husbands. In these struggles for honor, a woman's desire is taken as inconsequential. Once her physical purity is threatened, she becomes a source of shame to her male kin. They are obliged to defend her chastity, the primary determinant of their honor, regardless of her wishes. As an unstable chattel-like commodity she inspires distrust.

The tension between the two sets of relations continues throughout the woman's life. Although in the *Ālhā* women always remain loyal to their husbands, they cannot deter suspicion of harboring ties with their natal homes and of favoring their brothers. The affinal relative, especially the brother of a man's wife (*sālā,* also used as a term of abuse), attracts hostility and suspicion. Often the brother-in-law assumes the role of traitor in the unfolding of the narrative. If the husband and his family are suspicious of the brother-in-law, by the same token a brother cannot fully trust his sister because she has married into another family and become loyal to her husband.

The triangle of the woman, her husband, and her brother lies at the core of many a conflict in the *Ālhā*. The central narrative offers a good illustration. The queen Malhna, a character of great strength and dignity, is the protector of the Banaphar heroes and the "real ruler of the kingdom," to quote Grierson.[12] She is married to the weak king Parmal, lord of Mahoba and a member of the Chandel clan of Rajputs. The queen's brother, Mahil, belongs to a different clan, the Parihars. He holds a grudge against Parmal and the Banaphars because he considers himself Mahoba's rightful ruler. Being privy as her brother to Malhna's confidence, Mahil constantly plots ways to eliminate the heroes, to intervene treacherously in the events. In *Indal haraṇ,* for example, Mahil deceives Alha when the boy is kidnapped by Chittarrekha, alleging that Alha's brother (Udal) slept with Alha's wife (Machhla) and murdered their son (Indal). Alha almost kills his brother because of this allegation; curiously, he never consults his wife to see if it is true.

In the climactic incident leading to the final war of destruction, the clans do battle over Bela, the wife of Brahma, Parmal's son and heir. Although her marriage with Brahma has already been sanctified, Bela is still residing in Delhi with her father, the mighty Prithviraj, by now a sworn enemy of the Mahobans. When Brahma goes to fetch her for the *gaunā* he takes a large army, and in the first round he defeats Prithviraj's forces. At Mahil's instigation, however, Prithviraj resorts to treachery and devises a plan for Bela's brother Tahar to assassinate Brahma. Brahma is sorely wounded, but meanwhile the Mahobans have carried off Bela and brought her to him. Seeing her dying husband, she vows revenge on her brother Tahar. At the height of the entire epic, she dresses herself in Brahma's armor, rides on horseback leading the Mahoban army, and in single combat defeats and beheads Tahar. She carries his head back to Brahma, who now being satisfied breathes his last. When she mounts Brahma's funeral pyre to die as a *satī,* Bela's hair spontaneously catches fire. As the conflagration engulfs the bodies a tremendous battle rages between Prithviraj and the Mahobans in which almost all the major characters are killed.[13]

These triangles (Malhna-Parmal-Mahil and Bela-Brahma-Tahar) bring out two themes: the brother-in-law's treachery and the contest for the allegiance of the female. In the Bela episode, the attack by the woman's brother against her husband gives rise to a grand and horrific act of female aggression. Bela's grievance arises from the defense of her chastity by her own brethren, but it is an unwanted defense, a defense gone awry and carried out underhandedly. Tahar's duplicity triggers a counterdefense by Bela of her husband Brahma's honor. Bela seems to uphold Rajput chivalry and its code of fealty of wife to husband, but she also transforms the Rajput concept of female virtue, defending her husband—not her chastity or even her life—as her most precious possession. The warring aspect of female fury—the *vīrāṅganā* posture—is not a trivial or eccentric response; it emanates from immense reservoirs of rage and shame, appearing again and again in the Nauṭaṅkī literature as a positive image of female agency.

In another Rajput drama, *Amar siṁh rāṭhor,* brothers-in-law again play the part of treacherous advisors, while female characters instigate significant feats of valor. Salawat Khan, the noble who incites Shah Jahan against Amar Singh by manipulating Hindu-Muslim tensions, is the emperor's brother-in-law, whereas Arjun Gaur, the traitor who cuts Amar Singh's throat when he is defenseless, is related to Amar Singh as the brother of his first wife. In three instances women threaten to go into battle as a means of coaxing action from their reluctant partners. Shah Jahan's wife taunts the emperor when her brother Salawat is killed; she tells him to put on woman's dress—she herself will go to avenge her brother. Bhallu, the brother of Amar Singh, refuses to fight to regain Amar Singh's body, but his wife volunteers to take his place on the battlefield as repayment for a time when Amar Singh saved her; Bhallu is roused by her words to put up a show of bravery. Finally Hadi Rani, the wife of Amar Singh, prepares to retrieve her husband's corpse with Ram Singh, Amar Singh's nephew, but he refuses to allow her to come and takes two male friends instead. Women in this drama uphold the respect of their menfolk, motivate their heroism, and are ready to perform acts of self-sacrifice, but because of their pivotal position in the kinship structure, their loyalties can never be entirely trusted. The lack of security surrounding women's allegiance manifests itself in the warriors' constant fear of betrayal. Treacherous acts are almost always the instrument of the hero's final undoing, and they most frequently originate with the male kin of the wife, notably her brother.

Comparing the dangerous women of the preceding section with the heroines of the *Ālhā* and *Amar siṁh rāṭhor,* we perceive that certain traits characterize both groups, but on the whole female agency is more positively portrayed in the martial dramas. Virginal women pose a danger to chaste men in *Pūranmal* and *Rūp basant* as well as in *Indal haraṇ,* but the stepmothers turn to uncontrolled aggression whereas Chittarrekha uses sorcery, a magical force for good or evil. Bela's decapitation of her brother Tahar parallels Champa's beheading of her husband and the nameless sister's murder of Uttamchand, yet it proceeds not from lust but from a wellspring of outraged Rajput pride. Machhla disobeys Alha and takes Indal to Baithur, wreaking much havoc, yet she also inspires men to courageous action. The sister-brother tie is viewed with suspicion in both *Bhain bhaiyā* and *Amar siṁh rāṭhor;* in the first the *sister* is jealous, greedy, and treacherous, but in the second jealousy and greed motivate the *brothers* of Shah Jahan's wife and Amar Singh's first wife to perform their dastardly deeds.

Despite the wider range of actions allowed to women and the larger moral space within which they transact them, female virtue is linked explicitly in the martial dramas to self-sacrifice. Nowhere is this clearer than in the denouements of both the *Ālhā* and *Amar siṁh rāṭhor,* where Bela and Hadi Rani, the heroines of the two legends, perform self-cremation alongside their husbands' bodies. These events of *satī* are marked by extraordinary fanfare and supernatural occurrences (spontaneous combustion of the pyre). Whereas the dramas affirm the strength and heroism of a woman as chaste wife, the conclusions articulate the conviction that the purpose of a woman's existence ends with her husband's death. The best use of her body is to adorn his pyre and accompany him to the next world. Like the harridans of the previous set of narratives, these more exemplary wives leave the stage dead. They suffer demises that may be deemed glorious and spiritually meritorious but are still intensely public and painful. Once more, male honor is regained through destruction of the female body, an act that stands at the momentous point of closure.

The *Vīrāṅganā* and the Legitimation of Female Agency

While Rajput legend and in due course the Nauṭaṅkī theatre enshrined the *satī,* the virtuous wife who dies in the fires of self-sacrifice, North

Indian history also affords examples of women attuned to a greater glory—serving the homeland. Women such as Razia Sultana, Kurma Devi, Durgavati, Tarabai, Ahalyabai, and Lakshmibai, the Rani of Jhansi, chose to forego the path of *satī* and assumed power as queen-regents. Living in various periods and parts of the country, they shared certain experiences. Often they were tutored by their fathers, being educated in the arts of war and the skills of reading, writing, and administration; they rose to power at the death of a male kinsman, usually a husband. Once on the throne, they were reputed to be wise, just, and generous rulers. They attired themselves in masculine costume, adopted the perquisites of royal office, and exhibited military leadership and bravery in battle. Usually they died while defending the kingdom against an invader. These queens are known to Indian popular culture as *vīrāṅganās*, "warrior women," and they are celebrated in folk songs and legends, modern novels and poems, comic books and films. In popular iconography, they are usually depicted riding on horseback, wearing a turban and tunic with flowing trousers, and brandishing a sword high above their heads (figs. 17 and 18).[14]

If the ideology of *satī* sanctions destruction of the female body and exalts passive suffering, the *vīrāṅganā* ideal commends physical training and active deployment of the body in combat. The strength and efficacy of the *vīrāṅganā* are in many respects similar to those of the warring goddess Durga or Kali, her defeat of threatening enemies corresponding to the goddess's punishment of evil demons. What is remarkable in the *vīrāṅganā* concept is the different interpretation of "truth" (*sat*) in contrast to the *satī*'s "truth." While *sat* in the dominant gender ideology signifies sexual fidelity to one's husband (also identified as *pativrat dharm*), little emphasis is placed on the physical purity of the woman warrior. The *vīrāṅganā*'s status is not defined by her relationship to a man as wife, widow, or paramour but is consequent upon her valorous deeds. Because her virtue is not reducible to the sexual transactions of the female body, physical relations cannot impugn her truth. The *vīrāṅganā* thus conjoins physical prowess, moral strength, and sexual freedom in a startling counterparadigm of Indian womanhood.[15]

The historical evidence for the *vīrāṅganā* is supplied by queenly figures from the past. We have already encountered fictional Nauṭaṅkī characters who illustrate the ideal. The noble women from *Amar siṁh rāṭhor*, for example, entertained notions of charging into battle to avenge their husbands or family members, and their threat of doing so was a standard taunt to overcome male relations' cowardice. In the *Ālhā* epic, the heroine Bela not only threatened to but actually led her army into a

Fig. 17. The Indian woman warrior (*vīrāṅganā*), reprinted from Anil Rajkumar, *Bhāratīya vīrāṅganāeṁ*.

military clash with her brother Tahar and beheaded him on the battlefield. True, she did not take up the staff of rulership after her husband's death but instead converted her fighting stamina into the kindling of mass conflagration and blazed as a *satī*. Had she stepped onto the throne as a ruling queen, the epic would have taken a different, and more original, course.

The avenging heroine has also appeared in the romantic melodramas focusing on love between a princess and a commoner. In plays such as

Fig. 18. A *vīrāṅganā* from the nineteenth-century stage, reprinted from William Ridgeway, *The Dramas and Dances of Non-European Races* (Cambridge, 1915).

Nauṭaṅkī shāhzādī, Saudāgar vo syāhposh, and *Lākhā bañjārā,* the beloved at the beginning of the narrative is the ethereal beauty, dainty and difficult of access. Like a fairy occupying some realm between heaven and earth, she beckons to the lover from afar, inspiring him to cross boundaries of territory and social class. The ensuing love affair predictably leads to complications. The lover is discovered and sentenced to die for violating the woman's chastity—she is another man's possession. At this point in the dramas, to challenge the king's punishing arm the "violated" woman herself bursts onto the scene in a dark rider's disguise, sword in hand. Sweeping aside the state apparatus of trial and execution, the *vīrāṅganā* effects a justice of her own, which entails the marriage of the lovers according to mutual desire followed by their reintegration into society. The transformation from demure beloved to daredevil swordswoman shocks and confounds: How will the lover relate to such a brash avenger? The question is sidestepped, for the plot requires a dea ex machina, a goddesslike apparition to return the moral balance point to normal after the king's violent reaction to the simple discovery of love.

The *vīrāṅganā*-double in these dramas claims male positions for the female body; she rides on horseback, wears male dress, wields weapons ordinarily carried by men. She is an androgynous counterpart of the Rajput ideal, iconically identical to the male warrior. On the Nauṭaṅkī stage, the visual symbology of cross-dressing arguably possesses voyeuristic appeal, and like other character transformations based on physical disguise it plays into the theatregoer's fascination with illusion and deception. It disturbs gender boundaries and masks in confusion the essential difference between female and male, much to the delight of an audience socialized to rigid codes of gendered dress and gesture.

Yet there is a larger logic to the advent of the *vīrāṅganā* on the Nauṭaṅkī stage that connects this phantasm of female power with an enduring history of womanly fortitude. The *vīrāṅganā* arrives not simply when force is required but when moral order needs to be restored. Like the great goddess, she manifests her creative energy to return the world to righteousness. Hers is not a mission for destruction; her violence is radically different from that of the dangerous stepmothers and decapitating sisters in *Pūranmal, Rūp basant,* and *Triyā charitra.* She exercises her bravery in the cause of justice. Since the upholding of justice is customarily conceived as the duty of the head of state or the king, she bears the symbols of kingly office. The *vīrāṅganā*'s appropriation of masculine signs thus encodes the crossover from the confines of female morality with its emphasis on chastity and chatteldom (women's conventional "truth") to the more spacious morality allowed to males, that is, justice or "Truth."

The most popular *vīrāṅganā* story in the Nauṭaṅkī world appears to be *Vīrāṅganā vīrmatī.*[16]

> King Udiyaditya of Malwa has two wives, Baghelin and Solankin. Baghelin's son is a coward while Jagdev, son of Solankin, is brave and virtuous and his father's favorite. Baghelin fears that Jagdev may soon become king, and she forces the king to insult Jagdev by asking him to return the horse and swords the father had presented to him previously. As a result, Jagdev leaves the court followed by his wife, Virmati, who vows to be at his side no matter what difficulties lie ahead.
>
> After wandering for some time they reach a lake, and Jagdev leaves his wife while he goes to find lodging in the nearby city. Virmati is then approached by a prostitute and enticed to the brothel of Jamoti on the pretext that Jamoti is her husband's sister. Lalji, son of the *kotvāl* (chief of police), tries to seduce Virmati, but she gets him drunk and then kills him with his own sword. She dumps the body from the window, and when the *kotvāl* discovers his dead son, he rushes into the brothel to arrest her. However, Virmati, still holding the sword, proceeds to kill twenty-five of the *kotvāl*'s men. Jagdev eventually finds Virmati and the couple are welcomed by the king of the city.
>
> In the second part, Virmati proves herself capable of even greater courage when she beheads her own husband. Jagdev was tricked by the goddess Kankali into giving her his head, which she demanded as a religious gift (*dān*) in retribution for Jagdev's assault on her son, the demon Kalua. Virmati impresses even the bloodthirsty Kankali with her tearless fulfillment of duty, supplying the head upon demand. Eventually Kankali joins Jagdev's head back to his body and revives him. Through this test, Virmati proves herself to be a true daughter of the goddess, and Kankali addresses her as such while Virmati in return addresses Kankali as mother. In the end, Jagdev and Virmati return home, where Baghelin has repented, and they all live happily.

In the initial part of the narrative, the events uncannily resemble the *Rāmāyaṇa*. The rivalry between co-wives to determine whose son shall be heir, the exit of the favored son with his devoted wife, the wife's abandonment in the forest and her abduction—all parallel the well-known epic. At this point, however, the heroine's similarity to the patient Sita ends. She begins to fight back, using her wits to trick her assailant and then employing his own weapon against him. Inspired by these successes, she proceeds to take on a whole army of men, whom she engages like a lioness with bloodshot eyes and fierce roar. Virmati's bravery is explicitly directed toward protecting her chastity. She is sexually accosted by her captors and responds by unleashing her full powers of self-protection. The tale thus appears to fit with the set of narratives that define women's *sat* or truth in terms of *pativrat dharm*.

In the second half, however, Virmati overrides this interpretation when her higher allegiance to the goddess causes her to offer up her husband's head. She performs the act of decapitation stoically, as a difficult test of devotion to Kankali, unlike the greedy sister in *Bhain bhaiyā* and the lustful Champa in *Triyā charitra,* who also killed their own men. In consequence of her sacrifice, she earns the goddess's favor and the ultimate restoration of her husband's life. This incident makes evident the *vīrāṅganā*'s adherence to a higher truth than that prescribed by the customary gender ideology. Setting aside the passive behavior recommended to the epic wife, Virmati assumes heroic stature through active intervention in the events of the world and in so doing moves beyond the morality of husband worship and feminine modesty to the transcendent position of daughter of the goddess.

The fascination with warrior women in Nauṭaṅkī, especially in the years from 1910 to 1940, may be historically contextualized by reference to government restrictions on nationalist messages that were widely imposed on the print and entertainment media. Legislation incorporated into the Registration Act of 1867, the Dramatic Performances Act of 1876, the Vernacular Press Act of 1878, and the Press Act of 1910 formalized censorship of printed literature (dramatic texts, novels, and poems) as well as public performances, with severe consequences for any activity deemed seditious. Meanwhile, as the nineteenth-century sense of nationhood grew, a political symbolism developed in which female heroes and goddesses acquired significance. In Bengal, novelists such as Bankim Chandra Chatterjee reinstated the goddess as Mother India, savior of the future Indian nation. Slightly later in the Gangetic heartland, the legendary figure of the Rani of Jhansi became the symbol of resistance to colonial rule because of her perceived leadership of the 1857 rebellion against the British. The image of the Rani riding on horseback became so potent a rallying point for nationalist resistance that articles, poems, plays, and even Vrindavan Lal Varma's Hindi novel on the Rani's life were immediately banned upon publication.[17] Denied open reference to heroes like Lakshmibai, the public turned to fictional heroines from popular culture to voice their anticolonial sentiments. The popularity of the *vīrāṅganā* stories thus is partially attributable to their allegorical political meaning.

This process extended to the early cinema, for when Indian films began to displace the folk theatre in the 1920s and 1930s, a veritable spate on *vīrāṅganā* themes emerged. Some of these examined historical women warriors: silent movies of the 1920s and early 1930s include *Sati Veermat, Devi Ahalyabai,* and *Sultana Chand Bibi;* later talking versions were released of *Tara Sundari, Sultana Chand Bibi, Taramati,* and films on the Rajput heroines Padmini, Pannabai, and Minaldevi. Others featured more fanciful *vīrāṅganā*s; sample titles include *A Fair Warrior, Veerangana, Gallant Girl, Valiant Princess, Lioness,* and *Stree Shakti.*[18] Worthy of special mention are the films that star the actress Nadia: *Hunterwali, Sher Dil, Lutaru Lalna, Diamond Queen,* and others. In these Nadia plays the valiant heroine coming to the rescue, her most frequent entrance being on horseback. Stills from her films show her carrying every conceivable weapon—bow and arrow, sword, bullwhip, and pistol—as well as lifting men over her head and throwing them. The theatrical origins of Nadia's roles are suggested in the films' narratives, which typically focus on a besieged kingdom and include a restoration of righteousness at the eleventh hour by a daring princess.[19]

The most recent variation on the *vīrāṅganā* theme in Nauṭaṅkī is the female outlaw figure, the gendered equivalent of the dacoit hero discussed in chapter 5. Just as in folklore the dacoit (*ḍākū*) is like a king to followers and villagers within his territory, so the "bandit queen" (*dasyu sundarī*) shares the symbolic character of sovereignty with the historical queen. She is a woman of indomitable courage, a merciless executrix of justice. Former *vīrāṅganā*s defended their kingdoms against enemies of opposing ethnic and religious affiliation; the female outlaw of the twentieth century fights the police, landlords, and the wealthy in order to defend the rights of the poor and oppressed. Since the 1960s and 1970s, she is increasingly a low-caste heroine, in alliance with the disprivileged in rural society, in opposition to Brahmins, Ṭhākurs (members of the landlord caste), and government officials.

The female outlaw as a subtype of the *vīrāṅganā* appeared in several films of the thirties, for example, *Lady Robinhood, The Amazon,* and *Dacoit Damsel.* Numerous legends also grew up around Putli Bai, a famous one-armed dacoit of the 1950s.[20] Most widely publicized has been the story of Phulan Devi. Her career has been reported in *Time* and *Esquire* on the one hand and on the other has inspired Hindi Nauṭaṅkīs, *bārahmāsī*s, *birahā*s, and other folklore genres.[21] Several Bombay films have been produced about her, including the rather faithful version of her life, *Kahānī phūlvatī kī.* Clay idols of Phulan are sold together with images of gods and goddesses in local markets.[22] Her impact has been such that other women of her region have increasingly turned to banditry, and by 1986 gangs considered it de rigueur to have at least one female member.[23]

The following synopsis, based on the Nauṭaṅkī version by Svaminath, closely follows other folk and media sources.[24]

> Phulan was born a Mallāh (of the boatman caste) in a village in Jalaun district. When she was ten, her father married her to Puttilal, a lustful widower twenty years older. Escaping from him, Phulan returned to her village but was expelled by the panchayat. She went to live with an uncle whose sons and friends harassed and raped her. Seeking refuge with a cousin, she then met Kailash, a spy employed by the bandit Babu Gujar. Kailash and Phulan fell in love and got married, but Kailash later offered her to his friend Vikram and the gang leader for their sexual enjoyment.
>
> Visiting home, Phulan was falsely implicated in a robbery and was arrested by the police. She was repeatedly assaulted in custody. Released through the good graces of a Ṭhākur, she was afterwards forced to become his concubine. Kailash meanwhile had been killed by the police, and Phulan came under Vikram's protection. After killing Babu Gujar, Vikram established himself as gang leader with Phulan as his mistress. He taught her to shoot, and the two began a series of robberies and murders in the Chambal region.
>
> Internal feuding in the gang led to Vikram being killed by Sriram and Lalaram, two Ṭhākur gang members. They kidnapped Phulan Devi, took her to Behmai village, and kept her captive for twenty-two days while a number of Ṭhākurs raped her. Finally she escaped, hitting her guard in the face with a waterpot when she went to the fields to defecate.
>
> She met Mustaqim, a bandit of Robin Hood–like reputation, and they formed a new gang. They returned to Behmai to avenge the murder of Vikram and repay the Ṭhākurs for dishonoring Phulan. Phulan oversaw the selection of the men who raped her, led them to the edge of the river, slapped them and spat in their faces, and had them killed. She killed twenty-seven people in Behmai village, although Sriram and Lalaram were absent at the time. The police were busy playing volleyball, and by the time they arrived, Phulan and Mustaqim had escaped. The play ends with Phulan in hiding.

As told in the Nauṭaṅkī, the central theme of Phulan's life is repeated victimization, particularly sexual abuse. In multiple assaults, Phulan is looted of her chastity ("to rape" in Hindi is *izzat lūṭnā*, "to steal one's honor"). Phulan eventually turns to resistance and counterattack against the perpetrators; she takes to robbing and looting in return. The drama's obsessive concern with Phulan's sexual exploitation seems intended to supply an unambiguous moral ground for her violent deeds. She too is to be understood as a heroine defending her *sat,* the distinctive truth identified with the female body. But Phulan's struggle, like that of Virmati, is not simply a private affair. This drama introduces the perspective of class and caste, insofar as Phulan and the audience understand her violation to be a specific case of the more general violation of the poor and weak by the wealthy and powerful. A low-caste Mallāh, Phulan endures rape many times by upper-caste men, and it is toward them that she explicitly directs her avenging fury. As she states in the play, "Ṭhākurs have done whatever they wanted with me. High-caste men always played with my honor. Not until I shoot them all one by one will their oppression of me be repaid."[25]

In the popular imagination then, Phulan is a wronged woman. Like other *vīrāṅganā*s, she resorts to violence to restore her own and the larger world to moral order. Her act of truth extends, as it were, the physical boundaries of her own body to encompass others in her disprivileged position. She blends the examples of the historical queens—who defended their persons, their peoples, their kingdoms—with the male robbers who usurp authority in order to redistribute wealth within the underclass. A modern-day equivalent of the turbaned, sword-wielding *vīrāṅganā,* Phulan wears the khaki uniform of a police superintendent, a headband tied around her cropped hair and a rifle slung over her shoulder. She continues the narrative tradition of valiant women who protect themselves and also serve a higher morality through their own bloody deeds.

Beyond the dramatic text, Phulan's image has provoked a range of responses in the mass media in India and abroad. One reaction is to portray her as a dangerous but irresistible man-eater. *Esquire* described her as "a legendary six-foot-tall, raven-haired, one-armed beauty," "a beautiful femme fatale who had butchered twice as many men as she had bedded."[26] There is no doubt that a genuine terror of her (as of dacoits in general) existed in the countryside in the months following the Behmai massacre and preceding her capture in 1983. Yet we must deconstruct this representation in the light of folk narratives that portray female agency as dangerous and specifically as a sexual threat. The sensational reports of Phulan's ravishing appearance (proven false after her capture) parallel depictions in tales like *Pūranmal*—where Phulan's namesake is both attractive *and* sexually aggressive toward men. In the masculinist construction, be it folk theatre or popular journalism, female qualities such as strength and firm will that may challenge male domination are transposed into images of seductiveness in order to diminish their moral legitimacy.

It is noteworthy that Phulan has at the same time become a symbol of feminist resistance to rural women, cosmopolitan urban Indians, and women abroad. Phulan has removed the gender gap among Chambal Valley gangs; she and her sister bandits, Kusuma Nain, Meera Thakur, and others have been called "beacons of hope for countless young women who have a score to settle with society."[27] In Bombay and Delhi, Phulan "appeared to represent the ideas expressed by such feminists as Kate Millett, Betty Friedan, and Germaine Greer," rejecting the traditionally subservient position of the Indian female.[28] Her history has entered Western feminist annals via playwrights and artists such as Hélène Cixous and Carel Moiseiwitsch who have reimagined Phulan in their artistic productions.[29] The feminist response comments on and celebrates the truth contained at several levels in Phulan's life. As a revised *strī charitra* ("herstory"), Phulan's narrative acknowledges the injustice of society toward women, names the acts of violence committed by men against them, and asserts the power of women to survive abuse, defend themselves, and struggle for survival. However inadequate the Behmai killings may have been to bring gender equality to even a single village, they assume global proportions through the affirmative feminist reception of the legend of Phulan, the 1980s avatar of the *vīrāṅganā*.

Widows, Unwed Mothers, and Working Women

By the time Phulan Devi came into the public eye, women in North Indian society had begun to emerge from domestic seclusion. Beginning in the 1920s and in growing numbers during the decades following independence, women took their places beside men in schools and colleges, the workplace, and public life. The greater visibility of women and official encouragement for their increased participation hastened the changes proposed in nationalist agendas for social reform. In the 1930s and 1940s, both Nauṭaṅkī folk plays and Bombay films began to treat issues of feminist import, developing roles for women unthinkable several decades earlier. In this final section we examine three Nauṭaṅkī texts that address the topics of widow remarriage, unwed mothers and illegitimate children, and poor working women.

The moral dilemmas ensuing from gender-specific codes of sexual behavior that began this chapter's discussion reappear in two dramas, *Dukhiyā vidhvā* (The miserable widow) and *Dhūl kā phūl* (Flower in the dust). To varying degrees, these plays expose the injustice of prereform social practices. *The Miserable Widow* is a narrative set within the Seth mercantile class of Bombay and focuses on an atypical family consisting of a father, his two sons, and three widows: his widowed daughter, his widowed daughter-in-law, and a widow who is the mistress of his second son. By the end of the melodrama, one son has died of asthma and the other has been disinherited, while of the three widows, one has killed herself by jumping into a well and another has been run over by her brother's car. Although the drama ostensibly campaigns for allowing widows to remarry, these catastrophes reinforce the popular belief that widows are unruly and that their inauspicious presence brings bad fortune on the family.

> Ramnik Lal, a big businessman, lives with his two sons, Hari Das and Arun Kumar, and his widowed daughter, Raj Rani. Arun is in love with Usha, a widow, and he opposes the social prohibition against women's remarrying when men may marry as many times as they like. He decides to persuade his father to allow Raj Rani's remarriage, hoping it will pave the way for his own marriage with Usha. His father, however, is outraged and tells him not to even think of it.
>
> Raj Rani persuades the family doctor to become her lover, and they meet daily. Hari Das, who suffers from asthma, is to marry Chandra. Arun protests that this marriage will ruin the life of the girl, for Hari Das will soon die, but his father proceeds anyway; shortly after the wedding Chandra becomes a widow. Chandra is unhappy, and she and Raj Rani often have tiffs. Chandra gets scolded unjustly, and Arun takes her side against his father.
>
> Arun discovers the doctor and Raj Rani together in her room. When he reports this to his father, Raj Rani accuses Arun of pursuing Chandra. Ramnik Lal disowns Arun and expels him and Chandra from the house. Since Chandra's parents will not accept her back, Arun takes her to Usha's house, and he goes out to look for work. Meanwhile, the doctor visits Usha, and he alleges misbehavior between Arun and Chandra. Usha expels Chandra, and when Arun returns he goes out to find her.
>
> Raj Rani leaves her house to search for the doctor, but when she finds him he refuses to have anything more to do with her. In public, he then accuses Chandra, who is passing by, of making advances to him. Arun arrives and believes the malicious gossip about Chandra. In desperation, she jumps into a well and dies.
>
> Raj Rani is furious at the rejection by the doctor and stabs him to death. Running away, she is knocked down by a truck. She is taken

> home and sheltered by a sweeper. The police come after Raj Rani and as she flees from them, she dashes against the moving car of Arun and Usha and dies. Arun is miserable at his sister's death and promises to take up the fight for widows' remarriage. The bill allowing widows to remarry is passed in the assembly, and no reactionary pandit is able to put a stop to it.[30]

The chief advocate of widows' remarriage in this drama is Arun; his father, Ramnik Lal, represents the views of the orthodox. Arun is motivated by personal interest, namely his desire to marry his girlfriend Usha, and by sympathy for his widowed sister, Raj Rani, and later for his sister-in-law, Chandra. Arun is a prototypical male champion of women's rights. During the period of legislative reforms in the late nineteenth and early twentieth centuries, elite men took up the banner of female emancipation while few women agitated openly or received notice in the body politic. The Nauṭaṅkī drama, like most fictional documents of the period, does not express women's feelings about widowhood or articulate their experience. The sympathy it arouses for widows stems from patriarchal views of female sexuality and the assumed necessity of marriage and family life to women's happiness. The principal threat to the widows' well-being in *The Miserable Widow* is abandonment, specifically expulsion from the husband's home with no prospect of parental support. This perilous state does befall Chandra; left homeless, she falls prey to gossip and commits suicide in her anguish. Raj Rani, a more determined woman, runs away to be with the doctor. Finding herself unsheltered, she moves in with a sweeper family and earns her keep removing offal from the streets—a slap in the face of her high-caste father.

Named in the subtitle, Raj Rani is the most striking character. She could easily stand with Phulan of *Pūranmal;* sexually active, strong-willed and argumentative, she undermines family harmony with unruly conduct that leads to her own unnatural demise. Rejecting the lifelong celibacy and invisibility expected of widows by tradition, she stages a love affair right in her father's house, quarrels with her sister-in-law Chandra, and falsely accuses her brother, causing his and Chandra's exile from the family. Like the lustful young stepmother, she experiences boundless rage when her lover rejects her, and she murders him out of spite. Inevitably she comes to no good end. She dies in an accident fatefully involving the car of the brother whom she misused and who tried to aid her.

Raj Rani reacquaints the audience with the tenacity of the thwarted female. Her example both mirrors and maintains society's paranoia about unattached and unconfinable women, especially young widows. Chandra on the other hand plays the good widow in following the normative code of meekness and modesty. Her weakness sends forth signals calling for male protection, yet she is repeatedly victimized, ostracized, and left defenseless. Here the stereotype of woman as physically powerless (*abalā nārī,* "the weaker sex") buttresses the ideology of male superiority. The third widow, Usha, the partner of Arun, remains a shadowy figure throughout; even though a law passes allowing widows to marry, Arun and Usha do not get married.

The case for widows' remarriage sketched by these events in no wise challenges the system of male privilege or prevailing notions of woman's nature. Remarriage for women is urged because women can neither control nor support themselves. Their happiness depends not just on the presence of a husband; it requires the confinement and restraint provided by male dominance. The inequitable practices surrounding remarriage are explained away as the rigidity of social custom, not questioned as part of a reexamination of gender roles. As a result, although the drama purports to hold a progressive viewpoint, it portrays women in the same androcentric mode as most folktales. It reiterates attitudes of distrust, fear, and condemnation of widowed women as it extends them a modicum of condescending support.

In the somewhat more satisfying *Flower in the Dust,* discussed in chapter 6 in relation to Hindu-Muslim unity, the sexual advantage accorded men through multiple liaisons is forthrightly condemned. A respected citizen for years denies his paternity of an illegitimate child, but he is exposed in court and blamed for the sufferings of his wayward son and the son's mother. The narrative takes us into the urban middle class, where the college student Meena endures rebuffs and reverses after she and Mahesh fall in love. When she tells him of her pregnancy, Mahesh abandons her to marry another woman. Subsequently Meena gets thrown out by her aunt and uncle (she is already an orphan), tries to commit suicide, is rescued by Nandu Dai (a midwife and naive advocate of women's rights), and then is left alone when Nandu Dai dies. After her son is born, she returns to Mahesh to plea for support; he spurns her. Distraught, she leaves the baby in the forest and returns to the city to start life anew.

Despite the pain of rejection, Meena responds to her position with resourcefulness. She is neither reduced to a victim's passivity nor embittered by anger. The drama accords her dignity, and she pursues a pragmatic course, becoming a secretary to a barrister and eventually marrying him. In the drama's terms, neither Mahesh nor Meena is particularly to blame for the youthful sexual encounter; they both regret it as a momentary lapse. Mahesh becomes culpable when he turns against Meena and distances himself from her through deceit. He promises to ask her father for her hand, but he never does and from then on clings to a lie, disclaiming any connection with Meena. He refuses to help support his child although he is wealthy and Meena at that point is penniless. Pretending even to himself that he never sired a son, he chides his legitimate offspring, Ramesh, for befriending a schoolmate born out of wedlock (who happens to be Roshan, Mahesh's son by Meena). In court he claims that youthful criminal tendencies result from illegitimate birth and prepares to convict the unlucky Roshan until Meena's intervention reveals his own implication in the events.

In the restoration of moral order at the drama's climax, Mahesh is accused not only by Meena, who calls him a culprit for deserting her and remarrying, but by Malti, Mahesh's "second wife," who holds him indirectly responsible for the death of her son who she thinks was killed by Meena's curse. Mahesh repents and expresses willingness to welcome his illegitimate son back into the family, but the child ultimately goes with Meena; Mahesh, who once had two sons, is left heirless at the end of the play. The familial interrelationships here of husband, first wife, second wife, and two wives' sons curiously resemble the configurations found in *Pūranmal, Rūp basant,* and even the *Rāmāyaṇa*. In all these narratives, the husband in some sense abandons his first wife to marry a second, and in so doing opens up a chasm that leads to the traumatic separation of both parents from the son and a period of exile and wandering. Whereas in the older narratives the second wife has responsibility for the rupture, in *Dhūl kā phūl* the man bears the burden of guilt. The prior stories raise certain questions: Should the sexual behavior of men be governed by the same self-control as that of women? Should not a single standard of moral conduct apply to both? But those dramas prevaricate, introducing an unrighteous female as scapegoat for the erring hero. The twentieth-century Nauṭaṅkī, on the other hand, asserts the complicity of the polygynous husband in the spawning of unwanted children. The niceties of legal marriage do not absolve him of the moral consequences of his procreative acts, and he is brought to book for failing in his duty to protect his rejected kin.

These two dramas to some extent rework the moral issues surrounding male-female relationships, presenting modified guidelines within well defined problem areas (remarriage for widows, unwed motherhood). Men are asked to assume responsibility for women's welfare where women were once fated to suffer. There is no hint that women should claim the use of their bodies as a right or engage in sexual transactions according to their own desire. Sexuality is still hedged in by fear and danger, and the recommended attitude toward it is control and repression. The difference is that women are no longer automatically perceived as transgressors and condemned. Men are brought into focus as sexual players, becoming culpable for their actions. This may not seem a great advance for women's rights or for the acceptance of human sexuality. Nonetheless, these Nauṭaṅkī texts register the gradual dismantling of the fixation on female chastity, a cornerstone of the ideology that has obstructed the progress of women for centuries.

The last drama renews the discussion of woman's relationship to her affinal and natal families, an area of conflicted loyalty explored in a previous group of tales. In *Satī bindiyā* (The saintly Bindiya), the audience encounters not only a lower-class heroine but a working woman, successful wife and sister, and latter-day *satī* who holds together two families through the power of her goodness.

> Devraj works as an overseer for the contractor Rai Sahib, and among the laborers in his construction gang is Bindiya. Devraj has an errant brother, Raju, who is always in trouble at school; there is some mystery surrounding their parents. Bindiya is the sole support of her mother and her brothers, Chandan and Ramu. Devraj and Bindiya fall in love, and Devraj proposes to marry Bindiya, giving assurances to her family that he will care for them as well. Devraj marries her and brings her family home, assisting her brothers in finding jobs and schooling. Bindiya becomes a housewife, and when Devraj's fortunes increase, he credits it to the good luck she has brought to the home.
>
> Raju continues in his bad ways, stealing money from the Rai Sahib. Whereas Devraj usually beats his brother, Bindiya curbs him through kindness and instruction. Her brother Ramu is in direct contrast to Raju. An excellent student, he completes his B.A. and starts an engineering course. The Rai Sahib wants Ramu to marry his daughter Rama, but Ramu wishes to establish himself first.
>
> Devraj's past returns to haunt him when his stepmother and stepsister descend on the family after his father's death. Without revealing their identity, he takes them home where Bindiya readily agrees to shelter them. A wall in the newly constructed house literally cracks. The two women begin to alienate Devraj from Bindiya's family members.
>
> Meanwhile, Raju has decided he must marry Rama, and he appeals to Bindiya to give her consent. Bindiya requests her brother Ramu to

> forget Rama for the sake of family harmony, and he agrees. However, Rama and the Rai Sahib disapprove of the plan.
>
> Devraj's stepsister continues to create trouble in the family, and soon she acquires all the household keys. Raju steals a ring from Rama and drops it in Ramu's pocket, causing him to be falsely arrested. Finally, thanks to his female relatives' scheming, Devraj comes to suspect even Bindiya's fidelity, and he expels her and her brothers from the house. He realizes his error when he overhears the women complimenting each other on their victory.
>
> Devraj goes to find Bindiya, giving the women an opportunity to run off with all the valuables, but Raju appears in the nick of time to prevent the theft. All are forgiven and persuaded to return home, and Bindiya prevents Devraj's stepmother and sister from being handed over to the police. Rama and Ramu get married, a bride is found for Raju, and the play ends happily.[31]

This remarkably contemporary Nauṭaṅkī at first seems to give voice to female experience in a way not seen before. The heroine Bindiya is financially self-supporting, the provider for her mother and two brothers. Because of her family's dependence on her, her future husband must propose a more generous offer in exchange for her consent to marriage. Her family members accompany her into her new home, and she avoids the pain of separation from them experienced by most newly married women. Furthermore, they are hardworking and talented as well as devoted to her. Her brother is so upwardly mobile that her husband's boss proposes to marry his daughter to him. Her husband, although a capable man himself, is saddled with a miscreant brother and devious female relatives. The balance between the two families, usually tilted toward the husband by rules of hypergamy and patrilocality, favors the woman in this case. This may reflect the actualities of marital and economic relations among the working poor, where women arguably enjoy more independence than in the middle class. Uncharacteristically, the couple has no children, and this presents no problem. The attention that would be directed to bringing up children goes to the younger brothers of both the husband and wife.

Whatever the source of these initial anomalies, the emphasis of the drama eventually (and quite predictably) shifts to the virtue of the faithful wife and her ability to lessen discord through self-sacrifice. Naturally Bindiya quits her job as soon as her marriage is settled, molding herself easily to the role of housewife even though she once enjoyed financial security and independence. (Her job as a construction worker may not have been very enviable.) She still resides with her mother and brothers, but devotion to her husband becomes her foremost duty, and at crucial moments she sides with him and even the delinquent Raju rather than appearing to favor her own family. For some time, her forbearance and good counsel keep harmony and bring welfare to everyone, but ultimately she meets her match in Devraj's stepmother and stepsister. Bindiya's downfall is engineered by the jealousy of these outsiders, an example of women's supposed inability to coexist with one another in the joint family. Much as Sita did on her return from Lanka to Rama, Bindiya silently accepts her husband's command to leave home; through this self-sacrificing move she finally brings about a change of heart among all members of the family.

In mapping Bindiya's virtue and the steprelations' villainy, the drama resorts to comfortable categories of womanhood. Although she begins the drama as a laborer, a sort of lower-class heroine, Bindiya comes into her own only after marriage. Her name, which refers to the *bindī* or cosmetic dot on a woman's forehead, connotes the auspicious state of matrimony, a state enjoyed by women as long as their husbands live. Despite her impoverished origins, Bindiya fulfills the expectations associated with middle-class housewives, becoming a *grihlakṣhmī*, a manifestation of the goddess Lakshmi in the home (*grih*). According to this ideal, a woman's modesty and domestic talents bring prosperity, respect, and good luck on a household—the very opposite of what happens in the family containing three widows. By a materialistic but entirely accepted logic, the virtues of the *grihlakṣhmī* are measured by the family's increasing fortunes. Devraj's promotion, Ramu's academic success, and his engagement to Rama are all attributed to Bindiya's correct performance of wifely duties. The interloping second wife of Devraj's father and her daughter are as thoroughly evil as Bindiya is good. Their status as steprelations immediately discredits their motives; everything suggests that they intend to destroy the hero's happiness and rob him of his wealth. This polarization of roles indicates that even if a feminist imagination inspired Bindiya's worker status, it is one highly restricted by the conventional paradigms. Searching for a vocabulary of feminine excellence, the author invokes the ideology of self-sacrifice and the auspiciousness of marriage, as in situating discord and malice he latches onto the stereotype of the greedy stepmother. The drama thus shies away from the implications of Bindiya's independence and moral strength, redirecting her toward the nurture and instruction of those present in her home. It redefines the *satī* as a contemporary housewife perfect in her performance of domestic duty.

In this overview of Nauṭaṅkī's representation of women, the more recent examples show that women have begun to act differently from their mythical forebears. They seek higher education, have premarital sex, even become unwed mothers—and then marry and lead comfortable lives. They work side by side with men at rough outdoor jobs and raise families on their earnings—yet still maintain their virtue and status. Some are in the unfortunate position of being widowed, although this does not prevent them from seeking comfort, love, and remarriage. All these behaviors would have been considered disreputable several decades earlier; there is reason to believe that for many Nauṭaṅkī spectators they still touch chords of surprise or even outrage. Perhaps the biggest change is that most of these women survive: they stumble and fall but pick themselves up and keep going.

Looked at in this way, these texts suggest a stage of protofeminism that holds up for emulation positively valorized changes in women's lives. Certainly the cracks visible in the moral worlds of earlier narratives have widened. Male characters have lost the exclusive shelter of masculine privilege, and female characters have become capable of a range of initiatory, mediatory, and retaliatory behavior. The ground of moral action is still intersected by planes of contention, but the small space allotted to female-specific moral duty has expanded, and the larger arena of masculine righteousness has shrunk.

Yet we cannot but notice—and question—the texts' reinstatement of patriarchal concepts of womanhood. *Abalā nārī, satī, grihlakṣhmī,* and even the musty old *pativrat dharm* return in force although women get stronger, louder, and more visible. These "modern" heroines may not leave the stage in burial shrouds or flames as their ancestresses did, but whenever they can they pair off, get married, and raise families. Meena weds the barrister and reunites with her child; Bindiya reconciles with Devraj's nasty relatives, and both her son Ramu and his son Raju find brides; meanwhile not one of the widows (poor things) sees the face of a second husband. These unions are not just felicitous plot-closers. Each story, propelled in one direction by the winds of female emancipation, comes back to the culturally imposed necessity of male protection and guidance. Without it, female existence is unmanageable and unimaginable. Bindiya's evolution from construction worker to domestic angel is perhaps the best example of the circle back to patriarchy. The same narrative impulse guides Meena's path from unwed motherhood into the barrister's arms, and the absence of male protection leads Raj Rani and Chandra astray.

The reaffirmation of marital and family values so apparent in these recent Nauṭaṅkī tales summarizes the consensus achieved in contemporary Indian society on the "woman issue." Women are now allowed to get education, to work and bring in money for the family, and even occasionally to follow their hearts in love and marriage. But marriage remains a universal norm. Life without a male guardian is still an untenable proposition for all but the most adventuresome and resilient of women. Although the legal status of women continues to improve under the impact of feminist activism, the social conditions of women's lives are limiting and often oppressive. Remarriage for widows remains a near impossibility, divorce is available only under certain circumstances, and neither female celibacy nor childlessness is valorized as a choice. Women are constrained by male relations even when through some misfortune a husband is not present.

Within marriage the expected role for women is graceful submission and support. The tried-and-true concepts of *pativratā, abalā nārī,* and *grihlakṣhmī* continue to inform the socialization of young girls, shaping their self-image in adulthood. These ideals not only exert great influence on the reproduction of gender roles from generation to generation; they have become part of the distinctive cultural identity of a large section of the public in the postcolonial period. Viewed in this context, the more recent Nauṭaṅkī dramas do not simply expose viewers to modernity and teach them to adjust to change in women's roles. They advocate a modern *and* Indian response to change as opposed to an alienating and Westernizing response. To obliterate entirely the traditional vocabulary of womanhood might entail a deep cultural excision, a profound injury to national self-respect. But for how long can an emerging, purportedly secular and democratic, nation afford to base its sense of cultural distinctiveness on an ancient patriarchal ideology? This is a question with implications for millions of women's lives, and one that demands serious reflection from the architects of cultural policy, the designers and critics of culture, and the scholarly and feminist communities alike.

CHAPTER EIGHT

Melody, Meter, and the Musical Medium

The theatre, and especially the operatic or musical theatre, possesses a complex system of communication, combining in one integrated medium a number of separate subsystems. The union in theatre of various visual and auditory media was intimated by Bharata in the *Nāṭyaśāstra,* when he described how Brahma borrowed the best element of each of the four Vedas to fabricate his invention. To Bharata's *pāṭhya* (verbal recitation), *gīta* (music and song), *abhinaya* (gestures and movement), and *rasa* (sentiments and emotions) we might add other systems of theatrical communication: costumes and makeup, curtains and scenery, uses of space, props, and sound effects. The interplay of these systems creates a sensory bombardment, enriching levels of meaning and contributing both to theatre's distinctive identity and to its effect on an audience. In the vocabulary of semiotics, we can say that theatre engages the spectator by means of a "surplus of signifiers."[1] From this profusion of coded messages, we isolate different symbol sets or systems.

Even a preliminary overview of the traditional theatres of India suggests that these multiple systems of communication are ordered into hierarchies that vary from theatre to theatre. Abstract masks and songless speechless mime dominate the Seraikella Chhau of Bihar, while the shifting use of municipal space flavors the grand Rām Līlā at Ramnagar in Uttar Pradesh. In the Kuchipuḍi theatre (Andhra Pradesh) and the Bhāgavatamelā (Tanjore district, Tamilnadu), elaborate dance and stylized hand gestures prevail. Spectacular headdresses, costumes, and color-coded makeup distinguish both the Kathakaḷi theatre of Kerala and the Yakṣhagāna of Karnataka.

In Nauṭaṅkī, I contend, it is the music that constitutes the most important nonverbal system of communication, ranking above dance, acting techniques, or visual symbolism as a signifier of meaning. Further, the musical system of Nauṭaṅkī separates it from performance traditions that share its narratives, serving as a determinant of genre. A Nauṭaṅkī play based on the *Ālhā* story can be identified by its own music, different from that of an *Ālhā* epic recitation; the music similarly gives away a Nauṭaṅkī performance occurring at the edges of a Rās Līlā festival. Music in its alliance with poetic meter is the principal source of Nauṭaṅkī's aesthetic impact on its audience. The sound of Nauṭaṅkī resides in the hearer's consciousness, giving melody and rhythm to remembered snatches of words, aiding in their acquisition and retention. Musical and metrical structures weave through Nauṭaṅkī's treasury of hundreds of tales, conferring a unity on an outsized body of folklore. Furthermore, as Nauṭaṅkī has formed and reformed in the last hundred or more years, it is the music that has most clearly registered the radical shift in the relations between folk theatre and society.

This chapter treats first the more obvious features of Nauṭaṅkī's music: its distinctive instruments and vocal idiom, the manner in which singing and drumming combine, and the broad divisions of the sung text. The intention is to show that theatrical music constitutes a distinct category within the broader field of the Hindustani (North Indian) musical system, and that without being a classical style it incorporates certain features of the classical system and occupies a separate position comparable to folk music, popular music, or film music.[2] Proceeding from this is a more detailed examination of musical organization, including metrical and melodic analysis of the principal couplet and stanza forms and the variants and rhythmic patterns associated with them. A number of notational examples, possibly of greater interest to the musicologist than the lay reader, accompany this discussion. The musical analysis here supports the hypothesis that in theatre, as in recitational music forms, melodic construction is to a great extent determined by metrical composition within the larger parameters of regional style, historical period, and performative genre. The final section discusses the social, economic, and technological impacts on the traditional theatres, with reference to irrevocable changes in the structure and function of their music. Over the last hundred years, the context for Nauṭaṅkī music has altered from patron-supported open competition to production of a commercially-oriented commodity. Remnants of the historically discrete musical styles now coexist. The older Hathras style, to the extent that it survives, has maintained the improvised character and agonistic ethos of the traditional art, while in the Kanpur style and on recorded disks and cassettes, the music has become standardized, melodically and metrically simplified, and commodified to meet very different market conditions and listener expectations.

Music for the Outdoor Stage

We approach the overall character of Nauṭaṅkī music through consideration of the material culture of the folk stage and its requirements for communication. Until very recently, shows were performed outdoors mainly at night—on temporarily erected stages or platforms, on porches in market areas, in courtyards, or in tented arenas at fairs. Three sides of the stage were generally open to the public, and large crowds gathered, as many as ten thousand spectators by some accounts. In the absence of electricity and amplification, the foremost demand was that the music and voices of actor-singers be audible. Hearing was even more important than seeing, because sightlines would have been obstructed for many in the throng. Probably for these reasons, Nauṭaṅkī like other traditional theatres favored instruments with piercing timbres. The core of the Nauṭaṅkī ensemble consisted of a high-pitched reed instrument, such as the indigenous *shahnāī*, a relative of the oboe, or later the imported clarinet. Rhythm was maintained by the booming *nagāṛā*, a kettledrum played with sticks, supported by a second higher-pitched *nagāṛā* or a *ḍholak*, a popular double-faced hand-drum (figs. 19 and 20).

The *shahnāī* and *nagāṛā* were traditionally part of a processional ensemble known as the *naubat*, whose role was to lead military parades and announce the watches of the day in royal palaces.[3] As used in Nauṭaṅkī theatre, the *naubat* served first in its original function as marching band. It announced the show, playing in procession in the town or village beforehand and at the commencement of the evening's entertainment while the audience was assembling. Second, it served as "orchestra," accompanying the singers during the drama. Even today, the loud, rapid-fire drumming of the *nagāṛā* sums up the heroic and martial character of Nauṭaṅkī and serves as its ubiquitous trademark.[4] The thin piping tone of the *shahnāī*, by contrast, alerts the listener to

गत हरियाणा

सांगीत ओडकी का

गुरु मानसिंह जोगी साकिन सहदपुर जिला रोहतक के शिष्य
बणजारा मिठ्ठनलाल चुन्नीलाल कृत।

प्रकाशक—शम्भूदयाल दीनानाथ बुकसेलर, दरीबा कलाँ देहली।

शम्भूदयाल दीनानाथ के प्रबन्ध से दीनानाथ प्रेस
दरीबा कलाँ देहली में छपी।

Fig. 19. Title page of *Sāṅgīt oḍakī kā* by Mitthan Lal and Chunni Lal (Delhi, 1932). Musical instruments (left to right): *sāraṅgī*, harmonium, *ḍholak*. By permission of the British Library.

Fig. 20. Musical ensemble from *Amar siṁh rāṭhor*. Musical instruments (left to right): *nagāṛā*, *sāraṅgī*, *ḍholak*. By permission of the Sangeet Natak Akademi.

the romantic and feminine side of the theatre, signaling in particular the flirtatious games (*nakhre*) of the dancer-actress.

As with the instruments, the singing of the actors had to be very loud to project to the crowds. To reach this goal they cultivated an open-throated, forceful vocal style, dwelling primarily in the upper register (fig. 21). The recitatives of Nauṭaṅkī typically begin on the tonic in the upper octave and wind their way gradually downward to close on the lower tonic. The melodic "shadow" provided by the accompanying instrument anticipates the beginning, leading up to the high tonic at the end of the preceding phrase. Holding the breath on high notes is considered a feat of virtuosity, earning outbursts of praise from the audience.[5] At climactic moments, the singer conveys dramatic bursts of emotion by exploring the uppermost notes in his or her register; they are the ones most likely to cut through the ambient noise in the performance area and make an impact on the listeners. Male singers, especially female impersonators, may employ a falsetto voice quality. The most virtuosic Nauṭaṅkī singing is characterized by stirring florid passages charged with an almost erotic excess, an operatic overflow of passion. Rapid ornamental turns, melismatic ascents and descents, and other flourishes are used to adorn the vocal line and are much prized. The vibrato effects common to choral Sufi singing (*qavvālī*) and the folk singing of Haryana, Rajasthan, or the Punjab are usually absent.

The particular musical interaction that occurs between the singer-actors and the instrumental ensemble in Nauṭaṅkī reflects the demands of communication in an outdoor setting. Three types of poetic discourse characterize Nauṭaṅkī's sung text: these are narrative, dialogue, and lyric. Prose passages may also be introduced into the verbal texture but are never sung. Narrative and dialogue carry the forward movement of the story and must be clearly enunciated for audience comprehension. Perhaps for this reason, overlap between singers and instrumentalists in these sections is reduced to a minimum. The poetic lines are delivered one by one in recitative style, with percussion and the less audible melodic instruments entering after each line is concluded. These passages produce an antiphonal structure between the singer and the instrumental ensemble, the two alternating and taking turns throughout. During the recitative, the singer's meter does not follow the framework of *tāla* (rhythm cycle), as it would in Hindustani vocal music. He or she spontaneously matches the short and long weights of the metered line to the standard contours of the appropriate melody or freely improvises on an end rhyme using melismatic ornamentation. As soon as the singer fin-

Fig. 21. Singers in dialogue, from *Amar siṁh rāṭhor*. By permission of the Sangeet Natak Akademi.

ishes the line, and usually beginning with its last note, the percussion enters and plays a pattern in a regular rhythm cycle, ordinarily eight or sixteen beats. Melodic instruments such as *shahnāī*, flute, clarinet, *sāraṅgī*, or harmonium may shadow the singer during the recitative, lagging behind slightly and imitating the sung line. Customarily they repeat a refrain melody (comparable to the *laharā* of classical music) during the percussion solos. This antiphonal style contrasts with the style of the lyric passages, which exhibits simultaneous accompaniment (*sāth-saṅgat*). This style is found in the song forms of Nauṭaṅkī such as *dādrā, ṭhumrī,* and *ghazal.*

These three levels of poetic discourse and their differing modes of musical realization occur in the opening excerpt from *Sultānā ḍākū,* a commercial Nauṭaṅkī performance recorded on a 45 rpm Odeon disk (ex. 1).

> A narrative passage opens the story, several verses in which the narrator (*kavi*) describes the hero's character and fame (lines 1–6). A dialogue follows between Sultana and his guard (*sipāhī*), an episode that shows Sultana's character, in this case his merciless discipline (ll. 7–14). Here the speeches are short, and the passage is marked by rapid alternation between speakers. There follows another dialogue in which the villains are introduced, namely the notorious Mr. Young and one of his minions (*pulis*) (ll. 15–24). The humorous character of the passage lies in the British officer's imperfect success at speaking Hindi, indicated by the artificial retroflection of all dental consonants. In these three sections the singers are melodically shadowed by the clarinet, against the continuous drone and support of the harmonium. At the points indicated by an asterisk, the *nagāṛā* joins the clarinet to create an antiphonal response to each completed line. The melodies employed are all based on a diatonic mode of the Kalyāṇ-Bilāval-Khamāj type in Hindustani classical music, that is, a major scale occasionally touching the flatted seventh in descent and the raised fourth in ascent.
>
> A transition is announced by a flourish on the wind instruments and a change of mode, at which point a narrative *dohā* specifies the scene switch to Sultana's private quarters (ll. 25–26). The text moves into a lyrical section based loosely on conventions of love poetry found in Hindi and Urdu literature. The beloved woman (Phulkumvar) speaks in a Hindi idiom, suggesting a *dādrā* or *ṭhumrī* song form (ll. 27–28). After the vocal introduction of line 27, the instruments including *nagāṛā* accompany the singer in the lyrical fashion of *sāth-saṅgat* to the end of the song. Sultana, the lover, replies using the diction of the Urdu *ghazal* (note words like *tassavur, ulfat, judāī,* and *k͟hudāī*) (ll. 29–32). Both songs employ a minor mode that contrasts with the previous sections; in terms of Hindustani music, the mode is comparable to Bhairavī or Āsāvarī ragas with their flatted second, third, sixth, and seventh tones.

Although this passage is extremely compressed, it illustrates the episodic structure of the Nauṭaṅkī text and, wedded to that structure, a

EXAMPLE 1.   LEVELS OF POETIC DISCOURSE AND
MUSICAL ORGANIZATION

KAVI: sunā sabhoṁ ne hoigā sultānā kā nām,
               Everyone must have heard the name of Sultana.
               sher-e-nar ḍākū baṛā guzarā k͟hās-o-ām. (*)
               Like a lion, this dacoit was famed among rich and poor.
               madadgār rahtā garīboṁ kā har dam, (*twice, first time* *)
               He succored the poor at every chance.
               miṭātā thā bevāoṁ kā dukh alam gam. (*)
               He removed the great grief of widows.
               amīroṁ kā dhan lūṭṭā thā hameshā,   5
               He always stole the wealth of the rich;
               garīboṁ ke k͟hātir banāyā thā peshā. (*)
               He pursued his occupation for the sake of the poor.

SULTĀNĀ: chhoṛā pahrā merā ṭāl kar ke hukam,
               Leaving your duty and disobeying my order,
               ek sāgar ke pīne ko āyā yahāṁ.
               You have come here to drink an ocean.

SIPĀHĪ: is gharī māf merī k͟hatā kījiye,
               Please forgive my error this time.
               bhūl beshak huī, bak͟hshiye merī jāṁ. (*)   10
               I made a mistake of course. Please grant me my life.

SULTĀNĀ: māf kartā k͟hatāvār ko maiṁ nahīṁ,
               I don't forgive those who make mistakes.
               bhej detā hūṁ ik pal meṁ mulk-e-adam.
               I'll send you to the netherworld in an instant.
               zyādā bātoṁ kā sunne kā ādī nahīṁ,
               I'm not used to listening to much talk.
               ek golī meṁ kartā hūṁ qissā k͟hatam. *(shoots him)* (*)
               I'll end the story in one shot.

PULIS: baṛā hai sultānā hushiyār,   15
               Sultana is very clever.
               pulis us se jātī hai hār. (*)
               The police are defeated by him.
               giraftār karnā use yaṅg sāhab na khel
               It's no game to arrest him, Mr. Young.
               nikal bhāgtā har tarah leve jitanā gher.
               He escapes somehow no matter how you surround him.
               hai mushkil us se pānā pār,
               It's difficult to outwit him.
               baṛā hai sultānā hushiyār. (*)   20
               Sultana is very clever.

YAṄG SĀHAB: vel ṭum mujh ko jāṇṭā, hūṁ kiṭnā chālāk,
               Well, you know how smart I am.

EXAMPLE 1. *(continued)*

baṛoṁ baṛoṁ ko ekḍam kar ḍeṭā hūṁ khāk.
I reduce the biggest men to dust in an instant.
miṭā ḍālūṁgā us ko mār,
I'll kill him, wipe him out.
baṛā hai sulṭānā hushiyār.(*)
Sultana is very clever.

KAVI: jab jab fursat dekhtā sultānā ai yār,
Whenever Sultana had some free time, my friend,
phūlkuṁvar ke sāth meṁ kartā mauj bahār. (*)
He enjoyed himself with Phulkumvar [his mistress].

PHŪLKUṀVAR: rahe ho balamā kahāṁ sārī rain. (*twice, second time* *)
Where have you been all night, my beloved?
āye kahāṁ se mere dilārā, mad bhar jāge kahāṁ ke nain,
Where have you come from, my darling? Where did you get these wakeful, intoxicated eyes?
rahe ho balamā kahāṁ sārī rain.
Where have you been all night, my beloved?

SULTĀNĀ: terā hī tassavur rahtā hai, tū dil meṁ samāī rahtī hai. (*twice, first time* *)
I'm always thinking of you. You are in my heart constantly.
maiṁ rātoṁ ko jāgā kartā hūṁ, jab sotī khudāī rahtī hai. (*)
I lie awake at night when the rest of creation sleeps.
terī sūrat, terī chāhat, terī ulfat haiṁ pās sabhī,
Your face, desire for you, longing for you—all are near.
har chīz pās meṁ hote hue, kyoṁ tujh se judāī rahtī hai? (*)
When everything is near at hand, why am I separated still from you?

(*Sultānā ḍākū*, Odeon EP recorded disk)

---

* Instrumental interlude (melody and percussion)

continuous musical texture that supplies linkages and changes of scene and character. We see here as well that narrative, dialogue, and sections of song and dance alternate easily in a format that allows almost infinite extension in time. Each section engages different qualities of audience attention: the narrative passages move over events the most quickly, the dialogue brings into focus the dramatic interaction between characters; in the song and dance the action virtually stops. To the Western viewer bringing an Aristotelian concept of theatre, the song-and-dance portions appear to digress from the plot and distract the viewer, but the Indian audience does not rank the narrative and dialogue elements above song and dance. The song and dance in fact more often attract than distract, and viewers place a high entertainment value on them.[6]

Over the course of a performance the musical character of the recitatives varies markedly, first by alternating between contrasting metrical units associated with different modes, and second by gradually introducing a number of new modes, often in conjunction with action-related moods. These melodies in their diversity resemble some of the well-known ragas or scalar types of Hindustani classical music, for example, Yaman, Bilāval, Desh, Bhairavī, Kālingaṛā, and Āsāvarī. In addition, the lyric forms (popular songs) draw on the light classical and folk repertoires and, depending on the singer's knowledge, may develop scale patterns typical of the "mixed" ragas, particularly Khamāj, Pīlū, Pahāṛī, and Kāfī. The question then arises of the relationship of Nauṭaṅkī music to the Hindustani system. If the Hindustani system provides the substratum for theatrical music as for much folk music in this region, to what extent can we consider Nauṭaṅkī music "classical"?

Querying present-day Nauṭaṅkī singers about their musical training reveals that little direct transmission of the theoretical principles of Hindustani music occurs, at least through the channel of formal discipleship. Among currently performing Nauṭaṅkī artists, very few have had extensive instruction in vocal music, and few know the elaborate nomenclature of raga and *tāla* that demarcates the classical canon. Several performers mentioned a period of study with a guru or *ustād* as part of their life story. Giriraj Prasad emphasized his own classical training, as several directors who had worked with him also noted. In an interview recorded by the Sangeet Natak Akademi, Delhi, he summoned the names of a dozen ragas that he claimed to sing during his Nauṭaṅkī performances, but he erroneously attributed a Khamāj-type *chaubolā* he was demonstrating to Rāg Mālkauns, possibly because the verbal text also contains the heroic sentiment he was being asked to illustrate. Similarly, the *nagāṛā* player Atthan Khan performed as requested four or five *tāla*s; asked to play Dīpchandī, a relatively common rhythm cycle of fourteen beats, he did not do so correctly. These artists' assertions regarding their classical training may be as dubious as Malika Begam's alleged knowledge of the South Indian dance form, Bharata Nāṭyam, which she listed in the same breath with her qualifications in "*filmī* dance, Kathak, and the twist."

Nonetheless, we should neither discount the informal knowledge of the artists nor the structural similarities between Nauṭaṅkī's music and Hindustani music. Perhaps musicians and singers of Nauṭaṅkī are able to execute in practice what they are unable to discuss or name in theory. Although Nauṭaṅkī music does not conform to the raga system in its full form, it clearly employs a number of distinctive modes that are similar to classical Hindustani ragas as well as the mixed modes of light classical music. Melodies have contours based on stepwise descent and on *vakra* movements (skipping intermediate tones); they feature parallelisms between tetrachords and other types of patterning common to ragas. Structural features of classical composition found in Nauṭaṅkī include the *sthāyī-antarā* structure used in the lighter songs, rhythm cycles such as *tīntāl* for percussion interludes, and the frequent three-part rhythmic cadence (*tihāī*).[7] In these and other instances, Nauṭaṅkī music manifests its closeness to Hindustani classical music while maintaining a distinct character through its own specific musical grammar.

The musical dimensions of Nauṭaṅkī as a traditional outdoor theatre—its loudness, emphasis on drumming, high vocal register, antiphonal texture, mixture of recitation and song forms, and relatedness to the classical idiom—it shares with a number of other South Asian theatrical traditions. The ensemble of aerophones (especially reeds and brass) and drums is found in Gujarat in the *bhuṇgaḷ* (a five-foot-long copper pipe) and *nagāṛā* of Bhavāī; in Tamilnadu in Terukkūttu's *kurukuzhal* (small pipe similar to the *nāgasvaram*) and *maḍḍaḷam;* in the pipes and drums (*maḍḍaḷe* or *mridaṅga*) of Yakṣhagāna theatre, as well as in the more urbanized forms that use flutes, clarinets, trumpets, and nowadays (everywhere) the harmonium. High-pitched singing is common to most of the traditional theatres. The Jātrā of Bengal always began on a high note,[8] and in Tamāshā the higher the pitch, the more skillful the artists are considered to be.[9] The *bhāgavatha* or lead singer of Yakṣhagāna inspired Gargi to write: "He starts at a high pitch and raises his voice as if he were loudly calling, challenging, wailing. His high-crested voice constructs a many-pinnacled fortress."[10] The available accounts confirm the presence of multiple layers of recitation, dialogue, and song in all these theatres, as well as the predominance of question-response structures between actors and musicians.[11] Classical ragas similarly occur in the music of folk theatre throughout India, ranging from the mixed repertoire of 150 Hindustani, Karnatak, and regional Kannada ragas found in the Yakṣhagāna theatre, to the smaller selection of favored ragas and light melodies associated with Bhavāī, Jātrā, Khyāl, and Aṅkiyā Nāṭ in the north.[12]

We need to know more about the musical textures of South Asian theatres, and we must compare the function of music with other signifying systems across regions and genres. When more specific information becomes available, we may be able to construct a continuum of the traditional theatres to compare their musical components. On one end, we might provisionally place theatres like Chhau or Kathakaḷi where dance and mime are the actor's concern and singing is the function of a specialist offstage. At the other end, we might position the singer-actors of Nauṭaṅkī or Terukkūttu who carry the burden of continuous singing.

What consequences do various musical requirements have on the other signifying systems present in theatre? In Nauṭaṅkī, the amount of movement, gesture language, miming of emotions, and acting is small compared to other traditional theatres. Is this true for other music-dominated genres? How does the participation of actor-singers shift when other modes of communication become more important? These are areas in which comparative research could tell us much about the role of music as a system of communication within the theatre in South Asia.

Metrical Patterns and Melodic Contours

Although Nauṭaṅkī music resembles other South Asian theatrical music in general ways, it also possesses a distinctive blueprint: a configuration in sound that immediately labels this genre Nauṭaṅkī, even when compared to neighboring theatres such as Haryanvi Sāṅg or Rajasthani Khyāl. This blueprint is the music used for the ten-line stanza known as *dohā-chaubolā-dauṛ*, the basic building block of Nauṭaṅkī composition. It is significant that this identifying unit issues from the narrative level of the text, not the lyric. Nauṭaṅkī performance freely borrows lyric genres from various sources and incorporates them according to current fashion and the taste of the actors and audience. In older texts we find Hindi folk songs and semiclassical genres such as *dādrā, sāvan, holī, ṭhumrī,* and *māṇḍ,* as well as the Urdu *sher, ghazal, qavvālī, masnavī,* and so forth. Nowadays Bombay film tunes (*filmī gīt* or *gāne*) or film-influenced versions of the above genres tend to predominate. Popular songs are not exclusive to Nauṭaṅkī; they turn up in many performance contexts classified as "folk." Film-based musical quotations may lend a performance verve and status, but they do not distinguish Nauṭaṅkī as the old meters *dohā* and *chaubolā* do.

Dohā is a reputable Hindi meter with a long history. The *dohā-chaubolā* of Svāṅg and Nauṭaṅkī may be an outgrowth of the established

EXAMPLE 2. METRICAL STRUCTURE OF THE HINDI *dohā*

```
⏑   –  ⏑      –     –  –⏑  –/  (13)   –  –  –  –   –   ⏑  //   (11)
su-nā sa-bhoṁ ne ho-i-gā             sul-tā-nā kā nā-m(a),
 –  –  –   –  –  ⏑  –/         (13)   ⏑  ⏑  –   –   – –  ⏑  //  (11)
sher e nar ḍā-kū ba-ṛā               gu-za-rā khās o ā-m(a).
```

(*Sultānā ḍākū*, Odeon EP recorded disk)

Scansion code: The symbol ⏑ stands for a short syllable counted as one measure (*mātrā*), the symbol – for a long syllable counted as two measures.

dohā-chaupāī pattern of medieval Hindi narrative verse. In any case, nineteenth-century Sāṅgīt texts reveal that the *dohā-chaubolā* alone dominates Svāṅg composition from about 1850 to 1890. Beginning in the 1890s the six lines of *dohā-chaubolā* commonly add on an asymmetrical quatrain called *dauṛ* to form a ten-line unit; in the Hathras texts this becomes the standard.[13] *Dohā, chaubolā,* and *dauṛ* are scanned according to rules of Hindi prosody, by which every syllable bears either a short (*laghu*) or long (*guru*) weight or measure, indicated by the symbols ⏑ and –. The long weight counts as two measures, twice the short weight. Each line contains a fixed number of measures (*mātrās*) that vary in their arrangements of short and long but have specific patterns at line ends. Thus, the *dohā* meter is conventionally described as two rhyming lines of 24 measures, with a caesura after the first 13 measures of each line. In example 2, each line divides into two half-lines of 13 and 11 measures respectively. The lines end in a characteristic – ⏑ pattern and contain an *a a* rhyme scheme, carried in the words *nāma* and *āma.*[14]

In parallel fashion, the meter *chaubolā* consists of four lines of 28 measures each, ordinarily divided 14 + 14 and rhyming *b b b b.* The final two syllables of each line are generally weighted – –, and the rhyme occurs on the penultimate syllable (a "feminine" rhyme). The *dohā* and *chaubolā* are often interlinked, the final half-line of the *dohā* being repeated at the beginning of the *chaubolā.* The linkage of *dohā* to *chaubolā* is also one of sense; the *chaubolā* often repeats and expands on the content of the *dohā.* Characteristically following the *chaubolā* is a *dauṛ,* a Hindi meter of four lines, 13 + 13 + 13 + 28 measures, rhyming *c c d d,* again on two syllables. *Dohā-chaubolā-dauṛ* forms the speech of one character or a descriptive passage by the narrator (*kavi*). The *dauṛ* often

EXAMPLE 3. STRUCTURE OF *dohā-chaubolā-dauṛ*

Dohā: two lines of 24 measures, 13 + 11 each; rhymes *a a*
Chaubolā: four lines usually of 28 measures, 14 + 14 each, rhymes *b b b b;* interlinks with *dohā,* beginning with repetition of final half-line of *dohā*
Dauṛ: four lines, 13 + 13 + 13 + 28 measures, rhymes *c c d d*

dohā	Elizabeth *dvitīya* [the second] empress, good gracious strong,
	Prayer this ours is, may you live long long.
chaubolā	May you live long long, rule beneficent continue,
	Fortunate we are all having queen good like you.
	Under English sovereigns we received blessings new new,
	All of them had do good to us in their view.
dauṛ	Your gracious Majesty,
	Of the same dynasty,
	Your nature too kind:
	Long rule be yours, sincerely we pray combined.

Amar siṁh rāṭhor (Hathras: Shyam Press, 1981). The *maṅgalācharaṇ* appears in the text in Devanagari, with the English sounds rendered by their nearest Hindi equivalents. Instead of transliterating it, I restore the words to their standard English spellings without altering the grammar of the passage.

moves the action forward by forming an address to another character. Formally it provides for closure by returning to a final line of 28 measures, the same as the *chaubolā.*

Examples 3 and 4 illustrate these meters. The first is an homage (*maṅgalācharaṇ*) to Queen Elizabeth in the English language; the excerpt is from an actual Nauṭaṅkī text printed in Devanagari script. The overall structure of the ten-line stanza is readily visible here, freed from the technical details of Hindi scansion. Additionally, this passage shows how quickly Nauṭaṅkī performers adapted to changing patterns of patronage. The choice of English when seeking blessings from the British parallels the use of Sanskrit in invocations addressed to the Hindu deity Nārāyaṇa, or Perso-Arabic for those uttered to the Islamic god Khudā. One should, after all, address the gods in their own language. Example 4 is from the All-India Radio version of the Nauṭaṅkī *Rānī lakṣhmībāī.* In this telling of the story of the famous warrior queen, the dacoits are at first the villains, from whom the people require the Rani of Jhansi's protection. Later Sagar Singh, a dacoit leader, becomes an ally of the Rani in her fight against the British.

Whereas the *dohā-chaubolā-dauṛ* carries the weight of narration in

EXAMPLE 4. METRICAL STRUCTURE OF *dohā-chaubolā-daur̤*

dohā	(13)		(11)
khudā bakhsh(a) ghāyal(a) huā, /		ḍākū sab gaye bhāj(a), //	
khabar(a) lagī is(a) bāt(a) kī /	(13)	fauran(a) jhāṁsī rāj(a). //	(11)
chaubolā	(14)		(14)
fauran(a) jhāṁsī rāj(a) turat(a) /		rānī ne fauj(a) sajāī, //	
sun(a) kar(a) ke sandes(a) nahīṁ /	(14)	phir(a) pal(a) kī der(a) lagāī. //	(14)
lāī sahelī saṅg fauj(a) /	(14)	meṁ sab(a) se āge dhāī, //	(14)
baruā sāgar(a) machī dhūm(a) /	(14)	rānī jhāṁsī se āī. //	(14)
daur̤	(13)		
josh(a) harasoṁ apār(a) thā, /			
rānī ko sab se pyār thā, /	(13)		
milī janatā se rānī, /	(13)		

khudā bakhsh(a) se sāgar(a) siṁh kī sunane lagī kahānī. // (28)

Khuda Bakhsh became injured, and all the dacoits fled.
The news of this immediately reached the kingdom of Jhansi.
[The news of this] immediately [reached] the kingdom of Jhansi, and the queen summoned her army.
When she heard the message, she didn't delay an instant.
She brought her female companion, who rode with her at the head of the army.
In Barua Sagar, there was an uproar as the queen arrived from Jhansi.
The enthusiasm and delight [of the people] were unprecedented. The queen loved everyone.
She met with the public and heard from Khuda Bakhsh the story of Sagar Singh.

(*Rānī lakṣhmībāī,* AIR-Mathura recording)

Nauṭaṅkī, a shorter stanza useful for dialogue, known as *bahr-e-tavīl,* was introduced around 1910. This meter is based on Urdu prosody rather than Hindi, indicating the mixed linguistic heritage of this region and the presence of both Hindi and Urdu prototypes in the oral stratum

---

EXAMPLE 5. METRICAL STRUCTURE OF *bahr-e-tavīl*

Bahr-e-tavīl: two rhyming lines of 24 stresses (not *mātrās*) each, according to rules of Urdu scansion, that commonly occur in feet of long-short-long

– ⏑ – / – ⏑ – / – ⏑ – / – ⏑ – / – ⏑ – / – ⏑ – / – ⏑ – / – ⏑ – //
– ⏑ – / – ⏑ – / – ⏑ – / – ⏑ – / – ⏑ – / – ⏑ – / – ⏑ – / – ⏑ – //

Flexibility exists in determining the short and long stress of syllables, especially for grammatical endings signifying gender and case; ambiguous syllables carry the symbol ⏓

– ⏑ – – ⏓ – ⏓ ⏓ – – ⏑ – / – ⏑ – ⏓ ⏑ – – ⏑ – – ⏓ – //
ye araz me rī tum se hai māh-e-laqā / dil lagā ke na dil ko haṭā lenā tum //

– ⏑ – – ⏑ – – ⏑ – – ⏑ – / – ⏑ – – ⏑ – – ⏑ – – ⏓ – //
bevafāī na karnā kabhī bhūl(a) kar / gar muhabbat karo to nibhā denā tum //

I request this of you, oh moonfaced one: having given your heart, do not withdraw it.
Never be unfaithful, no matter what, and if you will love, fulfill your promise.
(*Lailā majnūn* [Hathras: Shyam Press, 1981])

---

from which Nauṭaṅkī arose. It can be described as two rhyming lines of 24 stresses each (according to rules of Urdu scansion), or four lines of 12 stresses each, arranged generally in feet of long-short-long.[15] The two long lines may be divided between two speakers to create a brisker pace of dialogue. Illustrating *bahr-e-tavīl* is example 5.

Other common meters include *bīr chhand,* also known as *ālhā chhand,* because of its use in the Hindi oral epic, the *Ālhā. Bīr chhand,* as used in Nauṭaṅkī, consists of two rhyming lines of 16 + 15 measures each (ex. 6). *Bīr chhand* is employed primarily for narration, as are several varieties of *lāvanī* such as *lāvanī laṅgaṛī, lāvanī chhoṭī, lāvanī baṛī,* and others. Additional forms favored for dialogue are *shair* (or *sher*), *qavvālī,* and even *ghazal,* which are essentially couplets or quatrains in various common Urdu meters. As occurring in Nauṭaṅkī, these terms appear to be somewhat interchangeable and may denote melodic rather than metrical units.

The foregoing description of the metrical patterning of the Nauṭaṅkī text is essential to an understanding of the musical dimension of performance, because music closely follows meter in this tradition. This is true in two primary senses. First of all, the meter of a passage reliably predicts the tune or type of tune to which it will be sung, within the con-

Example 6. Metrical Structure of *bīr chhand*

Bīr chhand (or *ālhā chhand*): a Hindi meter of two rhyming lines of 16 + 15 measures each

– –⏑– ⏑– ⏑ ⏑– –/ (16) ⏑⏑ – ⏑ ⏑ – –⏑ ⏑– ⏑ // (15)
jindā use nahīṁ rakhatā thā jis(a) se kuchh(a) ho jāi kasūr(a)

– ⏑ ⏑– – – –⏑ ⏑ –/ (16) ⏑⏑ – ⏑ ⏑ ⏑⏑– – – ⏑ // (15)
raub(a) kaho aise jālim(a) kā kis(a) se rah(a) sakatā hai dūr(a)

He allowed no one to live who might commit a wrongdoing.
Consider the defiance of such a tyrant! He avoided no man.

(*Sultānā ḍākū* [Hathras: Shyam Press, 1977])

ventional framework of the genre and the particular school or style of performance. Notably, the melodic rendering of the two most prevalent meter clusters, *dohā-chaubolā-dauṛ* and *bahr-e-tavīl,* is consistent in essentials over a wide range of performance examples collected. (Important differences between the Hathras, Kanpur, and more recent styles do emerge. The discussion here focuses on the Hathras singing style, and the next section treats developments in Kanpur and elsewhere.) Their divergent melodies place these two meter groups in sharp contrast. *Dohā, chaubolā,* and *dauṛ* almost always feature a tune based on the major scale, whereas the melody of *bahr-e-tavīl* uses a mode laden with minor tones, similar to the Bhairavī of Hindustani music. Because of this modal contrast, the audience perceives the shift from a narrative portion of the text (characteristically introduced by a *dohā*) to a dialogue passage (typically composed in *bahr-e-tavīl*). Furthermore, the contrast gives the performance a sufficient degree of melodic diversity. Both meter types are sung in the antiphonal manner, alternating between vocal and instrumental lines.

Second, music follows meter in the specific way in which the standard tune matches the words. The *dohā-chaubolā-dauṛ* and Hindi meters in general are sung in a recitative style corresponding to the weight of syllables, with long syllables receiving roughly twice the duration of short syllables. The rhythmic details of musical execution therefore vary from one line to another, insofar as the arrangement of long and short syllables varies. The meter also prescribes particular resting points where musical elaboration may occur. Syllables at the ends of lines or before caesuras are often elongated. Beyond the demands of the meter, moreover, Nauṭaṅkī singing favors an element of interpretive rubato that allows for individual expression. A passage may be slowed down for emphasis or speeded up to usher in the percussion response, usually set at a slightly faster tempo. In the examples with musical notation included here, I generally transcribe the time value of notes in accordance with their metrical weight, although the values attached to notes in ornamental passages are usually arbitrary. For ease of reading and comparison of modes, I transpose all melodies to a tonic of middle C. Similarly, I use the treble clef throughout, although the majority of examples are of male singers whose voices are pitched somewhat lower.

In example 7, the recitatives of the *dohā-chaubolā-dauṛ* from *Rānī lakṣhmībāī* (the metrical structure of which is in ex. 4) are transcribed to illustrate the melodies most frequently associated with these meters. This performance was produced for All-India Radio and was broadcast from its Mathura station in 1981. The singers and musicians come from the Braj area in western Uttar Pradesh and belong to the surviving performance traditions associated with the Hathras style.[16]

> The *dohā* begins in characteristic fashion on the high tonic, and after dwelling there for the first half-line, focuses on the fifth and then, in anticipation, moves down to the lower tonic at the end of the first line. In the second line the tune rises again to the high tonic at the caesura and returns to the lower at its completion. A drum interlude of eight bars follows, commencing at the utterance of the final syllable of the *dohā*. (Details of the drumming patterns will be discussed below.) The *chaubolā* is similarly structured in two-line pairs. The first line of the *chaubolā* echoes the opening of the *dohā*, beginning again on the high tonic. The second line carries the melody down from the high tonic to the lower in almost a purely stepwise descent, introducing a flatted seventh. After an eight-bar drum solo (not notated), the third line dwells on the fourth of the octave and moves down to the tonic after touching the fifth. The fourth line is a repeat of the second, essentially a descending scale with flatted seventh. The *chaubolā* concludes with a single drum beat, perhaps an indication of a solo that was edited out. The *dauṛ* in its own fashion imitates the *chaubolā;* the first line focuses on the high tonic and its leading tone, the major seventh, and the second line introduces the flatted seventh. The third line emphasizes the fourth tone of the scale, and the last line utilizes the descent pattern and melodic turns of the fourth line of the *chaubolā,* ending again on the lower tonic.

A schematic notation of the melodic range and contour of these lines is given at the end of example 7. Similar contours occur in a variety of

EXAMPLE 7. *Dohā-chaubolā-dauṛ*

EXAMPLE 7. (*continued*)

Melodic Contours

performances, and even when the singing line is highly ornamented, the same melodic orientation and tonal focus can be observed. Example 8 contains a transcription of the voice of Chunnilal, a master singer of the Braj area, singing from *Amar siṁh rāṭhor* during an All-India Radio interview; it includes the transcribed, scanned, and translated text. Chunnilal's *dohā* illustrates a common variant, beginning on the middle

EXAMPLE 8. *Dohā-chaubolā*

Example 8. *(continued)*

Melodic Contours

dohā

shahanshā jāpanāh(a) ko bande kā ādāb(a)
kamtarīn(a) pāmāl(a) kī hai ek [ye]* araz(a) janāb(a).

chaubolā

hai ek araz(a) janāb(a) irādā jo man(a) ṭhahrāyā hai
fāgun(a) badī pañchamī kā [merā]*gaunā qarār(a) pāyā hai.
khush(a) khabarī kā būndī[gaṛh]*se [jāpanā]* harkārā khat(a) lāyā hai
chhuṭṭī lene ko huzūr(a) se khāk(a)sār(a) āyā hai.

Greetings to the emperor, protector of the world, from your humble servant.
Your downtrodden slave has one request.
This one request, my lord, a desire that has lodged in my heart:
On the fifth day of the dark half of the month of Phagun, my wedding-consummation has been fixed.
A messenger brought the good news in a letter from Bundi.
This miserable slave has come to take leave of his master.

(*Amar siṁh rāṭhor* [Hathras: Shyam Press, 1979])

---

* Indicates word supplied by singer, not in printed text

third and working up to the high tonic in the first half-line, but otherwise conforming to the earlier pattern. In the *chaubolā*, both two-line phrases begin on the fourth tone, work to the higher tonic, and then close with a descent to the lower tonic. Example 9 contains a *dohā* and *chaubolā* sung by Giriraj Prasad, another famous Hathrasi singer, in a performance of *Lailā majnūn* recorded in the studio of the Sangeet Natak Akademi, Delhi, and its text. Although the excerpt is highly embellished, it too conforms to essentially the same pattern in the *dohā*. In the *chaubolā*, the singer exhibits his virtuosity in the first line by extending the range up to the fourth of the higher octave and dwelling on the high third tone, a phrase he repeats in the third line as well. Otherwise, the tonal emphasis and contour of these phrases corresponds to the earlier model.

EXAMPLE 9. *Dohā-chaubolā*

Example 9. *(continued)*

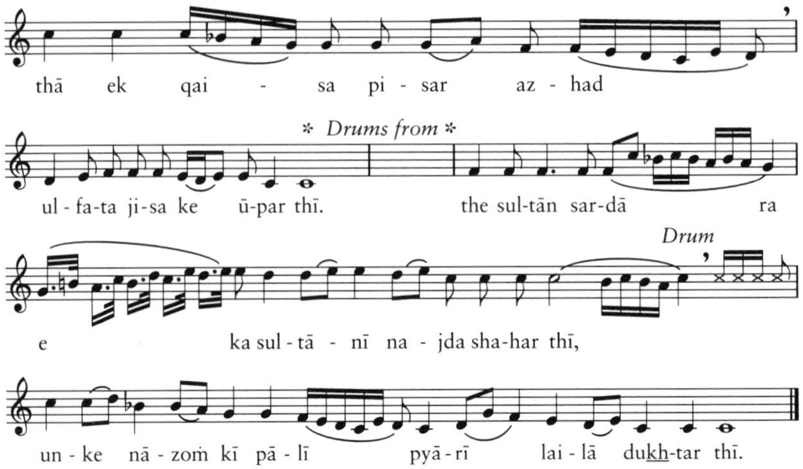

dohā

qissā hotā shurū ab(a) pāk(a) ishq(a) raṅgīn(a)
nām(a) amīr(a) damishq(a) ke the ek(a) takht(a) nashīn(a).

chaubolā

nek(a) bashar(a) the shāh(a) aur(a) raiyat(a) par(a) nek(a) nazar(a) thī
thā ek(a) qais(a) pisar azahad(a) ulfat(a) jis(a) ke ūpar(a) thī.
the sultān(a) sardār ek(a) sultānī najd(a) shahar(a) thī
unke nāzoṁ kī pālī pyārī lailā dukhtar(a) thī.

Here begins the story of a delightful pure love.
Once there was a king called Amir of Damascus.
This king was full of virtue, and he ruled his people well.
He had a son, Qais, who was very much in love.
There was also a chief and his queen in the town of Najd,
And their beloved daughter, raised in the lap of luxury, was Laila.

(*Lailā majnūn* [Hathras: Shyam Press, 1981])

Within the rather fixed bounds of the *dohā* and *chaubolā*, opportunities occur for a substantial amount of stylistic and expressive play. Certain places in the lines provide openings, positions for sustaining a syllable with melismatic ornamentation. These openings typically occur just before the caesuras in both lines and at the end of the first line. The end of the second line (the final word of the couplet in the case of the *dohā,* or the last two or three syllables in the *chaubolā*) is never used for melodic play. Its rhyme is anticipated by the first line, and it is therefore a point of closure. Furthermore, this rhyme point coincides with the entrance of the percussion; in practice, the singer often deletes the rhyme word, a maneuver performed with an upward flourish of the hand, indicating that it is up to the audience to supply the missing (but easily guessed) syllable(s) (fig. 22).

In these improvisatory passages, the type of vocal ornamentation varies from singer to singer, but in the main it incorporates embellishments such as short *tān*s (rapidly ascending and descending scalar patterns), *muṛkī*s (mordents, turns), *mīṇḍ* (glissando), and expressive breaks or inflections in the voice. The full repertoire of techniques known to Hindustani classical singing is not found here, nor is there the expansive freedom to improvise because of the exigencies of the text. Nonetheless, in comparison with certain popular *ghazal* or film songsters of today, the best Nauṭaṅkī artists are accomplished vocalists with their own considerable powers of expression. Without the benefit of training, they achieve a range of vocal modulation that is stirring and forceful, keeping the listener attuned to their words and endowing the performance with an aesthetic dimension.

In addition to the most frequent *dohā-chaubolā* melodies illustrated thus far, several other common types may occur. What is remarkable is that there should in fact be so few melodies available, and that these *dohā* variants should be so similar to one other. A degree of divergence from the most common tune certainly exists, yet any of these *dohā* melodies would still be clearly identifiable as "*dohā,*" especially in contrast to the tunes employed for other meters in the performance.

> For the most part, *chaubolā* tunes follow the *dohā*s to which they are attached. Therefore in example 10 I simply indicate the several varieties of *dohā* melodies alone. Here, for purposes of comparison, the *dohā* melody is rhythmically reduced to common time and each *dohā* fills the space of eight bars. (Actual renditions would dwell on these tones in the recitative style described earlier and employ ornaments.) I label the two types discussed above A and B. In C, the second half of the *dohā* melody is identical to the second and fourth lines of the *chaubolā* illustrated at the end of example 7. The same is true in D, although the first half is unique in beginning on the seventh tone and then dwelling on the high tonic. The melody E is identical to A but rests on the seventh rather than the fifth at the end of the first line, and in its descent in the

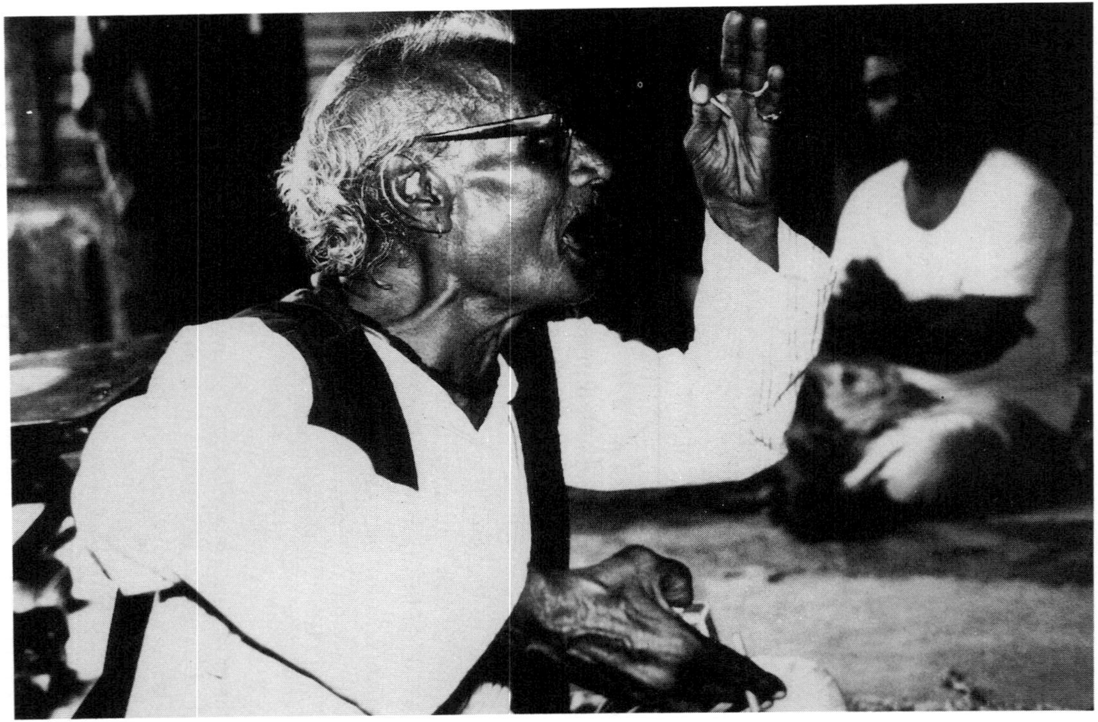

Fig. 22. Phakkar, former Nauṭaṅkī actor of Lucknow, gesturing at the end of a vocal line. Photographed in Lucknow in 1982.

EXAMPLE 10. TYPES OF *dohā* MELODIES

second line reaches only the third tone of the scale. Of particular interest are melodies F and G, both of which employ minor modes and seem to occur in narrative passages describing sad events. Though F opens in the same fashion as D, it touches several flatted notes in the descent, notably the sixth and third in addition to the seventh. Melody G rises from the lower tonic to the fifth using a set of flatted tones comparable to Rāg Āsāvarī, although in the second half it may use both the flatted and natural seventh. These two "mournful" *dohā*s are rare but significant for the contrast they create with the dominant "happy" sound of the major-scale *dohā* melodies.

Drumming patterns in the *dohā-chaubolā-dauṛ* section help to mark the completion of poetic sentences, giving the singers breathing space and keeping the performance moving vigorously ahead. In general, the percussion patterns follow an implicit eight- or sixteen-beat cycle, which usually breaks into two parts: the first part displays a characteristic motif or pattern, sometimes with variations, and the second part contains a rhythmic cadence.

In example 7 the drumming following the *dohā* features a dotted rhythm for the first four bars; this motif reappears in the *tihāī,* a cadence consisting of a six-beat pattern repeated three times, in such a way that the last stroke coincides with the *sam* or first beat of the next rhythm cycle. The drumming during the *dauṛ* is different from the drumming during the *dohā* and *chaubolā.* In this example, the first *dauṛ* drum solo (after the second line of the *dauṛ*) lasts eight bars and ends in a *tihāī.* The second solo, after the fourth line, contains a cross rhythm, grouping several accented three-beat phrases within four four-beat bars. Example 11 gives additional drumming patterns. Those that are played with *dohā* and *chaubolā* (A, B, C) all feature the dotted rhythmic motif; the *dauṛ* patterns (D, E) lack it but emphasize longer beat-length strokes with subsequent doubling and quadrupling of speed. The cadences here are often not true *tihāī*s but "crown" patterns, where a motif is played in progressively shorter phrases, leading to an anticipation of closure. Thus in pattern C, the phrase ♩ ♫ is played at the beginning of bar 5 and is followed by a continuous roll of drums to fill up eight beats; then it is played at the beginning of bar 7, followed by four beats, then twice in bar 8, each followed by two beats. Schematically the pattern is 8–4–2–2–1.

Example 11. Drumming Patterns

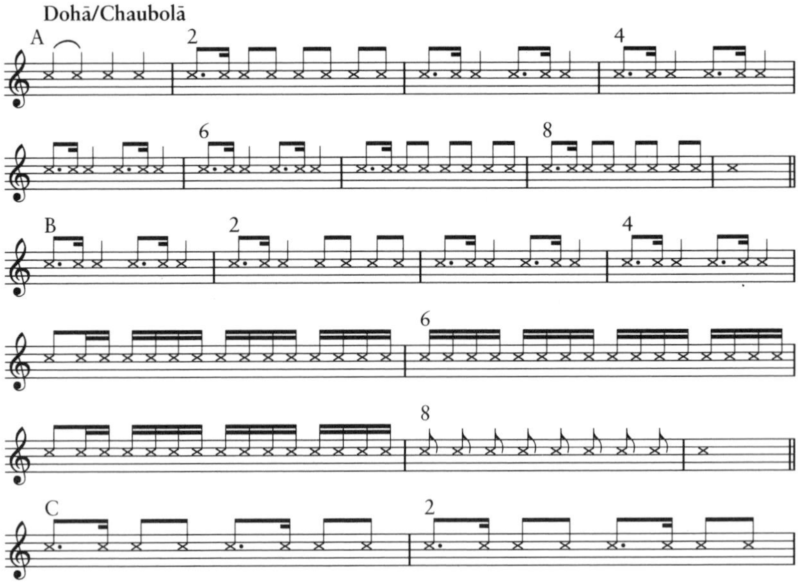

Example 11. *(continued)*

The melody of *bahr-e-tavīl* is distinctive, contrasting sharply with the *dohā* by virtue of its heavily flatted scale. Its supple sweep and dignity must be heard to be appreciated. Here musicality is not a simple matter of scale or pitch; it is often linked to declarations of powerful emotion. In example 12 I illustrate three standard *bahr-e-tavīl* renditions in the Hathras style, along with their texts. Each passage is emotionally charged—the first with *karuṇā ras,* the pathetic or tragic sentiment, the second two with *vīr ras,* or valor. In consequence, the singer in each case infuses the line with a high degree of musical expression. The techniques used for this purpose include repeating dramatic phrases, throwing or pushing the voice emphatically, breaking the voice with sighs or simulated tears, or accenting through exaggerated pronunciation. These passages suggest the heights to which Nauṭaṅkī music can soar.

Unlike the *dohā* with its several variants, the *bahr-e-tavīl* is sung to essentially one tune, with most of the variability occurring during the first phrase. Despite its very different modality, this tune shares the contours of the *dohā,* beginning on the high tonic, moving to the lower tonic at the end of the second phrase, then rising to the fourth tone and again to the high tonic in the third, and returning to the lower tonic at the conclusion. To some extent the recitative style of the *dohā* is also imitated, but the regular pattern of the Urdu meter, based on feet of – ⌣ –, tends to be interpreted rhythmically as 𝅗𝅥 ♩ ♩, with rhythmic accent rather than duration correlated with syllabic stress. These general features of the *bahr-e-tavīl* are illustrated in the schematic notation at the end of example 12.

Example 12. *Bahr-e-tavīl*

Example 12. (*continued*)

A. *Indal haraṇ* (AIR-Mathura)
chhaunā gaṅgā meṁ ḍūbā merī god se,
dekhte hī dekhte khā gayā kāl hai.
rūṭh ham se vidhātā hamārā gayā,
kyā kaheṁ ye sabhī bhāgya kī chāl hai.

The lad fell from my lap and drowned in the Ganges.
Even as I watched, Death [Time] swallowed him up.
The Creator is angry with me.
What can one say? This is all the course of fate.

B. *Amar siṁh rāṭhor* (film *Yamunā Kināre*)
matvāle kī golī se ghāyal karo,
vaise sar ko uṛā do ujar hī nahīṁ.
do ijāzat abhī jāke darbār meṁ,
dūṁ chukā khātā rakhūṁ kasar hī nahīṁ.

Example 12. *(continued)*

Shoot the madman and injure him,
And if you blow off his head, no matter.
Now please give me permission to leave,
I'll go to the court and settle the account completely.

C. *Rānī lakṣhmībāī* (AIR-Mathura)
apne kartabya pe hameṁ ān sabhī,
khokhlī bāt koī sunānī nahīṁ.
āñch jhāṁsī pe jīte jī āne na deṁ,
pīṭh raṇ meṁ ham ko dikhānī nahīṁ.

We all pride ourselves on our sense of duty.
No one needs to utter a hollow remark.
To the end of our lives, we will defend Jhansi.
We are not ones to show our backs in battle.

Schematic Notation

A number of other readily recognizable melodies populate the performances studied, but rather than prepare an exhaustive index I summarize the remaining narrative and dialogue meters by referring to two further examples. Most of these stanzas are structured by their rhyme schemes into either a rondo pattern (*a a b a c a,* etc.) or rhyming pairs (*a a b b c c,* etc.). As one might by now predict, the two-line meters are sung to two alternating melodies, distinguished primarily by register. In the meter type rhyming *a a b a,* a contrast between high and low melodies is created, and a melodic structure similar to the *sthāyī-antarā* pattern is used, where *sthāyī* is the melody in the lower register and *antarā*

that in the upper. The alternation is generated by repeating the first line twice; the first time it is sung to the *sthāyī* (A) and the second time to the *antarā* (B). Then line two is sung to the A melody, line three to B, line four to A and so on. This in effect reproduces the high-low contrast found in the previous examples. For an application, see example 13, an unidentified meter of 28 *mātrās* (possibly a *lāvanī* or *qavvālī*) sung frequently in the recording of *Rānī lakṣhmībāī.*

In the *a a b b* instance, each pair would again be rendered melodically by a contrasting set of tunes. The melodic structure for this type

---

EXAMPLE 13. *Sthāyī-antarā* STRUCTURE

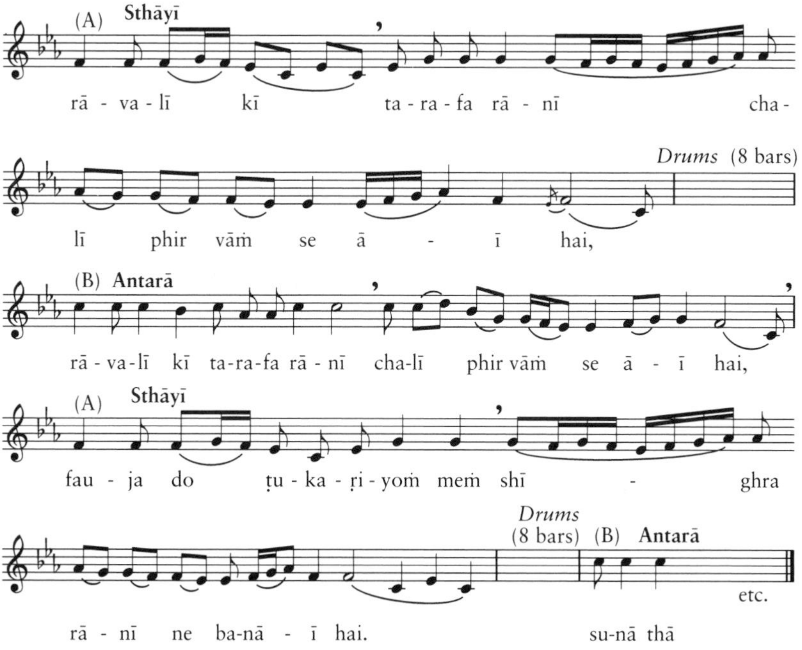

rāvalī kī taraf rānī chalī phir vāṁ se āī hai, [*repeated*]
fauj do ṭukṛiyoṁ meṁ shīghra rānī ne banāī hai.
sunā thā pās jaṅgal meṁ pahāṛoṁ meṁ hai kuchh ḍākū,
na kīnī der rānī ne turant senā sajāī hai.
achānak jo huā hamlā to ḍākū bhāg kar nikale,
chalā laṛne ko sāgar to paṛī rānī lakhāī hai.

Example 13. *(continued)*

The queen went toward Ravali and then returned from there.
She quickly divided her army into two platoons.
She had heard that there were some outlaws living in the mountains and in the wilds.
She made no delay; the queen quickly assembled her army.
When they were suddenly ambushed, the outlaws ran off and escaped.
Sagar Singh went to fight, and the queen found him out.

(*Rānī lakṣhmībāī*)

Rhyme scheme: *a (a) a b a c a*
Melody scheme: A B A B A B A

of meter in Nauṭaṅkī would be B A B A, where B represents a high-pitched melody, and A is in the lower register and ends on the tonic. Example 14 bears out these suppositions with a skeleton of the melody used for *bīr chhand* in Nauṭaṅkī. This narrative meter tends to be used for long passages, similar to its use in epic recitation. In the Ālhā singing style, however, the lower melody predominates, and the higher is used only occasionally for contrast; the melodic structure might be something like AA AA AA BA AA AA, and so forth. The melodies, we note, are essentially the same in the epic and Nauṭaṅkī renditions, but the meter in Nauṭaṅkī is sung in the higher register 50 percent of the time: BA BA BA BA. This indicates a process of adaptation, wherein a sung meter molds itself to the features of its musical environment. The direc-

---

Example 14. *Bīr chhand*

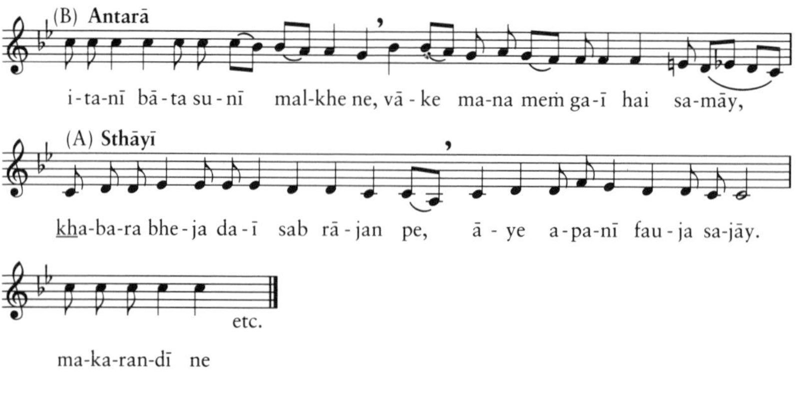
(B) Antarā
i-ta-nī bā-ta su-nī mal-khe ne, vā-ke ma-na meṁ ga-ī hai sa-māy,
(A) Sthāyī
kha-ba-ra bhe-ja da-ī sab rā-jan pe, ā-ye a-pa-nī fau-ja sa-jāy.
etc.
ma-ka-ran-dī ne

EXAMPLE 14. *(continued)*

itnī bāt sunī malkhe ne, vāke man meṁ gaī hai samāy,
khabar bhej daī sab rājan pe, āye apnī fauj sajāy.
makarandī ne māl lūṭ ko rasad sahit dīnī pahuṁchāy,
ūdal ko ghoṛā rakh līno jāko bendil nām kahāy.

When Malkhan heard this, he understood [what was needed].
He sent word to all the kings to come with their armies.
Makarandi distributed the provisions and foodstuffs.
They procured Udal's horse who was called Bendil.

(*Indal haraṇ*)

Rhyme scheme: *a a a a*
Melody scheme: B A B A

tion of adaptation, however, is not proven. The tune might have originated with epic recitation, and been embellished by emphasis on the *antarā* when it entered Nauṭaṅkī; or it could have been simplified in passing from the more musically intricate theatrical tradition to the recitational genre.

Further consideration of the origins of the many melodies and meters that make up the Nauṭaṅkī performance is beyond the scope of this research. Nonetheless, it is important to reiterate the degree of overlap that exists: many of these meters are found in other North Indian performance traditions and general characteristics may be present throughout South Asia. Musical treatment of the important narrative and dialogue meters so far seems unique to Nauṭaṅkī; however, definitive comparisons cannot precede research into other theatre music.

From Competition to Commodity

Within the seemingly prescribed limits of Nauṭaṅkī's metrical grammar we observe a substantial amount of melodic, rhythmic, and textually expressive play, especially in the most accomplished singing of the Hathras style. In the *ālāp*-like introductory flourishes and the elaboration of midline openings, the singer has the opportunity to demonstrate his or her virtuosity and personal creativity, while similar scope exists for the drummers in the spontaneous construction of rhythmic motifs and cadences. This "play" in the musical system—the flexibility, openness, and elasticity that allow improvisation—is closely related to audience responsiveness. The display of musical virtuosity actively solicits audience participation: the performers seek and expect vocal signs, calls of approbation. Techniques such as the deletion of the end rhyme or the repetition of key phrases engage the spectators in the ongoing construction of the sung text. Drawn in by the tension of anticipation, they too become players and poets. Together the performers and the audience articulate the high points of emotion in the story as they interact in the joint venture of creating the performance.

While an atmosphere of cooperation between audience and performers stimulates improvisation, equally important is the edge of challenge and competition that fuels the performance. Between audience and performers, the challenge is implicit in the guessing games that the singer initiates, as if daring the audience to "complete this if you can." The audience originates its own challenges as well, in its demands for passages to be repeated (at even greater levels of musical intensity or speed) or in requests for certain preferred items. If audience members are not pleased by the performance, they manifest disapproval in distractions such as talking, in avoidance (walking away), or in open jeering and disruption.

The interplay among the performers themselves is perhaps even more important to a full understanding of the process of improvisation. Music especially in its virtuosic dimension operates as a medium for acting out rivalries between singers and troupes. Melodic elaboration is prized because it "shows" the high calibre of the singer; the key verb in Hindi is *dikhānā,* to show not in the visual sense so much as to demonstrate or prove. The performance event is literally a "show," a proving ground, where a singer must demonstrate a sufficient degree of proficiency. The ability to hold one's breath, sing loudly, or high, or very quickly, establishes a singer's credentials as an expert, increasing his or her reputation. Improvisation is thus crucially tied to a competitive situation in which rewards are proffered for the achievement of special musical effects.

A further point, applicable to other musical styles in addition to theatre, is that improvisation is agonistic in nature; it relies on an opposition or contest between two individuals or parties. This competition generates the friction necessary for creative response. Folk theatrical forms like Nauṭaṅkī characteristically involve only two leading actor-singers on stage at the same time. Their dialogues are known as "question-answer" or *savāl-javāb;* the word *javāb* meaning "answer" or "response" occurs in the printed texts as a stage direction to refer to a character's speech. The *savāl-javāb* format has analogues in classical music performance and practices such as public debate of scripture (*shāstrārth*). The question-answer structure creates a dynamic of imitation and improvisation in performance, encouraging the continuously escalating elaboration of musical ideas. In contrast, epic recitational genres, in which there is one primary singer, inhibit improvisation and may therefore contain more static musical forms, at least as practiced at the village level. (One would expect more musical variety in an event like an Ālhā festival, in which different singers are competing against one another within the same arena.)

The intense rivalry that exists between Nauṭaṅkī actors and their troupes is manifest in the social organization of Nauṭaṅkī performers into *akhāṛā*s and is reproduced at every performance when the event is structured as a *daṅgal* or competition. An *akhāṛā* is an arena, gymnasium, or wrestling-pit—a ground for competitive play.[17] Sociologically speaking, it is an affiliative order based on adherence to a common activity or leader such as groups of amateur athletes (especially wrestlers and practitioners of martial arts), ascetics (sadhus and fakirs), and actors and folk performers in several regions of India. The possible historical connections between the martial and theatrical arts are particularly revealing here. Beginning as a site for physical training and male socializing, the *akhāṛā* acquired the characteristics of a cultural center where singing, dancing, and theatrical activities took place. In Orissa, Gotipua dancing boys were known as *ākhaḍā pilā* because of their attachment to particular gymnasia where they were taught athletics and dancing.[18] The consecrated dancing area in Seraikella Chhau is known as an *ākhaḍā;* the performers identify themselves by membership in two competing groups, the Bazar Shahi Akhada and the Brahmin Akhada.[19] The Bhagat, Khyāl, Māñch, Sāṅg, and Turrā-Kalagī are all traditions organized into *akhāṛā*s, as are nondramatic singers of forms such as Birahā.[20] An *akhāṛā* identifies itself by external symbols such as a distinctive banner, crest, color, or mark and internally binds itself through initiatory practices, common rituals, and an often secret body of knowledge.[21]

Nauṭaṅkī performers' discourse on their art provides further evidence of the competitive aspect. The early printed Sāṅgīts mention the poet's affiliation with a Turrā or Kalagī *akhāṛā* and the rivalry of actors in the theatrical arena, for example:

We bear the guise of the Turrā faction.
No one has achieved victory over those who wear the *turrā*.
Nattha the Brahmin and Madan enter the arena with the crest on their drum.
Raghuna leads the party in the *daṅgal.* / Flaunting the crest on the drum, he deals blows to the pride of the enemy.

The prefaces to some texts condemn Svāṅg and Khyāl performers for indulging in mutual namecalling and abuses, and in several places one reads of performances ending in physical violence—an extreme form of the *phaṭkebāzī* (bragging) employed to further group rivalry. On the positive side, competition produced a proliferation of performers and plays during the growth phase of Nauṭaṅkī (1890–1920). At least five major *akhāṛā*s were active in Hathras, and dozens of other parties were performing in the region.

What were Nauṭaṅkī performers competing for? As far as is known, theatrical shows in the Hathras heyday most often exhibited during fairs, festivals, and weddings, under the patronage of a prominent personage. Financial reward was thus guaranteed once a troupe was invited, but the troupe's survival depended on maintaining its reputation vis-à-vis rivals. Within the troupe, roles were graded, with the better singers playing the leads and receiving more money. Troupes tried to steal one another's stars so as to win the big bookings. Rewards or *inām* were also given for superlative performances. In short, competition seems to have flourished in the hopes of winning the name and fame always associated with show business.

It is likely that the Nauṭaṅkī theatre also operated as an arena for contesting political and social influence at the local and regional levels. The competition between actors and singers may have been part of larger processes of establishing dominance among communities. According to this analysis, the rivalry of Nauṭaṅkī troupes could be utilized and indeed fostered by opposing landlords, merchants, political factions, even religious patrons involved in their own contests for prestige and power. Unfortunately, little direct historical evidence has come to light to illustrate this process.

What I have said, in any case, should be sufficient to indicate a view at variance with that of Richard Schechner, when he states, "the occasion for theatre in India is not, nor was it ever, a competition among poets and actors."[22] Indeed, historical proof of dramatic contests is as old as the *Nāṭyaśāstra,* which lays out rules for how the king should award the banner of victory.[23] As I understand it, the Nauṭaṅkī performance in the days of the Hathras *akhāṛās* was very much a competition. Like a sporting event, it was dominated by a spirit of play and partisanship. For the audience, part of the entertainment consisted of taking sides, expressing approval and disapproval, and engaging in aesthetic judgments—especially of the singing by the leading actors. In accordance with these expectations, the musical style was soloistic, improvisatory, and almost unbounded in its use of time. To enable all sides of the audience to hear, for example, each verse was repeated three times on each side of the stage. Proceeding at this relaxed rate, performances could easily last all night.

In the 1920s with the rise of the Kanpur style, however, a process of commercialization began that fundamentally altered the theatre's musical culture. The "ticket-line system" involving box-office sales started to replace the old patronage patterns. Shrikrishna Khatri, a wrestler and tailor before his theatrical career blossomed, introduced changes to bring Nauṭaṅkī closer to the social dramas of the Parsi theatre. New topics on modern themes emerged, such as *Dhūl kā phūl,* in which two college students fall in love when their bicycles collide. In line with these changes, the music ensemble came closer to the model of Western orchestras by including instruments such as clarinets, trumpets, violins, even piano, banjo, mandolin, and bongos. Prose passages assumed a greater part in the verbal text, marked in Shrikrishna's plays by the English assignation *ḍrāmā*. Not surprisingly, the role of virtuosic singing and improvisation declined.

The Kanpur musical style is available on a number of commercial records and cassettes.[24] These miniature performances contain several recurring musical traits. The orchestral sound here is "fuller" than in the Hathras examples, using more instruments; it serves more frequently for sound effects and scene changes. The singing line reduces its range of pitches, its duration, and the amount of ornamentation. Metrical regularity replaces the free-floating unmetered recitative, with standard meters like *dohā-chaubolā* and *bahr-e-tavīl* molded to common time. The tunes associated with the various meters have become stereotyped, and the variety among them has diminished; recognition of metrical distinctions becomes more difficult. Fewer meters occur overall. The *bahr-e-tavīl* comes into prominence and by comparison the *dohā-chaubolā* fades into the background.

The most obvious indicator of the musical change to the Kanpur style is the virtual elimination of modal difference. It minimizes the contrast between the *bahr-e-tavīl* and *dohā-chaubolā,* for example, in two ways. First, it restricts the range of the *dohā* melody to the six notes of the descending scale, beginning with the high tonic and closing on the major third of the scale rather than the low tonic. The Kanpur *dohā* typically conforms to the type E outlined in example 10. Second, the *bahr-e-tavīl* is transposed from the tonic of C (with four accidentals) to the tonic of E (with no accidentals); thus, the final note of the *dohā* melody (the major third, E) becomes the tonic of the *bahr-e-tavīl*. The Kanpur *bahr-e-tavīl* in consequence uses the same range and tones as the *dohā*, extending from the high tonic to the third, with an occasional variant that stretches to the third in the higher octave (example 15). The transposition and removal of accidentals make the melodies easier for the orchestra to handle, especially for instruments with fixed intervals. The reduction of modal contrast also prepares the way for the most radical change: the introduction of Western harmony.

Before proceeding to that point, however, we return to the narrative of social, economic, and technological developments that precipitated musical change. Together with the breakdown of old patronage patterns, the 1920s witnessed the admission of women to the Nauṭaṅkī stage for the first time. Gulab Bai, who was awarded a Sangeet Natak Akademi prize in 1984, was one of the first to enter the field, beginning a trend whereby women now own and control most of the surviving companies in the Kanpur area. Although women performers in Nauṭaṅkī sing and enact roles in the same styles as men, the exhibition of the female body in public space—a cultural taboo—deflects attention from the music. The "male gaze" directed to the actress as fantasy object now dominates the popular stream of Nauṭaṅkī. This emphasis focuses on dance and the interspersed lyric portions of the text (song forms) and reduces the recitational styles of singing associated with the older Hathras art.

Further, the introduction of the talking motion picture shifted the whole arena of competition. At first folk theatre provided models for film production but then faced its own demise as cinema seized its audience. To keep pace, Nauṭaṅkī for years imitated the tunes and trends of the Bombay cinema, bringing the hits wholesale onto the stage or changing the words to fit the narrative situation. Musically this entailed the adoption of popular *gīt*s and *ghazal*s of urban origin, enhanced by simple Western harmonizations, as well as the diverse lot of regional folk dances and songs jazzed up for film presentation. With harmony creeping in through film music, harmonium players in Nauṭaṅkī parties

EXAMPLE 15. *Dohā* AND *bahr-e-tavīl* IN KANPUR NAUṬAṄKĪ

soon began to experiment with triads, adding a "modern" touch to the old recitatives.

More recently, Nauṭaṅkī listening (rather than viewing) has been turned into a leisure-time activity catering to the consumption habits of the semiurban populace. This trend has taken shape in the mass production of inexpensive audiocassettes and recorded LPs of Nauṭaṅkī

Fig. 23. Record jacket of *Bhakt pūranmal* on Brijwani Records, purchased in Lucknow in 1982.

songs (fig. 23). In this new package, Nauṭaṅkī offers to the consumer one more musical commodity available at the push of a button. Gone is the lively atmosphere of the *daṅgal* with the free play of improvisation it inspired. Instead, the soundtrack is a series of abbreviations: allusions to films, to sounds, to sentiments associated with prestige and pleasure. The new cassettes seem to be organized so that when casually dropped into a tape recorder, they offer hearers the first impression of a Hindi film score.

With widespread availability of amplification, instrumentation has changed drastically, both in live performances and recordings. One effect adopted from studio sound technology is the violin tremolo, used as background to prose dialogue, as found in an example from *Bhakt pūranmal,* one of the most venerable Nauṭaṅkī stories, in its latest incarnation on Brijwani Records. The worthy *nagāṛā,* a difficult instrument to record because of its resonance and low boom, has been replaced by *tablā, ḍholak,* and even castanets. The use of harmony and chords to accompany familiar *bahr-e-tavīl* tunes is another innovation. Other signs of the times are reverberation and special effects: the addition of ghoulish laughter (in an echo chamber) sets the scary mood for the opening of *Ḍākū dayārām gūjar* on a T-label cassette. The hallmark of these performances is the vicious speed at which the story and music proceed, imposed both by the limited availability and high cost of electromagnetic tape and by the hearers' preference for "modern," that is, fast-paced, music.

While the burgeoning audiocassette, film, and television industries have helped break up the old patron-performer-audience nexus that nurtured improvisatory folk music, they have attracted mass audiences seeking new symbols of social identity through hybridized forms of rural and regional music. Cassette technology, as Peter Manuel notes, may facilitate the access of rural audiences to folk music and even offer the potential for democratic control of the means of production.[25] In this sense, the mass media possess a regenerating force that may buttress dying folk arts and stimulate their recirculation. Meanwhile, for the recently urbanized seeking a palpable sense of place, the Nauṭaṅkī "hit" synthesizes nostalgia and modernity, negotiating the divide between distinctive regional cultural symbols and the homogenizing impulses of a larger public culture. Vestiges of the genre's identity remain, and the word Nauṭaṅkī still carries meaning. But a new arena has been created, and music now provides a ground for playing out the conflicts accompanying development, social dislocation, and economic change.

CHAPTER NINE

Conclusion

This inquiry into Nauṭaṅkī has opened up the field of indigenous secular theatre, a major area of cultural activity in South Asia for the last two hundred years and one that scholarship has largely overlooked. The period witnessed a complex transition from colonial rule to independence accompanied by realignments among social groups, changes in political and economic structures, and technological developments that irrevocably altered the premodern cultural fabric. As a consequence of these changes, some arenas of activity, including Nauṭaṅkī performance, lapsed to a great extent. However, the replacement of local expressive forms by Western-based models was neither immediate nor universal. Regional theatrical practices that predated British contact still exist in almost every linguistic region of India. Their continuation into the present derives from a combination of factors: the social distance that separates performers and audiences from the colonized stratum of urban society, the inappropriateness of imported cultural forms, and not least of all the resilience and adaptability of the theatres themselves. The persistence of these theatres albeit in transmuted shapes allows us to identify important, previously neglected aspects of the precolonial cultural system. Through forms such as Nauṭaṅkī we can glimpse the significant role of theatrical performance in producing shared values and symbols and hence in constructing community.

Secular theatre was obviously not the only traditional medium of communication. Religious dramas, epic recitations, folktales, popular songs, sermons, puppet shows, dances, almost every type of performance could transmit ideas to the unlettered. The formal and institutional sophistication of theatre, however, gave it unique scope. A relatively lengthy, complex form possessing its own sophisticated grammar, it possessed the internal capacity to expand complex ideas. Its external apparatus of costumes, scenery, music, dance, and other illusionary devices created a forceful impact, communicating its messages to large audiences.

The stress in this book upon a secular genre of theatre was not intended only as a corrective to earlier studies. By identifying Nauṭaṅkī as one among many similar theatres, I sought to indicate the large component of entertainment present in premodern forms of community life. This is not to say that the character of secular theatre was diametrically opposed to religious theatre or that the two occupied distinct temporal and spatial zones. The Rās Līlā and Nauṭaṅkī, for example, blended elements of each other and sometimes were staged side by side. Nonetheless, the secular theatres were preeminently designed for fun, not instruction or devotion. They offered a specific experience to their spectators, and they held an important position in social and cultural processes.

Before summarizing these aspects of Nauṭaṅkī, I wish to elaborate on the problematic position of secular theatre in educated discourse during the last century. As a result of European contact, a cultural stream developed in the late nineteenth century that in the literary field took the form of the urban drama, the novel, and the modern poetic genres. This emergent culture did not completely supplant indigenous theatrical genres, but the reformist discourse that resulted from the colonial experience pushed the theatre to the margins of respectability. In Bengal the Brahmo Samaj epitomized the trend toward puritanism. Meredith Borthwick notes, "It uncompromisingly condemned gambling, going to prostitutes, smoking, drinking, and the theater."[1] In the North Indian region, the Arya Samaj similarly abolished performances by dancing girls, introduced a purified form of the Holi festival, and condemned local theatrical forms.[2] Literary leaders like Bharatendu Harishchandra of Banaras declared most kinds of popular theatre "depraved" and lacking in theatricality.[3] Like other figures of the Indian renaissance, he championed a refined form of drama limited largely to drawing rooms and school auditoriums, whose purpose would be to assist in the moral regeneration of the nation.

It is worth asking how much effect such prohibitions actually had on the public who patronized traditional forms of theatre. The Nauṭaṅkī *akhāṛās* of Hathras entered their most prolific period around 1890, just as the reformist agenda began to reach western Uttar Pradesh. Publishers' exhortations to poets to produce pure verse seem to indicate the internalization of the pejorative discourse on theatre. Yet the Nauṭaṅkī as well as the Jātrā, Tamāshā, and Parsi theatres continued to flourish, and their audiences did not necessarily exclude aspirants to middle-class status acting in defiance of the reformers' dictates. Poets like Shrikrishna Khatri Pahalvan, who in his early career published under the imprint of the Āryā Sāṅgīt Samiti, illustrate the process of negotiation by which theatrical practitioners engaged with the dominant discourse and at the same time subverted it.

An additional difficulty is determining to what extent the "antitheatrical prejudice," to use Jonas Barish's phrase, was new.[4] As formulated in the self-purification campaigns of reformist elites, this prejudice would seem to have been an effect of British cultural colonialism. But was it an exclusively colonial discourse? Dating the construction of theatrical houses or the entrance of motion picture technology into the subcontinent is far easier than plotting the development of discursive formations now taken for granted. When were the performing arts conceptualized as either religious or secular? How can we identify the start of the distinction between "popular" and "elite" or find out when the prostitute-actress became the wife's rival? Indigenous terminology specifying these categories in fact precedes the arrival of the British. At what time these binary distinctions originated, and how such representations altered under the impact of historical conditions, including but not limited to colonialism, are significant questions that require further investigation. Nonetheless, it is beyond doubt that the theatre's ambiguous status in South Asia has an old record.

Although antecedent attitudes may have contributed to the theatre's disrepute, the marginalization of popular culture seems to have quickened in the colonial period. Sumanta Banerjee's research on the popular culture of nineteenth-century Calcutta indicates that the *bhadralok* (English-educated professional elite) increasingly associated popular forms with the "licentious and voluptuous tastes" of the "vulgar" populace, from whom they were at pains to differentiate themselves. Thus "the denunciation of popular culture was simultaneous with the formation of a new *bhadralok* culture." The urban audience for such forms had earlier contained large numbers of high-caste women who shared cultural usages, dialects, and idioms with women of lower socioeconomic groups.[5] Borthwick reports that a principal pastime of secluded women was attending Jātrā performances and other theatrical events.[6] As the male *bhadralok* consolidated their position, they exerted increasing pressure on their womenfolk to conform to British standards of ideal womanly conduct. They considered women's popular songs with their robust sense of humor and frank sensuality threatening to the new ideal of domestic order and heavily restricted elite women's association with female performers. Over time the campaigns against popular culture dramatically diminished the number of practitioners, leading to their eventual exile from urban society.[7]

As Amrit Srinivasan documents, female performers also came under attack in the well known Anti-Nautch campaign that culminated in 1947 in the outlawing of temple dancing and the prohibition on dedicating women as *devadāsī*s in South India. These professional performing women, living outside the model of companionate marriage favored by the British, practiced the regional dance form Sādir, an essential element in temple ritual and a component of the shared culture of Hindus in Madras province. Almost simultaneously the elite sections of society revived the "pure" art of Bharata Nāṭyam and, severing it from all association with the *devadāsī*, promulgated it as an appropriate pursuit for Brahmin women and girls.[8] In the process, they textualized the dance by invoking Sanskrit literature, eliminated the more erotic and bawdy songs, and created training institutions that supported upper-caste social practices.[9] A similar development occurred in the state of Orissa, where the temple dance performed by women of the Mahari community fell into disfavor and was displaced by the revived classical style known as Odissi.[10]

These examples among others illustrate a shared process: the maintenance and transmission of significant cultural forms by women performers in several parts of premodern India; the participation of women as well as men in their audiences and patronage networks; the relegation of these forms to the lower classes or popular culture by emergent elites or middle classes; the withdrawal of support coupled to the condemnation of female performers and viewers; and the construction of a new expressive culture with an altered representation of woman at its center. This sequence of events resembles the European experience that Armstrong and Tennenhouse discuss in their study of literature of conduct as a means of creating and regulating the concept of the "desireable" woman. Noting that the terms of desire change from one age to the next, they suggest "that the redefinition of the female was a crucial feature of the hegemony that brought the middle classes into power." If "the struggle to represent ideal female behavior indeed accompanied the struggle of an emergent middle class," then changes in the representation of women would be expected to accompany more extensive historical changes.[11] These statements acquire greater cogency if we understand "representations" not in the restricted sense of "images" lodged in literary texts but, following Chartier, as "the classifications, divisions and groupings that serve as the basis for our apprehension of the social world."[12] The representation of woman as public entertainer and locus of male desire no longer served the interests of the English-educated elite, which put in her place the Indian equivalent of the Victorian domestic angel, the *sugrihinī* or good housewife.[13]

The female performer, stigmatized in educated discourse as a "prostitute" and denied access to former sources of support, sought opportunity in the secular theatre and carried her marginalization with her. The Nauṭaṅkī theatre, chapter 1 suggested, owes its absence from the annals of literary history to its association with a prohibited category of womanhood. Demonstrated by such diverse sources as record jackets, cassette labels, chapbook covers, and modern fiction, the North Indian imagination unfailingly links Nauṭaṅkī with the alluring gestures of the dancer-actress. The feminine presence is also signaled by the nomenclature identifying the theatre. The genre is named for the aristocratic princess Nauṭaṅkī, the delicate, unattainable, and overpowering object of premodern desire.

In this way Nauṭaṅkī has been feminized in discourse and in practice. Its low status in the cultural system results from being identified with the devalued female gender. The continued participation of women in Nauṭaṅkī production, nowadays in managerial as well as star roles, reinforces the prejudice against the theatre. The presence and control of female performers meanwhile causes male performers to be viewed (and view themselves) as "effeminate" and inferior.

What I am suggesting is not, to use the words of Malika Begam that voice popular opinion, that "the wrong type of women . . . have fouled the atmosphere."[14] Since the second half of the nineteenth century it is doubtful whether there has been any "right type of women." This is not because earlier actresses were "pure," but because female performance at that juncture became problematic. It is not irrelevant or coincidental that Nauṭaṅkī's low status is "explained" by accusing those women who have sustained its existence of immorality. Popular cultural forms have been represented as marginal precisely because of the participation of women in them. The subordinate social status of women and their associations with the body and sexuality have been used to define these forms as "other" and establish the dominant group's superiority in relation to them.

Further work is needed to explore the representation of premodern Indian culture (later termed "popular" culture) as feminine vis-à-vis the emergent British-based modern culture as masculine. For now, an intriguing comparison may be made with one interpretation of modernism's development in western Europe. Andreas Huyssen argues that mass culture has typically been conceptualized as feminine in contradistinction to the masculine high culture.[15] Identifying women with pleasure and the "specious good," modernism "formed out of a desire to distance the threatening 'feminine' aspects of mass culture and the masses."[16] Huyssen details "the gendering of mass culture as feminine and inferior," which she dates to the late nineteenth century, "even though the underlying dichotomy did not lose its power until quite recently."[17] If this articulation rings true, then the parallel development in Indian discourse surely gains force. Further, it may at some level derive (to come full circle) from the colonial intervention.

One objective of this research then has been to reclaim Nauṭaṅkī and other forms of secular theatre from the neglect imposed on them by educated discourse. Once this discourse has been deconstructed, the overlooked cultural items actually revise our conceptualization of the system as a whole, revealing the selective nature of cultural tradition. As Raymond Williams asserts, tradition is constructed out of the "significant received and recovered elements of the past which represent not a necessary but a *desired* continuity."[18] My interpretation suggests that the association with female performers was the basis for Nauṭaṅkī's position shifting from desired to undesired element for certain social groups in the period under review.

Whereas colonial elites thus situated Nauṭaṅkī outside the cultural tradition that they reconstituted, I have contended that in practice Nauṭaṅkī was anything but marginal to social and cultural processes. This book suggests that Nauṭaṅkī functioned in integrative, mediatory, and oppositional ways, depending upon which aspect of the performance process we examine. Considered as a form of communication, Nauṭaṅkī operated as a mediating agency, crossing over several significant boundaries to transmit ideas back and forth among different groups. Sometimes this mediation occurred within a single arena, when spectators from several castes, classes, or religious backgrounds gathered to listen and watch together. Social divisions were not obliterated by the commingling in the audience; it is unlikely that social identity was radically transformed, or that there was a sense of fusion, or *communitas* to use Victor Turner's term, resulting from these performances. But by hearing the same stories spectators came to possess a culture in common. Themes were articulated, music was performed, symbols acquired meaning—and the community of spectators shared the experience.

Mediation also occurred across larger spaces as Nauṭaṅkī troupes traveled from one region to the next. The geographic linkage facilitated by itinerant entertainers was an important force in the construction of a common identity at the regional level. By employing specific linguistic, prosodic, musical, and narrative structures within a broad territory, the Nauṭaṅkī theatre extended recognition of them and ensured their survival. In this regard the theatre as a traditional medium of communication played a constitutive part in the production and preservation of North Indian culture. In the case of the Hindi-Urdu language based on the Khari Boli dialect, for example, the secular theatre likely contributed to its widespread acceptance as an oral speech form before it was canonically defined by literary usage.

Nauṭaṅkī also mediated between different levels of power and knowledge. Moving between villages with their extensive local lore and cities with their hybrid cultures, the theatre carried specific items of knowledge as well as larger structures of thought back and forth. Chapter 2 characterized Nauṭaṅkī as a conduit in the two-way cultural flow between urban centers and the hinterland. One important dimension of this process was the oral transmission of learned or literate culture, a flow not always synonymous with urban to rural contact. Literate culture of Sanskritic origin appears in the Nauṭaṅkī repertoire in texts such as *Harishchandra, Prahlād,* and other mythological stories; its Islamic counterpart is present in *Lailā majnūn, Shīrīn farhād,* and so on. These narratives with their ideological apparatus sometimes transmuted in the process of reaching the Nauṭaṅkī stage. Nevertheless, the performance medium facilitated their comprehension, with the result of popularizing the attitudes and concepts of high culture among large numbers of people. The practice of printing Nauṭaṅkī chapbooks similarly functioned as an incentive to the acquisition of basic literacy skills, making it possible for groups with little or no access to formal education to appropriate the substance of learned culture.

The reverse flow, from oral to literate culture, is more difficult to document without written texts. Nevertheless, it is probable that many of the better known Nauṭaṅkī narratives first circulated as oral tales in their own localities: *Hīr rāñjhā* in the Punjab, *Ḍholā mārū* in Rajasthan, *Soraṭh bījā* in Saurashtra, the *Ālhā* in Bundelkhand, even *Lailā majnūn* in the Arabian peninsula before it traveled to South Asia. In the same way that the folk drama repertoire incorporated these tales, so Nauṭaṅkī standardized and adapted the diverse melodies and meters drawn from oral culture to its purposes. The *lāvanī* of Maharashtra, the *māṇḍ* of Rajasthan, the *ṭhumrī* of Lucknow; the *sher* and *qavvālī* of Urdu poetry, the *dohā* and *chaubolā* of Hindi—all have enriched the oral performance style, blending with the formal characteristics of the ragas and *tāla*s of Hindustani classical music to create a rich composite.

The crossfertilization observable in these features of Nauṭaṅkī points to the intermediary character of this cultural form. It also suggests that Nauṭaṅkī (like all literary or performative genres, I would add) can be accurately delineated only in comparison and contrast to the genres that border it. Chapter 2 discussed a system of classification that allows us to place Nauṭaṅkī with reference to other major forms of the region. The idea of a "community of forms" as a conceptual basis for viewing cultural performance historically was the subject of chapter 3. Looking at the premodern modes of performance that were eclipsed during the reform phase of colonial history, I attempted to trace Nauṭaṅkī's emergence from a specific set of practices in an evolving social environment. Here too both literate and oral streams of culture left their impress upon the form.

The findings of this experiment in cultural archaeology were several. First, I established that secular theatre in North India predated the mid-nineteenth-century emergence of Khari Boli Svāṅg by at least a hundred years. The evidence of the Khyāl theatre of Rajasthan as well as a number of controversial Braj Bhasha dramas termed Svāṅg indicated that devotional dramas from the Līlā traditions were not the only possible models for the creation of Svāṅg and Nauṭaṅkī. Second, to the extent that the early Svāṅg was indebted to religious sources, I showed its connections to the iconoclastic practices of Yoga, Tantra, and Shaktism rather than the Vaishnava devotional cults. One proof of this link was the large number of narratives from the Nath yogi tradition that appear in the incipient Svāṅg corpus. Another was the formal similarity and historical connection between Svāṅg and Turrā-Kalagī, the tradition of spontaneous poetic contests of opposing heterodox sects. Third, I traced the distinctive Indo-Islamic character of Nauṭaṅkī to the impact of the nineteenth-century Urdu drama and the Parsi stage, suggesting that their pageantry contributed significantly to Nauṭaṅkī's character as a post-Mughal spectacle.

In chapter 4 I illustrated another method for gaining access to the historical context of cultural performance, namely the study of the printed literature of a folk genre. Nauṭaṅkī is a fortunate object of such study in that it possesses a large corpus of play scripts called Sāṅgīts published in cheap editions. Researchers now suggest that other South Asian performance traditions have an extensive history of publication. Carole Farber enumerates 374 Pālās or Jātrā texts that she collected during her fieldwork; she mentions that old Pālās are present in the National Library in Calcutta.[19] Similarly, Alf Hiltebeitel, on the basis of the research of Richard Frasca and A. N. Perumal as well as his own field collection, estimates that the literature of Terukkūttu could comprise up to 500 printed plays, beginning in the early 1800s.[20] These printed resources, once believed unavailable or considered inauthentic, permit a nuanced historical analysis far more comprehensive than that obtained from oral interviews and commissioned performances. We may hope that future investigations into South Asian theatre and other folklore genres will uncover more of these valuable texts and utilize them to construct a detailed understanding of cultural practices at the local and regional levels.

This study employed the printed Sāṅgīts to examine the social process of cultural production. The evolution of the printed text, its formats and geographical spread, the networks of publishers, and the association of authors into rival poetic lineages called *akhāṛā*s yielded information toward a sociology of culture. Comparison of these findings with other regions and traditions would substantially enhance the value of this information. As a warning, however, we must recall that such printed texts can be accurately interpreted only when referenced to an observed or documented performance practice. The difficulties the bibliographers in the British Museum and India Office Library faced in identifying the Sāṅgīt literature suggest the errors that may ensue when a performance text is unwittingly classified as an item of literate culture.

In the central section of this book, chapters 5 through 7, I expanded on the idea of Nauṭaṅkī theatre as a ground for exploring the moral tensions posed by the dilemmas of everyday life. The eminent Indian actor and playwright Girish Karnad recently stated, "To have any value at all, drama must at some level engage honestly with the contradictions that lie at the heart of the society it talks to and about."[21] Engagement with contradictions, I would stress, is equally the task of folk theatre and modern urban drama. In these chapters, I examined a range of Nauṭaṅkī narratives that confront areas of moral conflict: the exercise of political authority versus the practice of virtue, the spiritual perfection of love in contrast to loyalty to the community, the strength of women against the dangers of sexuality. Exposing the play of multiple meanings within dramatic texts, I illustrated that Nauṭaṅkī both upholds dominant or established values and challenges them. Through the creative involvement made possible by ludic activity, the theatre reworks the conflicts that riddle human experience, but it does not necessarily resolve them. Often a clash of viewpoints is highlighted by an unexpected narrative twist and then left unreconciled, or smoothed into an abrupt ending that masks a deeper confusion.

The terms of these perennial tensions were shown to shift as changing historical conditions offered new alternatives for individual and group behavior. In the early period of Svāṅg and Nauṭaṅkī, dramas about kingly renunciation phrased the popular conviction that the true king had no interest in material gain and privilege. Generosity and adherence to truth were the preeminent traits of the ideal ruler, yet these virtues ran up against the realities and responsibilities of power and proved almost impossible to fulfill, as the careers of Harishchandra and Gopichand demonstrated. For a later set of historically based heroes, the martial code of honor demanded loyalty, fearlessness, and benevolence. The independence and defiance of the warrior, however, kept him at a distance from the seat of power, where he was subject to insult, exile, and acts of betrayal. These dramas began to probe the injustice of the feudal system; simultaneously, their glorification of Rajput martyrs thinly disguised a bid to advance Hindu nationalism. The moral imperative to counter abuses of power, hinted at in these earlier plays, found its logical conclusion in the recent dacoit dramas. Here the underclass outlaw practiced almost the same virtues as the renunciant king, protecting the people by redistributing stolen wealth and enforcing justice at the point of a gun. For all his identification with the oppressed, however, he submitted ultimately to the higher power of the state, conceived simultaneously as the British Raj and the Congress party. His determination to create a counterstructure to established authority proved irreconcilable with his embrace of righteousness: much as the previous kings and warriors did, he chose truth and relinquished power in the end.

In the same manner that the moral basis of kingship, a doctrine of some antiquity, underlay these dramas, the premodern concept of love as a compelling spiritual goal united the second set of plays. Here too a progression toward contemporaneity was observable, but we must emphasize that the older dramas continued to command respectful followings; their moral formulations persisted despite external modifications. Thus the opposition between true love and social duty consistently structured these texts. In *Lailā majnūn,* the prototype of the subgenre, Majnun's excessive devotion to Laila led him beyond the bounds of civility and sanity. His search for the unattainable perfection of love, like the king's yearning for truth, collided with social arrangements; he too became a renunciant, leaving behind the fragile reality of the world.

Other dramas externalized the tension between familial bonds and inner conviction by positioning the lovers in different communities. Intercaste love was a common theme in older stories such as *Shīrīn farhād* as well as in modern Nauṭaṅkīs. Here the act of loving challenged the social hierarchy even more overtly, but the outcome often combined triumph over danger and social integration for the lovers through marriage. In recent tales the mistaken identity plot resolved the conflict between birth and desire, the initial dissimilarity of backgrounds heightening a romantic intensity that was finally compatible with social stability. In this way, Nauṭaṅkī dramas celebrated love and lauded its most unrealizable manifestations, as they upheld the order of family and community with which it so frequently clashed.

In the treatment of women and their lives, Nauṭaṅkī dramas again encoded seemingly mixed messages. Almost every drama contained utterances that belong to a discourse of female chastity and subservience, yet many of the characters (as well as the actresses who played their roles) were sexually active headstrong women. The earlier plays like *Pūranmal* posed dangerous aggressive women against saintly celibate men and punished most aggressors with violent death. A moral uncertainty lurked behind these events, however, for their premise was the polygynous family with its inherent instability traceable to the libidinous aging patriarch. Dramas of the *Ālhā* cycle, in a somewhat more positive vein, displayed the valor of the Rajput woman while distrusting her profoundly. A member of one clan by birth and another by marriage, she became the pretext of armed struggle between her husband's kin and her brother's, as both sides fought to protect her chastity. Her life typically ended in the horrifying act of *satī,* which marked the vindication of male honor through sacrifice of the female body.

A more expansive concept of female virtue (*sat*) found expression in the *vīrāṅganā,* who combined physical prowess with rectitude. Encountered in figures ranging from the mythic Virmati through the historical Rani of Jhansi and the contemporary bandit queen Phulan, she intervened at moments of moral crisis to restore righteousness. Contradiction still clung to her form: a frightening avenger, she could be ruthless and at the same time merciful to those under her protective care. But a conceptual separation had occurred between her morality and her chastity, paving the way for the emergence of new female roles. In recent plays widows, unwed mothers, and working women troubled the traditional concept of womanhood, raising issues of social justice and male culpability. Nonetheless, the auspicious state of matrimony was still painted as preferable to victimization by society, however unjust. Women thus acted in a wider range of roles, and morality was not exclusively indexed to their sexual behavior, yet patriarchal concepts were invoked to restate the code of womanly conduct within a liberal reformed framework.

My interpretation of these narratives contrasts with several recent discussions that assert the counterstructural character and function of popular practices. Cultural theorists of the West, including anthropologist Victor Turner, literary critic Mikhail Bakhtin, and historians of early modern England and France, have focused on a range of festive activities that they perceive as expressing opposition or resistance to dominant culture. Turner, in his earlier work on liminality and *communitas* and his later writing on theatre and cultural performance, stressed the antistructural character of ludic activity.[22] He viewed performance as a realm of transgressed boundaries and inverted symbols and considered periodic immersion in cultural forms of play to be regenerative, although basically he adhered to a functionalist position that omitted the perspective of change.

Bakhtin's notion of carnival similarly opposed the "two worlds" of official serious culture and the unofficial culture of laughter and "popular-festive forms." Carnival celebrated temporary liberation from the established order and marked suspension of hierarchical privileges and prohibitions.[23] Although both Turner and Bakhtin asserted that people use festive images to express criticism and distrust of official truth, Bakhtin's theory of carnival extended Turner's analysis of symbolic inversion by engaging with ideas of power. He maintained that the celebration of the carnivalesque helped remove the hierarchical authority of the medieval church and state and replace it with humanism and egalitarianism in the European Renaissance.[24] Similarly, recent studies of popular culture in early modern Europe have focused on its opposition to elite culture, looking in particular for elements of social protest and rebellion.[25]

Although these views differ as to whether performance can effect radical transformation (and whether that end is desirable), they are at one in their opinion that the content of popular performance is counterstructural. Yet the Nauṭaṅkī literature does not neatly fit this characterization. No doubt its narratives often pivoted on inversions of the North Indian social hierarchy. Motives of mistaken identity and disguise were prevalent, as was the inversion of ranked categories such as male-female, parent-child, and master-servant.[26] But Nauṭaṅkī presented no simple confrontation between "elite" and "popular" categories. Concepts that arguably articulate the interests of dominant groups (e.g., political authority, communal solidarity, gender difference) underwent challenge, debate, and reworking in the dramas, but by stressing everyday morality the dramas extended those concepts into normative categories for all groups. For example, the ideal of kingly renunciation became a model for virtuous behavior regardless of one's station. Is this a reversal of "dominant" ethics or its universalization?

Several commentators in India, including some of its prominent theatre directors, hold to an opposing view. These intellectuals, who have been active in creating new urban theatre movements, see no creative potential in the traditional theatres, which they consider backward looking, feudalistic, and irrelevant to contemporary needs. The avant-garde Bengali director Badal Sircar found folk theatre alien to his culture and to the urban experience, and he looked for inspiration to Western models like Grotowski's Poor Theatre.[27] Rajinder Nath, a Delhi theatre personality, felt that the fashion for folk theatre was simply a fad, a way of displaying a superficial "Indianness," and he resisted the trend to imitate its use of music and dance.[28] For Safdar Hashmi, an advocate of political street theatre, traditional theatres focused on reactionary values and empty ritualism, taking attention away from the situation of the common man.[29]

These interpretations proceed from the reflection and experimentation of committed theatre activists. It may not be fair to counterpose them to academic research. Yet we must look at the assumption underlying them, namely that the structure of traditional theatre is static and that it lacks the capacity for change. Again the Nauṭaṅkī literature points to a more complex possibility. Although perhaps not "transformative" or "revolutionary" in the sense suggested by Bakhtin (and wished for by Hashmi), the Nauṭaṅkī theatre has responded to the press of contemporaneity by updating its narrative content from decade to decade. Between 1880 and 1930, the cast of characters shifted from imaginary kings and queens to ordinary citizens of the present day. The stories increasingly incorporated social and political issues and commented upon the changing environment. The musical analysis in chapter 8 also showed that formal adaptation is a characteristic of the genre. Admittedly the genre is bound by a traditional grammar that separates the theatre from the realistic modes of representation of urban drama. This grammar, however, has always been somewhat malleable and need not restrict the innovative expansion of the form.

In conclusion then, I agree with Natalie Zemon Davis that "festive life can on the one hand perpetuate certain values of the community (even guarantee its survival), and on the other hand criticize political order."[30] The folk stage possesses a multivalent potential, like all media of communication, which we must neither condemn as reactionary nor laud as redemptive. Its content is multifarious, and it has the capacity to engage with contradictions and conflicts of many sorts. At the same time, I do not advocate a revival of some "pure" form of Nauṭaṅkī. Given the pace of change in modern India, Nauṭaṅkī is unlikely to regain the position it once enjoyed in public life; appropriation by urban elites can never recapture lost glamour. Raymond Williams points out the fallacy of "nostalgic reconstitution," the idea that past consciousness once revived and given contemporary trimmings can transform the present.[31] In the Indian case, the fact that popular films have usurped the idiom and audience of folk theatre makes its reemergence among the semiurban and rural populace particularly problematic. As Karnad has argued, theatre "does not exist in isolation but is a link in a long chain of reflexive relationships connecting different entertainment media." He speaks of the "high elasticity of substitution between the different performing media in India."[32] Films and television have taken over the modern cultural landscape, severely limiting the preservation and development of traditional art forms.

None of these observations rules out the creative synthesis of traditional and modern theatre forms that, despite the pessimism of Sircar and others, has flourished at the hands of directors like Habib Tanvir, Bansi Kaul, M. K. Raina, and Shanta Gandhi, to name a few.[33] In 1984 I attended a nationwide theatre festival sponsored by the Sangeet Natak Akademi in Delhi featuring "experimental productions which seek inspiration in the traditional/folk theatre forms, and thus through a process of artistic cross-fertilisation with modern sensibilities help contemporary theatre assimilate the heritage of the past."[34] The Nauṭaṅkī version of *Harishchandra* was here transformed into a new drama entitled *Harish channar kī laṛāī,* performed by Darpan of Lucknow under Urmil Kumar Thapaliyal's direction. Thapaliyal drew on Nauṭaṅkī scripts by Natharam Gaur and Shrikrishna Pahalvan, incorporating the meters, music, and grammar of traditional Nauṭaṅkī to construct the story of a twentieth-century man's attempts to live truthfully.

Even more recently, Anuradha Kapur transported the Nauṭaṅkī idiom abroad for an English-language version of Mudrarakshas's Hindi play *Ālā afsar,* itself an adaptation of Gogol's *The Inspector General.* Tara Arts, a London-based professional company, toured Britain in early 1989, and Kapur's experiment in transcultural theatre drew media attention in both India and England. "Kapur is attempting the weird and even more unlikely shift to an English version complete with the stylised bawdy folk forms of Northern Indian Nauṭaṅkī. Kapur is a specialist in traditional Indian performance techniques and her ostensible contribution is to familiarise her cast with the unusual vocals, movements and musical styles that have profoundly changed the texture of Gogol's play. . . . It's this healthy mix of what one can regard as the formal and the ridiculous that Kapur relates to with unhealthy relish. Her insistence that the Tara actors should not be strapped by her Nauṭaṅkī routines gives them the opportunity to develop their own ideas."[35] With these efforts, the organic process of artistic experimentation appears to be entering a stage in which Nauṭaṅkī, reshaped to meet a new set of requirements, plays yet another role.

Epilogue

CHUNNILAL: I must have been about ten years old. I was born in Aligarh, and I was living there at the time. One day it happened that a crowd of people were passing by, and I wondered where they were all going. I started to run after them. My father stopped me. He said, "Where are you going, young man, so late at night?" I made up an excuse and said, "Father, I'm just coming back in a minute." But then I followed the crowd. And what did I see, but a Svāṅg going on there in Jaiganj in Aligarh! I sat down at a corner of the stage. It seemed ever so fine to me, that Svāṅg. I don't remember a thing about it, and I didn't follow any of the sentiments, but I was so excited that I felt like singing right then and there. A tremendous wave of enthusiasm filled me. The next morning I made a vow that I was going to join the company, and I was going to sing in the Svāṅg. I went and met with them. I found the Svami and spoke to him myself—all by myself. I said, "Take me in, I want to join." He said, "What will you do here? It's a lot of work, there are many dangers." I said I would overcome everything with the help of God; just let me join. I stayed with them. The company was going to Bulandshahr, and in Bulandshahr, I mainly played the part of the sister-in-law in *Nauṭaṅkī*. And I don't know how, but it became so popular that people gave me a reward—a flashlight with batteries—and then I received various badges and medals. Well, my enthusiasm grew even greater after that. Ever since then, I've been in this line of work.[1]

To several generations of North Indians, the memory of running off to the theatre articulates an experience of freedom, a breaking away from rules. For Chunnilal, the boyhood encounter with Svāṅg revealed something hidden inside: his own voice, his penchant for role playing. At a turbulent moment he turned his back on the ways charted for him earlier. His life spun off in a new direction.

While presenting my findings on Nauṭaṅkī at conferences in North America, I met several Indian professors who recalled visitations of Nauṭaṅkī troupes to their hometowns in the 1940s. Their experiences of viewing Nauṭaṅkī as child spectators were remarkably similar to Chunnilal's. They recalled the excitement stirred by the arrival of the Nauṭaṅkī party. But of course Nauṭaṅkī was out of bounds; they were not allowed to attend. Late at night they sneaked off, usually accompanied by a servant from the household, to watch the shows with rapt attention. Unlike Chunnilal, these boys were taken home at the end of the evening's entertainment, but together with him they knew that chain of youthful fascination, parental disapproval, and escape to the realm of enchantment. The catalyst for each: a visiting theatrical troupe intruding into the quieter rhythms of daily life.

These recollections, loaded with adventure and defiance, were part of the shared cultural moorings of an age that grew up without television and cinema. Like the mythology of the circus in North America earlier in this century, such childhood lore continues to feed a sense of collective identity. It lends color and texture to the description of what it was like to grow up in the North India of that time.

It is difficult to say exactly what ignited the imaginations of both the child Chunnilal and the future professors. Their exposure to theatre occurred at moments of expanding awareness that entailed crossing over parental boundaries into a larger world. The transition was forbidden and fraught with risk. For them as perhaps for others in the audience, the theatre offered entry into an unexplored arena, a site of serious adult-style play. Perhaps a portion of liberation was also passed on to them, a release from the ordinary into the magic of the theatrical moment.

Chunnilal's encounter was decisive. There was no circling back to the familiar rhythms of the household; his embrace of Nauṭaṅkī lasted a lifetime. But even for those whose induction was temporary, the memory still sparkles. The recounting of it phrases an attraction to the theatrical world that lives even as the older theatrical forms recede from the common experience. Nauṭaṅkī remembered is a potent force in the popular mind of North India. It is a memory suffused with lost pleasure, abandon, and the taste of freedom.

A different sort of narrative accosted me when I was searching for the traces of the old Nauṭaṅkī. The memory bespeaks liberation and escape; the reality is one of destitution and decay.

Pandit Kakkuji is eighty-one years old when we meet in his costume shop-cum-residence (fig. 24). Lucknow, Ahiyaganj: a poor inner-city street accessible by cycle rickshaw. The threshold is crumbling but a crooked signboard announces the entrance. Beyond the steep stone stairs, bolts of spangled fabric tumble out of trunks. A huge *nagāṛā* hangs on the wall above the water pot. The shelves are packed with instrument cases, hat boxes, bedding, props. Yellowed strips of newspaper line the alcove that is crammed with jewelry chests. Outlining it, several dozen framed photographs picture the actors in leading roles from the old days.

Kakku's real name is Munindranath Goswami. He was born in 1901, the son of Ramnath Goswami, a painter of scenery for the Līlā dramas. He was influential in popularizing the Lucknow style of Nauṭaṅkī in the 1930s. Together with Ashiq Hussain and his wife, Malika Begam, he formed the Ashiq Company that was active until 1962. For the last twenty years or more, he has improvised a precarious existence stitching theatrical costumes.

Phakkar, another ex-Nauṭaṅkī singer of Lucknow, joins us midway through the interview. A toothless, wiry old man, Phakkar delights in demonstrating his powerful voice of yesteryear, contrasting it with his hoarse squeak now (see fig. 22).

> Eighty-six-year-old Phakkarji was a famous Nauṭaṅkī artist in his time. He captivated audiences with his acting and singing in many parts of North India. Audiences in places close to Lucknow still can't forget him. In 1965 he renounced this field because of the bad name of Nauṭaṅkī. Even at his age, he roams the alleys selling chapbooks and somehow ekes out a living. The thunderous range of his voice is without equal. He was so absorbed in his art that he didn't even know the meaning of "marriage." He is famous for his pure behavior in Nauṭaṅkī troupes.[2]

Phakkar and Kakkuji are both showcased on a television program in Lucknow aired the same night as our interview. The camera scans Phakkar's "home"—a hovel in the corner of a derelict building. The other featured artists are two Bhāṇḍ singers from Kashmir and a female

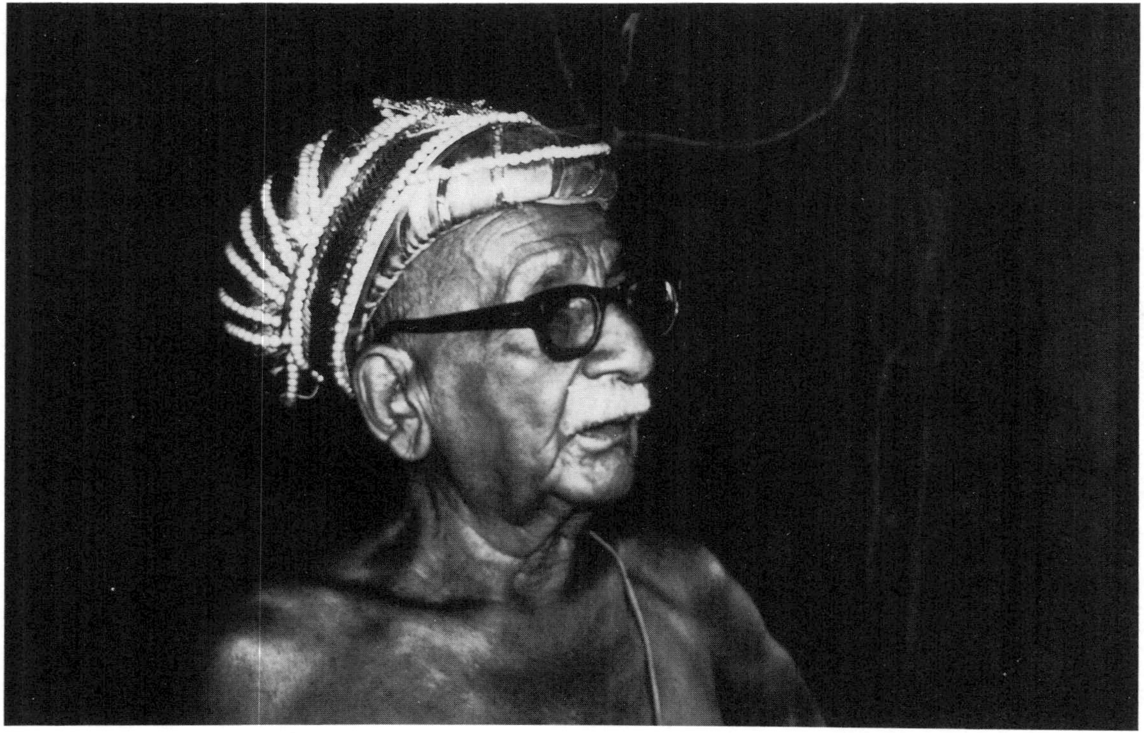

Fig. 24. Kakkuji, former Nauṭaṅkī actor of Lucknow, wearing a handcrafted headḍress. Photographed in Lucknow in 1982.

impersonator of the old Parsi stage. These are the human relics, survivors of the cultural wars of twentieth-century India. They are displayed like museum pieces for the duration of the broadcast, but their antics earn them no more than a few moments' respite. They are returned to the dusty streets to meet their own unmediated fates.[3]

The Nauṭaṅkī actors and actresses who performed in the bountiful days of the 1920s and 1930s are deceased, and hardly anyone remembers their names any more. The generation from the 1940s and 1950s is in its dotage—veterans like Kakku and Phakkar. Although they have experienced an unforeseen bit of fame in their final days as interesting subjects for television producers and foreign scholars, their economic situation is deplorable. Retirement is no different from unemployment for these artists; they have no pensions, surviving instead on their meager earnings as artisans and peddlers. Aside from the occasional government function or public appearance, they remain as unnoticed as the other lower-class citizens among whom they reside. They do not train their children in the art of Nauṭaṅkī singing. Malika Begam tries to ensure schooling for her daughters, because "you get nothing but disgrace in this work." Of the younger performers, those who are "professionals" also pull rickshaws, run tea stalls, or sell vegetables.

Nauṭaṅkī companies no longer tour the urban centers to entertain the crowds and allure the young. Without the visiting troupe, the nostalgia, the runaway experience, are not available to today's children. Young people in the urban north do not know the meaning of the word Nauṭaṅkī. If a troupe were to turn up suddenly, they would hardly prefer its outdoor stage to the air-conditioned comfort of the cinema hall. Meanwhile, in the countryside "song and dance parties" tour under the banner of Nauṭaṅkī, but scarcely a *dohā* or *chaubolā* gets sung. A nominal plot provides the pretext for the cabaret-style dancing imitated from Bombay films. The women who earn their livelihood supplying this entertainment may or may not be prostitutes, but their reputation is sullied and their art viewed as vulgar. Often these shows are restricted, taxed, or canceled by government authorities.

The objective of this book has been to describe Nauṭaṅkī as a definite form of life, a cultural organism emerging, growing, living, and dying within a community of related forms. That the old Nauṭaṅkī is now in a moribund state is beyond question. Although a research project inevitably draws attention to its subject, it has never been my aim to rescue Nauṭaṅkī. The complex cultural processes that brought about Nauṭaṅkī's slow attrition are probably beyond any human intervention. Yet even as one Nauṭaṅkī grows feeble and fades away, new uses of Nauṭaṅkī and other forms of traditional theatre emerge from the multilayered Indian cultural scene. Will Nauṭaṅkī be reborn into a changed world? In what guise will her next entrance be performed? These questions hold us suspended, waiting for the future.

The Kidnapping of Indal

Translation of *Indal haraṇ* (All-India Radio Recording)

NARRATOR: To the virgin goddess Sharada, the lord Ganapati, and the feet of the guru I bow my head, and having composed it, I tell the legend of the kidnapping of young Indal. Having composed it, I'll tell the legend. Uday Chand [Udal] arrived at the Ganges to bathe [on a festival day]. With him came his brother Alha's wife, Machhla, in order to have the ritual tonsure of her son Indal performed. They came to Bithur fort [in Kannauj] together with the brave Talan Saiyyad. Udal's brother was the paternal uncle of Lakhan of Kannauj [and thus they were cousins and were dissuaded from fighting]. Please quiet the noise and listen attentively now: this is the story. The queen Machhla, daughter of the Raghavas, spoke to the warrior Udal.

MACHHLA: Where are the tents of the Chauhans [the heroes' enemies], and where shall we encamp? [I.e., We should establish our camp where their tents are already set up.] Let the pride of the king of Delhi [Prithviraj Chauhan] be destroyed; I have decided.

NARRATOR: Hearing his sister-in-law's order, he waited not even an instant. Brave Udal drew his sword against the Chauhans. There was a terrible battle between the Chauhans and the men of Mahoba. Then the king of Delhi surrendered to Udal.

MACHHLA: My lord, Prithviraj has fled. The drums of victory have sounded. My lord, we rested at night. The morning star has appeared twinkling. My lord, go to the bank of the Ganges. Young Indal must get his head shaved. My lord, take Indal into your lap and bathe him in the river Ganges.

NARRATOR: Now from Balakh Bukhara came Abhinandan's daughter dear, wandering in search of a husband: Chittarrekha, disguised as a madwoman. When she saw Indal in Udal's arms, she lost her heart to him. Having turned him into a parrot by magic, this beautiful woman left [taking him]. When he didn't see Indal, Udal became very sad. Machhla stood there and became upset, saying "Where has my little Indal gone?" and repeating "Alas, alas!"

MACHHLA: Alas, alas, what has happened? Why has Fate burst the clouds? A terrible deed has occurred. Has someone drowned my dear little boy?

UDAL: Where has he flown from my lap? My dear child, the support of my life, the star of my eyes! Will I ever see the boy anywhere again?

MACHHLA: Oh king, without my son, I will expire. He is my eldest boy. Why has my home been laid waste?

UDAL: Without Indal, we cannot go back to Mahoba now. We can never return. Let's cross to the other side [of life], and die by stabbing ourselves in the milk-giving breast.

MACHHLA: Oh king, what are you doing? What kinds of thoughts are you thinking? Have patience, our dear Indal will not return [as a result of behaving] like this.

UDAL: How can I be patient? There is a stone on my heart, a weighty stone. My face has been blackened. In every way my fate has been destroyed.

TALAN: Udal, it won't do to cry like this. Have patience, Udal, within your heart. Come, let's go back to Mahoba and explain it. Let's go there and describe to Alha everything that happened. The parrot flew from our laps. We were left wringing our hands. What is destined to happen happens, oh warrior!

NARRATOR: With sad hearts, Udal, Machhla, and the rest set off toward Mahoba. Mahil arrived first and incited the anger of Alha, chief of the [Banaphar] clan. When Udal reached Mahoba and touched Alha's feet, Alha sternly spoke these words to Udal.

ALHA: Aren't you ashamed to come in front of me? Speak, where did you leave my son? Oh shameless one, the branch whose shade you enjoyed you have cut down with your own hands.

UDAL: The lad fell from my lap and drowned in the Ganges. Even as I watched, Death [Time] swallowed him up. The Creator is angry with me. What can one say? This is all the course of Fate.

ALHA: Tie him to a pillar and beat him with bamboos! Skin off all his hide. Just as he murdered my son, so let him be beaten unconscious.

NARRATOR: Everyone persuaded him greatly, but Alha would not change his mind. He turned Udal over to the hands of the executioners. When he turned Udal over, Machhla came to save Udal. Secretly she bribed the executioners, giving them her nine-*lākh* necklace. [A *lākh* is 100,000 rupees.] Through alleys and byways, Uday Chand [escaped and] came to Narvar fort. There Udal told the whole story to Makarandi [Udal's wife's brother]. Makarandi's mother prayed to the Mother Goddess. The Goddess herself appeared and revealed the whereabouts of Indal. Disguised as ascetics, Makarandi and Udal set out. They made their way to Bukhara, crying out "Om" and "Alakh, alakh" [begging alms] at every house.

When the queen heard that two enlightened ascetics had arrived, she sent a maidservant to invite them into the palace. Having entered the palace, the two sang the raga Mohani [a melody of enchantment]. They enchanted everyone and bewitched their hearts.

Chittarrekha invited both of them for dinner. Suddenly she changed Indal into a man and said to him, "You are not the only handsome one. This yogi is also under the sway of Maya [is beautiful]."

Indal said, "What do you mean? Whom are you calling a yogi? That is my maternal uncle Makarandi carrying the sitar, and this is my paternal uncle Udal, who makes the enemy tremble with fear." Indal embraced both Udal and Makarandi. Then Chittarrekha told [the visitors] the whole story of Indal [how she had captured him].

Having promised Chittarrekha [that he would return Indal to her], Udal took Indal and sent him back to Alha in Mahoba with Malkhan. "Here is your son Indal. Now bring back my Udal." In this way spoke Malkhan. Hearing these bitter words from Malkhan, Alha touched the ground [prostrated himself].

ALHA: Oh brother Malkhan, cut off my head! I was treacherous to Udal. From where shall I fetch Udal? He has gone to a terrible place. In exchange for Udal, you finish me off [kill me]. My life is torment, brother. I was treacherous to Udal.

MALKHAN: Why are you filled with remorse now, Alha? Listen closely to me. I've come from Balakh Bukhara where I gave my word, brother. Indal is to be married to Chittarrekha. Prepare Indal's wedding party—listen closely to me.

ALHA: O brother Malkhan, cut off my head! I was treacherous to Udal.

MALKHAN: Prepare Indal's wedding party—listen closely to me.

NARRATOR: Having said this much, Malkhan departed and didn't look back. The chief of the clan [Alha] performed his brother Udal's purificatory rites and lamented. Standing there, Alha thought about Indal's marriage and how it should be done. "Let Malkhan, Talan, Dheba, and Jagan come at my invitation and take the groom's procession to Narbar, stopping at my garden in Delhi." Udal spoke to Makarandi and he organized the procession. He sent Indal to Malkhan, because it wasn't in the paternal uncle's power [to take charge of a nephew's marriage].

[Indal said to Malkhan,] "Only you can get me married to Chittarrekha." When Malkhan heard this, he understood what was needed. He sent word to all the kings to come with their armies. Makarandi distributed the provisions and foodstuffs. They procured Udal's horse, who was called Bendil. They crossed place after place and finally reached Balakh Bukhara. Makarandi and Udal's army was spread out over three *kos* [six miles] of territory.

When Abhinandan got word he was incensed. "Oh father of Hamsa and Chhatrapal, what is troubling you?" He [Abhinandan] made Hamsa and Chhatrapal wage war [against the Mahobans]. Khatmal Khan captured the two brothers in battle, having raised his fist. When Abhinandan heard this, he was greatly angered. He climbed onto an elephant and rushed to do fierce battle. Abhinandan fought so brilliantly that his glory cannot be described. The Mahoba army got frightened and released his two sons. When Udal heard this, he was filled with rage. He quickly jumped onto Bendil's back and rode the horse through the sky. Brave Udal was a great fighter, and he fought fiercely. Whenever Udal went near other men, he broke several heads. He captured Chhatrapal and fought with Hamsa. Taking his sword in hand, Udal charged at Abhinandan.

[*break on tape*]

Leave this matter now and hear what happened next. When Alha saw this deed, he immediately recognized Udal. Approaching him swiftly, Alha embraced Uday Chand. Meanwhile, Abhinandan joined his palms and pleaded with Alha.

ABHINANDAN: Alha, my lord, listen to my plea, you are the chief of the clan. I am ready to marry my daughter to Indal. I am ready to marry her. Oh in-law, forgive me and release me together with my sons. Listen to my plea. I am happy to have the marriage performed between Indal and my daughter. Let the bridegroom and marriage party all enter my city. I'll entertain you with great hospitality. My daughter is ignorant, take her into your service.

NARRATOR: Alha released all three—Abhinandan, Chhatrapal, and Hamsa. Having embraced them, he respectfully bade them farewell. Chittarrekha and Indal were then married with the complete rites. Having obtained the life force from Guru Bichitra, Azad has sung this tale.

CHORUS: Hail to the mother Ganges!

Indal haraṇ (All-India Radio Recording)

Transcription prepared by Tara Sinha and Kathryn Hansen

KAVI: kumarī sāradā gaṇapati gurupad sīs navāy,
indal kuṁvar kī haraṇ kī gāthā kahūṁ banāy.
gāthā kahūṁ banāy, uday chand pahuṁche gaṅgā nhāne,
saṅg meṁ āī machhlā bhāvaj indal sut muṁṛvāne.
gaṛh biṭhūr āye saṅg meṁ tālan saiyyad mardāne,
kanvajiyā lākhan se tāū ūdal ke bhaiyā rahe.
band kar shorgul ab dhyān se suniye kahānī hai,
subhaṭṭ ūdal se bolī rāghav putrī machhlā rānī hai.

MACHHLĀ: kahāṁ tambū haiṁ chauhānoṁ ke, kahāṁ ḍerā lage apnā,
mān mardan ho dillī pat kā, maiṁ ne man meṁ ṭhānī hai.

KAVI: sunī āgyā jo bhābhī kī nahīṁ pal kī karī derī,
bali ūdal ne chauhānoṁ pe apnī teg tānī hai.
huā ghamsān chauhānoṁ mahobiyoṁ meṁ baṛā bhārī,
phir ūdal se dillī pat ne apnī hār mānī hai.

MACHHLĀ: mere svāmījī, bhāgo prithvīrāj, vijay ko bajo nagāṛo hai,
mere svāmījī, rāt kiyo bisrām, bhor ko chamko tāro hai.
mere svāmījī, jā gaṅgā ke tīr, kuṁvar indal muṁṛvāyo hai.
mere svāmījī, indal ko le god, gaṅg bhaṭṭ ūdal nhāyo hai.

KAVI: ab balakh bukhāre se āī abhinandan kī beṭī pyārī,
var kī talāsh meṁ ghūm rahī chittarrekhā ban matvārī.
ūdal kī god se indal ko dekhā to jiyarvā hārī,
jādū se suā banāy chalī indal ko sundar ye nārī.
nahīṁ jab dikhāī indal,
dukhī bhayo bhārī ūdal.
khaṛī machhlā ghabarāve,
kahāṁ gayo indal chhaunā kahe hāy hāy ḍaṭ āve.

MACHHLĀ: hāy hāy kahāṁ bhayo, kahāṁ ye bidh ne bādar phāṛo hai,
julam hai gujāro, kā ḍubakāyo chhaunā pyāro hai.

ŪDAL: godī se uṛ gayo kahāṁ sut indal prāṇī, prāṇ adhāro hai,
nainan tāro, kumar kāū meṁ kahūṁ nihāro hai.

MACHHLĀ: iday [uday] rāj, sut binā rahe na tan meṁ prāṇ, hamāro hai
chhaunā bāro, kahāṁ mere ghar ko ujiyāro hai.

ŪDAL: bin indal ke ab na mohabe jāno hoy, jāno hoy na hamāro hai,
karem kināro, mareṁ ur apne mār dudhāro hai.

MACHHLĀ: uday rāj, kahāṁ karoṁ, kahāṁ ye tum ne mato bichāro hai,
dhīraj dhāro, na aise āve indal pyāro hai.

ŪDAL: kaise dhārūṁ dhīr, paṛā hirday par bajar, bajar bhāro hai,
mukh bhayo kāro, har tarah phūṭo bhāgya hamāro hai.

TĀLAN: [*spoken*] ūdal, is tarah rone se kām nahīṁ chalegā.
[*sung*] dhīr dhar ūdal dil daramyān,
chalo mohabe ko kareṁ bahān.
ālhā ko jā kareṁ vahāṁ samjhāmeṁ sab bāt,
godī se totā uṛo, ham malte rah gaye hāth.
hot hai honhār balvān.

KAVI: ho dukhī hirday ūdal machhlā ādik mohabe ko dhāye haiṁ,
ā māhil ne pahle hī ālhā maṇḍalīk bhaṛkāye haiṁ.
mohabe ākar ūdal ne jab ālhā ke charaṇ dabāye haiṁ,
hokar kaṭhor ālhā ne yoṁ ūdal ko vachan sunāye haiṁ.

ĀLHĀ: sharam āī nahīṁ, ā gayā sāmne.
kah kahāṁ chhoṛ āyā merā lāl hai.
jiskī chhāyā meṁ baiṭhā, are besharam,
apne hāthoṁ se kāṭī vahī ḍāl hai.

ŪDAL: chhaunā gaṅgā meṁ ḍūbā merī god se,
dekhte hī dekhte khā gayā kāl hai.
rūṭh ham se vidhātā hamārā gayā,
kyā kaheṁ ye sabhī bhāgya kī chāl hai.

ĀLHĀ: bāndh khambe se bāṁsoṁ se māro ise,
iske tan kī uṛā do sabhī khāl hai.
jaise isne kiyā qatl, aur qatl ḍal merā
vaise hī iskā ho hāl behāl hai.

KAVI: sab ne samjhāyo bahut, ālhā māno nāy,
jallādan ke hāth meṁ ūdal diyo gahāy.
ūdal diyo gahāy, āye machhlā noṁ tāy bachāyo,
gupchup jallādan ko yāne nau lakh hār gahāyo.
dar manzil dar kūṅch uday chand narvar gaṛh meṁ āyo,
ye makarandī ko ūdal ne sāro ahvāl sunāyo.
māt debī ko makarandī kī mātā ne manāyā hai,
patā indal kā devī ne pragaṭ ho k͟hud batāyā hai.
banā kar bhes jogī kā chale makarand aur ūdal
bukhāre alakh oṁ jākar alakh ghar ghar jagāyā hai.
sunā rānī ne jab āye haiṁ do pahuṁche hue jogī
bhej bāndī ko mahārānī ne mahaloṁ meṁ bulāyā hai.
mahaloṁ meṁ ākar donoṁ ne mohanī rāg ko gāyā hai,
sab ko mohit kar ḍālā hai, sab ke man ko bharmāyā hai.
chittarrekhā ne donoṁ ko bhojan ke liye bulāyā hai,
indal ko jhaṭ ādmī banā kar aise bachan sunāyā hai.
tum hī ho nahīṁ ik rūpvān, jogī par bhī yah māyā hai,
bolā indal kyā kahtī ho, jogī kisko batlāyā hai.
o māmā makarandī mere jin hāth sitār suhāyā hai,
ye chāchā ūdal haiṁ jinke ḍar se dushman tharrāyā hai.
ūdal makarandī donoṁ ne indal ko gale lagāyā hai,
phir chittarrekhā indal ko sārā ahvāl sunāyā hai.
chittarrekha se bachan hār indal ko ūdal lāyā hai,

malkhe ke saṅg indal ko ālhā ke ḍhig mohabe pahuṁchāyā hai.
lyo sut apnā indal,
lā ab mero ūdal,
is tarah malkhe bole,
malkhe ke kaṭu bachan sune aur ālhā jamīṁ ṭaṭole.

ĀLHĀ: kāṭ sar mero malkhe bhrāt,
maiṁ ne ūdal saṅg kīnī ghāt.
ūdal lāūṁ kahāṁ se, vo pahuṁcho durdhām,
ūdal ke badle mero tū kar de kām tamām.
vrithā hai mero jīvan tāt,
maiṁ ne ūdal saṅg kīnī ghāt.

MALKHĀN: kāhe ko ab ālhā pachhtāt,
dhyān se sun lo merī bāt.
de āyo hūṁ bachan maiṁ balakh bukhāre bhāī,
chittarrekhā saṅg meṁ indal lījo byāy.
sajāo indal kī bārāt,
dhyān se sun lo merī bāt.

ĀLHĀ: kāṭ sar mero malkhe bhrāt,
maiṁ ne ūdal saṅg kīnī ghāt.

MALKHĀN: sajāo indal kī bārāt,
dhyān se sun lo merī bāt.

KAVI: itnī kah malkhe gayo, phir mukh debo nāy,
sudhi kar ūdal bhrāt kī maṇḍalīk bilakhāy.
kharā kharā ye ālhā soche kaise ho indal ko byāh,
malkhe tālan ḍheba jāgan mere bulāye āne āy.
le bārāt narbar meṁ āyo, bagiyā mere dillī ṭhahrāy,
ūdal ne makarandī se kah sab bārāt līnī juṭvāy.
indal bhejo malkhe ke ḍhig, chachā kahūṁ ke bas kī nāy,
chittarrekhā ke saṅg mero tum hī karāy sakyo ho byāh.
ye itnī bāt sunī malkhe ne ho vāke man meṁ gaī hai samāy,
khabar bhej daī sab rājan pe, āye apnī fauj sajāy.
makarandī ne māl lūṭ ko rasad sahit dīnī pahuṁchāy,
ūdal ko ghoṛā rakh līno jāko bendil nām kahāy.
manjil dar manjil dekh lī pahuṁche balakh bukhāre jāy,
tīn kos pe hai makarande ūdal ko rahyo lashkar chhāy.
abhinandan ko khabar paṛī to man meṁ gayo sanākoṁ khāy,
haṁsā chhatrapāl ke bābul, tum ko kaun paṛī parvāy.
haṁsā chhatrapāl ko unhoṁne dīno hai ghamsān machāy,
khaṭmal khān ne do bhaiyan kī līnī raṇ meṁ mushk chaṛhāy.
itnī khabar sunī abhinandan gussā gayo badan meṁ chhāy,
hāthī chaṛhke laṛve āyo dīnī mārāmār machāy.
aiso yuddh kiyo abhinandan jāke shobhā varaṇ na jāy,
fauj ḍar gaī ab mohabe kī līne haiṁ doū putra chhuṛāy.
itnī khabar sunī nar ūdal gussā gayo badan meṁ chhāy,

jhaṭ asavār bhayo bendul pe gayo bendulā gagan uṛāy.
baṛō laṛaiyā hai bhaṭṭ ūdal dīnī mārāmār machāy,
jiske nikaṭ jāt nar ūdal bhaiyā kāī sire phaṭ jāy.
chhatrapāl ko qaid kiyo phir haṁsā kī laṛī musk chaṛhāy,
gend lāl ke hāth teg le abhinandan se bhiṛ gayo jāy.
[*break*]
yahāṁ kī bāt yahīṁ par chhoṛo, ab āge kī suno bayān,
ye kartab jab dekhā ālhā, jhaṭ ūdal līno pahchān.
āge baṛh ke jhaṭ ālhā ne līyo uday chand gale lagāy,
it abhinandan hāth joṛkar ālhā se yoṁ bolo āy.

ABHINANDAN: vinay merī sun lījiye tū maṇḍalīk sardār,
indal saṅg nij sutā maiṁ byāhan ko taiyār.
taiyār hūṁ maiṁ byāh ko, samadhī kṣhamā kar dījiye,
chhoṛo mujhe putroṁ sahit, binatī merī sun lījiye.
indal ke saṅg mam sutā ko <u>kh</u>ush hai ki byāh rachāiye,
dulhā sahit bārāt sab mere nagar meṁ āiye.
jay jay baṛī <u>kh</u>ātir karūṁ, sirdār rājan kījiyo,
nādān hai beṭī merī, sevā meṁ apnī lījiyo.

KAVI: abhinandan chhatrapāl haṁsā tīnoṁ ālhā ne chhoṛ diye,
milkar ke gale sanmān sahit tīnoṁ phir vahāṁ se bidā kiye.
chittarrekhā indal kā phir vidhipūrvak byāh rachāyā hai,
guruvar bichitra kā āyus pā āzād ne ye kath gāyā hai.

CHORUS: bol gaṅgā maiyā kī jay!

Appendixes

APPENDIX A: Motif Analysis of *Sāṅgīt nauṭaṅkī shāhzādī* by Natharam

Based on motif index in Stith Thompson and Jonas Balys, *The Oral Tales of India* (Bloomington: Indiana University Press, 1958)

H 1222.	Prince a-hunting enters on quest
H 934.2.	Sister-in-law imposes task
W 165.	False pride (Phul Singh's)
W 185.6.	Insult worse than wound (sister-in-law's harsh words)
K 2212.2.	Treacherous sister-in-law
T 254.	Disobedient wife (elder brother's)
T 11.1.	Love from mere mention or description
H 455.	Chastity test: king weighs princess against flower
H 1301.1.1.2.	Quest for faraway princess
H 1301.1.	Quest for most beautiful bride
H 1381.3.1.2.3.	Quest for dangerous maiden as bride
T 50.1.	Girl carefully guarded from suitors
M 146.1.	Vow to marry queen of fairies (in this case, most beautiful woman) and not to eat or drink inside kingdom until this is done
H 1236.	Perilous path traversed on quest
H 1233.1.1.	Old woman helps on quest
N 825.3.	Old woman helper
H 971.1.	Tasks performed with help of old woman

H 90.	Identification by ornaments
H 94.9.	Identification through ring (here, gem) concealed in garland
D 12.	Transformation: man to woman
K 1836.	Disguise of man in woman's dress
K 1321.1.	Man disguised as woman admitted to women's quarters
D 658.3.	Transformation of sex to seduce
K 1816.	Disguise as a menial
K 1816.1.	Gardener disguise
K 1816.0.3.	Menial disguise of princess's lover
T 31.	Lovers' meeting: hero in service of heroine
D 1812.5.	Future learned through omens (throbbing arm)
T 3.	Omens in love affairs
T 24.	Symptoms of love
T 28.	Princess falls in love with a man disguised as a woman
T 55.	Girl as wooer
K 1970.	Sham miracle (sex change by invoking saint)
H 455.	Chastity test: king weighs princess against flower
T 84.	Lovers treacherously separated
Q 243.2.	Seduction punished
Q 256.	Punishment for clandestine lover of princess
Q 413.	Punishment: hanging
J 1192.	The bribed judge
W 35.2.	Upright judge refuses bribe
K 512.	Compassionate executioner
D 11.	Transformation: woman to man
K 1837.	Disguise of woman in man's clothes
K 1837.6.	Disguise of woman as a soldier
D 643.	Transformation so as to rescue
R 161.0.1.	Hero rescued by his lady
R 162.	Rescue by captor's daughter
T 97.	Father opposed to daughter's marriage
T 131.1.2.	Father's consent to daughter's marriage necessary
L 111.1.	Exile returns and is successful
L 10.	Victorious youngest son

APPENDIX B: Khyāl Literature in British Collections

1. From J. F. Blumhardt, *Catalogues of the Hindi, Panjabi, Sindhi, and Pushtu Printed Books in the Library of the British Museum* (1893)

Khyāl ḍholā mārū. n.a. Benares: 1882. 64 pp. lith. 14158.c.22(3). Blum1893:273.
Gopichand kā khyāl. Motī Lāl. Poona: 1881. 51 pp. lith. 14158.c.10(8). Blum1893:113. [VT1280]
Khyāl gopīchand. Sahdev. Benares: 1882. 56 pp. lith. 14156.h.29(1). Blum1893:152.
Maṇiyārī kā khyāl. Sahdev. Delhi: 1881. 24 pp. lith. 14158.c.9(8). Blum1893:153.
Pannā bīrande kā khel. Maṅgal Dās. Delhi: 1876. 60 pp. lith. 14158.c.3(7). Blum1893:104. [VT1134,1131]
Pinglā satī kā khyāl. Sahāshivkaran Darak. Bombay: 1881. 39 pp. 14158.c.22(2). Blum1893:153.
Rājā chitramukaṭ ko khyāl. Nānūlāl Rāṇā. Bombay: 1887. 91 pp. lith. 14156.h.29(3). Blum1893:117.
Khyāl rājā chitramukuṭ ko. Nānūlāl Rāṇā. Bombay: 1890. 79 pp. lith. 14156.h.28(2). Blum1893:276.
Khyāl rāṇā ratan siṁh kā. Chunnīlāl Ḍākot. Calcutta: 1887. 48 pp. 14156.h.34(1). Blum1893:36.
Rañjā hīr kā khyāl. Sevak Kīrat Rām. Bombay: 1875. 143 pp. lith. 14156.h.9. Blum1893:158. [VT49.A-33]
Khyāl saudāgar vazirzādī kā. Nānūlāl Rāṇā. Calcutta: 1887. 55 pp. 14156.h.34(2). Blum1893:117. [VT1566]
Khyāl sudavrachh sālaṅgyā kī. Jhālī Rām. Calcutta: 1886. 56 pp. 14158.d.25. Blum1893:274.

2. From J. F. Blumhardt, *A Supplementary Catalogue of Hindi Books in the Library of the British Museum, Acquired during the Years 1893–1912* (1913)

Khyāl chandrapratāp rājā ko. Bhān Jotgī. Calcutta: 1892. 57 pp. 14156.h.45(1). Blum1913:38.
Nakal devar bhujāī kī. Bālmukundjī. Bombay: 1894. 44 pp. 14156.h.44(2). Blum1913:31.
Pūrā khel māñch kā ḍholā mārūnī. Bālmukundjī. Delhi: 1895. 47 pp. lith. 14156.h.31(2). Blum1913:30.
Nakal gendā parī kī. Bālmukundjī. Bombay: 1894. 28 pp. 14156.h.44(3). Blum1913:31.
Khyāl hīr rāñjhā ko. Nānūlāl Rāṇā. Calcutta: 1892. 68 pp. 14156.h.45(3). Blum1913:202.
Khyāl jagdev kaṅkālī ko. Nānūlāl Rāṇā. Calcutta: 1892. 68 pp. 14156.h.45(4). Blum1913:203.
Khyāl pannā bīramde ko. Chunnīlāl Jotgī. Calcutta: 1892. 53 pp. 14156.h.45(2). Blum1913:62.

Pūrā khel māñch kā rājā bharatharī. Bālmukundjī. Delhi: 1897. 16, 80 pp. lith. 14156.h.66. Blum1913:30.
Khyāl ratan kuṁvar ko. Bichhulāljī. Bombay: 1892. 35 pp. 14156.h.39(2). Blum1913:50.
Pūrā khel māñch kā seṭh seṭhānī. Bālmukundjī. Delhi: 1895. 47 pp. lith. 14156.h.31(3). Blum1913:31.
Sultān marvaṇ bhāṭ kā khyāl. Ujīrām Telī. Bombay: 1893. 56 pp. 14156.h.44(1). Blum1913:320.
Khyāl tote mainā kā. Lālā Ghāsīrām. Moradabad: 1901. 10 pp. 14156.h.50(2). Blum1913:89–90.

3. From L. D. Barnett, J. F. Blumhardt, and J. V. S. Wilkinson, *A Secondary Supplementary Catalogue of Printed Books in Hindi, Bihari, . . . and Pahari in the Library of the British Museum* (1957)

Amar siṁh jī ko khyāl. Hariprasād Bhagīrath. Bombay: 1914. 127 pp. lith. 14158.ccc.5(3). Barn1957:24.
Khyāl āsā ḍābī arthāt, pachphūlā kā. Krishṇalāl. Jaipur/Mathura: 1923. 80 pp. 14158.ccc.30(5). Barn1957:494.
Khyāl chhailā diljān. Nandrām Paṁsārī Lāljī. Jaipur/Mathura: 1923. 16 pp. 14158.ccc.30(6). Barn1957:651.
Khyāl ḍholā marvaṇ ko. Nānūlāl Rāṇā. Jaipur/Mathura: 1930. 91 pp. 14158.c.71. Barn1957:652.
Khyāl ḍholā marvaṇ ko. Nānūlāl Rāṇā. Mathura: 1937. 96 pp. 14158.ccc.39. Barn1957:652.
Dūlā dhāḍvī ko khyāl. Nānūlāl Rāṇā. Bombay: 1914 (2d ed.). 87 pp. lith. 14158.ccc.5(4). Barn1957:652.
Nayā khyāl ḍuṅgar siṅg javār sīṅg kā. Nandrām Paṁsārī Lāljī. Nimach/Ahmedabad: 1914 (2d ed.). 15 pp. 14158.ccc.30(2). Barn1957:651.
Hiṛāū mairī kā khyāl. Rāmratandās Karnāṇī. Calcutta: 1914. 66 pp. 14158.ccc.29. Barn1957:853.
Khīmjī bālechā aur ābhalde kā baḍā khyāl. Sadāsukh Bhagvān Dās. Bholwada/Ahmedabad: 1916. 75 pp. 14156.h.50(3). Barn1957:883.
———Jaipur/Mathura:1928. 80 pp. 14158.ddd.9(2). Barn1957:883–4.
Navā khyāl nanand bhojāī kā. Pūnamchand Sikhvāl. Bombay: 1923. 15 pp. 14158.ccc.16(11). Barn1957:748.
Pannā bīramde kā khyāl. Nandrām Paṁsārī Lāljī. Nimach/Ahmedabad: 1914 (3d ed.). 47 pp. 14157.a.23(2). Barn1957:651.
Rājā kesar siṁh ko khyāl. n.a. Bombay/Jodhpur: 1926. 40 pp. 14158.ccc.30(7). Barn1957:475.
Khyāl rājā kesar siṁh rānī phūlān de kā. n.a. Jaipur/Mathura: 1924 (2d ed.). 44 pp. 14158.ddd.9(1). Barn1957:475.
Khyāl rājā risālu nopade kā. Jhālī Rām. Jaipur/Mathura: 1924. 64 pp. 14158.ccc.32(5). Barn1957:414.
Shrīkrishṇa avtār arthāt kaṁs rājā kā khyāl. Nandrām Paṁsārī Lāljī. Nimach/Moradabad: 1912. 65 pp. 14158.ccc.16(2). Barn1957:651.

Sultān marvaṇ kā bhāt kā khyāl. Vazīr Khān Telī. Jaipur/Mathura: 1927. 48 pp. 14158.ccc.30(9). Barn1957:1154.

4. From J. F. Blumhardt, *Catalogue of the Library of the India Office,* vol. 2, pt. 3, *Hindi, Panjabi, Pushtu, and Sindhi Books* (1902)

Navā khyāl bañjāre kā. n.a. Bombay: 1882. 52 pp. VT1202. Blum1902:37.
Khyāl bīñjārā kā. Prahlād Rāy. Calcutta: 1878. 25 pp. VT1213. Blum1902:68.
Ḍhol sultān ko khyāl. n.a. Delhi: 1879. 28 pp. VT1537. Blum1902:62.
———Delhi: 1879. 64 pp. VT1570. Blum1902:62.
Dūṅgar siṁh kā khyāl. n.a. Delhi: 1877. 20 pp. VT1137. Blum1902:67.
Gopīchand kā khyāl. Motī Lāl. Agra: 1869. 63 pp. VT1287. Blum1902:67.
———Bombay: 1869. 63 pp. VT1577. Blum1902:67.
———Poona: 1870. 57 pp. VT1579. Blum1902:67.
———Muttra: 1873. 63 pp. VT1127. Blum1902:67.
———Agra: 1874. 63 pp. VT1136. Blum1902:67.
———Delhi: 1875. 64 pp. VT1127. Blum1902:67.
———Poona: 1875. 60 pp. lith. VT1287. Blum1902:67.
———Delhi: 1876. 56 pp. VT1127. Blum1902:67.
———Delhi: 1879. 56 pp. VT1129. Blum1902:67.
———Poona: 1881. 51 pp. VT1280. Blum1902:67. [14158.c.10(8)]
Khyāl harishchandra kā. Shivprasād Poddār. Akola: 1886. 30 pp. VT1278. Blum1902:68.
Khyāl nal rājā kā. Nānūlāl Rāṇū. Calcutta: 1877. 78 pp. VT1287. Blum1902:30.
Pannā bīrande kā khel. Maṅgal Dās. Delhi: 1874. 61 pp. lith. VT1134. Blum1902:69.
——— Delhi: 1877. 60 pp. VT1131. Blum1902:69.
Khyāl pūran mal kā. Gaṇesh Prasād Sharmā. Calcutta: 1892. 78 pp. VT1274. Blum1902:30.
Rājā moti siṁh gul anārde kī khyāl. Kāshīnāth Mishra. Ajmer: 1878. 39 pp. VT1273. Blum1902:69.
Khyāl rājā risālu ko. Nānūlāl Rāṇā. Calcutta: 1878. 40 pp. VT1213. Blum1902:68.
Rañjhā hīr kā khyāl. Kīrat Rām. Bombay: 1875. 143 pp. 49.A-33. Blum1902:69. [14156.h.9]
Khyāl saudāgar vazīrzādī kā. Nānūlāl Rāṇā. Calcutta: 1887. 55 pp. VT1566. Blum1902:68. [14156.h.34(2)]
Khyāl shāhzāde benazir o badr-i munīr kā. n.a. Calcutta: 1881. 57 pp. VT1567. Blum1902:68.
Khyāl shāhzāde kā. Prahlād Rāy. Calcutta: 1877. 31 pp. VT1287. Blum1902:68.
Khyāl sīlosatvantī kā. Jagannāth Pujārī. Calcutta: 1884. 71 pp. VT1274. Blum1902:68.
Siṅgīvālā jarrāh kā khyāl. Shivkaraṇ. Delhi: 1879. 19 pp. VT1129. Blum1902:70.
Sudbudh sālaṅgyā kā khyāl. Baldev Juṅgarlāl. Poona: 1876. 14 pp. lith. VT1126. Blum1902:70.
Sultān shāh bādshāh kā khyāl. Nānūlāl Rāṇā. Calcutta: 1878. 45 pp. VT1274. Blum1902:70.

APPENDIX C: Sāṅgīt Literature in British Collections

1. From J. F. Blumhardt, *Catalogues of the Hindi, Panjabi, Sindhi, and Pushtu Printed Books in the Library of the British Museum* (1893)

Sāṅgīt ālhā mal khān. n.a. Delhi: 1882. 32 pp. lith. 14158.b.6(4). Blum1893:5.
Sāṅgīt basant kumār aur sāhukār bachchī kā. Faqīr Chand. Lahore: 1882. 52 pp. lith. 14158.b.6(5). Blum1893:48.
Sāṅgīt bīn bādshāhzādī. Jñānchandra. Meerut: 1877. 32 pp. lith. 14158.e.15(3). Blum1893:76.
Sāṅgīt budrī munīr. Hardev Sahāy. Meerut: 1876. 32 pp. lith. 14158.e.3(5). Blum1893:12.
Sāṅgīt chandravadan rūpakavār kā. n.a. Meerut: 1877. 32 pp. lith. 14158.e.15(5). Blum1893:32.
Sāṅgīt dhurūjī kā. n.a. Delhi: 1876. 32 pp. lith. 14158.e.8(14). Blum1893:43. [VT1536]
Dhurū līlā. n.a. Benares: 1875? 12 pp. lith. 14158.e.13(2). Blum1893:43.
Sāṅgīt dhurū līlā. n.a. Benares: 1880. 36 pp. lith. 14158.b.6(1). Blum1893:43.
Gopīchand bharatarī sāṅgīt. Kuṁvar Lakṣhmaṇ Siṁh. Delhi: 1868. 32 pp. lith. 14158.e.2(2). Blum1893:90.
Gopīchandra bharatarī. Kuṁvar Lakṣhmaṇ Siṁh. Delhi: 1870. 36 pp. lith. 14158.e.8(5). Blum1893:90. [VT1104]
———Delhi: 1874. 32 pp. lith. 14158.e.3(2). Blum1893:90. [VT1092]
———Delhi: 1877. 32 pp. lith. 14158.e.15(4). Blum1893:90.
———Meerut: 1878. 32 pp. lith. 14158.e.3(10). Blum1893:90.
———Meerut: 1878. 32 pp. lith. 14158.e.15(7). Blum1893:90. [VT1225]
———Benares: 1883. 32 pp. lith. 14156.i.24(3). Blum1893:90.
Sāṅgīt nānaksāī va sutresāī. Charaṇ Dās. Meerut: 1886. 12 pp. lith. 14156.i.26(2). Blum1893:32.
Prahlād sāṅgīt. Kuṁvar Lakṣhmaṇ Siṁh. Delhi: 1866. 48 pp. lith. 14156.i.11(1). Blum1893:90.
———Delhi: 1868? 48 pp. lith. 14156.i.18(2). Blum1893:90.
———Meerut: 1878. 48 pp. lith. 14158.e.15(8). Blum1893:90. [VT1092]
———Benares: 1882. 48 pp. lith. 14158.b.6(7). Blum1893:90.
Sāṅgīt puran mal kā. Rāmlāl. Meerut: 1878. 32 pp. lith. 14158.e.3(12). Blum1893:143. [VT1225]
———Meerut: 1879. 32 pp. lith. 14158.e.15(9). Blum1893:143.
Sāṅgīt raghbīr siṁh. Hardev Sahāy. Benares: 1882. 16 pp. lith. 14158.b.6(3). Blum1893:60.
Sāṅgīt rājā harichandra kā. Jainī Jīyā Lāl. Benares: 1877. 52 pp. lith. 14158.e.8(17). Blum1893:65.
Sāṅgīt rājā kārak kā. n.a. Meerut: 1878. 32 pp. lith. 14158.e.3(11). Blum1893:81.
———Benares: 1882. 32 pp. lith. 14158.b.6(6). Blum1893:81.
Sāṅgīt rājā mordhvaj. n.a. 24 pp. lith. Pers. char. Delhi: 1875? 14162.f.9(11). Blum 1893:274–5. [VT1090]
Sāṅgīt rānī nauṭaṅkī kā. Khushī Rām. Benares: 1882. 36 pp. lith. 14158.b.5(2). Blum1893:86.

Sāṅgīt rūp basant kā. Lakṣhmaṇ Siṁh and Hardev Sahāy. Meerut: 1876. 14158.e.8(13). Blum1893:60, 90. [VT1090]

———Meerut: 1877? 32 pp. lith. 14156.i.16(1). Blum1893:90.

———Benares: 1880? 32 pp. lith. 14158.b.6(2). Blum1893:90.

Sāṅgīt saudāgar vo syāhposh kā. Gurudayāl Siṁh. Delhi: 1875? 24 pp. lith. 14158.e.8(9). Blum1893:58.

——— Meerut: 1878. 24 pp. lith. 14158.e.3(9). Blum1893:58. [VT1225]

Sāṅgīt siyā svayaṁvar kā. Hardev Sahāy. Meerut: 1876. 24 pp. lith. 14158.e.3(4). Blum1893:61.

Sāṅg soraṭh. Ḍālchand. Delhi: 1888. 32 pp. lith. 14158.b.4(4). Blum1893:167.

2. From J. F. Blumhardt, *A Supplementary Catalogue of Hindi Books in the Library of the British Museum, Acquired during the Years 1893–1912* (1913)

Sāṅgīt anuruddh-ūṣhā charitra. Nanhūrām. Jabalpur: 1910. 32 pp. 14158.dd.23(2). Blum1913:202.

Sāṅgīt gopīchand arthāt bharatharī. Bālak Rām. Lahore: 1898. Gurm. char. 423 pp. 14158.ee.21. Blum1913:29.

Sāṅgīt gopīchand bharatharī. Lakṣhmaṇ Siṁh. Calcutta: 1907. Kaithi char. 92 pp. lith. 14158.cc.17(1). Blum1913:166.

Sāṅg gultāj māhtāj. Tansukh Rāy. Bulandshahr: 1907. 112 pp. 14158.e.30(3). Blum1913:306.

Sāṅgīt jān ālam. Prabhulāl Rāmchandra. Agra: 1904. 200 pp. 14157.b.2(1). Blum1913:245.

Sāṅgīt manoramā. n.a. Etawah: 1907 (2d ed.). 35 pp. 14154.h.36(2). Blum1913:185.

Sāṅgīt nauṭaṅkī shāhzādī. Muralīdhar Kavi. Kanpur: 1907. 53 pp. 14158.d.22(3). Blum1913:195.

Sāṅg pūran bhakt pūrā. Nārāyaṇ Prasād. Delhi: 1896. 220 pp. lith. 14156.i.32(2). Blum1913:204.

Sāṅgīt qatl jān ālam. Chirañjīlāl Nathārām. Mathura: 1910. 3 pts. 96, 155 pp. 14158.cc.26(4). Blum1913:117.

Sāṅg rājā amar siṁh rāṭhaur kā. Nānakchand Raīs. Moradabad: 1910. 138 pp. 14158.dd.28(1). Blum1913:201.

Sāṅgīt rājā bīr bahādur siṁh. Nārāyaṇ Dās. Mathura: 1910. 73 pp. 14158.dd.28(3). Blum1913:203.

Sāṅg shirīn farhād. Nathanlāl Jaḍiyā. Mathura: 1910. 182 pp. 14158.dd.28(2). Blum1913:205.

Ālhā Sāṅgīts

Sāṅgīt ālhā kā byāh yānī naināgaṛh kī laṛāī. Chirañjīlāl Nathārām. Kanpur: 1903. 168 pp. 14158.d.62(4). Blum1913:116.

Sāṅgīt ālhā nikāsī. Chirañjīlāl Nathārām. Kanpur: 1901. 68 pp. 14158.d.62(3). Blum1913:116.

Sāṅgīt bahoran kā byāh arthāt dillī kī laṛāī. Baṭuknāth Kalyāṇ/Chirañjīlāl Nathārām. Hathras/Kanpur: 1910. 131 pp. 14158.cc.26(11). Blum1913: 358,360.

Sāṅgīt belā kā gaunā. Muralīdhar Kavi. Mathura: 1911. 92 pp. 14158.cc.26(8). Blum1913:195.

Sāṅgīt bhārat arthāt jaitkhambh saṅgrām. Muralīdhar Kavi. Mathura: 1910 (2d ed.). 176 pp. 14158.cc.26(2). Blum1913:195.

Sāṅgīt brahmā kā byāh arthāt dillī kī laṛāī. Baṭuknāth Kalyāṇ. Mathura: 1902. 136 pp. 14158.d.40(6). Blum1913:33.

Sāṅgīt chandrāval kā jhūlā. Muralīdhar Kavi. Aligarh/Mathura: 1911. 114 pp. 14158.cc.26(7). Blum1913:195.

Sāṅgīt chandrāvalī kā vyāh. Muralīdhar Kavi. Kanpur: 1910. 14158.cc.26(6). Blum1913:195.

Sāṅgīt chandrāvalī kā jhūlā. Chirañjīlāl Nathārām. Kanpur: 1897. 76 pp. 14158.d.47(6). Blum1913:116.

———[4th ed.] Kanpur: 1901. 84 pp. 14158.d.40(3). Blum1913:117.

———Kanpur: 1906. 80 pp. 14158.cc.21(2). Blum1913:117.

Svāṅg indal haraṇ aslī arthāt ālhā kā pahilā bhāg. Nārāyaṇ Dās. Moradabad: 1906. 34 pp. 14158.dd.6(5). Blum1913:203.

Sāṅgīt indal haraṇ yānī balakhbukhāre kī laṛāī. Chirañjīlāl Nathārām. Kanpur: 1902 (2d ed.). 136 pp. 14158.d.40(9). Blum1913:117.

Sāṅgīt lākhan kā byāh arthāt kamrū kī laṛāī. Totā Rām Govind Chaman. Aligarh: 1910. 97 pp. 14158.cc.26(3). Blum1913:311.

Sāṅgīt machhlā haraṇ yānī pathrīgaṛh kī laṛāī. Govind Rām. Kanpur: 1909. 96 pp. 14158.cc.26(1). Blum1913:97.

Sāṅgīt malkhān kā byāh yānī kasaundī va pathrīgaṛh kī laṛāī. Baṭuknāth Kalyāṇ. Mathura: 1902. 87 pp. 14158.dd.5(4). Blum1913:33.

Sāṅgīt malkhān saṅgrām yānī sarsā kī laṛāī. Chirañjīlāl Nathārām. Kanpur: 1902. 80 pp. 14158.d.40(7). Blum1913:117.

Sāṅgīt māṛau kī laṛāī. Bholānāth. Kanpur: 1910. 52 pp. 14158.eee.1(2). Blum1913:45.

Sāṅgīt māṛau kī laṛāī. Chirañjīlāl Nathārām. Mathura: 1910. 96 pp. 14158.cc.26(5). Blum1913:117.

Naināgaṛh kī laṛāī arthāt ālhā kā byāh. Bholānāth. Kanpur: 1910 (4th ed.). 31 pp. 14158.eee.1(1). Blum1913:45.

Sāṅgīt pathrīgaṛh kī laṛāī arthāt machhlā haraṇ indal kā vivāh. Ghīsā Jāṭ. Meerut: 1910. 96 pp. 14158.eee.2(3). Blum1913:90.

Sāṅgīt samar malkhān. Muralīdhar Kavi. Kanpur: 1907. pt. iii. 100 pp. 14158.cc.20. Blum1913:196.

Shaṅkargaṛh saṅgrām yānī navale kā byāh. Nathārām Rāmchandra. Mathura: 1911. 94 pp. 14158.cc.26(10). Blum1913:363.

Sāṅgīt ūdal kā byāh arthāt narbargaṛh kī laṛāī. Baṭuknāth Kalyāṇ. Mathura: 1902. 75 pp. 14158.dd.5(5). Blum1913:33–34.

Sāṅgīt ūdal kā byāh yānī narbargaṛh kī laṛāī. Chirañjīlāl Nathārām. Kanpur: 1902. 152 pp. 14158.d.40(8). Blum1913:117.

3. From L. D. Barnett, J. F. Blumhardt, and J. V. S. Wilkinson, *A Second Supplementary Catalogue of Printed Books in Hindi, Bihari . . . and Pahari in the Library of the British Museum* (1957)

Sāngīt amar siṁh kā sākhā yānī āgre kī laṛāī. Chirañjīlāl Nathārām. Hathras/Mathura: 1912. 108 pp. 14158.cc.26(12). Barn1957:369–70.

———Aligarh/Kanpur: 1913. 94 pp. 14158.de.10(6). Barn1957:370.

———Hathras/Mathura: 1913. 108 pp. 14158.cc.26(12). Barn1957:370.

———Hathras/Mathura: 1915. 108 pp. 14158.de.12(8). Barn1957:370.

———Mathura: 1916. pt. i. 100 pp. 14158.de.20(8). Barn1957:370.

Sāngīt bāg-e jaliyān. Ustād Shivshaṅkar. Hathras: 1923. 40 pp. 14158.de.28(8). Barn1957:962.

Sāngīt bāṅkābīr amar siṁh rāṭhaur. Kāle Khān ("Aziz"). Aligarh: 1913. 96 pp. 14158.de.12(1). Barn1957:441. [Hin.D.3276]

Sāngīt bāp beṭā arthāt rāj siṁh va bhīm siṁh. Rūparām Sharmā. Hathras: 1923. 40 pp. 14158.de.28(9). Barn1957:879. [Hin.D.6127]

Sāngīt benazīr badr-e-munīr, gulzār ishq. Nathārām Gauṛ. Hathras: 1922. 14158.de.26(16). Barn1957:669. [Hin.D.1419]

Sāngīt bhain bhaiyā arthāt strī charitra. Totā Rām Govind Chaman. Aligarh/Kanpur: 1913 (4th ed.). 54 pp. 14158.de.10(5). Barn1957:1043. [Hin.D.3247]

Sāngīt bīramde rāv jodhpur. Baldev Sahāy. Chaprauli/Meerut: 1913. pts. i–ii, 108 pp. lith. 14158.de.6(1). Barn1957:68.

Sāngīt chachā bhatījā arthāt muñj aur rājā bhoj. Rūparām Sharmā. Salempur/Hathras: 1922. 48 pp. 14158.de.28(6). Barn1957:879. [Hin.D.1352]

Sāngīt chañchalā kumārī arthāt mahārānā rāj siṁh. Shrīkriṣhṇa Khatrī Pahalvān. Kanpur: 1921 (3d ed.). 43 pp. 14158.de.26(12). Barn1957:975.

Sāngīt chando dhobin. Ustād Shivshaṅkar. Hathras: 1920. 40 pp. 14158.de.26(10). Barn1957:962.

Sāngīt chhabīlī bhaṭiyārī. Gaṅgā Prasād Gupta. Aligarh: 1920. 34 pp. 14158.de.26(9). Barn1957:258.

Sāngīt chhatrapati shivājī. Shrīkriṣhṇa Varmā. Kanpur: 1916. 36 pp. 14158.de.20(3). Barn1957:977.

Sāngīt dayārām gūjar. Gaḍḍar Siṁh. Mathura: 1916. 74 pp. 14158.de.20(9). Barn1957:248.

Sāngīt dayārām gūjar. Totā Rām Govind Chaman. Aligarh/Kanpur: 1914 (6th ed.). 32 pp. 14158.de.10(9). Barn1957:1043–4.

Sāngīt dhruv charitra. Chirañjīlāl Nathārām. Hathras: 1918. 44 pp. 14158.d.22(11). Barn1957:178.

Sāngīt dūlā dhāṛvī yānī sindalgaṛh saṅgrām. Ghanshyām Dās Bhūdev Prasād Chaube. Sasni/Hathras: 1915. 81 pp. 14158.de.20(4). Barn1957:274.

Sāngīt gogā meṛī. Svāmī Rāmchandra. Sirsa/Benares: 1924. 44 pp. 14158.eee.16(9). Barn1957:796.

Sāngīt gopīchand bharatharī. Yogīshvar Bālak Rām. Saharanpur/Bara Banki: 1921 (2d ed.). 332 pp. 14158.eee.1(13). Barn1957:70.

Sāngīt gorakh machhandar nāth. Sādhūrām Mistrī Gaṇesh Dās. Khamgaon/Kanpur: 1915. 68 pp. 14158.de.12(6). Barn1957:885.

Sāngīt gul sanaubar. Pañcham Lāl Kāshīvāl Mahāvīr Prasād Shāir. Jhansi: 1923. 24 pp. 14158.df.14(2). Barn1957:693.

Sāngīt hardaul charitra. Shambhū Dayāl Nāyak. Jhansi: 1923. 21 pp. 14158.de.31(3). Barn1957:893.

Sāṅgīt jagdev kaṅkālī. Chandī Lāl. Kanpur: 1914. 34 pp. 14158.de.12(4). Barn1957:155.
Sāṅgīt jāhar pīr saṅgrām. Mishrīlāl Muralīdhar. Mathura: 1916. 48 pp. 14157.b.3(6). Barn1957:370.
Sāṅgīt jānī chor mahakde haran. Ṭhākur Devī Siṁh. Sikair/Bhiwani: 1925. pt. i. 50 pp. 14158.k.11(3). Barn1957:210.
Julmī ḍāyar yā jaliyāṁvālā bāg. Manohar Lāl Shukla. Kanpur: 1922. 41 pp. 14158.de.28(5). Barn1957:593.
Lailā majnūṁ yānī hushn kī bulbul. Devīdās Chhedīlāl. Kanpur: 1932. 40 pp. 14158.cc.27(5). Barn1957:207.
Sāṅgīt lākhā bañjārā yānī guñchā ishq. Totā Rām Govind Chaman. Mathura: 1916. 40 pp. 14157.b.3(5). Barn1957:1044.
Sāṅgīt mahārānī padminī arthāt chittorgaṛh saṅgrām. Shrīkriṣhṇa Khatrī Pahalvān. Kanpur: 1919. 42 pp. 14158.de.26(3). Barn1957:975–6.
Sāṅgīt mahārānī tārā. Ṭekchand Lakhmīchand Gauṛ. Delhi: 1932. pt. i. 24 pp. 14158.e.48(2). Barn1957:1034.
Sāṅgīt mañjhā kau desh nikārau yānī nal kā janm. Ghanshyām Dās Bhūdev Prasād. Sasni/Hathras: 1916. 35 pp. 14158.de.20(10). Barn1957:274.
Sāṅgīt maurdhvaj. Nathārām Gauṛ. Hathras: 1920. 32 pp. 14158.de.26(8). Barn1957:371.
Sāṅgīt mohanā rānī. Tejmaṇi Tivārī. Kanpur: 1916. 88 pp. 14157.b.20(2). Barn1957:1032.
Sāṅgīt mohanī kā jhūlā arthāt chhatrapur saṅgrām. Maṇnī Lāl Trimohan Lāl. Kannauj/Kanpur: 1920. 48 pp. 14158.de.26(11). Barn1957:592.
Sāṅgīt nauṭaṅkī. Chirañjīlāl. Mathura: 1922. 48 pp. 14158.de.28(2). Barn1957:178.
Sāṅgīt nauṭaṅkī. Shrīlāl Upādhyāy. Benares: 1922. 60 pp. 14158.de.31(1). Barn1957:977.
———Benares: 1923. 48 pp. 14158.de.28(7). Barn1957:977. [Hin.D.1613]
Sāṅgīt nauṭaṅkī shāhzādī. Muralīdhar Pahalvān. Aligarh: 1912. 52 pp. 14158.cc.42(5). Barn1957:636.
Sāṅgīt nauṭaṅkī yānī gulshan ishq. Govind Rām. Kanpur: 1915. 45 pp. 14157.b.20(1). Barn1957:299.
Sāṅgīt nihālde kā jhūlā. Chirañjīlāl Nathārām. Hathras: 1917. 52 pp. 14158.d.22(7). Barn1957:178.
Sāṅgīt oḍakī kā. Miṭṭhan Lāl Chunnī Lāl. Delhi: 1932. 14158.e.48(1). Barn1957:611.
Sāṅgīt padmāvatī ratnasen. Vishvambhar Sahāy. Meerut: 1916. 14157.c.7(3). Barn1957:1133–4.
Sāṅgīt prahlād charitra. n.a. Kanpur: 1914. 48 pp. 14158.ff.21. Barn1957:730.
Pūraṇmal bhakt kā sāṅgīt. Yogīshvar Bālak Rām. Bombay: 1912. 216 pp. 14154.ddd.3. Barn1957:70.
Aslī sāṅgīt pūranmal bhakt kā. Yogīshvar Bālak Rām. Mathura: 1934 (2d ed.). 268 pp. 14158.eee.22. Barn1957:70.
Sāṅgīt pūranmal jatī kā. Mātādīn Chaube. Kanpur/Mathura: 1915. iv pts. 64, 56, 78, 96 pp. 14158.de.20(1). Barn1957:597.
Sāṅgīt pūranmal pratham bhāg urf satsāgar, dūsrā bhāg urf satyashiromaṇi,

tīsrā bhāg urf satyavaktā, chauthā bhāg urf satyavādī. Nathārām Rāmchandra Gauṛ. Hathras: 1941–42. iv pts. 68, 36, 56, 32 pp. 14158.d.96. Barn1957:371–2.

Sāṅgīt qatl jān ālam. Kāle Khān. Aligarh: 1914. pt. i. 76 pp. 14158.de.26(1a). Barn1957:441.

Sāṅgīt qatl jān ālam yānī tarjumā gulshan jāfizāṁ. Chirañjīlāl Nathārām. Hathras/Mathura: 1910. iii pts. 96, 80, 155 pp. 14158.cc.26(4). Barn1957:371. [Hin.D.3169]

———Nathārām Sharmā. Hathras: 1924. pts. ii–iii. 79, 76 pp. 14158.de.26(1.b.c.). Barn1957:371.

Sāṅgīt raghupat siṁh saṅgrām akbar shāh kī laṛāī. Ustād Lakhan. Aligarh: 1922. 32 pp. 14158.de.31(2). Barn1957:515.

Sāṅgīt rājā bīr bahādur siṁh arthāt chandralatā chandrabhān. Nārāyaṇ Dās. Mathura: 1913. 73 pp. 14158.dd.28(7). Barn1957:657.

Svāṅgīt [sic] *rājā kārak.* Revānand. Saharanpur/Bara Banki: 1922 (4th ed.). 52 pp. 14158.eee.1(14). Barn1957:868.

Sāṅgīt rājā mordhaj bhakt. Miṭṭhan Lāl Chunnī Lāl. Delhi: 1932. 24 pp. 14158.e.48(3). Barn1957:611.

Aslī kaṛe sāṅgīt rānī mahakde va jānī chor. Dīpchand. Muzaffarnagar: 1927. 47 pp. 14158.eee.16(12). Barn1957:223.

Sāṅgīt rānī nihālde sultān siṁh kā. Āshārām Kavi. Hansi/Benares: 1930. 200 pp. 14158.eee.16(17). Barn1957:43.

Shahzādā jān ālam (svāṅg fisānā ajāyab). Pyāre Lāl. Saharanpur/Bara Banki: 1924. 273 pp. 14158.eee.10(4). Barn1957:765–6.

Sāṅgīt shiv pārvatī vivāh. Nathārām Gauṛ. Hathras: 1921. 43 pp. 14158.de.26(14). Barn1957:669.

Sāṅgīt baṛā silāde kā. Shrīrām. Sirsa/Benares: 1921. 94 pp. 14158.k.11(2). Barn1957:981.

Sāṅgīt sundarkāṇḍ rāh nauṭaṅkī. Shiv Nārāyaṇ Lāl Varmā. Jaitpur/Etawah: 1913. 26 pp. 14158.cc.42(7). Barn1957:955.

Sāṅgīt vīr bahādur yānī rājā ratan siṁh kā sākhā rānī padmāvat haran. Lālā Nāthūrām. Hathras: 1915. 85 pp. 14158.de.20(5). Barn1957:372.

Sāṅgīt vīr kesarī mahārāṇā pratāp. Shivdayāl Jāyasvāl. Padri/Lucknow: 1917. 81 pp. 14158.d.22(8). Barn1957:950.

Sāṅgīt vīrmatī. Shrīkriṣhṇa Khatrī Pahalvān. Kanpur: 1921. 48 pp. 14158.de.28(1). Barn1957:976.

Sāṅgīt yārmār. Gaṅgā Prasād Gupta. Aligarh: 1923. 48 pp. 14158.de.31(4). Barn1957:258.

Ālhā Sāṅgīts

Sāṅgīt ālhā haraṇ siyānand kā byāh yānī chandangaṛh saṅgrām. Totā Rām Govind Chaman. Hathras/Kanpur: 1913. 99 pp. 14158.de.10(4). Barn1957:1043.

Sāṅgīt ālhā kā byāh arthāt naināgaṛh kī laṛāī. Seḍhū Lāl Pūjārī. Aligarh/Kanpur: 1913. 128 pp. 14158.cc.42(13). Barn1957:928.

Sāṅgīt ālhā kā byāh yānī naināgaṛh kī laṛāī. Chirañjīlāl Nathārām. Hathras/Mathura: 1915. 168 pp. 14158.de.20(2). Barn1957:369.

Sāṅgīt ālhā manauā. Mannī Lāl Trimohan Lāl. Kannauj/Kanpur: 1920. 68 pp. 14158.de.26(5). Barn1957:591–2.

Sāṅgīt ālhā manauā. Nathārām. Kanpur: 1911. 72 pp. 14158.cc.42(2). Barn1957:369.

Sāṅgīt bahoran kā byāh arthāt dillī kī laṛāī. Vaṭuknāth Kalyāṇ. Hathras/Kanpur: 1910. pt. i. 131 pp. 14158.cc.26(11). Barn1957:1100.

——— Hathras/Kanpur: 1913. 14158.de.5. Barn1957:1100.

Sāṅgīt bahoran lāl kā gaunā . . . jaṅgamgaṛh saṅgrām. Muralīdhar Pahalvān. Hathras: 1916. 192 pp. 14158.de.20(11). Barn1957:634.

Sāṅgīt bahoran qatl arthāt tribenī haraṇ pratāpgaṛh saṅgrām. Seḍhū Lāl Pūjārī. Aligarh: 1911. 128 pp. 14158.de.26(2). Barn1957:928.

Sāṅgīt baṅgamgaṛh saṅgrām yānī jaṅgjīt jāgan ke beṭe kā byāh. Muralīdhar Pahalvān. Hathras/Kanpur: 1913. 127 pp. 14158.cc.42(10). Barn1957: 635.

Sāṅgīt baṅgamgaṛh saṅgrām yānī jaṅgjīt kā vivāh. Chirañjīlāl Nathārām. Hathras: 1920. 88 pp. 14158.de.26(6). Barn1957:370.

Sāṅgīt belā haraṇ yānī kāliñjargaṛh kī lūṭ. Sakṭū Siṁh. Hathras: 1924. 55 pp. 14158.de.28(11). Barn1957:889.

Sāṅgīt belā kā gaunā. Muralīdhar Pahalvān. Aligarh/Mathura: 1911. 92 pp. 14158.cc.26(8). Barn1957:635.

Sāṅgīt bhārat arthāt jaitkhambh saṅgrām. Muralīdhar Pahalvān. Hathras/Mathura: 1910. 176 pp. 14158.cc.26(2). Barn1957:635.

———[3d ed.] Aligarh/Kanpur: 1913. 166 pp. 14158.de.10(2).

Sāṅgīt bhārat jaitkhambh saṅgrām. Govind Rām. Hathras/Mathura: 1916. 144 pp. 14158.de.20(6). Barn1957:370.

Sāṅgīt bhayaṅkar qatl arthāt kañchangaṛh saṅgrām. Umā Charaṇ. Aligarh/Kanpur: 1914. 88 pp. 14158.de.12(5). Barn1957:1068.

Sāṅgīt chandrāval kā byāh yānī bāvangaṛh kī laṛāī. Totā Rām Govind Chaman. Aligarh/Kanpur: 1913. 89 pp. 14158.de.10(3). Barn1957:1043.

Sāṅgīt chandrāval kā jhūlā. Muralīdhar Kavi. Aligarh/Mathura: 1911. 114 pp. 14158.cc.26(7). Barn1957:635–6.

Sāṅgīt chandrāvali kā byāh. Muralīdhar Pahalvān. Hathras/Kanpur: 1910. 76 pp. 14158.cc.26(6). Barn1957:635.

Sāṅgīt chandrāvali kā gaunā yānī brahmā haran mahobe kī laṛāī. Ṭīkā Rām Ghāsī Rām. Hathras/Kanpur: 1912. 36 pp. 14158.cc.42(6). Barn1957:1039.

Sāṅgīt ḍhebā kā byāh yānī indargaṛh kī laṛāī. Totā Rām Govind Chaman. Aligarh/Kanpur: 1912. 116 pp. 14158.cc.42(8). Barn1957:1044.

———[4th ed.] Aligarh/Kanpur: 1914. 116 pp. 14158.de.10(10). Barn1957:1044.

Sāṅgīt indal haraṇ arthāt balakhbukhāre kā saṅgrām. Baṭuknāth Kalyāṇ. Hathras/Kanpur: 1913. 136 pp. 14158.cc.42(12). Barn1957:1100.

Sāṅgīt indal kā beṭā jaṅgbīr kā byāh yānī khañjargaṛh saṅgrām. Sakṭū Siṁh. Hathras: 1924. 37 pp. 14158.de.28(10). Barn1957:889.

Sāṅgīt jāgan kā byāh yānī uṛan bihār kī laṛāī. Muralīdhar Pahalvān. Hathras/Kanpur: 1914. 108 pp. 14158.de.10(8). Barn1957:636.

Sāṅgīt kañchangaṛh saṅgrām yānī ratan siṁh kā byāh. Muralīdhar Pahalvān. Hathras: 1915. 117 pp. 14158.de.12(7). Barn1957:636.

Sāṅgīt lākhan kā byāh arthāt kamrū kī laṛāī. Totā Rām Govind Chaman. Aligarh: 1910. 97 pp. 14158.cc.26(3). Barn1957:1044.

Sāṅgīt lākhan kā gaunā. Chirañjīlāl Nathārām. Hathras: 1917. 160 pp. 14158.d.22(10). Barn1957:178.

Sāṅgīt machhlā gajmotin phulvā jamanā kamalā pāñcho kā haran partāpgaṛh saṅgrām. Nathārām Rāmchandra. Hathras/Mathura: 1911. 98 pp. 14158.cc.42(3). Barn1957:371.

Sāṅgīt machhlā haraṇ yānī pathrīgaṛh kī laṛāī. Totā Rām Govind Chaman. Kanpur: 1910. 96 pp. 14158.cc.26(1). Barn1957:1044.

Sāṅgīt malkhān kā byāh yānī koṭ kasaundī kī laṛāī. Totā Rām Govind Chaman. Aligarh/Kanpur: 1913 (4th ed.). 152 pp. 14158.cc.42(12). Barn1957: 1044–5.

Sāṅgīt malkhān samar. Mannī Lāl Trimohan Lāl. Kanpur: 1922. 48 pp. 14158.de.28(3). Barn1957:1046.

Sāṅgīt malkhān samar yānī sarsāgaṛh kī laṛāī. Pannā Lāl Shrīkrishṇa Khatrī. Kanpur: 1920. 14158.de.26(7). Barn1957:699.

Sāṅgīt māṛau kī laṛāī yānī jambai va kaṛiyā se ālhā ūdal kī laṛāī. Chirañjīlāl Nathārām. Hathras/Mathura: 1910. 96 pp. 14158.cc.26(5). Barn1957:371.

Sāṅgīt māṛau kī laṛāī yānī jambai kaṛiyā se ālhā ūdal kī laṛāī. Totā Rām Govind Chaman. Aligarh/Kanpur: 1913. 86 pp. 14158.de.10(1). Barn1957:1045.

Sāṅgīt raghupat singh saṅgrām akbar shāh kī laṛāī. Ustād Lakhan. Aligarh: 1922. 32 pp. 14158.de.31(2). Barn1957:515.

Sāṅgīt rañjīt kā byāh arthāt pānīpat saṅgrām. Ṭhākur Lakham Siṁh. Aligarh/ Kanpur: 1913. 60 pp. 14158.cc.42(9). Barn1957:515.

Saṁyoginī svayaṁvar. Shivdayāl Jāyasvāl. Padri/Kanpur: 1924. 112 pp. 14158.de.31(5). Barn1957:950.

Sāṅgīt saṅkaldvīp saṅgrām yānī indal lekhā padminī kā vivāh. Chirañjīlāl Nathārām. Hathras: 1917. 64 pp. 14158.d.22(9). Barn1957:178–9.

Sāṅgīt shaṅkargaṛh saṅgrām navale kā byāh. Munshī Shāligrām. Aligarh: 1911. 116 pp. 14158.cc.42(1). Barn1957:890.

Sāṅgīt shaṅkargaṛh saṅgrām yānī navale kā byāh. Pannā Lāl Shrīkrishṇa Khatrī. Kanpur: 1922 (pts. i–ii). 39, 52 pp. 14158.de.28(4). Barn1957:699.

Sāṅgīt shaṅkargaṛh yānī navale kā byāh. Muralīdhar Pahalvān. Mathura: 1919. 129 pp. 14158.de.26(4). Barn1957:636.

Sāṅgīt sulkhe kā byāh. Gulzārī Lāl Lachhman Prasād. Hathras: 1916. 160 pp. 14158.de.20(7). Barn1957:307–8.

Sāṅgīt surjāvatī kā jhūlā yānī ūdal kā byāh bāndo saṅgrām. Totā Rām Govind Chaman. Aligarh/Kanpur: 1913. 79 pp. 14158.de.10(7). Barn1957:1045.

Sāṅgīt tribenī haraṇ. Totā Rām Govind Chaman. Aligarh/Kanpur: 1911. 106 pp. 14158.cc.42(4). Barn1957:1045.

Sāṅgīt ūdal kā byāh yānī narbargaṛh kī laṛāī. Mannī Lāl Trimohan Lāl. Kanpur: 1921 (pt. i). 50 pp. 14158.de.26(15). Barn1957:592.

Ūdalharan bahoran kā byāh. Govind Rām. Aligarh/Kanpur: 1911. 92 pp. 14158.d.22(6). Barn1957:299.

4. From J. F. Blumhardt, *Catalogue of the Library of the India Office,* vol. 2, pt. 3, *Hindi, Panjabi, Pushtu, and Sindhi Books* (1902)

Sāṅgīt badr-i munīr kā. n.a. Meerut: 1876. 32 pp. VT1091. Blum1902:69.

Sāṅgīt bālacharitra. Kuṁvar Sen. Delhi: 1874. 39 pp. VT1079. Blum1902:49.

Sāṅgīt chīrharaṇ līlā. n.a. Delhi: 1874. 26 pp. VT1134. Blum1902:49.
Sāṅgīt chitramukuṭ. n.a. Delhi: 1879. 56 pp. VT1106. Blum1902:69.
Sāṅgīt dhurūjī kā. n.a. Delhi: 1876. 32 pp. VT1536. Blum1902:69.
———Delhi: 1876. 36 pp. VT1079. Blum1902:69.
Gopīchand bharatarī/Sāṅgīt gopīchand kā. Lakṣhmaṇ Siṁh. Agra: 1867. 32 pp. VT1536. Blum1902:67.
———Delhi: 1867. 28 pp. VT1265. Blum1902:67.
———Agra: 1868. 32 pp. VT1539. Blum1902:67.
———Agra: 1868. 36 pp. VT1536. Blum1902:67.
———Delhi: 1869. 36 pp. VT1226. Blum1902:67.
———Agra: 1870. 32 pp. VT1239. Blum1902:67.
———Delhi: 1870. 36 pp. VT1104. Blum1902:67. [14158.e.8(5)]
———Agra: 1871. 32 pp. VT1106. Blum1902:67.
———Agra: 1871. 36 pp. VT1105. Blum1902:67.
———Meerut: 1871. 32 pp. VT1232. Blum1902:67.
———Delhi: 1873. 36 pp. VT1092. Blum1902:67.
———Delhi: 1874. 32 pp. VT1092. Blum1902:67. [14158.e.3(2)]
———Lucknow: 1874. 32 pp. VT1091 [1107]. Blum1902:67.
———Delhi: 1875. 32 pp. VT1090 [1091, 1093]. Blum1902:67.
———Delhi: 1875. 16 pp. Pers. char. VT1106. Blum1902:67.
———Lucknow: 1875. 20 pp. Pers. char. VT1554. Blum1902:67.
———Delhi: 1876. 32 pp. VT1092 [1538]. Blum1902:67.
———Delhi: 1877. 32 pp. VT1090 [1106]. Blum1902:67.
———Calcutta: 1878. 44 pp. VT1213. Blum1902:67.
———Delhi: 1878. 32 pp. VT1093. Blum1902:67.
———Meerut: 1878. 32 pp. VT1225. Blum1902:67. [14158.e.15(7)]
———Delhi: 1879. 32 pp. VT1094. Blum1902:67.
———Delhi: 1879. 16 pp. Pers. char. VT1090 [812]. Blum1902:67.
Sāṅgīt kaṁs līlā. Kuṁvar Sen. Delhi: 1875. 40 pp. VT1106. Blum1902:49.
Sāṅgīt lailā majnūn. Baldev. Meerut: 1874. 12 pp. VT1090. Blum1902:69.
———Delhi: 1879. 12 pp. VT1106. Blum1902:69.
Sāṅgīt nāg līlā. Kuṁvar Sen. Delhi: 1874. 15 pp. VT1079. Blum1902:50.
Sāṅgīt padmāvatī. n.a. Delhi: 1877. 32 pp. VT1091. Blum1902:69.
Sāṅgīt phulvantī kā. n.a. Delhi: 1877. 16 pp. VT1536. Blum1902:69.
Prahlād sāṅgīt. Lakṣhmaṇ Siṁh. Agra: 1869. 48 pp. VT1225. Blum1902:45.
———Delhi: 1869. 48 pp. VT1226. Blum1902:45.
———Delhi: 1869. 48 pp. Pers. char. VT1238. Blum1902:45.
———Delhi: 1870. 48 pp. VT1106. Blum1902:45.
———Delhi: 1874. 48 pp. VT1079. Blum1902:45.
———Delhi: 1875. 48 pp. VT1536. Blum1902:45.
———Delhi: 1876. 48 pp. VT1079. Blum1902:45.
———Delhi: 1877. 48 pp. VT1078. Blum1902:45.
———Delhi: 1877. 48 pp. Pers. char. VT1079. Blum1902:45.
———Delhi: 1878. 48 pp. VT1104. Blum1902:45.
———Meerut: 1878. 48 pp. VT1092. Blum1902:45. [14158.e.15(8)]
———Delhi: 1879. 48 pp. VT1532. Blum1902:45.
———Meerut: 1880. 48 pp. VT1239. Blum1902:45.

Sāṅgīt pūran bhagat. Bālak Rām. Gurum. char. Lahore: 1896. 238 pp. VT1555. Blum1902:69.
Sāṅgīt pūran mal kā. Rāmlāl. Meerut: 1878. 32 pp. VT1225. Blum1902:69.
Sāṅgīt rājā harichand kā. Jīyā Lāl. Delhi: 1877. 52 pp. VT1091. Blum1902:69.
———Delhi: 1879. 52 pp. VT1106. Blum1902:69.
Sāṅgīt rājā harichand kā. Kiḍhā Mishra. Meerut: 1880. 32 pp. VT1225. Blum1902:69.
———Meerut: 1882. 32 pp. VT1225. Blum1902:69.
Sāṅgīt rājā indra. Kuṁvar Sen. Delhi: 1874. 23 pp. VT1090. Blum1902:50.
———Delhi: 1875. 23 pp. VT1090. Blum1902:50.
———Lahore: 1879. 40 pp. VT1078. Blum1902:50.
Sāṅgīt rājā kaṁs kā. Khushī Rām. Delhi: 1879. 40 pp. VT1090. Blum1902:50.
Sāṅgīt rājā kārak kā. n.a. Meerut: 1878. 32 pp. VT1225. Blum1902:69. [14158.e.3(11)]
Sāṅgīt rājā mordhvaj kā. Jīyā Lāl. Delhi: 1876. 32 pp. VT1090. Blum1902:69.
———Delhi: 1877. 32 pp. VT1090. Blum1902:69.
Sāṅgīt rājā raghuvīr siṁh kā. Hardev Sahāy. Meerut: 1876. Devan., Pers. char. 16, 16 pp. VT1089. Blum1902:38.
———Meerut: 1876. 16 pp. VT1211. Blum1902:38.
———Meerut: 1877. Pers. char. 16 pp. VT1211. Blum1902:38.
Sāṅgīt rājā vajramukaṭ. Pheru Lāl. Delhi: 1875. 56 pp. VT1093. Blum1902:69.
Sāṅgīt rukmiṇī maṅgal. n.a. Delhi: 1874. 39 pp. VT1265. Blum1902:50.
———Meerut: 1876. 24 pp. VT1078. Blum1902:50.
Sāṅgīt rūp basant. Lakṣhmaṇ Siṁh and Hardev Sahāy. Meerut: 1874. 32 pp. VT1091. Blum1902:69.
———Delhi: 1875. 32 pp. VT1094. Blum1902:69.
———Delhi: 1876. 32 pp. VT1090. Blum1902:69.
———Meerut: 1876. 32 pp. VT1090. Blum1902:69.
———Delhi: 1877. 32 pp. VT1093. Blum1902:69.
———Delhi: 1879. 32 pp. VT1094. Blum1902:69.
Sāṅgīt saudāgar o siyāhposh kā. Gurudayāl Siṁh. Meerut: 1876/9. 24 pp. VT1091. Blum1902:69.
———Meerut: 1878. 24 pp. VT1225. Blum1902:69. [14158.e.3(9)]
Sāṅgīt siyā svayaṁvar kā. Hardev Sahāy. Meerut: 1875. 16 pp. VT1079. Blum1902:50.
Sāṅgīt soraṭh kā. Ḍālchand. Delhi: 1876. 32 pp. VT1090. Blum1902:70.
———Delhi: 1879. 32 pp. VT1090. Blum1902:70.
Sāṅgīt vīn bādshāhzādī. Jñānchandra. Meerut: 1877. 31 pp. VT1090. Blum1902:70.

APPENDIX D: Hansen Collection of Contemporary Sāṅgīts

Amar siṁh rāṭhor. Shrīkriṣhṇa Pahalvān. Kanpur: Shrikrishna Khatri, 1981. 48 pp.

Amar siṁh rāṭhor, sajild donoṁ bhāg. Nathārām Sharmā Gauṛ. Hathras: Shyam Press, 1979. 104, 80 pp.

Amar siṁh rāṭhor, sampūrṇ donoṁ bhāg. Yogeshvar Bālakrām. Delhi: Agraval Book Depot, n.d. 296 pp.

Andhī dulhin, jitendrī jaypāl. Nathārām Sharmā Gauṛ. Hathras: Shyam Press, 1980. 44 pp.

Aurat kā pyār, bahādur laṛkī. Shrīkriṣhṇa Pahalvān. Kanpur: Shrikrishna Khatri, 1975. 56 pp.

Bāṁsurī vālī, bevafā māshuq. Shrīkriṣhṇa Pahalvān. Kanpur: Shrikrishna Khatri, 1972. 48 pp.

Barsātī ḍākū, garīboṁ kā madadgār. Dhanuṣhdhar Yādav ("Mastānā"). Allahabad: Bombay Pustakalay, n.d. 48 pp.

Benazīr badr-e-munīr, gulzār ishq. Nathārām Sharmā Gauṛ. Hathras: Shyam Press, 1968. 44 pp.

Beqasūr beṭī, kālī nāgin. Nathārām Sharmā Gauṛ. Hathras: Shyam Press, 1976, 44 pp.

Bhain bhaiyā. Nathārām Sharmā Gauṛ. Hathras: Shyam Press, n.d. 40 pp.

Bhakt prahlād, rām kā dīvānā. Nathārām Sharmā Gauṛ. Hathras: Shyam Press, 1981. 32 pp.

Bhakt pūranmal, dūsrā bhāg. Bālakrām Yogeshvar. Delhi: Dehati Pustak Bhandar, n.d. 136 pp.

Bhakt pūranmal, sajild pāñchoṁ bhāg. Nathārām Sharmā Gauṛ. Hathras: Shyam Press, 1982. 64, 36, 56, 32, 40 pp.

Bhakt sūrdās, murīd-e tavāyaf. Nathārām Sharmā Gauṛ. Hathras: Shyam Press, 1970. 44 pp.

Bharatharī kā yog, shyāmdeī kā shok. Gayādīn Halvāī. Kanpur: Shrikrishna Pustakalay, 1979. 56 pp.

Chachā bhatījā, k̲h̲ud garaz muñj. Nathārām Sharmā Gauṛ. Hathras: Shyam Press, 1974. 40 pp.

Chhīn lo roṭī, chandan siṁh ḍākū. Rāmlochan Vishvakarmā. Allahabad: Bombay Pustakalay, n.d. 48 pp.

Chīn kī hasīnā, gulrū zarīnā. Nathārām Sharmā Gauṛ. Hathras: Shyam Press, 1953, 56 pp.

Ḍākū mān siṁh, bahādur rāṭhaur. Nathārām Sharmā Gauṛ. Hathras: Shyam Press, 1963. 54 pp.

Dayārām gūjar, bevafā dost. Nathārām Sharmā Gauṛ. Hathras: Shyam Press, 1981. 40 pp.

Dehlī darbār, san 1912. Nathārām Sharmā Gauṛ. Hathras: Shyam Press, 1965. 16 pp.

Dharmvīr haqīqat rāy, sachchī qurbānī. Nathārām Sharmā Gauṛ. Hathras: Shyam Press, 1976. 23 pp.

Dhobī kī beṭī, honī kā chamatkār. Nathārām Sharmā Gauṛ. Hathras: Shyam Press, 1970. 24 pp.
Ḍholā mārū, svarg kā kinārā. Nathārām Sharmā Gauṛ. Hathras: Shyam Press, 1981. 110 pp.
Dhūl kā phūl, matlabī insān. Nathārām Sharmā Gauṛ. Hathras: Shyam Press, 1977. 48 pp.
Dhūl kā phūl, muhabbat kī bhūl. Shrīkrishṇa Pahalvān. Kanpur: Shrikrishna Khatri, 1977. 52 pp.
Dil kī khatā, beṭe kī qurbānī. Shrīkrishṇa Pahalvān. Kanpur: Shrikrishna Khatri, 1972. 52 pp.
Dukhiyā vidhvā, rāj rānī. Nathārām Sharmā Gauṛ. Hathras: Shyam Press, 1951. 36 pp.
Garīb kā khudā. Shrīkrishṇa Pahalvān. Kanpur: Shrikrishna Khatri, 1954. 56 pp.
Garīb kī duniyā, nūrānī motī. Shrīkrishṇa Pahalvān. Kanpur: Shrikrishna Khatri, 1982. 52 pp.
Girand siṁh ḍākū, kālindrī kā sher. B. P. Saksenā ("Beḍhab"). Mainpuri: Anokhelal Saksena, 1965. 54 pp.
Gopīchand, jog kā updesh. Nathārām Sharmā Gauṛ. Hathras: Shyam Press, 1981. 47 pp.
Gopīchand bharatharī. Lakshmaṇ Dās. Delhi: Ratan and Company, n.d. 48 pp.
Gopīchand bharatharī. Lakshmaṇ Dās. Hathras: Gaur Book Depot, 1978. 48 pp.
Gul bakāvalī, shāhzādā yaman. Nathārām Sharmā Gauṛ. Hathras: Shyam Press, 1966. 48 pp.
Harishchandra, gulshan kā nāg. Nathārām Sharmā Gauṛ. Hathras: Shyam Press, 1981. 48 pp.
Hīr rāñjhā, sapne kā āshiq. Nathārām Sharmā Gauṛ. Hathras: Shyam Press, 1980. 56 pp.
Indal haraṇ, sajild do bhāg meṁ. Nathārām Sharmā Gauṛ. Hathras: Shyam Press, 1979. 128, 64 pp.
Indra sabhā amānat. Amānat. Delhi: Agraval Book Depot, n.d. 32 pp.
Jaṅgal kā sher, vafādār khazāñchī. Tasavvar Alī Khān. Kanpur: Shrikrishna Pustakalay, 1981. 48 pp.
Jay santoshī māṁ, abalā kī pukār. Vaṁshīdhar Chañchal. Kanpur: Ram Lakhan Gupta, 1977. 57 pp.
Khudādost sultān. Trimohan Lāl. Kanpur: Shrikrishna Pustakalay, 1977. 52 pp.
Krishṇa sudāmā, sachchī mitratā. Nathārām Sharmā Gauṛ. Hathras: Shyam Press, 1977. 44 pp.
Kshatrāṇī durgāvatī, khūnī kalāī. Nathārām Sharmā Gauṛ. Hathras: Shyam Press, 1973. 52 pp.
Lailā majnū, maktab kī yārī. Lakhmī Chand. Delhi: Agraval Book Depot, 1937. 24 pp.
Lailā majnūṁ, maktab kī muhabbat. Nathārām Sharmā Gauṛ. Hathras: Shyam Press, 1981. 40 pp.

Lākhā bañjārā, anokhī dulhin. Nathārām Sharmā Gauṛ. Hathras: Shyam Press, 1982. 36 pp.
Lāl-e-rukh gulfām, masnuī darvesh. Nathārām Sharmā Gauṛ. Hathras: Shyam Press, 1967. 52 pp.
Mahārānī lakṣhmībāī. Kriṣhṇa Mohan Saksenā. Lucknow: Nautanki Kala Kendra, 1985. 52 pp.
Mālī kā beṭā, shāhzādā firoz. Nathārām Sharmā Gauṛ. Hathras: Shyam Press, 1981. 32 pp.
Mān simh ḍākū, sher-e rāṭhaur. Ustād Maṅgal Siṁh. Gwalior: Chhotelal Kasautiya, n.d. 53 pp.
Māṛau kī laṛāī. Shrīkriṣhṇa Pahalvān. Kanpur: Shrikrishna Khatri, 1982. 60 pp.
Maut kā jhūlā, joṛ kā toṛ. Rāmlochan Vishvakarmā. Allahabad: Bombay Pustakalay, n.d. 43 pp.
Merā gāṁv merā desh, ḍākū jabbar siṁh. Abdul Raūf Khān. Allahabad: Bombay Pustakalay, n.d. 52 pp.
Mordhvaj, sher kā bhojan. Nathārām Sharmā Gauṛ. Hathras: Shyam Press, 1976. 36 pp.
Muhabbat kī putlī. Shrīkriṣhṇa Pahalvān. Kanpur: Shrikrishna Khatri, 1982. 52 pp.
Nāgin. Shrīkriṣhṇa Pahalvān. Kanpur: Shrikrishna Khatri, 1978. 48 pp.
Nauṭaṅkī. Lakhmī Chand. Delhi: Agraval Book Depot, n.d. 32 pp.
Nauṭaṅkī shahzādī, phūl siṁh panjābī. Nathārām Sharmā Gauṛ. Hathras: Shyam Press, 1975. 48 pp.
Nihālde, pratham bhāg: dil kā kāṇṭā. Nathārām Sharma Gauṛ. Hathras: Shyam Press, 1965. 52 pp.
Nihālde kā jhūlā, sajild pāñchoṁ bhāg. Nathārām Sharmā Gauṛ. Hathras: Shyam Press, 1979. 52, 40, 48, 46 pp.
Padmāvati, fariyād-e bulbul. Nathārām Sharmā Gauṛ. Hathras: Shyam Press, 1977. 72 pp.
Pāk dāman, anmol angūṭhī. Tasavvar Alī Khān. Kanpur: Shrikrishna Pustakalay, 1979. 40 pp.
Phūlan debī, maut kā naṅgā nāch. Svāmīnāth urf Nabīnkumār Barvar. Ayodhya: Ram Lakhan Gupta Bookseller, 1982. 58 pp.
Pūranmal, pratham bhāg: sat sāgar. Nathārām Sharmā Gauṛ. Hathras: Shyam Press, 1981. 64 pp.
Pūranmal bhakt. Bālakrām Yogeshvar. Delhi: Dehati Pustak Bhandar, n.d. 269 pp.
Qatl jān ālam, sajild tīnoṁ bhāg. Nathārām Sharmā Gauṛ. Hathras: Shyam Press, 1979. 96, 80, 76 pp.
Qismat kā dhanī, vafādār qātil. Tasavvar Alī Khān. Kanpur: Shrikrishna Pustakalay, 1981. 40 pp.
Rāmāyaṇ bāl kāṇḍ, rām janmotsav. Nathārām Sharmā Gauṛ. Hathras: Shyam Press, 1981. 28 pp.
Reshmī rūmāl, khasam joṛū kī noṅk jhoṅk. Nathārām Sharmā Gauṛ. Hathras: Shyam Press, 1963. 56 pp.
Rūp basant. Bālakrām Yogeshvar. Delhi: Dehati Pustak Bhandar, n.d. 192 pp.

Rūp basant, pratham bhāg: gend kī chorī. Nathārām Sharmā Gauṛ. Hathras: Shyam Press, 1981. 34 pp.
Rūp basant, sampūrṇ tīn bhāg meṁ. Nathārām Sharmā Gauṛ. Hathras: Shyam Press, 1982. 34, 48, 48 pp.
Sādhū aur shaitān, ḍākū alvar siṁh. Rāmlochan Vishvakarmā. Allahabad: Bombay Pustakalay, n.d. 40 pp.
Satī bindiyā, vafādār mazdūr. Nathārām Sharmā Gauṛ. Hathras: Shyam Press, 1975. 52 pp.
Satī mādhurī, ujjain kī shernī. Nathārām Sharmā Gauṛ. Hathras: Shyam Press, 1973. 32 pp.
Satī sāvitrī, husn kī devī. Nathārām Sharmā Gauṛ. Hathras: Shyam Press, 1982. 36 pp.
Satī shīlāde, rājā risālū va dīvān mahte shāh. Bālakrām Yogeshvar. Delhi: Agraval Book Depot, n.d. 208 pp.
Shāhī lakaṛhārā, nanhūnāī kī qismat. Shrīkriṣhṇa Pahalvān. Kanpur: Shrikrishna Khatri, n.d. 48 pp.
Shakuntalā vivāh, vishvāmitra yajña vidhvaṁsh. Nathārām Sharmā Gauṛ. Hathras: Shyam Press, 1978. 48 pp.
Shīlāde, rājā risālū aur mahtā dīvān. Bālakrām Yogeshvar. Delhi: Agraval Book Depot, n.d. 172 pp.
Shīrīṁ farhād. Shrīkriṣhṇa Pahalvān. Kanpur: Shrikrishna Khatri, 1968. 48 pp.
Shīrīṁ farhād, gulshan kī mulāqāt. Nathārām Sharmā Gauṛ. Hathras: Shyam Press, 1979. 52 pp.
Shiv pārvatī vivāh, duṣhṭ tārak badh. Nathārām Sharmā Gauṛ. Hathras: Shyam Press, 1981. 44 pp.
Shrīmatī mañjarī, gamzadā qaidī. Nathārām Sharmā Gauṛ. Hathras: Shyam Press, 1981. 48 pp.
Subhaṣh bos jīvan charitra, baṅgāl kā sher. Nathārām Sharmā Gauṛ. Hathras: Shyam Press, 1950. 44 pp.
Suhāg kī qurbānī, devar bhaujāī. Rāmlochan Vishvakarmā. Allahabad: Bombay Pustakalay, n.d. 39 pp.
Sultānā ḍākū, garīboṁ kā pyārā. Nathārām Sharmā Gauṛ. Hathras: Shyam Press, 1982. 60 pp.
Sultānā ḍākū, hāy re paisā. Muralīdhar. Hathras: Shrikrishna Press, n.d. 32 pp.
Sultānā ḍākū, hāy re paisā. Shrīkriṣhṇa Pahalvān. Kanpur: Shrikrishna Khatri, 1977. 64 pp.
Syāh posh, pāk muhabbat. Nathārām Sharmā Gauṛ. Hathras: Shyam Press, 1982. 63 pp.
Chhandoṁ kā syāhposh. Chhītarmal Jyotiṣhī. Hathras: N. S. Sharma Gaur Book Depot, 1948. 24 pp.
Ṭāvar sultān, zahrī sāṁp. Tasavvar Alī K͟hān. Kanpur: Shrikrishna Pustakalay, 1982. 31 pp.
Triyā charitra, qatl-e shauhar. Nathārām Sharmā Gauṛ. Hathras: Shyam Press, 1982. 40 pp.
Triyā charitra. Shrīkriṣhṇa Pahalvān. Kanpur: Shrikrishna Khatri, 1978. 40 pp.
Vidyā vinod, chamaktā jugnū. Nathārām Sharmā Gauṛ. Hathras: Shyam Press, 1951. 56 pp.

Vīr vikramāditya, jai kālī. Shrīkriṣhṇa Pahalvān. Kanpur: Shrikrishna Khatri, 1987. 48 pp.
Vīrāṅganā vīrmatī, pratham bhāg: khūn-e ayyāsh. Nathārām Sharmā Gauṛ. Hathras: Shyam Press, 1972. 48 pp.
Vīrāṇganā vīrmatī, dūsrā bhāg: jagdev kaṅkālī. Nathārām Sharmā Gauṛ. Hathras: Shyam Press, 1971. 47 pp.

APPENDIX E: A Brief History of Meters in Svāṅg and Nauṭaṅkī

The most prevalent meters in twentieth-century Sāṅgīt texts are the *dohā-chaubolā-dauṛ* sequence and *bahr-e-tavīl*. Current radio and commercial recordings also contain a preponderance of these meters. Examination of early Sāṅgīt texts shows that *dohā-chaubolā-dauṛ* assumed its present form in the early 1890s, and *bahr-e-tavīl* was introduced around 1910. Metrical analysis of dated play scripts confirms evidence from other sources for the history of the genre. For example, the rise of particular meters at certain times suggests the innovative role of popular poets and their influence on Nauṭaṅkī development, as well as trends in popular culture, shifts in patronage, or influence of regional or communal groups. The presence of a diversity of meters, furthermore, as in plays dated approximately 1910 to 1930, points to a phase of efflorescence and widespread support of the art. The later paucity of meters similarly indicates a decline in Nauṭaṅkī's status, associated with the advent of Hindi films and other sociological changes.

The earliest printed Sāṅgīts in the India Office and British Library collections, dated 1866 to 1892, are composed almost entirely in series of *dohā-chaubolā* units. The meter *dauṛ* that was later appended to the *chaubolā* is entirely absent, as are *bahr-e-tavīl* and the various meters from Urdu poetry and other traditions. Scenes are composed of dialogues in which one character's speech consists of a *dohā* and *chaubolā*, answered by the second character's *dohā* and *chaubolā*, and so on back and forth. The *dohā* and *chaubolā* are linked by repetition of the last half-line of the *dohā* at the beginning of the *chaubolā*, a feature characteristic of the Hindi meter *kuṇḍaliyā*, which is also composed of a two-line *dohā* followed by a four-line stanza. The *chaubolā* is also frequently called *kaṛā* in these texts. *Kaṛā* is identified with the classical Hindi meter *rolā*, consisting of four lines of 24 measures (*mātrā*s). Many *chaubolā*s and *kaṛā*s in early Sāṅgīt texts do contain 24 measures, but *chaubolā*s of 20 and of 28 measures are also present. Rhyme is similarly variable; the four lines of the *chaubolā/kaṛā* may rhyme *a a b b* or *a a a a*. The *dohā* meter conforms to the traditional pattern of two rhymed lines of 13 + 11 measures, ending long-short. Apart from these, the meters *chhand, rekhtā,* and several types of *rāganī* or song occur, but too infrequently for generalization on their metrical character. The *rāganī*s are often indicated to be sung in specific melodies, such as *bihāg, soraṭh, holī, āsāvarī,* or *bahār*.

A pivotal text in the history of Sāṅgīt meters is *Pūranmal kā khyāl,* dated 1892, which is probably the first typeset printed play in the Hindustani Svāṅg tradition (despite its title *khyāl,* and as opposed to the Marwari *khyāl*s that were first typeset earlier). This is perhaps also the first play ascribed to the poet Indarman or written by a poet of his school, as Indarman's name recurs in signature lines throughout the text. In this playscript the meter *dauṛ* first appears, and the sequence *dohā-chaubolā-dauṛ* becomes established as the primary compositional unit of the play. The *chaubolā* consists of four lines of 28 measures rhyming *a a a a,* which is the form that continues up to the present. The *dauṛ* consists of four lines, 13, 13, 13, and 28 measures, rhyming *a a b b*.

Other meters contained in the play are *chhand* (known as *harigītikā* in classical Hindi prosody), which shows the traditional line length of 28 measures, *dubolā* of 30 measures per line, and *jhūlnā* of 40 measures. No Urdu or folk meters are present.

From the advent of Indarman, a great flowering of metrical forms takes place. The Hathras style of Svāṅg flourished under Indarman's disciples Chiranjilal and Natharam, who appear to have introduced many meters and songs from various sources current in popular culture. *Indal haraṇ,* composed by Chiranjilal and Natharam in 1900, contains over twenty metrical varieties drawn from Hindi classical and folk poetry, Urdu literature, light classical music, and religious music. The Hindi meters include *dohā, chaubolā, dauṛ, kaṛā, dubolā, chhand, rekhtā, soraṭhā, belmā, kavitt,* and *chhappay.* Urdu influence is present in the use of *qavvālī, ghazal,* and *sher.* Folk songs such as *dādrā, jhūlnā, lāvanī, māṇḍ,* and *ālhā* as well as various *bhajans* are also amply represented. A number of classical ragas are indicated: *khamāj, soraṭh* and *bhairavī.* Even a Sanskrit meter, *shikhariṇī,* finds its way into the highly peppered text. Comparable metrical diversity is found in *Syāhposh,* composed by "Natharam in his childhood" according to the colophon (1901 is the probable date).

The meter *bahr-e-tavīl,* which comes to dominate Nauṭaṅkī composition later, is not present in these early Hathras texts. It makes its first appearance in *Qatl jān ālam,* dated 1908, where a sprinkling of *bahr-e-tavīl* examples concludes part one, like a final flourish to the author's display of metrical virtuosity. About 25 meters are indicated in this text, illustrating again the merging of older theatrical styles into the newly expanding Svāṅg-Nauṭaṅkī form. Thus we find here *thiyeṭar* and *dādrā thiyeṭar,* tunes borrowed from the Parsi theatre, as well as a meter from the popular Urdu play *Indarsabhā,* simply called *shair indra sabhā kī bahr,* "a verse in the meter of *Indarsabhā.*" The frequent use of *ṭhumrī, dādrā, lāvanī,* and *khyāl* forms also illustrates the incorporation of regional musical styles in the stage singing evolving at the time.

Natharam's version of the famous *Harishchandra* is also from this period (dated 1917), and it too illlustrates the Hathrasi poet's penchant for metrical variety. The Hindi meters present are *dohā, chaubolā, dauṛ, kaṛā,* and *chhand. Bahr-e-tavīl* is commonly employed, especially in dialogues of moderate length, as is *qavvālī,* used mostly for rapid exchanges. Influence of the Parsi theatre is again marked by the inclusion of several songs entitled *thiyeṭar, dādrā thiyeṭar,* and *dhun thiyeṭar. Bahr indrasabhā* makes its appearance, as do numerous varieties of *lāvanī, ṭhumrī, bhajan,* and *dādrā.* The play concludes with two Sanskrit meters, *shārdūlavikrīḍita* and *harigītikā.*

The use of meter in Shrikrishna Khatri's Nauṭaṅkīs (Kanpur *akhāṛā*) differs substantially from that of the Hathras tradition associated with Natharam and others. The most striking difference is that the sequence *dohā-chaubolā-dauṛ* is entirely absent from some of Shrikrishna's plays (such as *Aurat kā pyār*) and present only rarely in most (*Amar siṁh rāṭhor, Bāṁsurī vālī, Dhūl kā phūl, Sultānā ḍākū*). *Dohās* frequently introduce meters other than *chaubolā,* especially *qavvālī, sher,* or *chhand,* and thus *dohā* occurs in greater numbers than *chaubolā* and *dauṛ.* For example, the first twenty pages of *Shirīn farhād* contain 26 *dohās,* 13 *chaubolās,* and 9 *dauṛs.* The meters that dominate most of Shrikrishna's plays are the common Urdu ones: *qavvālī, bahr-e-tavīl, sher,* and *ghazal.* It is noteworthy that this *akhāṛā* uses Urdu meters regardless of the theme of the play, in stories featuring Hindu characters and themes (*Shāhī lakaṛhārā, Triyā charitra*), as well as in Islamic romances like *Shīrīn farhād.*

Prose passages also occupy a larger percentage of Kanpur texts than their Hathras counterparts. The prose sections, which may be rhymed or unrhymed, are termed *ḍrāmā,* a coinage attributed to Shrikrishna; these *ḍrāmā*s are found in every play but one in the sample of ten. In that single case, the prose speech is called by the name *vārtā,* the appellation common in Hathras texts for unmetered passages. Another unique feature of the Kanpur tradition is the opening chorus, *koras,* which appears in six of the ten plays. The chorus is sung by all members of the cast as an invocation, and is similar to the usual *maṅgalācharaṇ.*

Tunes from the Parsi theatre, *tarz-e-thiyeṭar, thiyeṭar,* or *theṭar,* are very common in Shrikrishna Khatri's plays. Authors like Agraval and Gargi have mentioned the greater influence of Parsi theatre on the Kanpur Nauṭaṅkī than on Hathras Svāṅg; this observation is certainly borne out by the metrical evidence as well as the scenery and stagecraft techniques to which they allude. Similarly, film songs (*filmī, filam,* or simply *gānā*) often figure in these plays. Nine out of the ten plays contain *lāvanī*s of various types: *lāvanī langṛī, lāvanī chhoṭī raṅgat,* or *lāvanī baṛī. Bahr shikast* is also a popular meter in the Kanpur style. Certain meters in these plays are not encountered in the Hathras school. Typically enough, one is called *kānpurī,* a two-line meter of 32 measures rhyming *a a.* Another peculiar to Kanpur is *ḍeṛh tukī,* literally "one-and-a-half rhymer," composed of a line of 24 measures followed by a half-line of 11 measures, repeated, rhyming *a a a a.* Also unique to this *akhāṛā* is *raṅgat bāg,* apparently a four-line stanza of 30 measures rhyming *a a a a.* One common meter that occurs in many of Shrikrishna's plays (but in very few Hathrasi compositions) is *bashīkaran.* This is a unique meter (a type of *lāvanī,* according to Agraval), constituted by a pair of 16-measure rhymed lines, followed by a *dohā* (two lines of 24 measures each), followed by another pair of 16-measure lines, the last of which is identical with the second line of the entire stanza. The rhyme scheme is thus *a a b b a a.*

APPENDIX F: Nauṭaṅkī Performances

1. Recordings of All-India Radio (Mathura), produced by Tribhuvan Sharma. Copies of recordings donated by Alan Entwistle. The eleven performances are listed alphabetically by title; running time; length of transcription; author, if known; singers and instrumentalists, if known; and instrumentation.

Amar siṁh rāṭhor. 25 min. 13 pp. *Sāraṅgī,* clarinet, harmonium, *nagāṛā, ḍholak.*

Bhaktā mīrābāī. 23 min. 12 pp. Satyanarayan Kishoriya. Giriraj Prasad, Ram Dayal Sharma, Madan Mohan Brijbasi, Krishna Lal Sharma, Mamta Gupta, Pushpa Avasthi; Atthan Khan (*nagāṛā*). *Nagāṛā, sāraṅgī,* harmonium, *ḍholak.*

Ghanshyām darshan. 26 min. 7 pp. Rameshvari Devi. Shyam Sundar Varma, Bhairo Singh Brijbasi, Premlata Chaudhuri, Chunnilal, Mukhtiyar Ahmad. Harmonium, *nagāṛā.*

Indal haraṇ. 55 min. 15 pp. B. Azad. Vishnu Kumar Sharma, Bhuresh Kumar Varma, Saras Kaul; Kamal Kishor Sharma (harmonium), Madan Lal Varma (clarinet), Chidda Lal (*nagāṛā*), Madan Lal Jaipuri (*ḍholak*).

Kissā seṭh tārāchand kā. 21 min. 11 pp. *Sāraṅgī,* harmonium, drums.

Nyāy aur kartavya (rānī lakṣhmībāī). 29 min. 11 pp. Ramji Lal Bhatt. Kamalesh Lata, Bhuresh Kumar Varma, Chunnilal, Ram Dayal Sharma; Tulsiram, Chidda Lal, Babu Khan, Madan Lal Jaipuri, Shanta Prasad. Flute, clarinet, harmonium, *nagāṛā, ḍholak.*

Padminī kā jauhar. 30 min. 12 pp. B. Azad Mathuravi. Bhuresh Kumar Varma, Samant Lal, Chunnilal, Indira Bhargav; Madan Lal Jaipuri, Chidda Lal, Hari Babu Kaushik, Babu Khan, Shanta Prasad. Harmonium, *sāraṅgī,* flute, clarinet, *nagāṛā, ḍholak.*

Rājā gopīchandra. 36 min. 12 pp. Raj Bahadur Srivastav. Madan Mohan Brijbasi, Ram Dayal Sharma, Madan Lal Sharma, Saras Kaul, Kamini Devi; Atthan Khan (*nagāṛā*), Abdul Rahman Khan (*ḍholak*), Babu Khan (clarinet). *Nagāṛā, ḍholak,* clarinet.

Rambhā-shuk saṁvād. 26 min. 11 pp. Krishna Gopal Dikshit. Manohar Lal Sharma, Giriraj Prasad, Madan Lal Sharma, Chunnilal, Ram Dayal Sharma, Saras Kaul; Abdul Rahman (*ḍholak*), Atthan Khan (*nagāṛā*). *Ḍholak, nagāṛā,* flute, *sāraṅgī,* harmonium.

Satī anusūyā. 22 min. 11 pp. Satyanarayan Kishoriya. Krishna Lal Sharma, Bhole Lal Sharma, Kamini Srivastav; Atthan Khan. *Nagāṛā.*

Satyavādī harishchandra. 55 min. 19 pp. Raj Bahadur Srivastav. Ramesh Shravat, Madan Lal Sharma, Chunnilal, Saras Kaul; Atthan Khan, Natthu Singh, Babu Khan, Shanta Prasad, Madan Lal Jaipuri. Clarinet, flute, *nagāṛā, ḍholak.*

2. Extended play commercial disks (45 rpm), purchased at Punjab Gramophone House, Lucknow

Amar siṁh rāṭhor
Anārkalī
Andhī dulhan
Bhakt pūranmal
Dahīvālī
Ḍākū dayārām gūjar
Indal haraṇ
K͟hudādost sultān
Kriṣhṇa avtār
Muhabbat kī putlī
Prithvīrāj chauhān
Rājā harishchandra
Santoṣhī mā
Satyavān sāvitrī
Shravaṇ kumār
Sultānā ḍākū (A)
Sultānā ḍākū (B)
Syāhposh
Vīr abhimanyu

3. Cassette tapes, purchased in Palika Bazaar, New Delhi

"Nautanki 3"—*Jālim siṁh, Indal haraṇ, Muhabbat kī putlī, Dahīvālī, Vīr abhimanyu*
"Nautanki 4"—*Syāh posh, Ḍākū dayārām gūjar, Prithvīrāj chauhān, Anārkalī, K͟hudādost sultān*
"Nautanki 5"—*Satyavān sāvitrī, Santoṣhī mā, Bhakt pūranmal, Shravaṇ kumār, Dhanuṣh yajña*
"Hindi Nautanki Hits, Vol. 2"—*K͟hudādost sultān, Sultānā ḍākū, Santoṣhi mā, Muhabbat kī putlī, Vīr abhimanyu*
Nauṭaṅkī amar siṁh rāṭhor (Ishtiyak Varsi, Zahid Husain Varsi, Chanda)
Sāṅg shāhī lakkaṛhārā (Gulab Singh)
Jālim siṁh nauṭaṅkī; Dhanuṣh yajña

Notes

Introduction

1. Victor W. Turner, "Social Dramas and Stories About Them," in *From Ritual to Theatre,* 61–88.

2. Raymond Williams refers to British newspapers, but his phrases are equally suitable here. *Communications,* 37.

3. Communication is here understood as the transmission and reception of ideas, information, and attitudes. Ibid., 9.

4. James W. Carey, *Communication as Culture,* 23.

5. Ibid., 30.

6. These ideas are elaborated by James Carey in response to John Dewey. Ibid., 13–23.

7. Ibid., 65.

8. Roger Chartier has emphasized differences in the appropriation of cultural forms; see Lynn Hunt's introduction, *The New Cultural History,* 12–14.

9. Carey, *Communication as Culture,* 9.

10. Swann collected about 150 Sāṅgīts from pavement sellers in the early 1970s while researching traditional theatre forms in Uttar Pradesh; listed in the bibliography, Darius Leander Swann, "Three Forms of Traditional Theatre," 463–469. Working on the *qissā,* a narrative genre printed in chapbooks, for comparative purposes Frances W. Pritchett acquired about 100 Sāṅgīts and donated them to the Regenstein Library of the University of Chicago; personal communication to author.

11. Partial references to the British collections appear in Frances W. Pritchett, *Marvelous Encounters,* 24; Ronald Stuart McGregor, *Hindi Literature of the Nineteenth and Early Twentieth Centuries,* 91–93.

12. Teresa de Lauretis, ed., *Feminist Studies/Critical Studies,* 2.

Chapter One

1. The description of the princess Nauṭaṅkī and synopsis of her story is a composite of verses from Chiranjilal and Natharam, *Sāṅgīt nauṭaṅkī* (1904), later known as *Sāṅgīt nauṭaṅkī shahzādī urf, phūl siṁh panjābī* (e.g., 1975 ed.); Muralidhar, *Sāṅgīt nauṭaṅkī shāhzādī* (1909); Govind Ram, *Sāṅgīt nauṭaṅkī* (1915).

2. Govind Rajnish, *Rājasthān ke pūrvī āñchal kā lok-sāhitya,* 130–134. Phulan De is also the subject of two Rajasthani folk plays, *Khyāl rājā kesar siṁh rānī phūlān de kā* (1924) and *Rājā kesar siṁh ko khyāl* (1926), both in the British Museum collection. In these *khyāl*s her suitor's name is Kesar Singh.

3. Frances W. Pritchett, "Śīt Basant: Oral Tale, Sāṅgīt and Kissā," *Asian Folklore Studies* 42, no. 1 (1983): 53. See also Frances W. Pritchett, *Marvelous Encounters,* appendix B, 191–192, for versions of the Sit Basant story from all over India. Phulvanti's story is also contained in *Sāṅgīt phulvantī kā* (1877), a Marwari folk play in the India Office collection.

4. Charles Augustus Kincaid, "Rupsinh and the Queen of the Anardes," in *Folk Tales of Sind and Guzarat,* 90–101.

5. Mary Frere, ed., "Panch-Phul Ranee," as told by Anna Liberata de Souza, in *Hindoo Fairy Legends,* 95–141. In this tale she is sought by a prince exiled by his stepmother. William Crooke, "The Tale of Pañchphūlā Rāṇī," in *Indian Antiquary* (Sept. 1895): 272–274. Here she lives in the land of China and is wooed by the youngest of seven brothers. Several *khyāl*s also exist on Panchphula Rani: Krishnalal, *Khyāl āsā ḍābī, arthāt pachphūlā kā* (1923) in the British Museum, and perhaps by the same author, but catalogued as Kishanlal Nasirabadi in the India Office Library, *Khyāl pachaphūlā* (1923, 1928, 1931).

6. In "A Survey of the Incidents in Modern Indian Aryan Folk-tales," the "delicate heroine" type is characterized as "ordinary form: five-flower princess: heroine weighs five flowers only." See Flora Annie Steel and R. C. Temple, *Tales of the Punjab,* 302. The Miyan Bhunga ("Sir Buzz") story is in the same volume, 9–15. Here her suitor is a poor soldier's son.

7. The earliest known manuscript of the Nauṭaṅkī drama in Hindi is Khushi Ram, *Sāṅgīt rānī nauṭaṅkī kā* (1882) in the British Library. Richard Carnac Temple in the preface to vol. 3 of *Legends of the Panjab* lists "Rani Nautanki and the Panjabi Lad" as one of the stories he had collected but not translated or published.

8. Passages describing the Nauṭaṅkī performance at the fair and the interview with Master Surkhi are adapted from Surendra Sukumar, "Mele meṁ nauṭaṅkī," *Dharmyug,* Aug. 28, 1977, 43–46. I am grateful to Bruce Pray for a copy of this article.

9. The interview with Gulab Bai was conducted by an anonymous interviewer and was published in the Hindi newspaper *Navbhārat Times,* Delhi, May 8, 1985, 5. I am indebted to Ashok Aklujkar for a copy of this interview.

10. Malika Begam together with Pandit Kakkuji and Phakkar, all veteran Nauṭaṅkī artists of Lucknow, were interviewed by Kathryn Hansen and Jugal Kishor on July 15, 1982. Sound recording was done by Kay Norton, transcription by Tara Sinha, and translation by Kathryn Hansen.

11. Excerpts from Phanishwarnath Renu's short story "Tīsrī kasam" are abridged from the translation by Kathryn Hansen in *The Third Vow and Other Stories,* 49–88. The original story was published in *Ṭhumrī* in 1959.

12. The various etymologies for the word *nauṭaṅkī* are discussed by Ram Narayan Agraval in *Sāṅgīt: ek loknāṭya paraṁparā,* 135–137.

13. The publication history of *Sāṅgīt nauṭaṅkī shāhzādī* reveals its expanding territory and continuous influence over a hundred-year period. I located a total of twenty versions of the drama in the British Museum, India Office Library, University of Chicago Regenstein Library, and the private collections of Frances Pritchett, Darius Swann, and Kathryn Hansen. Chronologically ordered, the texts were authored by Khushi Ram (Banaras: 1882), Chiranjilal Natharam (Kanpur: 1904), Muralidhar (Kanpur: 1907, 1909; Aligarh: 1912, 1923, 1924), Govind Ram (Kanpur: 1915), Chiranjilal (Mathura: 1922), Shrilal Upadhyay (Banaras: 1922, 1923, 1930), Natharam Sharma Gaur (Hathras: 1925, 1975, 1982), Shivdulare Shukla (Kanpur: 1926), Muhammad Ismail "Shauda" (Banaras: 1930), Dipchand (Muzaffarnagar: 1932), Shrikrishna Pahalvan (Kanpur: n.d.), and Lakhmi Chand (Delhi: n.d.).

14. Scholarly opinion as well as oral sources corroborate the transference of the heroine's name to the theatre. "Nauṭaṅkī must originally have been the delicate heroine of a certain romance who weighed only nine *ṭaṅk.* That story was presented as a musical drama and in this form became so prevalent that now every musical drama or *svāṅg* has come to be called a *nauṭaṅkī.*" Dhirendra Varma et al., eds., *Hindī sāhitya kosh,* 1:358. See also Balwant Gargi, "Nautanki," in *Folk Theater of India,* 37; Mahendra Bhanavat, *Lokraṅg,* 319–320; Kapila Vatsyayan, *Traditional Indian Theatre,* 165. Several Nauṭaṅkī performers told the same story to Surendra Sukumar in the interview, "Mele meṁ nauṭaṅkī," 44.

15. Ved Prakash Vatuk, "Poetics and Genre-Typology in Indian Folklore," in *Studies in Indian Folk Traditions,* 38–47; George A. Grierson, introduction to *The Lay of Alha,* trans. William Waterfield, 9–25; Anil Santram, *Kanaujī lok-sāhitya,* 142–147.

16. Susan S. Wadley, "Ḍholā: A North Indian Folk Genre," *Asian Folklore Studies* 42, no. 1 (1983): 3–25.

17. Unlike *ālhā* and *ḍholā, nauṭaṅkī* does not denote a particular meter or song type. *Chaubolā* is the metrical and musical signature of Nauṭaṅkī performance, but a number of other meters including *ālhā* and *ḍholā* are also employed.

18. Jonas Barish, *The Antitheatrical Prejudice,* 4.

19. See appendix A for a detailed motif analysis.

20. The use of the dissuasion motif as a self-referencing device in a body of folklore is discussed by Stuart Blackburn, citing the Tamil bow-song tradition, in his introduction to *Another Harmony,* 22–23.

21. The Tamil *ulā* is discussed in David Dean Shulman, *The King and the Clown in South Indian Myth and Poetry,* 312–324.

22. Brenda E. F. Beck, *The Three Twins,* 24.

23. "The Man Who Changed Sexes," in J. A. B. van Buitenen, trans., *Tales of Ancient India,* 25–32.

24. This behavior was considered an educational task, part of the male's necessary preparation and "warming up" for marriage, not viewed as sexual aggression on the part of the sister-in-law, according to my female Indian informant.

25. Kathryn Hansen, "The *Virangana* in North Indian History, Myth and Popular Culture," *Economic and Political Weekly* 23, no. 18 (Apr. 30, 1988), WS25–33.

Chapter Two

1. Women and *mlecchas* are not mentioned in the *Nāṭyaśāstra* passage, but they were by this time also outside the Vedic community. In the earlier Vedic period, women performed sacrifices and recited rituals, but by the time of the lawgiver Manu (around 200 B.C.), they were classed with Shudras and prohibited access to Vedic learning.

2. G. K. Bhat, *Theatric Aspects of Sanskrit Drama,* 32; A. K. Warder, *Indian Kavya Literature,* 1:15.

3. Manomohan Ghosh, trans., *The Nāṭyaśāstra ascribed to Bharata-Muni,* 2–4.

4. Elsewhere in the *Nāṭyaśāstra,* the secondary function of education, especially moral education, is mentioned; see Ghosh, *Nāṭyaśāstra,* 14–15.

5. Ibid., 15.

6. V. Raghavan, "Sanskrit Drama in Performance," in Rachel Van M. Baumer and James R. Brandon, eds., *Sanskrit Drama in Performance,* 18.

7. Lachman M. Khubchandani, *Plural Languages, Plural Cultures,* 6.

8. Darius Leander Swann, "Rās Līlā and the Sanskrit Drama," in Baumer and Brandon, eds., *Sanskrit Drama in Performance,* 264.

9. Kapila Vatsyayan, *Traditional Indian Theatre,* 10.

10. On the Guga legend, see William Crooke, "A Version of the Guga Legend," *Indian Antiquary* (Feb. 1895): 49–56; Elwyn C. Lapoint, "The Epic of Guga: A North Indian Oral Tradition," in Sylvia Vatuk, ed., *American Studies in the Anthropology of India,* 281–308; Richard Carnac Temple, "Guru Gugga," in *Legends of the Panjab,* 1:121–209; John Campbell Oman, *Cults, Customs and Superstitions of India,* 67–82.

11. For further discussion on the distinctions between northern and southern recitational and dramatic traditions, see John D. Smith, "Scapegoats of the Gods: The Ideology of the Indian Epics," in Stuart H. Blackburn et al., eds., *Oral Epics in India,* 176–194. Certain North Indian epic genres such as the Pabuji recitation with the scroll (*phaṛ*) may involve possession by Bhopa specialists. See Komal Kothari, "Performers, Gods, and Heroes in the Oral Epics of Rajasthan," in Stuart H. Blackburn et al., eds., *Oral Epics in India,* 102–117.

12. For an overview of recent activity in the modern Hindi theatre, see Birendra Narayana, *Hindi Drama and Stage;* Nemichandra Jain, ed., *Ādhunik hindī nāṭak aur raṅgmañch;* Susham Bedi, *Hindī nāṭya: prayog ke sandarbh meṁ.*

13. Kathryn Hansen, "Indian Folk Traditions and the Modern Theatre," *Asian Folklore Studies* 42, no. 1 (1983): 77–89.

14. Susan Wadley, in her study of the western Uttar Pradesh village of Karimpur, does not mention Nauṭaṅkī or its primary meters (*dohā* and *chaubolā*) among the categories of song known to the villagers. Curiously, in a table she lists *vahrat* as an unglossed category; *vahrat* or *bahrat* is the abbreviation of the tune or metrical type *bahr-e-tavīl* typical of Nauṭaṅkī texts and performance. Discussing performances of traveling drama groups, she mentions only the "folk opera" Ḍholā and the Rām Līlā. Susan S. Wadley, *Shakti,* 38–49. Similarly, in a review of village musical genres in the Bhojpuri-speaking area of eastern Uttar Pradesh and western Bihar, Edward Henry does not mention Nauṭaṅkī, although he does discuss Ālhā, Qavvālī, and Muslim "entertainment bands." Edward O. Henry, "Correlating Musical Genres and Social Categories in Bhojpuri-speaking North India," paper delivered at the South Asia Regional Studies Seminar, Univ. of Pennsylvania, Nov. 18, 1987.

15. Personal communication to author from Ron Hess, 1981, detailing results of his fieldwork for the documentary film, *Ajuba Dance and Drama Company.*

16. It is not entirely clear whether these caste names are ascribed to the women after they take up performing or whether they represent hereditary groups.

17. As an example, note the title of the Hindi monograph, *Sāṅgīt: ek lok-nāṭya paraṁparā.*

18. Roger D. Abrahams, "Folk Drama," in Richard M. Dorson, ed., *Folklore and Folklife,* 354.

19. For a discussion of the Sāṅg of Haryana, see Daniel M. Neuman, "Country Musicians and Their City Cousins: The Social Organization of Music Transmissions in India," *Proceedings of the Twelfth International Musicological Conference,* 603–608.

20. Abrahams, "Folk Drama," 354.

21. Ross Kidd, "Folk Media, Popular Theatre and Conflicting Strategies for Social Change in the Third World," in Ross Kidd and Nat Colletta, eds., *Tradition for Development,* 281.

22. Witness this use in J. S. R. Goodlad, *A Sociology of Popular Drama.*

23. Raymond Williams discusses a similar set of meanings of "popular culture" in Stephen Heath and Gillian Skirrow, "An Interview with Raymond Williams," in Tania Modleski, ed., *Studies in Entertainment,* 4–5.

24. Stuart H. Blackburn and A. K. Ramanujan, eds., *Another Harmony,* 24–25.

25. A. J. Gunawardana used the term "intermediary theatre" as the second element in a tripartite scheme for classifying Asian theatres: traditional, intermediary, and modern. Within the intermediary category he included Kabuki, Chinese Opera, Jātrā, Nauṭaṅkī, Tamāshā, and Ludruk. The present usage differs somewhat from Gunawardana's definition. He explained the intermediary theatres as those that "are traditional in form but project secular values" and defined the "traditional" theatres as liturgical or ritualistic. A. J. Gunawardana, "From Ritual to Rationality: Notes on the Changing Asian Theatre," in *The Drama Review* 15, no. 3 (1971): 48–62.

26. Blackburn and Ramanujan, eds., *Another Harmony,* 14–23.

27. For a discussion of Kūṭiyāṭṭam and its relationship to the performance practice of Sanskrit drama, see Rachel Van M. Baumer and James R. Brandon,

eds., *Sanskrit Drama in Performance,* 260–262, and Pragna Thakkar Enros's essay in the same volume, "Producing Sanskrit Plays in the Tradition of Kūṭiyāṭṭam," 275–298.

28. Raghavan, "Sanskrit Drama in Performance," 25.

29. Carla Rae Petievich, "The Two School Theory of Urdu Literature," in particular 293–304.

30. Blackburn and Ramanujan, eds., *Another Harmony,* 15.

31. Ibid., 19.

32. Baumer and Brandon, eds., *Sanskrit Drama in Performance,* 260.

33. Raghavan, "Sanskrit Drama in Performance," 41. For further details on the *uparūpakas*, see V. Raghavan, "Uparūpakas and Nrttyaprabandhas," *Sangeet Natak* 2 (April 1966): 5–25.

34. According to Vatsyayan, the term *saṅgītaka* is mentioned in the *Caturbhāṇi,* Bana's *Kādambarī,* Bana's *Harṣacarita, Vaijayantī* by Yadava Prakasha, and Subhankara's *Saṅgīta dāmodara.* Vatsyayan, *Traditional Indian Theatre,* 100, 182.

35. Hansen, "Indian Folk Traditions and the Modern Theatre."

36. Roger D. Abrahams, "The Complex Relations of Simple Forms," in Dan Ben-Amos, ed., *Folklore Genres,* 195.

37. Abrahams, "Folk Drama," 351.

38. As an example of genre theory in South Asian folklore studies, see A. K. Ramanujan, "Two Realms of Kannada Folklore," in Stuart H. Blackburn and A. K. Ramanujan, eds., *Another Harmony,* 41–75.

39. The theoretical limitations of using Eurocentric analytical categories are discussed by Ben-Amos in "Analytical Categories and Ethnic Genres," *Folklore Genres,* 215–242. To my knowledge, however, there is no comparable critique of Western use of indigenous taxonomies. Such a critique might consider issues such as the criteria for selection of individuals who provide taxonomic information, the number of informants required for reliability, the basis for interpreting informants' statements about the meaning of categories, the influence of social, economic, and cultural processes on the naming of categories, the limitations of ethnographers' linguistic and interpretive abilities, the need for corroboration by observation of performance practices, and so on. Several recent folklore studies illustrate some of the problems. In *The Three Twins,* Brenda E. F. Beck never defines her use of the term "epic" in reference to the *Aṇṇanmār katai* but draws an analogy between English ballads and Tamil ballads, suggesting that her use is Western-derived (3–7). In a later chapter, she does not distinguish between recitations of the tale by bards in street clothes and dramatic performances by itinerant troupes involving costumes, makeup, and stage props, claiming that native classification makes no distinction (87). She apparently did not document through audiovisual recording and transcription the dramatic performances she viewed in the village or study them as separate performance practices, or examine the text of an early printed dramatic version of the Aṇṇanmār story in the British Museum, *Ponnara and Caṅkarar Nāṭakam* (1902), a text that would seem to provide evidence of a theatrical tradition of some duration. Susan S. Wadley, in "Ḍholā: A North Indian Folk Genre," *Asian Folklore Studies* 42, no. 1 (1983): 3–25, defines Ḍholā as a unified genre ap-

parently on the basis of village informants, although her textual sources include medieval courtly poems, folk lyrics, dramas, and a contemporary bardic recitation. She concludes that "Ḍholā is, in terms of text, texture and performance, drama, and most critically, a drama to be performed" (20). However, in more recent work she describes Ḍholā not primarily as a drama but as an oral epic. See Susan S. Wadley, "Choosing a Path: Performance Strategies in a North Indian Epic," in Stuart H. Blackburn et al., eds., *Oral Epics in India,* 75–101.

40. Gene H. Roghair, *The Epic of Palnāḍu,* 7.

41. Frances W. Pritchett, "Śīt Basant: Oral Tale, Sāṅgīt and Kissā," *Asian Folklore Studies* 42, no. 1 (1983): 45–62.

42. Abrahams, "Complex Relations of Simple Forms," 195.

43. Ibid., 196; Ben-Amos, "Analytical Categories and Ethnic Genres," 227.

44. Ved Prakash Vatuk, "Poetics and Genre-Typology in Indian Folklore," in *Studies in Indian Folk Traditions,* 38–47.

45. Ramanujan, "Two Realms of Kannada Folklore," especially 42–51.

46. Abrahams, "Complex Relations of Simple Forms," 205.

47. Personal observation of performance, Delhi 1982.

Chapter Three

1. For a discussion of how modern playwriting in Hindi as initiated by Bharatendu Harishchandra created a separate space for itself in contradistinction to the practices of the late nineteenth-century indigenous theatre, see Kathryn Hansen, "The Birth of Hindi Drama in Banaras, 1868–1885," in Sandria B. Freitag, ed., *Culture and Power in Banaras,* 62–92.

2. Raymond Williams, *Culture,* 156.

3. Shrikrishna Lal, *Ādhunik hindī sāhitya kā vikās,* 181.

4. For a background on the history and performance style of the Rām Līlā, see Norvin Hein, *The Miracle Plays of Mathura,* 70–125; Norvin Hein, "The Rām Līlā," in Milton Singer, ed., *Traditional India,* 73–98; Kapila Vatsyayan, *Traditional Indian Theatre,* 110–135; Balwant Gargi, *Folk Theater of India,* 90–113; Anuradha Kapur, "Actors, Pilgrims, Kings, and Gods: The Rāmlīlā at Ramnagar," *Contributions to Indian Sociology,* n.s., 19, no. 1 (1985): 57–74; Induja Avasthi, *Rāmlīlā: paraṁparā aur shailiyāṁ;* Richard Schechner and Linda Hess, "The Rāmlīlā of Ramnagar," in *The Drama Review* 21, no. 3 (Sept. 1977): 51–82; Richard Schechner, *Performative Circumstances,* 238–305; Linda Hess, "Rām Līlā: The Audience Experience," in Monika Thiel-Horstmann, ed., *Bhakti in Current Research,* 171–194; Philip Lutgendorf, "Ram's Story in Shiva's City: Public Arenas and Private Patronage," in Sandria B. Freitag, ed., *Culture and Power in Banaras,* 34–61.

5. The principal sources on the history and performance of the Rās Līlā are Hein, *Miracle Plays,* 129–271; Vatsyayan, *Traditional Indian Theatre,* 121–135; Gargi, *Folk Theater,* 114–131; John Stratton Hawley, *At Play with Krishna;* Ram Narayan Agraval, *Braj kā rās raṅgmañch.*

6. Typical of this folk Līlā tradition are the Rām Līlā companies cited by Hein and the Rāsdhārīs of Mewar discussed by Samar and Bhanavat. Hein,

Miracle Plays, 71; Devilal Samar, "Rāsdhārī: Folk Theatre of Rajasthan," *Sangeet Natak* 20 (April–June 1971): 50–57; Mahendra Bhanavat, *Mevāṛ ke rāsdhārī.* See also Gargi, *Folk Theater,* 113.

7. The Ram and Krishna stories have little place in the Sāṅgīt literature, appearing only in certain nineteenth-century examples, e.g., the *Sāṅgīt bālacharitra, Sāṅgīt kaṁs līlā,* and *Sāṅgīt nāg līlā,* all by Kumvar Sen, and *Sāṅgīt siyā svayaṁvar kā* by Hardev Sahay. Publication dates and library locations of these dramas are given in appendix C pt. 4.

8. These distinctions would be less marked in village and neighborhood Līlā performances.

9. Kabir also mentions the caste of actors called *naṭ,* the playing of the *ḍaṅk* (a type of drum), and the changing of costume (*bheṣh*). Ram Narayan Agraval, *Sāṅgīt: ek loknāṭya paraṁparā,* 22.

10. Yadunath Sarkar, trans., Abul Fazl's *Āʿīn-e-akbarī,* 3:272, cited in Agraval, *Sāṅgīt,* 41.

11. Agraval, *Sāṅgīt,* 42–44; Shivkumar Madhur, *Bhārat ke loknāṭya,* 27; Somnath Gupta, *Hindī nāṭak sāhitya kā itihās,* 16; Gopinath Tivari, *Bhāratendukālīn nāṭak sāhitya,* 77.

12. On *bhāṇḍ*s and popular entertainers during the Mughal period, see Abdul Halim Sharar, *Lucknow: The Last Phase,* 34, 100, 142–145. On *naṭ*s, minstrels, and acrobats in central India in the early nineteenth century, see John Malcolm, *A Memoir of Central India,* 195–197. On *naqāl*s, see Gargi, *Folk Theater,* 183–186.

13. Among the translations from Sanskrit are ten versions of the religious allegory *Prabodha chandrodaya,* originally written in the eleventh century. There are also two secular compositions based on Sanskrit works, *Śakuntalā* (two versions) and *Mādhava vinoda* (based on Bhavabhuti's *Mālatīmādhava*).

14. Tivari, *Bhāratendukālīn nāṭak;* chap. 3 (46–93) is devoted to proving that the Braj Bhasha plays were performed as dramas.

15. *Svāṅga,* derived from Sanskrit *su* or *sva* + *aṅga* (good or self + limb, part) and meaning "disguise" or "mime," was first used by Kalidasa in his drama *Mālavikāgnimitram.* Speech of Raja to Parivrajika in scene 1, cited in ibid., 73–74. Jayasi, Tukaram, Kabir, and others employed the term in medieval literature. Agraval, *Sāṅgīt,* 22–23.

16. According to internal evidence, *Hāsyārṇava* was transcribed after it was performed before a king of Telangana by a *naṭ* named Kamarup. *Mahārāja tailaṅgapati ati prasiddha chahuṁ dāga / kāmarūpa naṭa soṁ kahyau hamahiṁ dikhāvahu svāṅga. / Mahārāja mahipāla mani jo kachhu āyasu dīna / anayasindha naranātha kau sakalā svāṅga maiṁ kīna* (Agraval, *Sāṅgīt,* 23–24).

17. *Mādhava vinoda* was written at the request of Bahadur Singh, king of Bharatpur. Agraval claims that the poet wrote it down after seeing it performed "in Svāṅg style." Ibid., 26.

18. Tivari, *Bhāratendukālīn nāṭak,* 93. *Aura svāṅga kī tahaṁ bhaī avandanī niradhāra / āyo svāṅga siṅgāra.*

19. Tivari lists eight uses of the word in Brajvasi Das's 1759 version, as well as examples contained in subsequent plays on the same theme by Nanak Das (1789) and Gulab Singh (1789). Ibid., 8–9, 93–94.

20. For a brief history and definition of *khyāl* music, see chaps. 1–2 of Bonnie C. Wade, *Khyal.*

21. Platts's *Dictionary of Urdu* derives *Khayāl* from Arabic "to think, to fancy," and includes in its meanings, "Thought, opinion, fancy; apparition, vision, spectre, delusion; a kind of song" (497), and derives *khyāl* or *khai'āl* from Hindi and defines it as "A kind of song; a species of measure in (Hindi) versification; play, sport, fun, frolics" (885). According to the *Hindī shabd sāgar, khyāl* derived from the Arabic includes in its meanings both the classical music form and "a manner of singing *lāvanī*," whereas derived from Hindi *khel* it denotes "game, amusement"; Surdas and Tulsidas used it in that sense (1188).

22. The *dohā* quoted by Agraval, *Sāṅgīt*, 29, is *Mādhava aura mālatāya ke prema kathā kau khyāla / Baranata so sasinātha kavi hukuma pāya tatakāla.* As usual, Agraval gives no reference for his source. Tivari, however, has another reading that omits the reference to *khyāl: Mādhava aru mālati ke prema kathā rasāla / Barananu so sasinātha kavi hukuma pāi ke hāla.* He also notes that Sasinath was the poet's pen name; Tivari, *Bhāratendukālīn nāṭak*, 29.

23. *Tihiṁ khyāla kī rachanā aba hama karihemi tāke āge.* Tivari, *Bhāratendukālīn nāṭak*, 94, 9.

24. John Robson, *A Selection of Khyals or Marwari Plays*, vi–vii.

25. Robson's selections include two martial or political stories, *Dūṅgar siṁh* and *Aṅgrez aur paṭhān*, the latter a polemic against British rule composed for the Raja of Kishengarh. Also included are the nineteenth-century classics of asceticism, *Gopīchand* and *Bharatarī*, and the popular romance *Hīr rāñjhā.*

26. "They are not written by persons pretending to scholarship or even education, and I was unable to get a copy of any of them fully written either in Ajmer or Kishengarh. The different roles of some of them were written and were in the possession of the actors, but in other cases the pundit whom I asked to get the pieces for me, had to write them down from the dictation of the players who could not read or write." Robson, *A Selection of Khyals*, xv, vi, iii.

27. Ibid., iv–v.

28. Note the phrase "in the middle of the last century." Robson also states that the form of the *khyāl* had "not changed much during the last hundred years." Ibid., vii.

29. "There is seldom anything in them beyond dialogue, and sometimes only one actor sings through several scenes, while numbers of others may be carrying on the action of the piece. A new scene is introduced with a new refrain. If there is dialogue, each of the singers sings his own refrain first, and then they continue singing alternate stanzas, each repeating, at the end of each stanza he sings, his opening refrain." Ibid., vii–viii.

30. Vatsyayan dates Khyāl to the eighteenth century (*Traditional Indian Theatre*, 160), as does Gargi (*Folk Theater*, 48).

31. See appendix B for nineteenth-century printed Khyāls in British collections.

32. Samar states that Khyāl players of the Shekhawati style traveled regularly to Bombay and Calcutta. Devilal Samar, *Rājasthānī lok-nāṭya*, 18.

33. Ibid., 16–20. See also D. R. Ahuja, *Folklore of Rajasthan*, 141, and Gargi, *Folk Theater*, 48, for mention of Nanulal Rana, Jhali Ram (Jhaliram

Nirmal), Prahladi Ram (Prahlad Ray Purohit), Ujira or Ujiram, and Lachhi Ram.

34. Devilal Samar, "The Dance Dramas of Rajasthan," *Cultural Forum* 6, no. 3 (May 1964): 44. Whereas the nineteenth-century plays were published all over North India, in the twentieth century they come mostly from Rajasthan, according to the British Museum and India Office Library catalogues.

35. Samar, *Rājasthānī lok-nāṭya,* 18.

36. Agraval, *Sāṅgīt,* 34–38. See also Vatsyayan, *Traditional Indian Theatre,* 160.

37. The *akhāṛās* of Turrā and Kalagī bear some striking similarities to the *akhāṛās* of renunciants (*sādhūs*) organized on a paramilitary basis, who also identify themselves with distinctive banners and insignia. See Romila Thapar, *Ancient Indian Social History,* 89.

38. According to Tulpule, the Kalagī tradition was founded by Vadavalasiddha Nagesa in the fourteenth century, whereas Turrā originated with Haradasa. Shankar Gopal Tulpule, *Classical Marathi Literature,* 440. Several North Indian sources, however, name Tukun Giri and Shah Ali as founders of Kalagī and Turrā respectively, dating them to four hundred years ago. A nineteenth-century lithographed collection of Hindi *lāvanīs* in the British Library contains a foreword that supports this view: "Some call this Lāvanī and some Marhaṭhī or Khyāl. Actually, its composition and singing come from the south, and its two originators were Tukan Giri and Shah Ali who founded the two sects, Turrā and Kalagī." Kashigir Banarasi, *Lāvanī* (Banaras: Munshi Ambe Prasad, 1877). Similar information is contained in Devilal Samar, "The Khyals of Rajasthan," in P. N. Chopra, ed., *Folk Entertainment in India,* 57; and in Mahendra Bhanavat, *Rājasthān ke turrākalaṅgī,* 2–3. Agraval says that Tukhangiri (his spelling) was a *nirguṇvādī sādhū* and Shah Ali a Sufi *faqīr*. They were residents of Madhya Pradesh and were given their crests by the king of Chanderi following a court performance. Tukhangiri's disciple Rasalgiri came to Uttar Pradesh in the eighteenth century and spread the *khyāl* form there. He was especially welcomed in Agra where *akhāṛās* of *khyāl* and *lāvanī* were started at his instigation. Agraval, *Sāṅgīt,* 30–31.

39. The Turrā and Kalagī parties may have been heirs to older confrontations between Naths and rival Siddha or Mahanubhava groups. See Tulpule, *Classical Marathi Literature,* 440; Bhanvat, *Rājasthān ke turrākalaṅgī,* 17.

40. Vatsyayan, *Traditional Indian Theatre,* 170; Tulpule, *Classical Marathi Literature,* 345, 433.

41. Vatsyayan, *Traditional Indian Theatre,* 174; Gargi, *Folk Theater,* 79. Dhyaneshwar Nadkarni, however, reports that the *savāl-javāb* form of musical repartee has long disappeared from the Tamāshā. See his "Marathi Tamasha, Yesterday and Today," in Durgadas Mukhopadhyay, ed., *Lesser Known Forms of Performing Arts in India,* 53. See also M. L. Varadpande, "Tamasha: Folk Theatre of Maharashtra," in Chopra, ed., *Folk Entertainment in India,* 61–67; Chandrashekhar Jahagirdar, "Marathi Folk Literature," in K. M. George, ed., *Comparative Indian Literature,* 1:103–104.

42. Hemendra Nath Das Gupta, *The Indian Theatre,* 145.

43. Ibid., 151.

44. Shivkumar Madhur reports that Turrā-Kalagī parties now exist in Ujjain, Indore, and other towns of Madhya Pradesh, and he describes their performance style in *Madhyapradesh kā lok nāṭya māch,* 17. I viewed a videotape of a Turrā-Kalagī troupe from Madhya Pradesh performing *Abhimanyu droṇāchārya saṁvād* in the Sangeet Natak Akademi archives in December 1984.

45. Ramgharib Chaube, "On Popular Singers in Saharanpur," *Indian Antiquary* 39 (Feb. 1910): 64.

46. The plays of Guru Gopalji, one of the originators of Māch, bear rubrics such as *khyāl māch kā* and *nakal khyāl māch ki* (play or poem of the Māch stage, impersonation-play or poem of the Māch stage). Gopalji's successor, Balmukund, established the conventions of the present day and popularized the use of the name Māch. Five of Balmukund's plays are contained in the British Library, where three of them are termed *pūra khel māñch kā* (complete play of the Māch stage) and two are styled *nakal* (impersonation). These editions of Balmukund's plays were published in Delhi and Calcutta between 1894 and 1897. See appendix B pt. 2.

47. Bhanavat, *Rājasthān ke turrākalaṅgī,* 15–21. Samar, "The Khyāls of Rajasthan," 55.

48. The Kalagī troupe of Bhagvati Prasad is mentioned as one of the *akhāṛās* of folk theatre in Agra in the second half of the nineteenth century. Ashok Chakradhar, "Nautanki," in Durgadas Mukhopadhyay, ed., *Lesser Known Forms of Performing Arts in India,* 121.

49. Sadhuram Mistri, *Sāṅgīt gorakh machhandar nāth* (1915), 3; Chiranjilal Natharam, *Sāṅgīt chandrāvalī kā jhūlā* (1901), 84; Batuknath Kalyan, *Sāṅgīt brahmā kā byāh* (1902), 136.

50. Batuknath Kalyan, *Sāṅgīt brahmā kā byāh,* 136; Chhitarmal Jyotishi, *Chhandoṁ kā syāhposh* (1948), 1.

51. [Ustad Indarman], *Khyāl pūran mal kā* (1892), 1.

52. The first printed play of the Indarman *akhāṛā* in the India Office Library, possibly written by Indarman himself, is entitled *Khyāl pūran mal kā,* although it is written in the distinctive metrical form of Svāṅg, the *dohā-chaubolā-dauṛ,* and is in Khari Boli Hindi.

53. *Jo sajjan aslī chāheṁ indarman krit khyāla / likhau muhar meṁ lai paḍhi nām chirañjīlāla.* Chiranjilal Natharam, *Amar siṁh kā sākhā* (1915). See also Chiranjilal Natharam, *Malkhān saṅgrām* (1902), cover page.

54. *Yah baidya chirañjīlāl khyāl kath gāyā / din sāt mahīṁ rachi pachi ke svāṅg banāyā.* Vaidya Chiranjilal, *Brahma kā byāh* (1902), final page.

55. Describing contemporary Khyāl, Ahuja writes, "Two principal actors have a question-answer session on the stage and in poetical dialogue they do what would require many actors to perform." Ahuja, *Folklore of Rajasthan,* 139. Vatsyayan similarly notes, "The characteristic feature of all these performances whether in Punjab or Haryana or Rajasthan or U.P. is . . . the wordy battle which takes place between two groups or between two characters." Vatsyayan, *Traditional Indian Theatre,* 159. Robson's reference to this practice was mentioned above (note 29).

56. Published anthologies of *lāvanīs* appear in the British Library from 1866 on. Some of these carry cover sketches of groups of *lāvanī* singers gathered

around a drum player, as in fig. 6 where one member of the party smokes a *chilam* (clay pipe).

57. The texts indicate that the term *lāvanī* was used interchangeably with *khyāl* to refer to a song type (e.g., the phrase *iti khyāl sampūrṇam,* "the end of the *khyāl,*" at the conclusion of a poem labeled *lāvanī*). The British Library texts examined were Nanhu Lal, *Lāvanī navīn bilās* (Banaras: Munshi Ambe Prasad, ca. 1873); Kashigir Banarasi, *Lāvanī* (Banaras: Munshi Ambe Prasad, 1877); and *Suddh bilās, pahilā bhāg* (Fatehgarh, 1882) by various authors.

58. "Lower class people had also evolved special literary interests according to their tastes. For instance, one practice arose which was known as *khayal.* People composed extemporary verses and recited them when sitting in a circle. The name *khayal* was given to the feat of everyone producing a masterpiece from his imagination and creating some new idea. Several exponents of this art achieved great success and although they had no connection with the best society or with educated people, still, if one considers the matter, one must admit that they produced real and natural poetry." Sharar, *Lucknow: The Last Phase,* 93.

59. Madan Gopal, *The Bharatendu,* 28.

60. On the current practice of *lāvanī* singing in Urdu, see Mohammad Hasan, "Urdu Folk Literature," in K. M. George, ed., *Comparative Indian Literature,* 1:144; and also Azhar Ali Faruqi, *Uttar pradesh ke lok gīt,* 425–447. In eastern Rajasthan, folk poets continue to compose verses (classed in general as *khyāls*) in a large number of *lāvanī* meters, which have been described in detail by Bhanavat, *Rājasthān ke turrākalaṅgī,* 4–15, and Govind Rajnish, *Rājasthān ke pūrvī āñchal kā lok-sāhitya,* 53–73.

61. The uniqueness of these tenets can be adjudged from Charlotte Vaudeville's discussion in her *Kabir,* 126–127, 134.

62. Gorakhnath was probably born between A.D. 1000 and 1200 in either the Punjab or eastern Bengal. His name is closely linked with several other Siddhas, namely Machhendarnath (Matsyendranath), Jalandharnath (Jalandharipa), and Kanipa, who may have been his teachers. Although the early stages of the Nath sect are dim, Gorakh's primary significance lay in synthesizing Buddhist and Tantric doctrines with Shaivism. He codified the system of Hatha yoga and authored the *Gorakṣaśataka* and possibly other texts. Nath influence on medieval poets like Kabir, Nanak, and Jnandev was considerable, and a host of lesser poets in Hindi, Marathi, and Bengali were also followers of the Nath cult. For general background on the dates and teachings of Gorakhnath, see J. N. Farquhar, *An Outline of the Religious Literature of India;* George Weston Briggs, *Gorakhnāth and the Kānphaṭa Yogīs,* 228–257; Vaudeville, *Kabir,* 85–89.

63. Briggs, *Gorakhnāth,* 78–124.

64. C. A. Bayly, *Rulers, Townsmen and Bazaars,* 140–143. See also David N. Lorenzen, "Warrior Ascetics in Indian History," *Journal of the American Oriental Society* 98, no. 1 (1978): 61–75.

65. Bayly, *Rulers, Townsmen and Bazaars,* 126; Briggs, *Gorakhnāth,* 6.

66. Briggs, *Gorakhnāth,* 24–25, 55, 183–207.

67. K. Raghunathji, "Bombay Beggars and Criers," *Indian Antiquary* (Nov. 1880): 279.

68. M. A. Sherring, *Hindu Tribes and Castes,* 261.

69. Elwyn C. Lapoint, "The Epic of Guga," in Sylvia Vatuk, ed., *American Studies in the Anthropology of India,* 281–308. Daniel Gold and Ann Grodzins Gold, "The Fate of the Householder Nath," *History of Religions* 24, no. 2 (Nov. 1984): 113–132.

70. *Jogīs* in Rajasthan sing the ballad of Amar Singh; see Ocora LP #31, "Inde—Rajasthan—Musiciens professionels populaires," recorded 1971–72. The importance of *jogīs* in the medieval ballad traditions of the Punjab is mentioned by Adya Rangacharya, *The Indian Theatre,* 66. On the dominance of the Nath cult in Rajasthani folklore and the role of the *jogis*, see Ahuja, *Folklore of Rajasthan,* 47, 120. The Naths' singing of *Pingla Jhurapo,* a version of the tale of Raja Bhartari in Malawi, is mentioned in Shyam Parmar, *Folklore of Madhya Pradesh,* 93. *Jogīs*' singing of the *Nihalde* legend in Haryana is reported by Devi Shankar Prabhakar, "Folk Entertainment in Haryana," in P. N. Chopra, ed., *Folk Entertainment in India,* 28.

71. J. Abbott, "On the Ballads and Legends of the Punjab," and "Rifacimento of the Legend of Russaloo," *Journal of the Asiatic Society of Bengal,* nos. 1 & 2 (1854): 59–163. William Crooke, "A Version of the Guga Legend," *Indian Antiquary* (Feb. 1895):49–56. Flora Annie Steel and R. C. Temple, "How Raja Rasalu Was Born" and other stories in *Tales of the Punjab,* 159–161. Charles Swynnerton, *Romantic Tales from the Panjab,* "The Love Story of Hir and Ranjha," 1–24; "Raja Rasalu," 51–151; "The Story of Puran Bhagat," 230–245.

72. William Ridgeway, *The Dramas and Dramatic Dances of Non-European Races,* 190.

73. Ibid., 194. The Svāṅg of Puran is reported to be presented most commonly at Dashahara and Holi. The different styles of dramatic representation are described as follows: "The story of Hakikat Rai has been turned into a regular play and staged as such. But the accounts of Gopi Chand and Puran are mostly known in dialogue forms only, in which they are represented not only in the Punjab, but in the United Provinces and Rajputana as well. The difference is that the latter are staged on modern lines. There are, of course, actors representing the personages connected with the story, each taking his turn in time, but they may not come and go with scenes or curtains or other contrivances." Ibid., 197.

74. Jagdish Chandra Mathur, "Hindi Drama and Theatre," in *Indian Drama,* 23.

75. Suniti Kumar Chatterji, introduction to *Indian Drama,* 8. Twenty-five of these plays in Devanagari with critical introductions by Jagdish Chandra Mathur and Dasharath Ojha are found in Mata Prasad Gupta, ed., *Prāchīn bhāṣhā nāṭak saṁgrah.*

76. A Bengali version of *Gopīchandra* found in Nepal, written in 1712, is mentioned by Das Gupta, *The Indian Theatre,* 164.

77. Chatterji, introduction to *Indian Drama,* 8.

78. Hein, *Miracle Plays,* 121–123. According to Hein, three drama manuscripts from seventeenth-century Nepal, including the *Harishchandra nrityam,* are preserved in the library of the German Oriental Society.

79. Shardadevi Vedalankar, *The Development of Hindi Prose Literature,* 188–198. A manuscript of the play is reportedly contained in the Hodgson Collection in the India Office Library.

80. Joyce Lebra-Chapman, *The Rani of Jhansi,* 17.

81. Mahesh Anand, "Bhāratenduyugīn raṅgmañch," in Nemichandra Jain, ed., *Ādhunik hindī nāṭak aur raṅgmañch,* 53, 61. See also Krishna Mohan Saksena, *Bhāratenduyugīn nāṭya-sāhitya meṁ loktattva,* 133–134.

82. Preoccupation with the arts has conventionally been viewed as the cause of Wajid Ali's loss of power, but recent historiography has reexamined the dynamics of the Awadh Nawabi and considered the role of cultural patronage in legitimizing rulership. See Richard B. Barnett, *North India between Empires;* Michael H. Fisher, *A Clash of Cultures;* and Carla Rae Petievich, "The Two School Theory of Urdu Literature." Also of interest is the controversy within India about Wajid Ali's actions vis-à-vis the British, as represented in Satyajit Ray's film based on the Premchand short story, "Shatrañj ke khilāṛī" (The chessplayers). Satyajit Ray, "My Wajid Ali Is Not 'Effete and Effeminate,' " *Illustrated Weekly of India,* Dec. 31, 1978, 49–51 (and Rajbans Khanna's rejoinder in the same issue, 53).

83. On *ṭhumrī* and Kathak, see Sharar, *Lucknow: The Last Phase,* 137–142; Peter Manuel, "The Evolution of Modern *Ṭhumrī,*" *Ethnomusicology* 30, no. 3 (Fall 1986): 470–490; Nirmala Joshi, "Wajidali Shah and the Music of His Time," *Sangeet Natak Akademi Bulletin* 6 (May 1957): 36–38; Ragini Devi, *Dance Dialects of India,* 167; Nandita Haksar, "Kathak," *Indian Horizons* 29, no. 3 (1980): 34–39.

84. Adib asserts that *rahas* or *rās* originally referred to the dances of Krishna and the *gopīs*, but later it came to be a general term for drama and was used as such on the title pages of Amanat's *Indarsabhā.* Masud Hasan Rizvi ("Adib"), *Urdū ḍrāmā aur istej,* pt. 2: *Lakhnaū kā ʿavāmī istej,* 45–46. Platts's *Dictionary of Urdu* includes the following as meanings of the word *rahas:* "a secret, mystery, mystical or religious truth"; "sexual intercourse, copulation"; "pleasantry, merriment, sportive sallies"; and "a kind of ballet or theatric representation of Krishna and the Gopis (a similar entertainment was invented by Wajid ʿAli Shah of Lakhnau and given in his court)" (609). In his *Annals and Antiquities of Rajasthan* (1829) James Tod refers to the Rāsdhārīs as *Rahus-d'harees,* an indication of the earlier pronunciation (cited in Hein, *Miracle Plays,* 133).

85. The text of *Rādhā kanhaiyā kā qissā* is printed in Masud Hasan Rizvi ("Adib"), *Urdū ḍrāmā aur istej,* pt. 1: *Lakhnaū kā shāhī istej,* 212–224.

86. The principal source on Wajid Ali Shah's involvement with the theatre is Rizvi, *Urdū ḍrāmā aur istej,* pt. 1, especially 71–194. For a brief English synopsis, see Syed Masud Hasan Rizavi, "On *Urdu Drama aur Stage,*" *Indian Literature* (Oct. 1959–Mar. 1960): 138–140. The issues are also discussed at length in M. Aslam Qureshi, *Wajid Ali Shah's Theatrical Genius.* A Hindi summary appears in Agraval, *Sāṅgīt,* 68–76. See also Sharar, *Lucknow: The Last*

Phase, 64, 85, 146; Tivari, *Bhāratendukālīn nāṭak,* 115–117; and Somnath Gupta, *Pārsī thiyeṭar,* 227–229.

87. Ram Babu Saksena, *A History of Urdu Literature,* 350–351; Somnath Gupta, *Hindī nāṭak sāhitya,* 8; Annemarie Schimmel, *Classical Urdu Literature,* 213–214. Saksena, however, does not claim complete reliability, suggesting that the story of the Nawab's participation was based on hearsay.

88. Rizvi, *Urdū ḍrāmā aur istej,* pt. 2, 42–45.

89. Saksena states, "One of the French companions [of Wajid Ali Shah] mooted the idea of stage and presented the scheme of opera which was in the heyday of popularity in France." *History of Urdu Literature,* 351. Muhammad Sadiq declares, "Indar Sabha is a musical comedy modelled on European opera" (Sadiq, *A History of Urdu Literature,* 2d ed., 607), and earlier he states, "The revival of drama in India in the middle of the nineteenth century owes nothing to the discovery of an indigenous tradition. It is essentially an exotic" (606).

90. John Pemble, *The Raj, the Indian Mutiny, and the Kingdom of Oudh,* 265; see also 23–24, 265–266.

91. Agraval argues that the *Indarsabhā* ought not to be called an Urdu play (*nāṭak*) but rather a folk play of the old *rāsak* tradition. *Sāṅgīt,* 69–70, 78–79. The *Indarsabhā* is commonly included in histories of Hindi dramatic literature and is discussed in the context of older Indian folk drama traditions. See Somnath Gupta, *Hindī nāṭak sāhitya,* 8; Tivari, *Bhāratendukālīn nāṭak,* 117; Suresh Avasthi, "Indar sabhā: ek rūpgat adhyayan," *Naṭraṅg* 9 (1969): 23–29.

92. An illustration of Indra's court as symbolic of the Nayaks' reign in Madurai is given in David Dean Shulman, *The King and the Clown,* 229.

93. The *dāstān* was coming to occupy an important place in the literature of nineteenth-century Urdu. See Frances W. Pritchett, *Marvelous Encounters,* 1–8.

94. Sadiq, *A History of Urdu Literature,* 607; and Schimmel, *Classical Urdu Literature,* 214.

95. By 1893, fifty-four editions had been published, in Devanagari and Gujarati scripts as well as in Urdu. James Fuller Blumhardt, *Catalogue of Hindustani Printed Books,* 1889, 29–30; James Fuller Blumhardt, *Catalogue of the Library of the India Office,* 1900.

96. The British Museum's first edition by Madarilal was published in Agra in 1860.

97. Somnath Gupta, *Pārsī thiyeṭar,* 229–236.

98. A possibly incomplete edition of *Bandar sabhā* is contained in Shivprasad Mishra, ed., *Bhāratendu granthāvalī,* 1:729–731. Blumhardt 1889 catalogues *Bandar sabhā* (47) but lists no author. This edition was printed in Gujarati script, published in Bombay in 1877, 24 pp.

99. I am grateful to Bruce Pray for a copy of the first edition of Friedrich Rosen's *Die Indarsabha des Amanat,* which became the basis for the operetta, *Im Reiche des Indra.* See Schimmel, *Classical Urdu Literature,* 214.

100. The Parsis practice the pre-Islamic Persian religion founded by Zoroaster. They emigrated from Iran to Gujarat in the eighth century and settled

in Bombay under British encouragement soon after 1660. In the nineteenth century Parsis achieved prominence in education, law, and business; they became one of the most Westernized communities in India. Eckehard Kulke, *The Parsees in India,* 26–34.

101. Y. K. Yajnik, *The Indian Theatre,* 93; Somnath Gupta, *Pārsī thiyeṭar,* 245. See also Kulke, *Parsees in India,* 106–107.

102. Birendra Narayana, *Hindi Drama and Stage,* 38; Saksena, *History of Urdu Literature,* 354–355. Schimmel calls the Delhi company the "Balliwala Theatrical Company," in *Classical Urdu Literature,* 236.

103. Somnath Gupta, *Pārsī thiyeṭar,* 14.

104. Ibid., 196. The Parsi Curzon Theatrical Company of Calcutta, in addition to its Indian tours, went to Burma, Straits Settlements, and Penang. See A. Yusuf Ali, "The Modern Hindustani Drama," *Transactions of the Royal Society of Literature,* 2d s., 35 (1917): 85.

105. Yajnik, *Indian Theatre,* 97–102.

106. Ibid., 113. Yusuf Ali, "Modern Hindustani Drama," 95–96.

107. Yajnik, *Indian Theatre,* 111–115.

108. See Kulke, *Parsees in India,* 105–108, regarding the "extensive anglicization" of the Parsis.

109. Somnath Gupta, *Pārsī thiyeṭar,* 33–51.

110. At least four of some twenty-five plays of Raunaq's are housed in the British Museum collection. These were published in Bombay in 1879–1880 and are printed in Gujarati script. The four plays concern favorite themes found in the nineteenth-century Svāṅg tradition: *Hīr rāñjhā, Benazīr badr-e-munīr, Lailā majnūn, Pūran bhagat.* According to Somnath Gupta, most of Zarif's plays are unavailable (*Pārsī thiyeṭar,* 60). Thirty plays are attributed to him by Saksena, following Nami (*History of Urdu Literature,* 354).

111. For a discussion of Talib's works and examples of his language, see Somnath Gupta, *Pārsī thiyeṭar,* 71–85. Gupta indicates that Talib's plays were published by Khurshedji Balliwala and bases his comments on personally owned manuscripts. On Betab see ibid., 85–86; and Vidyavati Lakshmanrao Namre, *Hindī raṅgmañch aur paṇḍit nārāyaṇprasād betāb.*

112. Lakshmi Narayan Lal, *Pārsī-hindī raṅgmañch,* 20. For a more detailed discussion of Urdu playwrights of the Parsi stage, see Saksena, *History of Urdu Literature,* 353–366.

113. Further information on Radheyshyam is found in Lakshmi Narayan Lal, *Pārsī-hindī raṅgmañch,* 42–52.

114. Somnath Gupta, *Pārsī thiyeṭar,* appendix 2, 13–17; Yajnik, *Indian Theatre,* 92–93.

115. Yajnik has an extensive discussion of Indian adaptations of Shakespeare in *Indian Theatre,* 125–216. His appendix C lists approximately two hundred versions of twenty-nine plays of Shakespeare translated or adapted into various Indian languages, 270–278.

116. Yusuf Ali, "Modern Hindustani Drama," 96.

117. Yajnik, *Indian Theatre,* 112.

118. Narayana, *Hindi Drama and Stage,* 40; Yajnik, *Indian Theatre,* 115.

119. Somnath Gupta, *Pārsī thiyeṭar*, appendix 2, 40–50.
120. Yusuf Ali, "Modern Hindustani Drama," 96.
121. Narayana, *Hindi Drama and Stage*, 40–41.
122. Yajnik, *Indian Theatre*, 109–110.
123. These include *Gopīchandra, Harishchandra, Prahlād, Pūran bhagat, Lailā majnūn, Shīrīn farhād, Gul bakāvalī, Benazīr badr-e-munīr, Nal daman, Satī sāvitrī*, and *Shakuntalā*.
124. See Yajnik, *Indian Theatre*, 106: "The phenomenal success of *Harishchandra* in all the provinces of India was largely due to Parsi effort in Urdu."

Chapter Four

1. Ved Prakash Vatuk and Sylvia Vatuk, "The Ethnography of *Sāṅg*, A North Indian Folk Opera," in Ved Prakash Vatuk, ed., *Studies in Indian Folk Traditions*, 33.
2. Robson reports that he acquired copies of the *khyāl* plays he published from the Raja of Kishengarh and that "the different roles of some of them were written and were in the possession of the actors." John Robson, *A Selection of Khyals or Marwari Plays*, xiii, xv.
3. From street sellers of Delhi, Lucknow, Mathura, and Jaipur and from publishers' warehouses I accumulated a personal collection of ninety-nine contemporary Nauṭaṅkī Sāṅgīts bearing cover dates between 1950 and 1982. For a catalogue of this collection, see appendix D.
4. See N. Gerald Barrier, *Banned: Controversial Literature*, 5.
5. A. J. Arberry, *The India Office Library*, 67.
6. Catalogues in the British Museum (BM) include James Fuller Blumhardt, *Catalogues of the Hindi, Panjabi, Sindhi, and Pushtu Printed Books in the Library of the British Museum* (1893); Blumhardt's supplement for Hindi books in 1913; a second supplement in 1957 by L. D. Barnett, J. F. Blumhardt, and J. V. S. Wilkinson; some Urdu Sāṅgīts and related items are in Blumhardt's *Catalogue of Hindustani Printed Books* (1889) and his 1899 catalogue of Hindi, Panjabi, and Hindustani manuscripts. Hindi acquisitions in the India Office Library (IOL) are listed in James Fuller Blumhardt, *Catalogue of the Library of the India Office*, vol. 2, pt. 3: *Hindi, Panjabi, Pushtu, and Sindhi Books* (1902); Hindustani books are listed in Blumhardt's vol. 2, pt. 2 (1900).
7. The early lithographed texts appear to be preserved with greater care in the British Museum, and facilities for photographing and photocopying are more readily available there. Publication details and library locations of Sāṅgīts cited in the notes are listed in appendix C.
8. George A. Grierson, "Two Versions of the Song of Gopī Chand," *Journal of the Asiatic Society of Bengal* 54, no. 1 (1885): 35.
9. Jaini Jiya Lal, *Sāṅgīt rājā harichandra kā* (1877), 51. The poet then relates how the publisher Ambe Prasad requested him to correct a manuscript written earlier by Bhagvan Das, providing verses at the beginning and end to replace lost pages. Jiya Lal attests that his own work is limited to five *chaubolā*s at the beginning and five *chaubolā*s at the end, and thus he disclaims responsi-

bility for poetic flaws anywhere else in the play. This long explanation fills the place at the end of a composition where a poet normally asks forgiveness for any errors he may have committed.

10. Roger Chartier, "Culture as Appropriation: Popular Cultural Uses in Early Modern France," in Steven L. Kaplan, ed., *Understanding Popular Culture,* 229–253.

11. Thomas R. Metcalf, *Land, Landlords, and the British Raj,* 144.

12. "In the fortress market of Hatras buoyant growth maintained its momentum even after the great Raja had been driven from his dominions by British power in 1817. In 1830, it was 'bursting at the seams' and traders who had accumulated capital in the days of Diaram's opulence began to invest their resources in the purchase of land-rights in the vicinity." C. A. Bayly, *Rulers, Townsmen and Bazaars,* 208.

13. Ram Narayan Agraval, *Sāṅgīt,* 114.

14. On the history of the Indarman *akhāṛā,* see Agraval, *Sāṅgīt,* 108–111, 280–281. Also Radhavallabh Gaur, "Hāthras kī nauṭaṅkī, svāṅg va bhagat paraṁparā," in Radheyshyam "Pragalbh," ed., *Braj kalā kendra ke vārṣhik adhiveṣhan,* 105–111; and Radhavallabh Gaur, newspaper article, *Amar ujālā* (Agra), Jan. 20, 1980, 2.

15. The first instance is, "The servant of the people, Indraman, says: What the Creator wills is what will happen (*jandās indraman kahai kartā karai hogī vahī*)." *Khyāl pūran mal kā* (1892), 22.

16. *Dauṛ* constitutes the closing four lines added to the standard six-line *dohā-chaubolā*. *Dauṛ* is used extensively throughout the play in the same metric array as its later usage (13 + 13 + 13 + 28 *mātrās*).

17. Chiranjilal Natharam, *Chandrāvalī kā jhūlā* (1897), back cover.

18. This idea was also expressed by the current publisher of the Indarman *akhāṛā,* Natharam's son, Radhavallabh Gaur, in an interview with Pritchett. Frances W. Pritchett, "Śīt Basant: Oral Tale, Sāṅgīt, and Kissā," *Asian Foklore Studies* 42, no. 1 (1983): 47.

19. Publication list on back cover of Chiranjilal Natharam, *Malkhān saṅgrām* (1902).

20. Chiranjilal Natharam, *Ūdal kā byāh* (1902), 152.

21. Chiranjilal Natharam, *Indal haraṇ* (1901), pt. 1, 128.

22. *The ustād govind chirañjīlāl shahr hāthras mukām. Qatl jān ālam,* pt. 3 (1908), 76.

23. *Sāṅgīt nauṭaṅkī,* for example, was first published in 1904 under both authors' names. The same play reprinted by Chiranjilal's son, Bankelal, in 1922 was credited to Chiranjilal alone (see fig. 2), whereas from 1925 on it was reprinted from Shyam Press as if it were a work by Natharam.

24. Ruparam also published at least two Sāṅgīts on his own, *Chachā bhatījā* (1922) and *Bāp beṭā* (1923), both published in Hathras.

25. Twenty-five of "Natharam's" texts examined bear Rupa's signature, and the total number of his compositions is without doubt much greater than Natharam's, although other poets may have been working under him, particularly in his later years. Agraval lists a total of 147 Sāṅgīts by Ruparam. *Sāṅgīt,* 272–273.

26. These entries include only Sāṅgīts in London collections and the personal collections of Hansen and Pritchett.

27. The Sāṅgīts attributed to Govind Chaman in the London collections include ten Ālhā episodes published between 1909 and 1916, plus *Bhain bhaiyā* (4th ed., 1913), *Dayārām gūjar* (6th ed., 1914), *Nauṭaṅkī* (1915), *Lākhā bañjārā* (1916), and others.

28. Tota Ram Govind Chaman, *Malkhān kā byāh* (1913), 1–2.

29. Tota Ram Govind Chaman, *Machhlā haraṇ* (1916), 95–96.

30. *Jo sajjan aslī chahaiṁ indarman krit khyāl / likhau muhar meṁ laī paḍhi nām chirañjīlāl. Malkhān saṅgrām* (1902). For an illustration of a similar *dohā* of Chiranjilal, see fig. 2.

31. *Indarman krit khās jo chāhat khyāl amol / nathārām paḍh muhar meṁ sajjan lo dil khol. Kishan rasiyā amar siṁh rāṭhor* (1914).

32. The title page of Basudev's *Sāṅgīt siyeposh* explicitly mentions Muralidhar as Basam's disciple. Agraval says the Basam-Muralidhar *akhāṛā* was the first to appear in Hathras, sometime around 1870, according to an oral account of Lala Khachermal Atevala that cites Basam's *Syāhposh* as the first Svāṅg ever performed there. Agraval, *Sāṅgīt*, 106–107. However, the printed text of Basam's *Siyeposh* in the London collections is dated 1907; as the *akhāṛā*'s other printed plays in London are dated from between 1907 and 1915, these texts cannot prove Agraval's assertion.

33. Agraval states that the name of Basam's guru was Saligram, but that he was better known as Sarju Das or Serhu. In the *maṅgalācharaṇ* of *Sāṅgīt siyeposh*, the poet Basudev mentions his gurus Sedhu Singh and Salig as if they were two individuals. Pandit Basudev, *Sāṅgīt siyeposh*, 3d ed. (1907).

34. Muralidhar, *Sāṅgīt samar malkhān* (1907).

35. *Shaṅkargaṛh saṅgrām* (1911) is composed by Munshi Shaligram, master of the Tahsil school in Aligarh, but it contains no reference that might link it with Muralidhar's lineage. Another text is *Ālhā kā byāh* (1913), published under the following heading: "The *akhāṛā* of the famed poet of Hathras, Shri Muralidhar, composed by Ustad Sedhu Lal Pujari." The phrase "composed by" (*krit*) ordinarily refers to the guru or head of the *akhāṛā*, not the actual author. The author in this case is named below the title as Pandit Ganeshi Lal, master of the branch high school in Hathras. In a *lāvanī* at the end of this text, Shaligram is mentioned as the brother of the bookseller, Master Nihalchand. Another play listed as composed by Sedhu Lal Pujari is *Bahoran qatl* (1911), which is marked in the catalogues "edited by Munshi Shaligram."

36. Muralidhar, *Sāṅgīt bhārat* (1913), facing p. 1.

37. *Niskalaṅk nirmāṇ kiya shrī ustād mukand, / bhaneṁ chhand shivlāl shuchi muralīdhar harnand.*

38. Agraval, *Sāṅgīt*, 112–113. See opposite 76 for a photograph of the *maṇḍap* erected by Hanna Singh.

39. *Chintāmaṇī ko grahaṇ kar matī kharīdau kāñch / asal nakal mālum paḍai ādi ant tak vāñch.* Batuknath Kalyan, *Brahmā kā byāh* (1902), title page.

40. Agraval, *Sāṅgīt*, 112.

41. Kale Khan ("Aziz"), *Sāṅgīt bāṅkābīr amar siṁh rāṭhaur* (Aligarh: 1913), facing p. 1.

42. Shiv Narayan Lal, *Sāṅgīt sundarkāṇḍ rāh nauṭaṅkī* (Etawah: 1913), 26. Within the play, the composition is said to be in *rāh chaubolā,* indicating that the unique style or manner (*rāh*) of Nauṭaṅkī is the use of the poetic and musical unit *chaubolā. Sundarkāṇḍ rāh chaubolā tat raqam kartā hūṁ. Sāṅgīt sundarkāṇḍ,* 1.

43. For the historical background to the Dramatic Performances Act, see Hemendra Nath Das Gupta, *The Indian Stage,* 2/3:253–292, and Nikhat Kazmi, "Obsolete Theatre Act Stops the Action," in *The Times of India,* Apr. 15, 1990, 12. My thanks to Harjot Singh Oberoi for giving me a copy of the latter article.

44. Shaligram, *Shaṅkargaṛh saṅgrām* (1911), back cover.

45. Ibid., inside front cover.

46. Bayly, *Rulers, Townsmen and Bazaars,* 216.

47. Ibid., 444.

48. Chandi Lal, *Sāṅgīt jagdev kaṅkālī* (1914).

49. His Sāṅgīts bear Indarman's name on their covers.

50. Agraval, *Sāṅgīt,* 131, 286.

51. *Naklī pustak se bacho, idhar dījiye dhyān / aslī kā hai yah patā, lo phoṭū pahichān.*

52. The London collections contain six Sāṅgīts by Trimohan Lal, all published in Kanpur between 1920 and 1924.

53. Agraval notes Yasin Khan was employed as the chief writer for Trimohan Lal. He lists twenty-nine plays published under Trimohan's name. *Sāṅgīt,* 273–274.

54. The London collections contain forty-five titles by Shrikrishna published between 1919 and 1938. The earliest Sāṅgīt by Shrikrishna may be the *Chhatrapati shivājī* attributed to one Shrikrishna Varma and published in Kanpur in 1916. This play and six others are listed on a back cover of a Sāṅgīt of Shrikrishna's published in 1920.

55. Shrikrishna Khatri Pahalvan, *Mahārānī padminī* (1919), 42.

56. For further information on the history of the Haryana Sāṅg, see Agraval, *Sāṅgīt,* 121–124. A general treatment of contemporary Sāṅg performance is contained in Vatuk and Vatuk, "The Ethnography of *Sāṅg.*"

Chapter Five

1. Based on Jaini Jiya Lal's *Sāṅgīt rājā harichandra kā* (1877) and Natharam Sharma Gaur, *Sāṅgīt harishchandra, urf gulshan kā nāg* (1981). On the dating of the Natharam *Harishchandra,* see Kathryn Hansen, "*Sultānā the dacoit* and *Harishchandra:* Two Popular Dramas of the Nauṭaṅkī Tradition of North India," *Modern Asian Studies* 17, no. 2 (1983): 320.

2. The old story was first mentioned in the *Mahābhārata* and recounted in detail in the *Mārkaṇḍeya purāṇa.* See Cornelia Dimmitt and J. A. B. van Buitenen, eds. and trans., *Classical Hindu Mythology,* 274–286; John Dowson, *A Classical Dictionary of Hindu Mythology,* 118–119.

3. The Harishchandra story first makes its appearance as a Sāṅgīt in both Hindi and Urdu in the late nineteenth century. Jaini Jiya Lal's version was published as *Sāṅgīt rājā harichandra kā* in Devanagari in Banaras in 1877 and as

Svāṅg rājah harichand in Urdu (Persian characters) in Delhi in 1881. Another Hindi Sāṅgīt edition is that of Kidha Mishra, published in Meerut in 1880. Temple's "Legend of Hari Chand," collected from a bard in Meerut district, is evidence of its circulation as an oral tale at this time. Ramabhadra Sarman's *Harishchandra nrityam,* written in 1651 in Maithili and other dialects, was performed in the Indrayatra festival in Kathmandu. A drama on the same theme was exhibited in the court at Jhansi, Madhya Pradesh, during the reign of Gangadhar Rao (1835–1853). It was known in the folk theatre of Rajasthan, as seen from Shivprasad Poddar's published Khyāl dated 1886, and versions also circulated in Gujarati, Bengali, and other North Indian languages.

4. Trimohan Lal, *Khudādost sultān* (1977).

5. The two most influential Sāṅgīt versions, that of Lakshman Das dating to 1866 or earlier and that of Chiranjilal Natharam, perhaps written in 1925, are quite similar. The narrative presented above comes primarily from the Lakshman Das version but includes some differences from the later text where they clarify the meaning. For other versions and historical context, see discussion of narrative folklore in chapter 3 end of lithographed Sāṅgīts in chapter 4.

6. Hardev Sahay, *Sāṅgīt rājā raghuvīr siṁh kā* (1876).

7. Two Nauṭaṅkī versions of the Puranmal story are Balakram Yogeshvar, *Pūranmal bhakt* (n.d.); and Natharam Sharma Gaur, *Pūranmal* (1981). On Risalu, see Balakram Yogeshvar, *Satī shīlāde, rājā risālū va dīvān mahte shāh* (n.d.).

8. Gandhi had personal contact with the story when theatrical troupes performed it during his childhood in Gujarat. His reaction must have been shared by thousands of spectators over the years: "To follow truth and go through all the ordeals Harishchandra went through was the one ideal it inspired in me. I literally believed in the story of Harishchandra. The thought of it all often made me weep." Mohandas K. Gandhi, *An Autobiography,* 7.

9. Shalini Reys, "Dancing on a String: Kathputlis, Marionettes of Rajasthan," *The India Magazine* 5, no. 3 (Feb. 1985): 52–59; D. R. Ahuja, *Folklore of Rajasthan,* 5, 122, 143–144.

10. Synopsis adapted from Natharam Gaur, *Sāṅgīt amar siṁh rāṭhor, sajild donoṁ bhāg* (1979).

11. For a summary of the story, see George A. Grierson's introduction to the translation of William Waterfield, *The Lay of Alha,* 13–20.

12. In order to fit the Indian legal definition, a dacoit must operate with a gang of at least five. See Shyam Sunder Katare, *Patterns of Dacoity in India,* 6. A number of Indian studies discuss the various sociological aspects of the dacoit problem. These include R. P. Garg, *Dacoit Problem in Chambal Valley;* Taroon Coomar Bhaduri, *Chambal: The Valley of Terror;* R. G. Singh, *Terror to Reform;* D. P. Jatar and M. Z. Khan, *The Problem of Dacoity in Bundelkhand and the Chambal Valley;* and M. Z. Khan, *Dacoity in Chambal Valley.*

13. The synopsis is based on Natharam's text, *Sāṅgīt dayārām gūjar, urf bevafā dost* (1981). The story first appears in the Sāṅgīt literature in a version by Tota Ram Govind Chaman, *Dayārām gūjar* (1914), and in Gaddar Simh, *Dayārām gūjar* (1916).

14. The text on which this synopsis is based is that of Natharam Sharma

Gaur, *Sultānā ḍākū, urf garīboṁ kā pyārā* (1982). Other Sāṅgīt versions of the play are Shrikrishna Pahalvan, *Sultānā ḍākū, urf hāy re paisā* (1977); and Muralidhar, *Sultānā ḍākū, hāy re paisā* (n.d.). For nondramatic versions, see Hansen, *"Sultānā the dacoit* and *Harishchandra,"* 319.

15. Natharam, *Sultānā ḍākū,* 1, 8.

16. Ibid., 60.

17. Jim Corbett, *My India,* 98.

18. Shrikrishna Pahalvan, *Sultānā ḍākū,* 62.

19. The text used for this analysis is from Natharam's *akhāṛā, Sāṅgīt ḍākū mān siṁh* (1963). A second version in my possession is that of Ustad Mangal Simh's *akhāṛā, Sāṅgīt mān siṁh ḍākū* (n.d.).

20. Bhaduri, *Chambal: The Valley of Terror,* 28.

21. M. Radhakrishnan, *Indian Police Journal,* quoted in Bhaduri, *Chambal: The Valley of Terror,* 29.

22. Khan, *Dacoity in Chambal Valley,* 78.

23. Natharam, *Ḍākū mān siṁh,* 51.

24. The classic study of "social banditry" based on European folk and historical materials is Eric Hobsbawm's *Bandits.* For examples from the folklore of Gujarat, see Charles Augustus Kincaid, *The Outlaws of Kathiawar and Other Studies;* Tara Bose, *Folk Tales of Gujarat.* For the Deccan, J. F. Richards and V. N. Rao, "Banditry in Mughal India: Historical and Folk Perceptions," *Indian Economic and Social History Review* 17, no. 1 (Jan.–Mar. 1980): 95–120. For Tamilnadu, N. Vanamamalai, "Dacoits and Robbers in Tamil Ballads," *Folklore* 12, no. 2 (Feb. 1971): 66–72; Stuart H. Blackburn, "The Folk Hero and Class Interests in Tamil Heroic Ballads," *Asian Folklore Studies* 37, no. 1 (1978): 131–149. For Kerala, Vilanilam, "Robinhood of Kerala," *Folklore* 13, no. 8 (Aug. 1972): 308–317. And Bangladesh, Ashraf Siddiqui, *Folkloric Bangladesh,* 50–51.

Chapter Six

1. Natharam Sharma Gaur, *Lailā majnūṁ, urf maktab kī muhabbat* (1981). Other Sāṅgīt editions include Baldev, *Sāṅgīt lailā majnūn* (1874); Devidas Chhedilal, *Lailā majnūṁ yānī hushn kī bulbul* (1932); and Lakhmi Chand, *Sāṅgīt lailā majnū yānī maktab kī yārī* (1937).

2. R. Gelpke, translator of the Persian poet Nizami's *Layla and Majnun,* considers the tale "probably the best known . . . among the legendary love stories of the Islamic Orient." He mentions a book that has so far evaded my search, M. Gh. Hilal's *The Development of the Majnun-Layla Theme in the Literatures of the Orient* (Cairo: 1954). Nizami, *The Story of Layla and Majnun,* ed. and trans. R. Gelpke, 200–201.

3. Note the opening *dohā* of the Nauṭaṅkī: *qissā hotā shurū ab* pāk ishq *raṅgīn / nām amīr damishq ke the ek ta*<u>*kh*</u>*t nashīn.* "Here begins the story of a delightful *pure love.* Once there was a king called Amir of Damascus" (emphasis mine). The Urdu phrase does not specify an avoidance of carnal attachment, as the English equivalent might. Although *pāk* connotes something that is sa-

cred or clean, the phrase emphasizes the perfection of the spirit required to love with ideal intensity rather than physical relations or their absence.

4. A feud "dating back to generations" is mentioned in Gurbakhsh Singh's version in *Immortal Lovers.*

5. The *Sāṅg soraṭh* of Dalchand is found in several editions in the IOL and the BM (1876, 1879, 1888).

6. Natharam Sharma Gaur, *Sāṅgīt hīr rāñjhā, urf sapne kā āshiq* (1980). Folk retellings include those of Gurbakhsh Singh in *Immortal Lovers,* Masud ul-Hasan, *Famous Folk Tales of Pakistan,* 24–34, and Charles Swynnerton, *Romantic Tales from the Panjab,* 1–24. An oral ballad version by Asa Singh was recorded by H. A. Rose in Punjabi and translated into English in "A Version of Hir and Ranjha," *Indian Antiquary* (Sept. 1925): 176–179, (Nov. 1925): 210–219.

7. On the Damodar version, see Sant Singh Sekhon, trans., *The Love of Hir and Ranjha (Waris Shah),* 6–7. The version of the bard Sher, recited in Abbottabad to Swynnerton in 1889, similarly has the two lovers transported in the end on *pālkīs* to Mecca, where they lived happily for many years and may still be living. Swynnerton, *Romantic Tales,* 24.

8. The Waris Shah text is perhaps best known through the English translation of Charles Frederick Usborne, *The Adventures of Hir and Ranjha.*

9. The pattern of divine guidance for the hero and performance of magical feats en route to union with the beloved recapitulates the Persian *dāstān* tradition, although it is not lacking in tales of Indian origin. See Frances W. Pritchett, *Marvelous Encounters,* 7–11.

10. Again events differ in the Waris Shah poem, but the characterization is essentially the same. Ranjha takes on the guise of a fakir or yogi after Hir has been married away, contriving a plan to elope with her when she supposedly falls victim to snakebite and is sent to him to be cured.

11. Natharam Sharma Gaur, *Shīrīṁ farhād, urf gulshan kī mulāqāt* (1979). From the Kanpur school, Shrikrishna Pahalvan, *Shīrīṁ farhād* (1968). An early edition is Nathanlal Jadiya, *Sāṅg shirīn farhād* (1910).

12. Gurudayal Simh, *Sāṅgīt saudāgar vo syāhposh kā,* several copies in the IOL and BM (1875, 1876, 1878).

13. Natharam Sharma Gaur, *Lākhā bañjārā, urf anokhī dulhin* (1982).

14. See discussion of the *vīrāṅganā* in chapter 7, and Kathryn Hansen, "The *Virangana* in North Indian History, Myth and Popular Culture," *Economic and Political Weekly* 23, no. 18 (Apr. 30, 1988), WS25–33.

15. Natharam Sharma Gaur, *Mālī kā beṭā, urf shāhzādā firoz* (1981).

16. Natharam Sharma Gaur, *Andhī dulhin, urf jitendrī jaypāl* (1980).

17. Natharam Sharma Gaur, *Dharmvīr haqīqat rāy, urf sachchī qurbānī* (1976).

18. Natharam Sharma Gaur, *Shrīmatī mañjarī, urf gamzadā qaidī* (1981).

19. Shrikrishna Pahalvan, *Dhūl kā phūl, urf muhabbat kī bhūl* (1977). Another version is Natharam Sharma Gaur, *Dhūl kā phūl, urf matlabī insān* (1977).

Chapter Seven

1. The account of Jacobson's informant, Bhuri, a Brahmin village woman from Madhya Pradesh, suggests that the "chaste wife" norm is honored more in the breach than otherwise. Doranne Jacobson, "The Chaste Wife: Cultural Norm and Individual Experience," in Sylvia Vatuk, ed., *American Studies in the Anthropology of India,* 94–138.

2. Kishwar and Vanita, pioneers of feminist journalism in India in the 1970s and 1980s, express dismay at the "pervasive popular cultural ideal of womanhood" conveyed through mythic role models such as Sita, Savitri, and Anusuya. Madhu Kishwar and Ruth Vanita, eds., *In Search of Answers,* 46.

3. For an introductory discussion of Hindu goddesses, see David Kinsley, *Hindu Goddesses.*

4. Sandra P. Robinson proposes that the Hindu goddess's function may be best viewed as "revelatory," in contrast to the role played by the epic heroines as "exemplary" women. See her treatment of these two types in "Hindu Paradigms of Women: Images and Values," in Yvonne Yazbeck Haddad, ed., *Women, Religion, and Social Change,* 181–215.

5. Liddle and Joshi go even further, connecting goddess worship with a strong self-image of women and a matriarchal worldview. Joanna Liddle and Rama Joshi, *Daughters of Independence,* 55–56.

6. Vatuk and Vatuk's study presents not only a useful survey of the worldwide spread of the motif but also an excellent analysis of the theme in the folklore of Uttar Pradesh and Haryana, based on a number of Sāṅg librettos and ballads which they collected in 1970. See Ved Prakash Vatuk and Sylvia Vatuk, "The Lustful Stepmother in the Folklore of Northwestern India," *Journal of South Asian Literature* 11, nos. 1–2 (1975): 19–44.

7. The synopsis is based on the version of Natharam Sharma Gaur, *Bhakt pūranmal, sajild pāñchoṁ bhāg* (1982).

8. Natharam Sharma Gaur, *Rūp basant, sampūrṇ tīn bhāg meṁ* (1982).

9. Natharam Sharma Gaur, *Sāṅgīt triyā charitra, urf qatl-e shauhar* (1982). Another version is Shrikrishna Khatri Pahalvan, *Sāṅgīt triyā charitra* (1978).

10. Natharam Sharma Gaur, *Bhaiṅ bhaiyā* (n.d.).

11. While this retelling follows the Natharam edition, it may be compared with the transcription and translation of the All-India Radio version of *Indal haraṇ,* following the epilogue.

12. George A. Grierson, introduction to *The Lay of Alha,* trans. William Waterfield, 15.

13. Ibid., 18–19.

14. Kathryn Hansen, "The *Virangana* in North Indian History, Myth and Popular Culture," *Economic and Political Weekly* 23, no. 18 (Apr. 30, 1988), WS25–33.

15. History preserves the names of several of the warrior queens' lovers and companions. Razia Sultana fell in love with Yaqut, an Abyssinian slave, and promoted him from master of horse to general in chief, an event that caused dissatisfaction among the nobles. Later she won over her captor Altuniya and married him. John J. Pool, *Famous Women of India,* 87–88; Swami Madha-

vananda and Ramesh Chandra Majumdar, eds., *Great Women of India,* 382. The Rani of Jhansi was always accompanied by a female companion, Mundar, who was with her when she died. Shyam Narain Sinha, *Rani Lakshmi Bai of Jhansi,* 89; Madhavananda and Majumdar, eds., *Great Women of India,* 398; Joyce Lebra-Chapman, *The Rani of Jhansi,* 112, 116, 135, 147, 154.

16. The tale of Virmati and her husband, Jagdev, was first recorded in dramatic form in 1876, but it reached prominence in the 1920s when the two most commonly performed versions of it were published, those of Shrikrishna Khatri Pahalvan and of Natharam Sharma Gaur. The present discussion follows Natharam's text. Other narrative versions of it are contained in Richard Carnac Temple, *The Legends of the Panjab,* 2:182–203; and in Anil Rajkumar, *Bhāratīya vīrāṅganāeṁ,* 58–71.

17. Lebra-Chapman, *Rani of Jhansi,* 145–147.

18. This information is drawn from Firoze Rangoonwalla, *Indian Filmography,* and Rajendra Ojha, ed., *Seventy-Five Glorious Years of Indian Cinema.*

19. Girish Karnad, "This One is for Nadia," *Cinema Vision India* 1, no. 2 (Apr. 1980): 84–90.

20. Taroon Coomar Bhaduri, *Chambal: The Valley of Terror,* 54–66.

21. In addition to Nauṭaṅkī versions, published folk texts and oral performances on Phulan Devi I have collected include the printed *Bārahmāsī phūlandevī,* no author listed, courtesy of the Archives and Research Centre for Ethnomusicology of the American Institute of Indian Studies, Delhi; oral performance of *Phūlan devī birahā* by Ramji and Party of Ramman Akhara, Varanasi, and oral performance of *Phūlan devī birahā,* by Hans Raj and Party, Varanasi, both courtesy of Scott Marcus.

22. "Phoolan Fever," *Times of India,* Oct. 24, 1984.

23. "The Bullet Queens," *Times of India,* Aug. 18, 1985; "Day of Reckoning," *India Today,* Oct. 31, 1986, 33.

24. Svaminath urf Nabinkumar Barvar, *Sāṅgīt phūlan debī* (1982).

25. Ibid., 46.

26. Jon Bradshaw, "The Bandit Queen," *Esquire,* October 1985, 73.

27. *Times of India,* Aug. 18, 1985.

28. Bradshaw, "The Bandit Queen," 86.

29. An example is Hélène Cixous's operatic production of *Phulan* in Paris in 1988; I thank Françoise Burger for this information. Carel Moiseiwitsch, *Fugitive,* a site-specific work at the University of British Columbia Fine Arts Gallery, October 1987. "This Art Evokes Lost History," review by Oraf, *The Georgia Straight,* Sept. 25–Oct. 2, 1987, 20.

30. Natharam Sharma Gaur, *Dukhiyā vidhvā* (1951).

31. Natharam Sharma Gaur, *Satī bindiyā* (1975).

Chapter Eight

1. Barbara Babcock, cited in Frank E. Manning, ed., *The Celebration of Society,* 27.

2. The authors of the "India" section in Stanley Sadie, ed., *New Grove Dictionary of Music and Musicians* include "representational music" as a Basic

Musical Category together with "ritual and ceremonial music" and "devotional songs" (9:73–75). Most musicological surveys, however, overlook the category.

3. For further information on the *naubat-k͟hānā* ensemble, see "India" in *New Grove Dictionary,* 9:114–115, 150; Nazir A. Jairazbhoy, "A Preliminary Survey of the Oboe in India," *Ethnomusicology* 14, no. 3 (Sept. 1970): 375–388; Nazir A. Jairazbhoy, "Colloquy: The South Asian Double-Reed Aerophone Reconsidered," *Ethnomusicology* 24, no. 1 (Jan. 1980): 147–156.

4. Outside of theatre, the *nagāṛā* has been replaced by its heir the *tablā* in most classical performance contexts and by the *ḍholak* in folk music. It is occasionally heard at temples, Sufi shrines, and weddings. See Komal Kothari, "Rural-Urban Transitions," in *Proceedings of the Twelfth International Musicological Conference,* 598. On the probable evolution of the *nagāṛā* into the *tablā,* see "India," *New Grove Dictionary,* 9:137; and James Kippen, *The Tabla of Lucknow,* 17.

5. This technique is known as *ḍāt lagānā;* and actors practice it by going down into a well and singing long notes for hours, according to my informant, Ram Dayal Sharma.

6. Indeed, some Nauṭaṅkī shows today are essentially cabaret acts containing only vestiges of narrative material. In a short story published in 1988, a Nauṭaṅkī troupe is named the "Shyam Dancing Party." A. Asaphal, "Nepathya kā gīt," *Gaṅgā,* January 1988, 34.

7. Gargi mentions the singer doubling and quadrupling the tempo in the refrain portion of the *bahr-e-tavīl* (Balwant Gargi, *Folk Theater of India,* 38); and Wade cites this feature as evidence of the shared rhythmic structures of classical and folk theatre music ("India: Folk Music," *New Grove Dictionary,* 9:149). However, none of my performance examples bear this out. Perhaps what Gargi refers to is the illusion of doubling and quadrupling the tempo by drumming in *dugun* and *chaugun* (two strokes per beat and four strokes per beat).

8. Kapila Vatsyayan, *Traditional Indian Theatre,* 144.

9. Gargi, *Folk Theater,* 77.

10. Ibid., 158.

11. In Yakṣhagāna, the *bhāgavatha* conducts dialogues between himself and the leading actor (Vatsyayan, *Traditional Indian Theatre,* 40); in traditional Jātrā, the singing was divided between the actors and the *juri* singers (Gargi, *Folk Theater,* 27; Vatsyayan, 145). See also Gargi, 173–174.

12. *New Grove Dictionary,* 9:148–149; Vatsyayan, *Traditional Indian Theatre,* 41, 61–62, 154; Gargi, *Folk Theater,* 66, 81, 134, 159.

13. For a brief history of meters in Svāṅg and Nauṭaṅkī, see appendix E.

14. For a standard introduction to the principles of Hindi prosody, see S. H. Kellogg, *A Grammar of the Hindi Language,* 546–584.

15. A useful reference work on Urdu prosody is Frances W. Pritchett and Kh. A. Khaliq, *Urdu Meter.*

16. Appendix F pt. 1 lists the All-India Radio Nauṭaṅkī performances I collected in the course of this research.

17. Platts's dictionary derives it from Sanskrit *akṣa* + *pāṭa* + *kaḥ,* meaning "gambling table; place of contest, arena."

18. Sunil Kothari, "Gotipua Dancers of Orissa," *Sangeet Natak* 8 (April-June 1968): 33.
19. Gargi, *Folk Theater*, 179; Vatsyayan, *Traditional Indian Theatre*, 69.
20. On the *akhāṛās* of Birahā, see Scott L. Marcus, "The Rise of a Folk Music Genre: Birahā," in Sandria B. Freitag, ed., *Culture and Power in Banaras*, 93–113.
21. Chapter 3 discusses the Turrā-Kalagī *akhāṛās* and their historical relation to Svāṅg and Nauṭaṅkī.
22. Richard Schechner, "Performers and Spectators Transported and Transformed," in *Performative Circumstances*, 110.
23. Manomohan Ghosh, trans., *The Nāṭyaśāstra*, 526–527.
24. Appendix F pts. 2, 3 contain lists of Nauṭaṅkī performances on commercial disks and cassettes collected during my fieldwork in India.
25. Peter Manuel, *Popular Music of the Non-Western World*, 6–7.

Chapter Nine

1. Meredith Borthwick, *The Changing Role of Women in Bengal*, 117.
2. Kenneth W. Jones, *Arya Dharm*, 95, 99. Vatuk and Vatuk state, "The movement's founder, Dayanand, was quite explicit in his writings about the evils of dramatic performances." Ved Prakash Vatuk and Sylvia Vatuk, "The Ethnography of *Sāṅg*, A North Indian Folk Opera," in Ved Prakash Vatuk, ed., *Studies in Indian Folk Traditions*, 30.
3. Kathryn Hansen, "The Birth of Hindi Drama in Banaras," in Sandria B. Freitag, ed., *Culture and Power in Banaras*, 86.
4. Jonas Barish, *The Antitheatrical Prejudice*.
5. Sumanta Banerjee, "Marginalization of Women's Popular Culture in Nineteenth-Century Bengal," in Kumkum Sangari and Sudesh Vaid, eds., *Recasting Women*, 131, 130.
6. "*Zenana* women were said to sustain the existence of the Calcutta theater. If men were to stop their wives from going, many theaters would have had to close down." Borthwick, *Changing Role of Women*, 268; see also 18, 269.
7. Banerjee, "Marginalization of Women's Popular Culture," 132.
8. Amrit Srinivasan, "The Hindu Temple-Dancer: Prostitute or Nun?" *Cambridge Anthropology* 8, no. 1 (1983): 73–99; Amrit Srinivasan, "Reform and Revival: The Devadasi and Her Dance," *Economic and Political Weekly*, Nov. 2, 1985, 1869–1876.
9. Srinivasan, "Reform and Revival," 1875.
10. "The transformation of Odissi from a regional traditional form of dance to a nationally recognized 'classical' form of dance . . . also meant the creation of a new ideological framework . . . one that fitted the new national consciousness of the educated elite. That consciousness made it impossible for the revivalists to invite the devadasis to participate in the seminars which took place in the 1950s to establish Odissi as a classical form of dance." Frédérique Apffel Marglin, *Wives of the God-King*, 28.
11. Nancy Armstrong and Leonard Tennenhouse, eds., *The Ideology of Conduct*, 21, 20.

12. Roger Chartier, *Cultural History,* 4–5.

13. Borthwick, *Changing Role of Women,* 194–197.

14. Malika Begam, personal interview by Kathryn Hansen and Jugal Kishor, Lucknow, July 15, 1982.

15. "It is indeed striking to observe how the political, psychological, and aesthetic discourse around the turn of the century consistently and obsessively genders mass culture and the masses as feminine, while high culture, whether traditional or modern, clearly remains the privileged realm of male activities." Andreas Huyssen, "Mass Culture as Woman: Modernism's Other," in Tania Modleski, ed., *Studies in Entertainment,* 191.

16. Tania Modleski, introduction to *Studies in Entertainment,* xviii.

17. Huyssen, "Mass Culture as Woman," 205.

18. Raymond Williams, *Culture,* 187.

19. Carole M. Farber, "Performing Social and Cultural Change: The Jatra of West Bengal, India," *South Asian Anthropologist* 5, no. 2 (1984): 124.

20. Alf Hiltebeitel, *The Cult of Draupadi,* 1:153.

21. Girish Karnad, "Theatre in India," *Daedalus* 118, no. 4 (Fall 1989): 336.

22. Victor W. Turner, *The Ritual Process,* chaps. 3–5, and *From Ritual to Theatre.*

23. Mikhail Bakhtin, *Rabelais and His World,* 10.

24. Ibid., 268–275.

25. David Hall summarizes and critiques these studies in his introduction to Steven L. Kaplan, ed., *Understanding Popular Culture,* 5–18.

26. Some familiar examples of status reversal include the king becoming an ascetic (*Gopīchand, Raghuvīr siṁh*), the king becoming an untouchable (*Harishchandra*), the child becoming a preacher to adults (*Prahlād, Dhurū*), the outlaw becoming a respected leader (*Sultānā ḍākū*), the man becoming a woman and the woman becoming a man (*Rānī nauṭaṅkī*).

27. Badal Sircar, *The Third Theatre,* 25–27.

28. Rajinder Nath, foreword to Girish Karnad, *Hayavadana,* trans. B. V. Karanth.

29. Safdar Hashmi, *The Right to Perform.*

30. Natalie Zemon Davis, *Society and Culture in Early Modern France,* 97.

31. Stephen Heath and Gillian Skirrow, "An Interview with Raymond Williams," in Tania Modleski, ed., *Studies in Entertainment,* 10.

32. Karnad, "Theatre in India," 338, 349.

33. For a discussion of their work, see Vasudha Dalmia-Lüderitz, "To Be More Brechtian is to be more Indian: On the Theatre of Habib Tanvir," in Erika Fischer-Lichte et al., eds., *The Dramatic Touch of Difference,* 221–235; Kathryn Hansen, "Indian Folk Traditions and the Modern Theatre," *Asian Folklore Studies* 42, no. 1 (1983): 77–89.

34. Natya Samaroh 1984 festival brochure.

35. James Christopher, "Going for Gogol," in *Time Out* (London), Jan. 11–18, 1989. This clipping and one by David Spark entitled "Indian theatre bridges cultural gulf" (*The Hindu,* Feb. 28, 1989) were kindly given to me by Bill Buxton.

Epilogue

1. Interview with Chunnilal recorded for All-India Radio, Mathura; copy provided courtesy of Alan Entwistle. Transcription by Tara Sinha.

2. From a brochure for the performance of the Nauṭaṅkī *Bhikhārin,* played in Lucknow, July 7, 1982.

3. Personal interview by author with Pandit Kakkuji, Malika Begam, and Phakkar, conducted on July 15, 1982, in Lucknow. Television interview the same night on Doordarshan, Lucknow.

Bibliography

English Sources

Abbott, J. "On the Ballads and Legends of the Punjab," and "Rifacimento of the Legend of Russaloo." *Journal of the Asiatic Society of Bengal*, nos. 1 and 2 (1854): 59–163.

Abrahams, Roger D. "The Complex Relations of Simple Forms." In *Folklore Genres*, ed. Dan Ben-Amos, 193–214. Austin: University of Texas Press, 1976.

———."Folk Drama." In *Folklore and Folklife: An Introduction*, ed. Richard M. Dorson, 351–362. Chicago: University of Chicago Press, 1972.

Abrams, Tevia. "Tamasha: People's Theatre of Maharashtra State, India." Ph.D. dissertation, Michigan State University, 1974.

Ahuja, D. R. *Folklore of Rajasthan*. Delhi: National Book Trust, 1980.

Arberry, A. J. *The India Office Library: A Historical Sketch*. London: Commonwealth Office, 1967.

Armstrong, Nancy, and Leonard Tennenhouse, eds. *The Ideology of Conduct: Essays on Literature and the History of Sexuality*. New York: Methuen, 1987.

Babcock, Barbara A. *The Reversible World: Symbolic Inversion in Art and Society*. Ithaca: Cornell University Press, 1978.

Bakhtin, Mikhail. *Rabelais and His World*. Trans. Helene Iswolsky. Bloomington: Indiana University Press, 1984.

Banerjee, Sumanta. "Marginalization of Women's Popular Culture in Nineteenth-Century Bengal." In *Recasting Women: Essays in Colonial History*, ed. Kumkum Sangari and Sudesh Vaid, 127–179. Delhi: Kali for Women, 1989.

Barish, Jonas. *The Antitheatrical Prejudice*. Berkeley: University of California Press, 1981.

Barnett, L. D., J. F. Blumhardt, and J. V. S. Wilkinson. *A Second Supplementary Catalogue of Printed Books in Hindi, Bihari . . . and Pahari in the Library of the British Museum*. London: British Museum, 1957.

Barnett, Richard B. *North India between Empires: Awadh, the Mughals, and the British, 1720–1801*. Berkeley: University of California Press, 1980.

Barrier, N. Gerald. *Banned: Controversial Literature and Political Control in British India, 1907–1947*. Columbia: University of Missouri Press, 1974.

Baskaran, S. Theodore. *The Message Bearers: The Nationalist Politics and the Entertainment Media in South India, 1880–1945*. Madras: Cre-A, 1981.

Baumer, Rachel Van M., and James R. Brandon, eds. *Sanskrit Drama in Performance*. Honolulu: University of Hawaii Press, 1981.

Bayly, C. A. *Rulers, Townsmen and Bazaars: North Indian Society in the Age of British Expansion, 1770–1870*. Cambridge: Cambridge University Press, 1983.

Beck, Brenda E. F. *The Three Twins: The Telling of a South Indian Folk Epic*. Bloomington: Indiana University Press, 1982.

Bedi, Sohinder Singh. *Folklore of the Punjab*. Delhi: National Book Trust, 1971.

Ben-Amos, Dan, ed. *Folklore Genres*. Austin: University of Texas Press, 1976.

Bhaduri, Taroon Coomar. *Chambal: The Valley of Terror*. Delhi: Vikas, 1972.

Bhat, G. K. *Theatric Aspects of Sanskrit Drama*. Poona: Bhandarkar Oriental Research Institute, 1983.

Blackburn, Stuart H. "The Folk Hero and Class Interests in Tamil Heroic Ballads." *Asian Folklore Studies* 37, no. 1 (1978): 131–149.

Blackburn, Stuart H., Peter J. Claus, Joyce B. Flueckiger, and Susan S. Wadley, eds. *Oral Epics in India*. Berkeley: University of California Press, 1989.

Blackburn, Stuart H., and A. K. Ramanujan, eds. *Another Harmony: New Essays on the Folklore of India*. Berkeley: University of California Press, 1986.

Blumhardt, James Fuller. *Catalogues of the Hindi, Panjabi, Sindhi, and Pushtu Printed Books in the Library of the British Museum*. London: British Museum, 1893.

———. *Catalogue of the Hindi, Panjabi, and Hindustani Manuscripts*. London: British Museum, 1899.

———. *Catalogue of Hindustani Printed Books in the Library of the British Museum*. London: British Museum, 1889.

———. *Catalogue of the Library of the India Office*. Vol. 2, pt. 2, *Hindustani Books*. London: India Office Library, 1900.

———. *Catalogue of the Library of the India Office*. Vol. 2, pt. 3, *Hindi, Panjabi, Pushtu, and Sindhi Books*. London: India Office Library, 1902.

———. *A Supplementary Catalogue of Hindi Books in the Library of the British Museum Acquired during the Years 1893–1912*. London: British Museum, 1913.

Borthwick, Meredith. *The Changing Role of Women in Bengal, 1849–1905*. Princeton: Princeton University Press, 1984.

Bose, Tara. *Folk Tales of Gujarat*. Delhi: Sterling Publishers, 1971.

Bradshaw, Jon. "The Bandit Queen." *Esquire*, October 1985, 73–88.

Briggs, George Weston. *Gorakhnāth and the Kānphaṭa Yogīs*. 1938. Reprint. Delhi: Motilal Banarsidass, 1982.

Burke, Peter. *Popular Culture in Early Modern Europe.* New York: Harper and Row, 1978.
Carey, James W. *Communication as Culture: Essays on Media and Society.* Boston: Unwin Hyman, 1989.
Chakradhar, Ashok. "Nautanki." In *Lesser Known Forms of Performing Arts in India,* ed. Durgadas Mukhopadhyay, 118–123. Delhi: Sterling Publishers, 1978.
Chartier, Roger. *Cultural History: Between Practices and Representations.* Trans. Lydia G. Cochrane. Cambridge: Polity Press, 1988.
———. "Culture as Appropriation: Popular Cultural Uses in Early Modern France." In *Understanding Popular Cultural: Europe from the Middle Ages to the Nineteenth Century,* ed. Steven L. Kaplan, 229–253. Berlin: Mouton Publishers, 1984.
Chatterji, Suniti Kumar. Introduction to *Indian Drama,* 1–11. 2d rev. ed. Publications Division, Ministry of Information and Broadcasting, Government of India, 1981.
Chaturvedi, Mahendra, and B. N. Tiwari. *A Practical Hindi-English Dictionary.* 15th ed. Delhi: National Publishing House, 1987.
Chaube, Ramgharib. "Note on Origin of Swang." *Indian Antiquary* 39 (Jan. 1910): 32.
———. "On Popular Singers in Saharanpur." *Indian Antiquary* 39 (Feb. 1910): 64.
Chopra, P. N., ed. *Folk Entertainment in India.* Delhi: Ministry of Education and Culture, Government of India, 1981.
Corbett, Jim. *My India.* Madras: Oxford University Press, 1983.
Crooke, William. *An Introduction to the Popular Religion and Folklore of Northern India.* Allahabad: Government Press, 1894.
———. "The Tale of Pañchphūlā Rāṇī." *Indian Antiquary* (Sept. 1895): 272–274.
———. "A Version of the Guga Legend." *Indian Antiquary* (Feb. 1895): 49–56.
Dalmia-Lüderitz, Vasudha. "To Be More Brechtian Is to Be More Indian: On the Theatre of Habib Tanvir." In *The Dramatic Touch of Difference: Theatre, Own and Foreign,* ed. Erika Fischer-Lichte, Josephine Riley, and Michael Gissenwehrer, 221–235. Tübingen: Gunter Narr Verlag, 1990.
Das Gupta, Hemendra Nath. *The Indian Theatre.* 1946. Reprint. Delhi: Gian Publishing House, 1988.
———. *The Indian Stage.* Vol. 2/3, rev. ed. Calcutta: M. K. Das Gupta, 1946.
———. *The Indian Stage.* Vol. 4. Calcutta: M. K. Das Gupta, 1944.
Davis, Natalie Zemon. *Society and Culture in Early Modern France.* Stanford: Stanford University Press, 1975.
de Lauretis, Teresa. *Alice Doesn't: Feminism, Semiotics, Cinema.* Bloomington: Indiana University Press, 1984.
———, ed. *Feminist Studies/Critical Studies.* Bloomington: Indiana University Press, 1986.
Desai, Sudha R. *Bhavai: A Medieval Form of Ancient Indian Dramatic Art as Prevalent in Gujarat.* Ahmedabad: Gujarat University, 1972.
Devi, Ragini. *Dance Dialects of India.* Delhi: Vikas, 1972.

Dimmitt, Cornelia, and J. A. B. van Buitenen, eds. and trans. *Classical Hindu Mythology: A Reader in the Sanskrit Purāṇas*. Philadelphia: Temple University Press, 1978.

Dimock, Edward C., Jr. *The Thief of Love: Bengali Tales from Court and Village*. Chicago: University of Chicago Press, 1963.

Dorson, Richard M., ed. *Folklore and Folklife: An Introduction*. Chicago: University of Chicago Press, 1972.

Dowson, John. *A Classical Dictionary of Hindu Mythology*. 12th ed. Ludhiana: Lyall Book Depot, n.d.

Elam, Keir. *The Semiotics of Theatre and Drama*. London: Methuen, 1980.

Enros, Pragna Thakkar. "Producing Sanskrit Plays in the Tradition of Kūtiyāṭṭam." In *Sanskrit Drama in Performance*, ed. Rachel Van M. Baumer and James R. Brandon, 275–298. Honolulu: University of Hawaii Press, 1981.

Farber, Carole M. "Performing Social and Cultural Change: The Jatra of West Bengal, India." *South Asian Anthropologist* 5, no. 2 (1984): 121–135.

———. "Prolegomenon to an Understanding of the Jatra of India: The Travelling Popular Theatre of the State of West Bengal." Ph.D. dissertation, University of British Columbia, 1979.

Farquhar, J. N. *An Outline of the Religious Literature of India*. 1920. Reprint. Delhi: Motilal Banarsidass, 1967.

Fischer-Lichte, Erika, Josephine Riley, and Michael Gissenwehrer, eds. *The Dramatic Touch of Difference: Theatre, Own and Foreign*. Tübingen: Gunter Narr Verlag, 1990.

Fisher, Michael H. *A Clash of Cultures: Awadh, the British and the Mughals*. Riverdale, Md.: Riverdale Company, 1987.

Freitag, Sandria B., ed. *Culture and Power in Banaras: Community, Performance, and Environment, 1800–1980*. Berkeley: University of California Press, 1989.

Frere, Mary, ed. *Hindoo Fairy Legends (Old Deccan Days)*. [1881?] New York: Dover, 1967.

Gandhi, Mohandas K. *An Autobiography: The Story of My Experiments with Truth*. Boston: Beacon Press, 1957.

Garg, R. P. *Dacoit Problem in Chambal Valley*. Banaras: Gandhian Institute of Studies, 1965.

Gargi, Balwant. *Folk Theater of India*. Seattle: University of Washington Press, 1966.

George, K. M., ed. *Comparative Indian Literature*. Vols. 1 and 2. Trichur: Kerala Sahitya Akademi, 1984.

Ghosh, Manomohan, trans. *The Nāṭyaśāstra ascribed to Bharata-Muni*. Vol. 1, 2d ed. Calcutta: Granthalaya Private, 1967.

Gold, Daniel, and Ann Grodzins Gold. "The Fate of the Householder Nath." *History of Religions* 24, no. 2 (Nov. 1984): 113–132.

Goodlad, J. S. R. *A Sociology of Popular Drama*. London: Heinemann, 1971.

Gopal, Madan. *The Bharatendu: His Life and Times*. Delhi: Sagar Publications, 1972.

Grierson, George A. Introduction to *The Lay of Alha.* Trans. William Waterfield, 9–25. London: Oxford University Press, 1923.
———. "Two Versions of the Song of Gopī Chand." *Journal of the Asiatic Society of Bengal* 54, no. 1 (1885): 35–55.
Gunawardana, A. J. "From Ritual to Rationality: Notes on the Changing Asian Theatre." *The Drama Review* 15, no. 3 (1971): 48–62.
Haddad, Yvonne Yazbeck, ed. *Women, Religion, and Social Change.* Albany: State University of New York Press, 1985.
Haksar, Nandita. "Kathak." *Indian Horizons* 29, no. 3 (1980): 34–39.
Hall, David. Introduction to *Understanding Popular Culture: Europe from the Middle Ages to the Nineteenth Century,* ed. Steven L. Kaplan, 5–18. Berlin: Mouton Publishers, 1984.
Hansen, Kathryn. "The Birth of Hindi Drama in Banaras, 1868–1885." In *Culture and Power in Banaras: Community, Performance, and Environment, 1800–1980,* ed. Sandria B. Freitag, 62–92. Berkeley: University of California Press, 1989.
———. "Indian Folk Traditions and the Modern Theatre." *Asian Folklore Studies* 42, no. 1 (1983): 77–89.
———."*Sultānā the dacoit* and *Harishchandra:* Two Popular Dramas of the Nauṭaṅkī Tradition of North India." *Modern Asian Studies* 17, no. 2 (1983): 313–331.
———. "The *Virangana* in North Indian History, Myth and Popular Culture." *Economic and Political Weekly* 23, no. 18 (Apr. 30, 1988), WS25–33.
———. "Nautanki Chapbooks: Written Traditions of a Folk Form." *The India Magazine* 6, no. 2 (Jan. 1986): 64–72.
ul-Hasan, Masud. *Famous Folk Tales of Pakistan.* Lahore: Ferozsons, 1976.
Hasan, Mohammad. "Urdu Folk Literature." In *Comparative Indian Literature,* ed. K. M. George, 1:142–146. Trichur: Kerala Sahitya Akademi, 1984.
Hashmi, Safdar. *The Right to Perform: Selected Writings of Safdar Hashmi.* Delhi: Sahmat, 1989.
Hawley, John Stratton. *At Play with Krishna: Pilgrimage Dramas from Brindavan.* Princeton: Princeton University Press, 1981.
Heath, Stephen, and Gillian Skirrow, "An Interview with Raymond Williams." In *Studies in Entertainment: Critical Approaches to Mass Culture,* ed. Tania Modleski, 3–17. Bloomington: Indiana University Press, 1986.
Hein, Norvin. *The Miracle Plays of Mathura.* New Haven: Yale University Press, 1972.
———. "The Rām Līlā." In *Traditional India: Structure and Change,* ed. Milton Singer, 73–98. Philadelphia: American Folklore Society, 1959.
Henry, Edward O. "Correlating Musical Genres and Social Categories in Bhojpuri-speaking North India." Paper delivered at the South Asia Regional Studies Seminar, University of Pennsylvania, November 18, 1987.
Hess, Linda. "Rām Līlā: The Audience Experience." In *Bhakti in Current Research, 1979–1982,* ed. Monika Thiel-Horstmann, 171–194. Berlin: Dietrich Reimer, 1983.
Hiltebeitel, Alf. *The Cult of Draupadi.* Vol. 1. Chicago: University of Chicago Press, 1988.

Hobsbawm, Eric. *Bandits*. New York: Delacorte Press, 1969.

Hunt, Lynn, ed. *The New Cultural History*. Berkeley: University of California Press, 1989.

Huyssen, Andreas. "Mass Culture as Woman: Modernism's Other." In *Studies in Entertainment: Critical Approaches to Mass Culture,* ed. Tania Modleski, 188–207. Bloomington: Indiana University Press, 1986.

Indian Drama. 2d rev. ed. Publications Division, Ministry of Information and Broadcasting, Government of India, 1981.

Jacobson, Doranne. "The Chaste Wife: Cultural Norm and Individual Experience." In *American Studies in the Anthropology of India,* ed. Sylvia Vatuk, 94–138. Delhi: Manohar, 1978.

Jahagirdar, Chandrashekhar. "Marathi Folk Literature." In *Comparative Indian Literature,* ed. K. M. George, 1:100–105. Trichur: Kerala Sahitya Akademi, 1984.

Jairazbhoy, Nazir A. "Colloquy: The South Asian Double-Reed Aerophone Reconsidered." *Ethnomusicology* 24, no. 1 (Jan. 1980): 147–156.

———. "A Preliminary Survey of the Oboe in India." *Ethnomusicology* 14, no. 3 (Sept. 1970): 375–388.

Jatar, D. P., and M. Z. Khan. *The Problem of Dacoity in Bundelkhand and the Chambal Valley*. Delhi: S. Chand, 1980.

Jones, Kenneth W. *Arya Dharm: Hindu Consciousness in Nineteenth-Century Punjab*. Berkeley: University of California Press, 1976.

Joshi, Nirmala. "Wajidali Shah and the Music of His Time." *Sangeet Natak Akademi Bulletin* 6 (May 1957): 36–38.

Kaplan, Steven L., ed. *Understanding Popular Culture: Europe from the Middle Ages to the Nineteenth Century*. Berlin: Mouton Publishers, 1984.

Kapur, Anuradha. "Actors, Pilgrims, Kings, and Gods: The Rāmlīlā at Ramnagar." *Contributions to Indian Sociology,* n.s., 19, no. 1 (1985): 57–74.

Karnad, Girish. "Theatre in India." *Daedalus* 118, no. 4 (Fall 1989): 331–352.

———. "This One is for Nadia." *Cinema Vision India* 1, no. 2 (April 1980): 84–90.

Katare, Shyam Sunder. *Patterns of Dacoity in India* Delhi: S. Chand and Company, 1972.

Kellogg, S. H. *A Grammar of the Hindi Language*. Delhi: Oriental Books Reprint, 1972.

Khan, M. Z. *Dacoity in Chambal Valley*. Delhi: National Publishing House, 1981.

Khubchandani, Lachman M. *Plural Languages, Plural Cultures*. Honolulu: University of Hawaii Press, 1983.

Kidd, Ross. "Folk Media, Popular Theatre and Conflicting Strategies for Social Change in the Third World." In *Tradition for Development: Indigenous Structures and Folk Media in Non-Formal Education,* ed. Ross Kidd and Nat Colletta, 280–301. Berlin: German Foundation for International Development and International Council for Adult Education, 1980.

Kincaid, Charles Augustus. *Folk Tales of Sind and Guzarat*. Karachi: Daily Gazette Press, 1925.

———. *The Outlaws of Kathiawar and Other Studies.* Bombay: The Times Press, 1905.
Kinsley, David. *Hindu Goddesses: Visions of the Divine Feminine in the Hindu Religious Tradition.* Berkeley: University of California Press, 1986.
Kippen, James. *The Tabla of Lucknow: A Cultural Analysis of a Musical Tradition.* Cambridge: Cambridge University Press, 1988.
Kishwar, Madhu, and Ruth Vanita, eds. *In Search of Answers: Indian Women's Voices from Manushi.* London: Zed Books, 1984.
Kothari, Komal. "Performers, Gods, and Heroes in the Oral Epics of Rajasthan." In *Oral Epics in India,* ed. Stuart H. Blackburn, Peter J. Claus, Joyce B. Flueckiger, and Susan S. Wadley, 102–117. Berkeley: University of California Press, 1989.
———. "Rural-Urban Transitions." In *Proceedings of the Twelfth International Musicological Conference,* 595–603. Berkeley: American Musicological Society, 1981.
Kothari, Sunil. "Gotipua Dancers of Orissa." *Sangeet Natak* 8 (Apr.–June 1968): 31–43.
Kulke, Eckehard. *The Parsees in India: A Minority as Agent of Social Change.* Munich: Weltforum Verlag, 1974.
Lapoint, Elwyn C. "The Epic of Guga: A North Indian Oral Tradition." In *American Studies in the Anthropology of India,* ed. Sylvia Vatuk, 281–308. Delhi: Manohar, 1978.
Lebra-Chapman, Joyce. *The Rani of Jhansi: A Study in Female Heroism in India.* Honolulu: University of Hawaii Press, 1986.
Liddle, Joanna, and Rama Joshi. *Daughters of Independence: Gender, Caste, and Class in India.* London: Zed Books, 1986.
Lorenzen, David N. "Warrior Ascetics in Indian History." *Journal of the American Oriental Society* 98, no. 1 (1978): 61–75.
Lutgendorf, Philip. "Ram's Story in Shiva's City: Public Arenas and Private Patronage." In *Culture and Power in Banaras: Community, Performance, and Environment, 1800–1980,* ed. Sandria B. Freitag, 34–61. Berkeley: University of California Press, 1989.
McGregor, Ronald Stuart. *Hindi Literature of the Nineteenth and Early Twentieth Centuries.* Wiesbaden: Otto Harrassowitz, 1974.
Madhavananda, Swami, and Ramesh Chandra Majumdar, eds. *Great Women of India.* Almora: Advaita Ashrama, 1953.
Malcolm, John. *A Memoir of Central India including Malwa.* London: Parbury, Allen, and Company, 1832.
Manning, Frank E., ed. *The Celebration of Society: Perspectives on Contemporary Cultural Performance.* Bowling Green, Ohio: Bowling Green University Popular Press, 1983.
Manuel, Peter. "The Evolution of Modern *Ṭhumrī.*" *Ethnomusicology* 30, no. 3 (Fall 1986): 470–490.
———. *Popular Music of the Non-Western World.* New York: Oxford University Press, 1988.
Marcus, Scott L. "The Rise of a Folk Music Genre: Birahā." In *Culture and*

Power in Banaras: Community, Performance, and Environment, 1800–1980, ed. Sandria B. Freitag, 93–113. Berkeley: University of California Press, 1989.

Marglin, Frédérique Apffel. *Wives of the God-King: The Rituals of the Devadasis of Puri.* Delhi: Oxford University Press, 1985.

Mathur, Jagdish Chandra. *Drama in Rural India.* New York: Asia Publishing House, 1964.

———. "Hindi Drama and Theatre." In *Indian Drama,* 23–34. 2d rev. ed. Publications Division, Ministry of Information and Broadcasting, Government of India, 1981.

Metcalf, Thomas R. *Land, Landlords, and the British Raj.* Berkeley: University of California Press, 1979.

Miller, Barbara Stoler. *Phantasies of a Love-Thief.* New York: Columbia University Press, 1971.

Modleski, Tania, ed. *Studies in Entertainment: Critical Approaches to Mass Culture.* Bloomington: Indiana University Press, 1986.

Mukhopadhyay, Durgadas, ed. *Lesser Known Forms of Performing Arts in India.* Delhi: Sterling Publishers, 1978.

Nadkarni, Dhyaneshwar. "Marathi Tamasha, Yesterday and Today." In *Lesser Known Forms of Performing Arts in India,* ed. Durgadas Mukhopadhyay, 51–57. Delhi: Sterling Publishers, 1978.

Narayana, Birendra. *Hindi Drama and Stage.* Delhi: Bansal and Company, 1981.

Neuman, Daniel M. "Country Musicians and Their City Cousins: The Social Organization of Music Transmissions in India." In *Proceedings of the Twelfth International Musicological Conference,* 603–608. Berkeley: American Musicological Society, 1981.

Nizami. *The Story of Layla and Majnun.* Ed. and trans. R. Gelpke. Boulder: Shambhala, 1978.

Ojha, Rajendra, ed. *Seventy-Five Glorious Years of Indian Cinema.* Bombay: Screen World Publication [1989].

Oman, John Campbell. *Cults, Customs and Superstitions of India.* London: T. Fisher Unwin, 1908.

Pani, Jiwan. "The Female Impersonator in Traditional Indian Theatre." *Sangeet Natak* 45 (July–Sept. 1977): 37–42.

Parmar, Shyam. *Folklore of Madhya Pradesh.* 2d ed. Delhi: National Book Trust, 1981.

———. *Folk Music and Mass Media.* Delhi: Communication Publications, 1977.

———. *Traditional Folk Media in India.* Delhi: Geka Books, 1975.

Pemble, John. *The Raj, the Indian Mutiny, and the Kingdom of Oudh, 1801–1859.* Sussex: Harvester Press, 1977.

Petievich, Carla Rae. "The Two School Theory of Urdu Literature." Ph.D. dissertation, University of British Columbia, 1986.

Platts, John T. *A Dictionary of Urdu, Classical Hindi, and English.* 2d. Indian ed. 1884. Reprint. Delhi: Munshiram Manoharlal, 1988.

Pool, John J. *Famous Women of India.* Calcutta: Susil Gupta, 1954.

Prabhakar, Devi Shankar. "Folk Entertainment in Haryana." In *Folk Entertainment in India,* ed. P. N. Chopra, 27–36. Delhi: Ministry of Education and Culture, Government of India, 1981.

Pritchett, Frances W. *Marvelous Encounters: Folk Romance in Urdu and Hindi.* Riverdale, Md.: Riverdale Company, 1985.

———. "Śīt Basant: Oral Tale, Sāṅgīt and Kissā." *Asian Folklore Studies* 42, no. 1 (1983): 45–62.

Pritchett, Frances W., and Kh. A. Khaliq. *Urdu Meter: A Practical Handbook.* Madison: University of Wisconsin, 1987.

Qureshi, M. Aslam. *Wajid Ali Shah's Theatrical Genius.* Lahore: Vanguard Books, 1987.

Raghavan, V. "Sanskrit Drama in Performance." In *Sanskrit Drama in Performance,* ed. Rachel Van M. Baumer and James R. Brandon, 9–44. Honolulu: University of Hawaii Press, 1981.

———. "Uparūpakas and Nṛttyaprabandhas." *Sangeet Natak* 2 (Apr. 1966): 5–25.

Raghunathji, K. "Bombay Beggars and Criers." *Indian Antiquary* (Oct. 1880): 247–250; (Nov. 1880): 278–280; (Mar. 1881): 71–75; (May 1881): 145–147; (Oct. 1881): 286–287; (Jan. 1882): 22–24; (Feb. 1882): 44–47; (May 1882): 141–146; (June 1882): 172–174.

Ramanujan, A. K. "Two Realms of Kannada Folklore." In *Another Harmony: New Essays on the Folklore of India,* ed. Stuart H. Blackburn and A. K. Ramanujan, 41–75. Berkeley: University of California Press, 1986.

Rangacharya, Adya. *The Indian Theatre.* 2d ed. Delhi: National Book Trust, 1980.

Rangoonwalla, Firoze. *Indian Filmography: Silent and Hindi Films (1897–1969).* Bombay: J. Udeshi, 1970.

Ray, Satyajit. "My Wajid Ali Is Not 'Effete and Effeminate.' " *Illustrated Weekly of India,* Dec. 31, 1978, 49–51.

Renu, Phanishwarnath. *The Third Vow and Other Stories.* Trans. Kathryn Hansen. Delhi: Chanakya Publications, 1986.

Reys, Shalini. "Dancing on a String: Kathputlis, Marionettes of Rajasthan." *The India Magazine* 5, no. 3 (Feb. 1985): 52–59.

Richards, J. F., and V. N. Rao. "Banditry in Mughal India: Historical and Folk Perceptions." *Indian Economic and Social History Review* 17, no. 1 (Jan.–Mar. 1980): 95–120.

Ridgeway, William. *The Dramas and Dramatic Dances of Non-European Races, in special reference to the Origin of Greek Tragedy.* Cambridge: Cambridge University Press, 1915.

Rizavi, Syed Masud Hasan. "On *Urdu Drama aur Stage.*" *Indian Literature* (Oct. 1959–Mar. 1960): 138–140.

Robinson, Sandra P. "Hindu Paradigms of Women: Images and Values." In *Women, Religion, and Social Change,* ed. Yvonne Yazbeck Haddad, 181–215. Albany: State University of New York Press, 1985.

Robson, John. *A Selection of Khyals or Marwari Plays with an Introduction and Glossary.* Beawar, Rajasthan: Beawr [*sic*] Mission Press, 1866.

Roghair, Gene H. *The Epic of Palnāḍu.* New York: Oxford University Press, 1982.

Rose, H. A., trans. "A Version of Hir and Ranjha." *Indian Antiquary* (Sept. 1925): 176–179; (Nov. 1925): 210–219.

Sadie, Stanley, ed. *New Grove Dictionary of Music and Musicians*. London: Macmillan Publishers, 1980.

Sadiq, Muhammad. *A History of Urdu Literature*. 2d ed. Delhi: Oxford University Press, 1984.

Saksena, Ram Babu. *A History of Urdu Literature*. 2d ed. Allahabad: Ram Narain Lal, 1940.

Samar, Devilal. "The Dance Dramas of Rajasthan." *Cultural Forum* 6, no. 3 (May 1964): 44–48.

———. *Folk Entertainments of Rajasthan*. Udaipur: Bharatiya Lok Kala Mandal, 1979.

———. "The Khyāls of Rajasthan." In *Folk Entertainment in India*, ed. P. N. Chopra, 55–60. Delhi: Ministry of Education and Culture, Government of India, 1981.

———. "Rāsdhārī: Folk Theatre of Rajasthan." *Sangeet Natak* 20 (Apr.–June 1971): 50–57.

Sangari, Kumkum, and Sudesh Vaid, eds. *Recasting Women: Essays in Colonial History*. Delhi: Kali for Women, 1989.

Schechner, Richard. *Essays on Performance Theory, 1970–1976*. New York: Drama Book Specialists, 1977.

———. *Performative Circumstances from the Avant Garde to the Rāmlīlā*. Calcutta: Seagull Books, 1983.

Schechner, Richard, and Linda Hess. "The Rāmlīlā of Ramnagar." *The Drama Review* 21, no. 3 (Sept. 1977): 51–82.

Schimmel, Annemarie. *Classical Urdu Literature from the Beginning to Iqbal*. Wiesbaden: Otto Harrassowitz, 1975.

Sekhon, Sant Singh, trans. *The Love of Hir and Ranjha (Waris Shah)*. Ludhiana: Punjab Agricultural University, 1978.

Sharar, Abdul Halim. *Lucknow: The Last Phase of an Oriental Culture*. Trans. and ed. E. S. Harcourt and Fakhir Hussain. Boulder: Westview Press, 1976.

Sherring, M. A. *Hindu Tribes and Castes, as Represented in Benares*. 1872. Reprint. Delhi: Cosmos Publications, 1974.

Shulman, David Dean. *The King and the Clown in South Indian Myth and Poetry*. Princeton: Princeton University Press, 1985.

Siddiqui, Ashraf. *Folkloric Bangladesh*. Dacca: Bangla Academy, 1976.

Singer, Milton, ed. *Traditional India: Structure and Change*. Philadelphia: American Folklore Society, 1959.

Singh, Gurbakhsh. *Immortal Lovers: Tender Tales of Great Love*. Delhi: Sterling Publishers, 1973.

Singh, R. G. *Terror to Reform (A Study of Dacoits of Central India)*. Delhi: Intellectual Book Corner, 1980.

Sinha, Shyam Narain. *Rani Lakshmi Bai of Jhansi*. Allahabad: Chugh Publications, 1980.

Sircar, Badal. *The Third Theatre*. Calcutta: Badal Sircar, 1978.

Smith, John D. "Scapegoats of the Gods: The Ideology of the Indian Epics." In *Oral Epics in India*, ed. Stuart H. Blackburn, Peter J. Claus, Joyce B. Flueckiger, and Susan S. Wadley, 176–194. Berkeley: University of California Press, 1989.

Srinivasan, Amrit. "The Hindu Temple-Dancer: Prostitute or Nun?" *Cambridge Anthropology* 8, no. 1 (1983): 73–99.

———. "Reform and Revival: The Devadasi and Her Dance." *Economic and Political Weekly,* Nov. 2, 1985, 1869–1876.

Steel, Flora Annie, and R. C. Temple. *Tales of the Punjab, Told by the People.* 1894. Reprint. London: Bodley Head, 1973.

Subramaniam, V., ed. *The Sacred and the Secular in India's Performing Arts: Ananda K. Coomaraswamy Centenary Essays.* Delhi: Ashish Publishing House, 1980.

Swann, Darius Leander. "Rās Līlā and the Sanskrit Drama." In *Sanskrit Drama in Performance,* ed. Rachel Van M. Baumer and James R. Brandon, 264–274. Honolulu: University of Hawaii Press, 1981.

———. "Three Forms of Traditional Theatre of Uttar Pradesh, North India." Ph.D. dissertation, University of Hawaii, 1974.

Swynnerton, Charles. *Romantic Tales from the Panjab with Indian Nights' Entertainment.* London: Archibald Constable and Company, 1908.

Temple, Richard Carnac. *Legends of the Panjab.* 3 vols. Bombay: Education Society's Press, 1884–1900.

Thapar, Romila. *Ancient Indian Social History: Some Interpretations.* Delhi: Orient Longman, 1978.

Thiel-Horstmann, Monika, ed. *Bhakti in Current Research, 1979–1982.* Berlin: Dietrich Reimer, 1983.

Thompson, J. T. *Dictionary in Hindee and English.* 2d ed. Calcutta: Sarasvati Press, 1862.

Thompson, Stith, and Jonas Balys. *The Oral Tales of India.* Bloomington: Indiana University Press, 1958.

Tulpule, Shankar Gopal. *Classical Marathi Literature.* Wiesbaden: Otto Harrassowitz, 1979.

Turner, Victor W. *From Ritual to Theatre: The Human Seriousness of Play.* New York: Performing Arts Journal Publications, 1982.

———. *The Ritual Process: Structure and Anti-Structure.* Chicago: Aldine Publishing Company, 1969.

Vanamamalai, N. "Dacoits and Robbers in Tamil Ballads." *Folklore* 12, no. 2 (Feb. 1971): 66–72.

van Buitenen, J. A. B., trans. *Tales of Ancient India.* Chicago: University of Chicago Press, 1959.

Varadpande, M. L. "Tamasha: Folk Theatre of Maharashtra." In *Folk Entertainment in India,* ed. P. N. Chopra, 61–67. Delhi: Ministry of Education and Culture, Government of India, 1981.

Vatsyayan, Kapila. *Traditional Indian Theatre: Multiple Streams.* Delhi: National Book Trust, 1980.

Vatuk, Sylvia, ed. *American Studies in the Anthropology of India.* Delhi: Manohar, 1978.

Vatuk, Ved Prakash, ed. *Studies in Indian Folk Traditions.* Delhi: Manohar, 1979.

Vatuk, Ved Prakash, and Sylvia Vatuk. "The Ethnography of *Sāṅg,* A North Indian Folk Opera." In *Studies in Indian Folk Traditions,* ed. Ved Prakash Vatuk, 15–37. Delhi: Manohar, 1979.

———. "The Lustful Stepmother in the Folklore of Northwestern India." *Journal of South Asian Literature* 11, nos. 1–2 (1975): 19–44.

Vaudeville, Charlotte. *Kabir.* Oxford: Clarendon Press, 1974.

Vedalankar, Shardadevi. *The Development of Hindi Prose Literature in the Early Nineteenth Century (1800–1856 A.D.).* Allahabad: Lokbharti Publications, 1969.

Vilanilam. "Robinhood of Kerala." *Folklore* 13, no. 8 (Aug. 1972): 308–317.

Wade, Bonnie C. *Khyal: Creativity within North India's Classical Music Tradition.* Cambridge: Cambridge University Press, 1984.

Wadley, Susan S. "Choosing a Path: Performance Strategies in a North Indian Epic." In *Oral Epics in India,* ed. Stuart H. Blackburn, Peter J. Claus, Joyce B. Flueckiger, and Susan S. Wadley, 75–101. Berkeley: University of California Press, 1989.

———."Ḍholā: A North Indian Folk Genre." *Asian Folklore Studies* 42, no. 1 (1983): 3–25.

———. *Shakti: Power in the Conceptual Structure of Karimpur Religion.* Delhi: Munshiram Manoharlal, 1985.

Warder, A. K. *Indian Kavya Literature.* Vol. 1, *Literary Criticism.* Delhi: Motilal Banarsidass, 1972.

Waris Shah. *The Adventures of Hir and Ranjha.* Ed. Mumtaz Hasan, trans. Charles Frederick Usborne. Karachi: Lion Art Press, 1966.

Waterfield, William, trans. *The Lay of Alha.* London: Oxford University Press, 1923.

Williams, Raymond. *Communications.* 3d ed. London: Penguin Books, 1976.

———. *Culture.* Glasgow: Fontana Press, 1989.

Yajnik, Y. K. *The Indian Theatre.* London: George Allen and Unwin, 1933.

Yusuf Ali, A. "The Modern Hindustani Drama." *Transactions of the Royal Society of Literature,* 2d s., 35 (1917): 79–99.

Hindi Sources

Agraval, Ram Narayan. *Braj kā rās raṅgmañch.* Delhi: National Publishing House, 1981.

———. *Sāṅgīt: ek loknāṭya paraṁparā.* Delhi: Rajpal and Sons, 1976.

Anand, Mahesh. "Bhāratenduyugīn raṅgmañch." In *Ādhunik hindī nāṭak aur raṅgmañch,* ed. Nemichandra Jain, 51–64. Delhi: Macmillan Company of India, 1978.

Avasthi, Induja. *Rāmlīlā: paraṁparā aur shailiyāṁ.* Delhi: Radhakrishna Prakashan, 1979.

Avasthi, Suresh. "Indar sabhā: ek rūpgat adhyayan." *Naṭraṅg* 9 (1969): 23–29.

Banarasi, Kashigir. *Lāvanī.* Banaras: Munshi Ambe Prasad, 1877.

Bedi, Susham. *Hindī nāṭya: prayog ke sandarbh meṁ.* Delhi: Parag Prakashan, 1984.

Bhanavat, Mahendra. *Lokraṅg: bhāratīya loknāṭyoṁ kī pratinidhi vidhoṁ kā prāmāṇik vivechan.* Udaipur: Bharatiya Lok Kala Mandal, 1971.

———. *Mevāṛ ke rāsdhārī.* Udaipur: Bharatiya Lok Kala Mandal, 1970.

———. *Rājasthān ke turrākalaṅgī.* Udaipur: Bharatiya Lok Kala Mandal, 1968.
———. *Rājasthān kī rammateṁ.* Vdaipur: Bharatiya Lok Kala Mandal, 1975.
Das, Shyam Sundar, ed. *Hindī shabd sāgar.* Varanasi: Nagari Pracharini Sabha, 1968.
Gaur, Radhavallabh. "Hāthras kī nauṭaṅkī, svāṅg va bhagat paraṁparā." In *Braj kalā kendra ke vārṣhik adhiveṣhaṇ 1964 kā sampūrṇ vivaraṇ,* ed. Radheyshyam "Pragalbh," 105–111. Hathras: Suruchi Udyan, 1965.
Gupta, Mata Prasad, ed. *Prāchīn bhāṣhā nāṭak saṁgrah.* Agra: Agra University, 1968.
Gupta, Somnath. *Hindī nāṭak sāhitya kā itihās.* Allahabad: Hindi Bhavan, 1958.
———. *Pārsī thiyeṭar: udbhav aur vikās.* Allahabad: Lokbharati Prakashan, 1981.
Hansen, Kathryn. "Bhāratīya lok paraṁparāeṁ aur ādhunik raṅgmañch." *Naṭraṅg* 46 (1986): 22–29.
Jain, Nemichandra, ed. *Ādhunik hindī nāṭak aur raṅgmañch.* Delhi: Macmillan Company of India, 1978.
Karnad, Girish. *Hayavadana.* Trans. B. V. Karanth, foreword by Rajinder Nath. Delhi: Radhakrishna Prakashan, 1975.
Lal, Lakshmi Narayan. *Pārsī-hindī raṅgmañch.* Delhi: Rajpal and Sons, 1973.
Lal, Nanhu. *Lāvanī navīn bilās.* Banaras: Munshi Ambe Prasad, ca. 1873.
Lal, Shrikrishna. *Ādhunik hindī sāhitya kā vikās.* 4th ed. Allahabad: Hindi Parishad, 1965.
Madhur, Shivkumar. *Bhārat ke loknāṭya.* Delhi: Vani Prakashan, 1980.
———. *Madhyapradesh kā lok nāṭya māch.* Delhi: Ankur Prakashan, 1980.
Mishra, Shivprasad, ed. *Bhāratendu granthāvalī, pahlā khaṇḍ.* Varanasi: Nagari Pracharini Sabha, 1974.
Mohan, Braj, and Badrinath Kapur, eds. *Mīnākṣhī hindī-angrezī kosh.* Delhi: Meenakshi Prakashan, 1980.
Namre, Vidyavati Lakshmanrao. *Hindī raṅgmañch aur paṇḍit nārāyaṇprasād betāb.* Varanasi: Vishvavidyalay Prakashan, 1972.
Ojha, Dasharath. *Hindī nāṭak: udbhav aur vikās.* Delhi: Rajpal, 1954.
Radheyshyam "Pragalbh," ed. *Braj kalā kendra ke vārṣhik adhiveṣhaṇ 1964 kā sampūrṇ vivaraṇ.* Hathras: Suruchi Udyan, 1965.
Rajkumar, Anil. *Bhāratīya vīrāṅganāeṁ.* Delhi: Kitab Ghar, 1984.
Rajnish, Govind. *Rājasthān ke pūrvī āñchal kā lok-sāhitya.* Jaipur: 1974.
Renu, Phanishvarnath. *Ṭhumrī.* Delhi: Rajkamal Prakashan, 1959.
Saksena, Krishna Mohan. *Bhāratenduyugīn nāṭya-sāhitya meṁ loktattva.* Allahabad: Abhinav Bharati, 1977.
Samar, Devilal. *Rājasthān ke rāval.* Udaipur: Bharatiya Lok Kala Mandal, 1967.
———. *Rājasthānī lok-nāṭya.* Udaipur: Bharatiya Lok Kala Mandal, 1957.
Santram, Anil. *Kanaujī lok-sāhitya.* Delhi: Abhinav Prakashan, 1975.
Shukla, Bhanudev. *Bhāratendu ke nāṭak.* Kanpur: Grantham, 1972.
Sukumar, Surendra. "Mele meṁ nauṭaṅkī." *Dharmyug,* Aug. 28, 1977, 43–46.
Tivari, Gopinath. *Bhāratendukālīn nāṭak sāhitya.* Jalandhar: Hindi Bhavan, 1959.
Varma, Dhirendra, Vrajeshvar Varma, Dharmvir Bharti et al., eds. *Hindī sāhitya kosh.* Vol. 1. 3d ed. Varanasi: Jnanmandal, 1985.

Varma, Kalyan Prasad. *Karaulī kṣhetra kā khyāl sāhitya*. Udaipur: Bharatiya Lok Kala Mandal, 1972.
Varma, Ramchandra, ed. *Mānak hindī kosh*. 5th ed. Allahabad: Hindi Sahitya Sammelan, 1964.
———. *Prāmāṇik hindī kosh*. 2d ed. Allahabad: Hindi Sahitya Sammelan, 1951.

Urdu Sources

Faruqi, Azhar Ali. *Uttar pradesh ke lok gīt*. Delhi: Taraqqi Urdu Bureau, 1981.
Nami, Abdul Alim. *Urdū thiyeṭar*. Karachi: Anjuman Taraqqi Urdu Pakistan, 1970.
Rizvi, Masud Hasan ("Adib"). *Urdū ḍrāmā aur istej*. Pt. 1, *Lakhnaū kā shāhī istej*. Lucknow: Kitab Ghar, 1957.
———. *Urdū ḍrāmā aur istej*. Pt. 2, *Lakhnaū kā ʿavāmī istej: Amānat aur indarsabhā*. Lucknow: Kitab Ghar, 1957.

Index

Salag (Salig, Saligram), 102, 325n.33
Salawat Khan, 131, 187
Salig/Saligram. *See* Salag
Samaj, Arya. *See* Arya Samaj
Samaj, Brahmo. *See* Brahmo Samaj
Sāma Veda, 33
Sāṅg, 56, 68, 90, 245; of Haryana, 41, 65, 113
Sangeet Natak Akademi, 6, 112, 218, 231, 248, 265–66
Sāṅgīt (term), 56, 67–68, 87, 90, 307n.10
Sāṅgīt (texts), 5, 57, 73, 79, 86–116, 260, 286–300, 323–26; Hathras, 79, 95–104, 106, 324–26; on Hindu-Muslim relations, 163–64; Kanpur, 104–13, 326n.54; lithographed, 90–94, 323n.7; meters in, 113, 221, 301–3; political themes of, 92, 118–43; and Ram and Krishna stories, 314n.7; recent developments, 113–14; sources of, 87–90
Saṅgītaka, 47
Sāṅgīt budre munīr kā, 94
Sāṅgīt julmī ḍāyar, 116
Sāṅgīt nauṭaṅkī, 15, 324n.23
Sāṅgīt nauṭaṅkī shāhzādī, 281–82, 309n.13. See also *Nauṭaṅkī shāhzādī*
Sāṅgīt oḍakī kā (Mitthan Lal & Chunni Lal), 211
Sāṅgīt phulvantī kā, 308n.3
Sāṅgīt puranmal kā (Ramlal), 71
Sāṅgīt rānī nauṭaṅkī kā (The musical drama of Queen Nauṭaṅkī) (Khushi Ram), 13, 14, 29, 308
Sāṅgīt samar malkhān, 102
Sāṅgīt siyeposh (Basudev), 325nn.32,33
Sāṅgīt sundarkāṇḍ rāh nauṭaṅkī (The musical play "Sundarkāṇḍ" in the Nauṭaṅkī manner), 104–5
Sāṅgīt vīr vikramāditya, 112, 114
Sāṅg soraṭh, 153–54
Sanskrit drama, 62, 258; class of audience, 37; as classical, 37, 43–44, 46–47; decline of, 57, 61; and *Indarsabhā,* 76; lust in, 28; and Parsi theatre, 82; *rasa* theory of, 36; similarities with traditional or folk theatre, 46–47; themes of, 27
Sanskrit language, 62, 222, 314n.13
Sanskrit love poetry, 144, 151
Sarasvati, Dayanand, 110
Sarju Das, 325n.33
Sarman, Ramabhadra, 74–75, 327n.3
Sastri, Pandit Hiranand, 73
Sat, 30, 119, 189, 197, 262–63. *See also* Truth
Sati, 172, 176, 183
Satī, 174, 188–89, 190, 262
Satī bindiyā (The saintly Bindiya), 203–5
Sati Veermat, 195
Satyagraha, 127
Saudāgar vo syāhposh, 92, 158, 192. See also *Syāhposh*
Saurashtra, 259
Savaiyā, 62
Savāl-javāb structure, 66, 244–45, 316n.41
Sāvan, 50, 220
Savitri, 7, 172, 176, 183, 330n.2
Scale patterns, 218. See also *Rāganī;* Ragas
Schechner, Richard, 246
Schimmel, Annemarie, 76
Secular theatre, 1–2, 21, 37–39, 252–53, 256, 257, 259; folk, 57, 61–73; Nauṭaṅkī as, 1, 37–38, 252, 253, 256, 257
Sedhu Lal (Sedhu), 102. *See also* Serhu
Sedhu Singh, 325n.33
Self-sacrifice: devotees, 38; female, 188, 204–5; and love, 151–57, 162–63, 168, 169, 170. *See also* Renunciation
Semiotics, 208
Separation: of audience and performer, 53–54; story themes of, 26, 27, 202. *See also* Renunciation
Seraikella Chhau, 208, 245
Serhu, 325n.33
Seth, Lala Natthumal, 92–93
Seths, 112, 199
Sexuality: dangerous, 174–84, 188, 197–98; and Hindu-Muslim relations, 166, 167; men's, 27–32, 173–84, 201–3; rape, 196–97; same-sex, 30; women's, 21, 27–32, 148–49, 173–88, 189, 196–203 passim, 262, 263. *See also* Chastity, female
Shah Jahan, 128, 131, 134–35, 187, 188
Shahnāī, 50, 210–13
Shair indra sabhā kī bahr, 302
Shaivism, 66, 318n.62
Shakespeare, William, 40, 83, 322n.115
Shakti/*shakti,* 66, 172, 185
Shaktism, 70, 259
Shakuntalā/Śakuntalā, 28, 75, 314n.13
Shaligram, 102, 105, 325n.35
Shaṅkargaṛh saṅgrām (Shaligram), 325n.35
Sharar, Abdul Halim, 68
Sharma, Ganesh Prasad, 95
Shekhawati Khyāl, 65, 315n.32
Sher, 51, 220, 224, 259, 302, 303
Sher Dil, 195
Sherring, M. A., 72

Compositor:	Maple-Vail Composition Services
Text:	10/13 Sabon
Display:	Sabon
Printer:	Maple-Vail Book Manufacturing Group
Binder:	Maple-Vail Book Manufacturing Group